THE RISE OF THE AGRICULTURAL WELFARE STATE

PRINCETON STUDIES IN AMERICAN POLITICS:
HISTORICAL, INTERNATIONAL, AND COMPARATIVE PERSPECTIVES

SERIES EDITORS

IRA KATZNELSON, MARTIN SHEFTER, THEDA SKOCPOL

A list of titles
in this series appears
at the back of
the book

THE RISE OF THE AGRICULTURAL WELFARE STATE

INSTITUTIONS AND INTEREST GROUP
POWER IN THE UNITED STATES,
FRANCE, AND JAPAN

Adam D. Sheingate

PRINCETON UNIVERSITY PRESS   PRINCETON AND OXFORD

Library of Congress Cataloging-in-Publication Data

Sheingate, Adam D., 1969–
The rise of the agricultural welfare state : institutions and interest group power in the United
States, France, and Japan / Adam D. Sheingate.
p. cm. — (Princeton studies in American politics)
Includes bibliographical references and index.
ISBN 0-691-00983-X (alk. paper)
1. Agriculture and state—United States. Agriculture and state—France. 3. Agriculture and
state—Japan. 4. Pressure groups—United States. 5. Pressure groups—France. 6. Pressure
groups—Japan. I. Title. II. Series.
HD1761 .S49 2000
338.1'8—dc21   00-038501

This book has been composed in Sabon

The paper used in this publication meets the minimum requirements
of ANSI/NISO Z39.48-1992 (R1997) (*Permanence of Paper*)

www.pup.princeton.edu

Printed in the United States of America

1   3   5   7   9   10   8   6   4   2

For Marisa

AS YOU WISH

Contents

Illustrations

FIGURES

TABLES

I AM OFTEN ASKED why I chose to study agricultural policy. To the disappointment of most who ask, I did not grow up on a farm, nor did any of my family. The initial choice was motivated more by necessity than by any particular attraction to the subject matter. Faced with the task of finding a dissertation topic, I looked for an empirical case study with which to test propositions derived from the literature in historical institutionalism and American political development. A prominent theme in the field at the time was that the federal government of the United States was institutionally weak. Generally, this weakness manifested itself in two ways. First, institutional fragmentation supposedly diminished government capacity for certain types of policies, such as encouraging the economic development of a particular sector. A second consequence of this fragmentation was that interest groups dictated the terms of public policy.

Agriculture, it occurred to me, did not fit either proposition particularly well. The argument about policy capacity did not stand up to historical scrutiny. Beginning in the late nineteenth century, the federal government created a nationwide system of research institutions—land-grant agricultural colleges, experiment stations, and the Extension Service—that promoted the development and dissemination of agricultural technology. Federal grants encouraged railroad construction and other transportation links that completed the interior market for agricultural products and made export markets accessible for domestic producers. U.S. institutions did not impede government promotion of commercial agriculture.

The argument about interest group power did not stand up to comparative scrutiny. Agricultural interest groups in France and Japan—countries usually placed on the opposite end of the institutional spectrum from the United States—routinely make life difficult for politicians and policy makers responsible for subsidy programs or engaged in multilateral trade negotiations. In the United States, agricultural interest groups certainly enjoy access to policy, but they must compete for attention with a variety of other interests whose concerns are often contrary to their own, such as consumer or business groups. Although far from powerless, agricultural interests in the United States do not dictate the terms of farm policy to the same degree as their counterparts in France or Japan.

These two observations form the core argument and methodology of this book. By adopting a historical approach to the study of policy and institutions, I argue that government capacity in agriculture varied over time, according to the tasks policy makers undertook. At times, institutional fragmentation was an asset to policy makers, at other times a liability. By adopting a comparative perspective to the study of policy and institutions, I argue that agricultural interest groups exercise greater influence over policy in centralized institutional environments, such as France and Japan, than in the United States. However, like institutions, the effect of interest group influence on government capacity also depends on the policy task at hand. The incorporation of interest groups in the policy process can present government actors with both opportunities for and obstacles to effective action.

I received support from many individuals over the past years, from the initial conception of this project as a dissertation prospectus through its final product as a completed book. At Yale, I had the great fortune to find faculty advisers who encouraged me to pursue an ambitious dissertation topic. Stephen Skowronek sparked my interest in institutions and historically informed political science. As the chair of my dissertation committee, he read my draft chapters with the same diligence and high standard of excellence he applies to his own work. David Cameron and Frances Rosenbluth, although they warned me of the pitfalls, encouraged my desire to examine U.S. institutions in comparative perspective. Jim Scott, Mary Summers, and everyone associated with the Program in Agrarian Studies impressed on me the distinctiveness of agriculture and rural life, although some readers may conclude otherwise. Agrarian Studies also provided financial support for some of my research, for which I am grateful. Soo Yeon Kim and the regular participants in the graduate research colloquium provided valuable comments on every chapter, as well as invaluable commiseration during the arduous task of finishing a dissertation.

I could not have transformed my doctoral thesis into a book were it not for my time as a Prize Research Fellow at Nuffield College, Oxford, from 1997 to 2000. Nuffield provided me with financial resources, time away from teaching responsibilities, and the opportunity to be a member of a very special academic community. Few people are so lucky at the beginning of their careers. At Nuffield, Byron Shafer was extremely helpful concerning various aspects of this project.

Graham K. Wilson of the University of Wisconsin read the entire manuscript and provided useful comments and criticisms. I also thank the anonymous reviewers for Princeton University Press. All errors and omissions are my own.

The debt I owe to my wife, Marisa, is obvious to our friends and family. Without her love, patience, wisdom, and financial support during graduate school, many things, least of all this book, would not have been possible.

THE RISE OF THE AGRICULTURAL WELFARE STATE

Introduction

IN 1933, the United States Congress passed the Agricultural Adjustment Act (AAA). A cornerstone of the New Deal, the AAA offered government payments to farmers who cut production of basic crops such as wheat, cotton, and corn. Although originally conceived as an emergency measure to lift agriculture out of the depths of the Great Depression, government farm programs evolved over the next several decades into a complex policy regime of price supports, acreage controls, and government loans. Together, these policies constituted an agricultural welfare state that regulated the production and prices of one of life's basic elements—food.

The term *agricultural welfare state* situates farm policies within the larger context of American political development. First, as just noted, the historical provenance of agricultural commodity programs is rooted in the expansion of government authority over the economy during the Great Depression. Along with the 1935 Social Security Act, the AAA stands as one of the longest surviving policy legacies of the New Deal. Second, in their operation, federal commodity programs resemble a sector-specific form of social insurance. Through the regulation of agricultural markets, the U.S. government provided countercyclical spending during times of low prices. Production controls and price supports operated as a social safety net designed to protect farmers' incomes. Third, like other welfare state programs, agricultural subsidies have been at the center of debates over how to cut spending and reduce government intervention in the economy.

In fact, agriculture provides us with an example of successful welfare state retrenchment. Beginning in the 1970s, agricultural policy came under attack from a variety of quarters. Over a two-decade period, consumer advocates, budget hawks, and other critics of farm programs successfully pressed for reductions in agricultural subsidies. In 1996, more than sixty years after passage of the AAA, President Clinton signed the Federal Agriculture Improvement and Reform Act (FAIR). For major field crops such as corn, soybeans, and wheat the FAIR Act removed nearly all restrictions on production: farmers were left free to decide what, and how much, to produce. Income supports, previously tied to market prices, were replaced by fixed annual payments unrelated to current market prices or production levels.[1] Although a federal role in agriculture persists, the 1996 legislation followed more than two decades of attempts to cut

---

[1] USDA, *Provisions of the Federal Agriculture Improvement and Reform Act of 1996*, 3.

budgetary costs, reduce government control over agricultural markets, and remedy various problems—ranging from surplus commodity production to environmental degradation—caused by federal farm programs.

Institutions facilitated agricultural retrenchment in the United States. A pluralist interest group environment granted easy access to a variety of interests hostile to farm programs. The location of policy authority in Congress and the decline of rural representation through periodic redistricting transmitted access into influence as agricultural policy came to reflect the growing urban and suburban characteristics of U.S. House districts. Institutional changes in Congress, such as the post-1974 budget rules, undermined agricultural committee autonomy over policy and forced rural lawmakers to make policy decisions within the fiscal constraints of deficit reduction.

But these recent developments in agriculture run counter to mainstream views of U.S. institutions. Standard treatments of American politics often argue that institutions—separated powers and routine conditions of divided government, federalism, bicameralism, and congressional committees—detract from the capacity of policy makers to cut programs, remove subsidies, or deregulate markets.[2] Yet institutions *did not* hamstring efforts to dismantle federal commodity programs. The capacity to cut off generous entitlements to farmers, many of them in existence since the New Deal, represents an important instance of welfare state retrenchment.

Second, U.S. institutions did not secure farmer control over agricultural policy or insulate farm program decisions from the influence of nonagricultural interests. Despite the geographic concentration of certain groups of producers, the decentralization of policy authority, and the supposed capacity of small groups, like farmers, to overcome obstacles to collective action, agriculture is a pluralistic policy domain. Agricultural policy was supposed to be highly parochial, an example of clientele politics par excellence where producer interests successfully "captured" public policy.[3] Yet the influence enjoyed by diffuse interests such as consumers, environmentalists, and taxpayers runs counter to the received wisdom.

The mainstream view of American institutions, in effect, associates government (in)capacity with interest group access. Institutional fragmentation supposedly creates opportunities for private interests to control the policy process, thereby limiting the capacity of politicians and bureaucrats to impose losses or make policies contrary to the desires of well-organized groups. On its face, agriculture should conform to a Pierson-like account of policy feedback: years of government intervention in agriculture gave rise to powerful farm groups that "retain a substantial ability to inflict political retribution . . . for visible assaults on programs they favor." The

---

[2] Pierson, *Dismantling the Welfare State?*
[3] McConnell, *Private Power and American Democracy*; Lowi, *The End of Liberalism*.

inability "to dislodge the extensive interest group networks that have grown up around social programs" should make agricultural retrenchment particularly difficult.[4]

Yet in agriculture, I argue, retrenchment took place *precisely because* advocates of policy change could draw on the very same institutional characteristics so widely criticized as inimical to government capacity. Political institutions did not preserve the policy status quo. Nor did institutions isolate policy decisions in the hands of rural politicians, conservative farm organizations, or agricultural specialists. The central policy role of Congress in a separated system and a highly pluralistic interest group environment facilitated retrenchment.

By tracing the rise of the agricultural welfare state, I endeavor to show how the historical development of political institutions structures the relationship between interest groups and the government. The central hypothesis of this book is that government capacity is a function of this relationship between interest groups and the state as mediated by institutions. From the inauguration of subsidies in the 1930s to the struggles over retrenchment in the 1990s, government capacity has been shaped by the historical evolution of institutions that influence interest group formation, the pattern of interest group participation in policy, and the political relationship between interest groups and political parties.

Agriculture is not simply a curious anomaly but an important challenge to how we understand the impact of institutions on interest group power and government capacity. Agricultural policy was thought to exemplify the pathologies of American institutions. Influential students of American politics such as Grant McConnell and Theodore Lowi pointed to agriculture as an example of agency capture and policy sclerosis. Other fields of inquiry, in particular comparative analysis of political institutions, drew heavily on the views of McConnell and Lowi that institutional fragmentation, agency capture, and government incapacity were causally related. Consequently, a reassessment of agricultural policy requires us to rethink some of our assumptions about the relationship between institutions, interest group power, and government capacity in the United States and abroad.

AGRICULTURE, INSTITUTIONS, AND INTEREST GROUP POWER

It is due perhaps to the long history of government involvement in agriculture that such a wide range of empirical studies of institutions and interest group power use farm policy as a case study.[5] For the early pluralists,

---

[4] Pierson, *Dismantling the Welfare State?* 160–61.

[5] For a more comprehensive survey of the literature on interest groups, see Baumgartner and Leech, *Basic Interests*.

agriculture illustrated how political organizations formed around common economic interests in order to influence public policy. In the 1960s, critics of pluralism such as Lowi and McConnell used agriculture to illustrate the pathologies of American democracy and the propensity for interest group capture of public policy. Lowi and McConnell influenced much subsequent work on institutions and interest group power, ranging from the economic theory of regulation to comparative studies of institutions in advanced capitalist countries. Some of these later works also used agriculture to exemplify the *decline* of policy subgovernments in U.S. politics and the rise of so-called issue networks. Finally, New Deal agricultural policy has been called an island of state strength, a policy domain that exhibited a greater degree of government autonomy from interest group influence than other areas of New Deal activity.

For pluralists such as David Truman, agriculture exemplified the group nature of politics. Farmers were one of the first occupations to establish "political interest groups," which Truman defined as "those that make their claims through or upon governmental institutions." According to Truman, "The relative weakness of the farmer's bargaining position in the market and the relative strength resulting from the overrepresentation of rural areas in State and national legislatures combine to explain the readiness of these groups to resort to the government in order to achieve their objectives."[6] Farmers established political interest groups because they could not achieve economic ends without recourse to public power and because their wide geographic distribution ensured overrepresentation in legislative bodies.

Truman understood, therefore, that the structure of U.S. political institutions shaped the distribution of power and influence among interest groups in American society: "It is obvious . . . that a group such as the American Farm Bureau Federation, which can cover a great many rural States, can gain readier access [to Congress] than urban groups."[7] Over time, Truman acknowledged, access becomes institutionalized to the point that close and congenial relations develop between interest groups, like-minded politicians on well-placed congressional committees, and executive branch bureaucrats. Again, farm groups were exemplary of what subsequent analysts referred to as the "iron triangle." As Truman noted, "One of the most instructive sets of established and highly inflexible relationships in the Federal government is that involving the Department of Agriculture, . . . the Farm Bureau, and, of course, congressmen (especially committee chairmen) from important farm States. The relationships among these are especially revealing because of their strength and their

[6] Truman, *The Governmental Process*, 107.
[7] Ibid., 322–23.

complexity."[8] Although Truman recognized that institutionalized influence by private interests could have a negative effect on American democracy, consideration of this threat was only accorded a small place in his analysis. In his conclusion on the future of group politics, Truman placed his confidence in "the vitality of . . . potential groups" that could exercise countervailing power against more entrenched interests.[9]

Skeptics, however, became increasingly disenchanted with the prospects that "outsiders" or disadvantaged groups could counter the influence wielded by organized interests. As Grant McConnell argued, "The result [of interest group influence] has been the . . . exercise of public authority by the private groups. . . . The process amounts in some situations to the capture of government."[10] Once again agriculture provided a critical case study. Describing the administration of grazing rights on public lands, McConnell referred to "the almost diagrammatic simplicity of their political system," adding that "in probably no other public program of substantial size are the elements of power and control [by private interests] so easily visible or so stark."[11] For McConnell, however, it was the way the Farm Bureau undermined the Farm Security Administration and other government efforts to help the rural poor that exemplified agency capture. "Farm policy," McConnell argued, "had been taken into the possession of the private organization."[12]

For the other great critic of pluralism, Theodore Lowi, agriculture exemplified what he called "interest group liberalism." The control of public policy by organized groups undermined the legitimacy of democratic institutions. According to Lowi, "Agriculture is that field of American government where the distinction between public and private has come closest to being completely eliminated. This has been accomplished not by public expropriation of private domain . . . but by private expropriation of public authority."[13] Like McConnell, Lowi emphasized the "triangular trading pattern" between the United States Department of Agriculture (USDA), the Farm Bureau, and the agriculture committees of Congress: "As in geometry and engineering, so in politics the triangle seems to be the most stable type of structure." As a result of these relationships, farm programs were "the exclusive province of those who are most directly interested in them."[14]

---

[8] Ibid., 469.

[9] Ibid., 535.

[10] McConnell, *Private Power and American Democracy*, 7.

[11] Ibid., 211.

[12] McConnell, *The Decline of Agrarian Democracy*, chap. 9; McConnell, *Private Power and American Democracy*, 235.

[13] Lowi, *The End of Liberalism*, 67.

[14] Ibid., 75.

For both McConnell and Lowi, the structure of American government was a critical factor in interest group power. Federalism, separated powers, and congressional committees divided authority over public policy among a number of institutions. This decentralization narrowed the size of political constituencies, resulted in a more homogeneous set of interests, and increased the likelihood that a single group could capture public policy. According to McConnell, "Decentralization means weakness of public officers in contests with private organizations and the elites these represent."[15] In short, decentralization undermined democratic processes, prevented coherent policy, and threatened government sclerosis.

Once a radical critique of pluralist theory, the views of McConnell and Lowi eventually became the orthodox approach to American politics.[16] For example, the economic theory of regulation developed by George Stigler and others offered a formal, mathematical explanation for the capture of public policy.[17] Stigler and his progeny built on the work by Mancur Olson, who explored the asymmetric capacity among potential groups to overcome obstacles to collective action.[18] This asymmetric capacity to organize underlies the propensity for regulatory capture. In order to maximize votes, politicians reward those groups who supply reelection resources. Because regulations potentially impact producers a great deal but affect consumers and taxpayers very little, producer groups are more likely to overcome collective action problems and supply resources to politicians. As a reward for these reelection resources, politicians design regulatory policies that subsidize production, reduce competition, or otherwise advance the economic interests of the regulated.

Agriculture may provide the best example of this phenomenon. In fact, agricultural economists often use the political marketplace model to explain commodity programs and other forms of agricultural protection. As the size of the agricultural labor force declines in industrial countries, the costs of farm subsidies are diffused more widely among consumers or taxpayers.[19] At the same time, the benefits of protection become more concentrated in the hands of fewer producers. Thus, as farm sector employment declines, farmers have both greater incentives to lobby government for protection and a greater capacity to overcome obstacles to collec-

---

[15] McConnell, *Private Power and American Democracy*, 245.

[16] Summers, "Putting Populism Back In."

[17] Stigler, "The Theory of Economic Regulation"; Peltzman, "Toward a More General Theory of Regulation"; Becker, "A Theory of Competition among Pressure Groups."

[18] Olson, *The Logic of Collective Action*.

[19] When farmers are 50 percent of the population, the cost of a $100 transfer from consumers (or taxpayers) to producers is $50/50 \times \$100 = \$100$ per nonfarmer. When farmers are 5 percent of the population, the cost of a $100 transfer is $5/95 \times \$100 = \$5.26$ per nonfarmer. Lindert, "Historical Patterns of Agricultural Policy," 57.

tive action. When politicians translate the costs and benefits of agricultural policy into an electoral calculus, they subsidize farmers and tax consumers. Agriculture fits nicely within the predictions of the economic theory of regulation.[20]

Some empirical studies of agricultural protection estimate econometric models based on the economic theory of regulation. Masayoshi Honma and Yujiro Hayami examined agricultural protection levels in fifteen industrial countries between 1955 and 1980. For explanatory variables, Honma and Hayami used the percentage of farmers in the male workforce, agriculture's contribution to gross domestic product, the comparative advantage of the farm sector, and the international terms of trade for agricultural commodities.[21] According to their findings, the level of agricultural protection rises as the share of agriculture in the economy declines, as comparative advantage shifts away from agriculture, and as the international terms of trade turn against agricultural commodities. These findings lend some empirical support to the economic theory of regulation as applied to the agricultural case. Honma and Hayami also help account for the fact that farmers in industrialized countries receive higher levels of protection than farmers in developing countries, ceteris paribus.[22]

However, other studies that model the effect of sector size or comparative advantage on agricultural subsidy levels have yielded less conclusive results. Peter Lindert, who used much of the same data as Honma and Hayami, found that "sector size alone does not reliably explain the developmental pattern." And as for comparative advantage, Lindert expresses "doubts about whether greater relative poverty of the farm sector would explain why policy favored farmers more in higher-income countries."[23]

[20] Anderson, Hayami, and Honma, "The Growth of Agricultural Protection"; Hayami, "The Roots of Agricultural Protection"; Gardner, "Causes of U.S. Farm Commodity Programs"; Tolley et al., "What We Know about Agricultural Prices," 133–51.

[21] For comparative advantage, Honma and Hayami use two proxies: a labor-productivity ratio and a factor-endowment ratio. The international terms of trade are expressed as the ratio of indexes of world unit export values of agricultural products and manufacturing goods. "The Determinants of Agricultural Protection Levels," 40–43.

[22] Ibid., 44–45.

[23] Lindert, "Historical Patterns of Agricultural Policy," 66–67. In addition, Lindert reports an R^2 of between .29 and .48, in contrast to an R^2 of between .6 and .7 reported by Honma and Hayami. This raises the possibility of an inflated R^2 in the Honma and Hayami study. Honma and Hayami use ordinary least squares (OLS) regression for time-series data (protection levels over time). Autocorrelation (protection levels at T_1 influence protection levels at T_2) violate the OLS regression assumption of the independence of cases (in this case, years). Consequently, an insignificant equation could appear statistically significant (see Janoski and Isaac, "Introduction to Time-Series Analysis," 33). Because Honma and Hayami do not include a lagged dependent variable or report any standard tests used to diagnose autocorrelation, we must interpret their results with some caution.

As Tolley et al. remark in their review of this literature, "The importance of free riding and organizing costs in explaining policy differences . . . is unclear."[24] The exact mechanism that links sectoral characteristics (size, geographic concentration, etc.) to agricultural policy outcomes continues to elude empirical testing by economists.

John Mark Hansen, again using agriculture, employed a historical methodology to study the rational bases of interest group influence in the policy process. In a study that spans farm politics from 1919 to 1981, Hansen traced how the Farm Bureau came to occupy a privileged place in congressional farm politics. Specifically, the Farm Bureau gained access through its capacity to supply politicians with reliable information on constituency preferences. When the Farm Bureau's competitive advantage began to wane in the late 1950s, commodity organizations emerged as the most reliable source of constituency preference and, as a result, became the principal representative of agricultural interests.[25] Hansen's findings were consistent with those of Charles O. Jones, who nearly thirty years earlier found that members of the House Agriculture Committee tended to vote according to the specific commodity interests in their constituencies. Jones added that the structure of the House Agriculture Committee, especially its division into commodity-specific subcommittees, allowed "a maximum of constituency-oriented representation."[26] Both Hansen's meticulous historical treatment and Jones's careful case study illustrate the electoral connection in interest group politics and public policy theorized by Stigler and others.

But other have scholars have challenged the policy subgovernment model of American politics. Again, agricultural case studies figured prominently in the critiques of interest group capture. Graham K. Wilson argued, in his study of U.S. agriculture, that party and ideology rather than narrow constituency interest were often more important determinants of votes on agricultural subsidies.[27] And with the proliferation of interest groups in the 1960s and 1970s, particularly of the public interest variety, the notion that pro-industry interests dominated the policy process came under scrutiny. Rather than a system of "cozy little triangles," the interest group environment in Washington was more akin to "sloppy large hexagons."[28] William Browne, in his work on agriculture, found not only that

[24] Tolley et al., "What We Know about Agricultural Prices," 147.

[25] Hansen, *Gaining Access*.

[26] Jones, "Representation in Congress," 367.

[27] Wilson, *Special Interests and Policymaking*.

[28] Jones, "American Politics and the Organization of Energy Decision Making," 105; Heclo, "Issue Networks in the Executive Establishment"; Walker, "The Origins and Maintenance of Interest Groups."

producer groups are only one among a wide range of interests involved in farm policy but also that members of Congress have come to rely less and less on organized interests in the policy process.[29] One implication of an overcrowded policy process is that interest groups, far from controlling outcomes, in fact see their influence diminished as access to Congress becomes easier. As Salisbury argues, interest groups are "awash in access but often subordinate in influence."[30]

A different challenge to the view of interest group dominance comes from the work of Kenneth Finegold and Theda Skocpol on New Deal agricultural policy. According to this view, government officials in the USDA did enjoy enough autonomy from societal pressure to formulate policy independently and possessed the administrative capacity to implement programs at times over the opposition of domestic groups. Finegold and Skocpol compare New Deal agriculture to industrial policies of the National Recovery Administration (NRA). In the case of the NRA, policy makers lacked the institutional capacity enjoyed in agriculture, which explains why industrial policy failed in the United States and agricultural policy did not just succeed but survived beyond the New Deal.[31]

Debates about institutions, interest group power, and government capacity in the United States influenced the study of comparative institutions as well. In many cases, this comparative work bears the mark of Lowi and McConnell—that interest group access undermines policy capacity. The "strong" state/"weak" state dichotomy of the late 1970s, for example, viewed the United States as unable to execute coherent policy because it was "permeated by political pressure groups."[32] In contrast, countries such as France and Japan could "pursue a coherent set of objectives because bureaucrats had "the dominant voice in policy deliberations" and institutions prevented "infiltration from the bottom."[33]

This view continues to hold sway, even if scholars do not employ the value-laden terms of "strong" and "weak" states. For example, Pierson notes that, "as observers have long noted, the diffusion of authority exhibited by the American political system allows [interest] groups to flourish and makes them relatively resistant to centralized control."[34] Helen Milner summarizes the view this way: "The key issue . . . becomes how autonomous the governmental administration is from political and social

---

[29] Browne, *Private Interests, Public Policy, and American Agriculture*; Browne, *Cultivating Congress*.

[30] Salisbury, "The Paradox of Interests in Washington, D.C.," 213.

[31] Finegold and Skocpol, *State and Party in America's New Deal*.

[32] Krasner, "United States Commercial and Monetary Policy," 60.

[33] Ibid., 61; Katzenstein, "Conclusion," 314–23.

[34] Pierson, *Dismantling the Welfare State?* 161.

pressure. When policymaking structures are . . . insulated from the legis-lature and interest groups, . . . then policy will be coherent and broadly based."[35]

Similarly, the policy network or policy community approach, with its discussion of pluralism, corporatism, and other varieties of state-society relations, frequently associates interest group pluralism with ad hoc, overly politicized policy making.[36] Again, agriculture provided a useful case study. For example, Coleman, Skogstad, and Atkinson contrast a "pluralist policy network where group self-interest will be dominant" and "policy-making is reactive rather than anticipatory" with a corporatist network that promotes "the long term collective interest of the sector rather than the short term interest of specific groups."[37] Whereas plural-ism tends to preserve the status quo, corporatist arrangements—whereby bureaucrats and leaders of peak associations make policy through negoti-ation and consensus—enhance government capacity in an area such as industrial policy.

But Coleman and his coauthors also recognize that corporatism can produce clientele relations between interest groups and the government that inhibit policy change. In matters of retrenchment, government ca-pacity might be greater "when interest groups are highly fragmented and restricted to pressuring pluralist policy networks, [because] they are less able to defend programs than those that are vertically integrated and engaged in corporatist networks."[38] This suggests that government capacity might vary across policy types—for instance, industrial policy versus retrenchment—within the same institutional and interest group environment.

In sum, the literature on institutions and interest group power—partic-ularly as it is applied to agriculture—is mixed in its conclusions. Scholars have used U.S. farm policy to exemplify the autonomy of government actors (Finegold and Skocpol), the capture of public policy (Lowi, McConnell), the evolution of a relatively closed policy subsystem (Han-sen, Jones), and the expansion of an issue network (Browne). Compara-tive work on institutions (with agriculture as an occasional case study) bears the distinct mark of pluralist critics such as Lowi and McConnell but is unclear about whether U.S. institutions and interest group politics diminish government capacity for effective policy or may, in fact, enhance it (Coleman, Atkinson, and Montpetit).

---

[35] Milner, "Maintaining International Commitments," 349–50.
[36] See, for example, Atkinson and Coleman, "Strong States and Weak States," 60.
[37] Coleman, Skogstad, and Atkinson, "Paradigm Shifts and Policy Networks," 279.
[38] Coleman, Atkinson, and Montpetit, "Against the Odds," 455.

This diversity of opinion reveals that the relationship between institutions, interest group power, and policy capacity remains unclear. More specifically, at least three basic questions remain unanswered. First, does this relationship change over time? This may account for the temporal pattern of observations in the U.S. case: relative autonomy in the 1930s, capture/subgovernment in the 1950s and 1960s, and a pluralistic issue network since the 1970s. Second, does this relationship vary according to the types of policies governments pursue? This question takes seriously Pierson's argument that welfare state retrenchment is a distinct political task from welfare state expansion. Third, does this relationship vary across countries? This question asks whether institutional arrangements such as federalism or the separation of powers provide interest groups with any particular advantages in access or influence and with what consequence for government capacity.

I attempt to address these questions by tracing the rise of the agricultural welfare state in the United States, France, and Japan. Through the study of institutions and interest group power in both historical and comparative perspective, I argue that U.S. institutions did not give agricultural interest groups any particular advantages and, in fact, may have impeded agricultural interest group capture of the policy process. The ramifications for government capacity were, however, variable. In some policy contexts, the configuration of institutions and interest groups in the United States enhanced government capacity; at other times, the configuration was detrimental to the fulfillment of policy goals.

CHAPTER 1

History, Policy, and Institutions

IN THE FOLLOWING CHAPTERS, I adopt a threefold research design to the study of institutions, interest group power, and government capacity in agriculture. I examine agricultural policy from a longitudinal (change over time), cross-sectional (variation across policy types), and comparative (variation across countries) perspective. The longitudinal study covers agricultural policy from the second half of the nineteenth century—beginning with the creation of the U.S. Department of Agriculture (USDA) in 1862—and ending in the late 1990s. Over this long period the objectives of government policy changed considerably, from the promotion of commercial agriculture to the regulation of agricultural markets and eventually the retrenchment of farm subsidies. The secular trend in farm policy provides the basis for a cross-sectional study of agriculture. Different policy objectives required distinct relationships between the government and farm organizations. However, institutions structure these relationships and shape government capacity to achieve policy goals. Institutional effects become clear when we compare agricultural policy in the United States, France, and Japan.

THE AGRICULTURAL WELFARE STATE: A LONGITUDINAL PERSPECTIVE

The scope and purpose of agricultural policy in advanced capitalist countries has changed considerably over the past 125 years. Whether caused by endogenous technological developments or exogenous economic shocks, changes in economic conditions required governments to develop new policy instruments.[1] In the nineteenth century, agricultural policies were largely promotional. In order to encourage commercial farming, governments built roads, provided credit, and established agricultural research facilities. In the 1920s and 1930s, the policy emphasis switched from promotion to market intervention: governments introduced production con-

---

[1] This interpretation of agricultural change borrows from rural sociologists who adapted key concepts of the French Regulation school to their analysis of capitalist agriculture. See the collection of essays, in Friedland et al., *Towards a New Political Economy of Agriculture*. On the regulation school, see Noël, "Accumulation, Regulation, and Social Change."

trols and price supports in an attempt to lift farm income out of the depths of the Great Depression. After World War II, these depression-era policies formed the substantive core of a mature subsidy regime in agriculture. With the more stable incomes provided by farm subsidies, the postwar agricultural welfare state fueled a tremendous growth in productivity. But beginning in the 1970s, the economic and political cost of government farm programs became onerous. Rising public expenditures, chronic surpluses, environmental degradation, and international conflict over domestic farm programs brought deregulation and retrenchment to the forefront of agricultural policy debates. Despite structural differences in the farm economies of the United States, France, and Japan, agricultural policies in these three nations display this secular trend.

In the second half of the nineteenth century, improved transportation links between rural hinterlands and urban centers opened new markets for farm products. It was at this time that governments in the United States, France, and Japan established departments or ministries of agriculture designated to promote and disseminate research and technology that enhanced agricultural production. In addition, land improvement schemes and transportation projects were an important component of nineteenth-century policy.[2]

In the United States, the federal government established the U.S. Department of Agriculture in 1862. That same year, Congress passed the Homestead Act to encourage westward expansion and the Pacific Railway Act to link newly developed areas of agricultural production with urban markets in the East. The 1862 Morrill Act and the 1887 Hatch Act created a system of state-level agricultural colleges and experiment stations for the conduct of agricultural research.[3] These promotional policies helped commercial agriculture spread steadily westward during the second half of the nineteenth century. Acreage for field crops such as wheat, cotton, and corn increased dramatically.[4] By the end of the century, regional product specializations were clear: the Corn Belt stretched from western Ohio through Indiana, Illinois, and Iowa; wheat dominated from the Canadian border to the Texas Panhandle; the Upper Midwest specialized in dairy; and the South specialized in cotton, tobacco, and rice.[5]

Meanwhile, in France, agricultural promotion was an important policy focus of the early Third Republic. The creation of the Ministry of Agricul-

---

[2] Friedmann and McMichael, "Agriculture and the State System," 93–117.

[3] Gates, *Agriculture and the Civil War,* 293; Benedict, *Farm Policies of the United States,* 19; Curry, *Blueprint for Modern America,* chap. 5.

[4] Between 1870 and 1914, acreage devoted to corn increased 157 percent, wheat acreage increased 161 percent, and cotton acreage increased 290 percent. Calculated by author from USDA, *Yearbook of Agriculture, 1935,* 349–50, 378–79, 390–91, 425–26.

[5] Cochrane, *The Development of American Agriculture,* 65–76, 87–92.

ture in 1881 was one of the first acts of the new Gambetta government. State promotion of railroad construction, such as the 1878 Freycinet Plan, ended isolation for many rural communities and made possible interregional trade in agricultural commodities.[6] According to geographer Hugh Clout, land improvement projects in Brittany, Poitou, and Touraine during the late nineteenth century "served to fill out the interior colonies of middle and northwestern France."[7] With agricultural development and commercial exchange came regional specializations: wheat production in the Paris Basin, cattle in Poitou and the Massif Central, and wine in the Languedoc.[8] Finally, French colonization of Algeria and Tunisia added two million hectares of land devoted principally to wheat and wine—an area equivalent to 10 percent of the arable land in metropolitan France.[9]

In Japan, the Meiji government also established an agriculture ministry in 1881. Research conducted at the network of regional experiment stations developed improved rice varieties amenable to the colder climates and shorter growing seasons of northern Japan.[10] Government funds also underwrote improvement of rice paddies in the north and extreme south.[11] Meanwhile, the large, northern island of Hokkaido came under increased cultivation in the late nineteenth century.[12] Through such measures, rice output increased by 70 percent and wheat output by 98 percent between 1880 and 1910.[13] Finally, the colonization of Taiwan and Korea in the late nineteenth century doubled the area of arable land under Japanese control and increased the supply of rice available to consumers in Japan.[14]

The economic crisis in agriculture after World War I precipitated a shift in government policy. The end of the war in Europe and the continued expansion of production in the United States and other exporting nations flooded world markets with huge stocks of wheat and other grains. Between 1914 and 1939, world wheat production outpaced consumption by a two to one margin.[15] By the early 1930s, nominal prices for U.S.

---

[6] See Duby and Wallon, *Histoire de la France rurale*, 190–93; Price, *The Modernization of Rural France*, 208–59.

[7] Clout, *The Land of France*, 70.

[8] Price, *The Modernization of rural France*, 370; Duby and Wallon, *Histoire de la France rurale*, 119–20; Clout, *The Land of France*, 76–82, 102, 108–10, 112–13.

[9] Miette, *L'Evolution de l'agriculture algerienne*, 79–93; Barral, *Les Agrariens*, 63–65.

[10] Ogura, *Agricultural Development in Modern Japan*, 435–47, 500–508.

[11] Francks, *Technology and Agricultural Development*, 81.

[12] Ogura, *Agricultural Development in Modern Japan*, 481–87.

[13] Calculated by author, Bank of Japan, *Historical Statistics of the Japanese Economy*, 37.

[14] Ogura, *Agricultural Development in Modern Japan*, 481–87.

[15] Malenbaum, *The World Wheat Economy*, 237, 239, 247.

corn, French wheat, and Japanese rice had declined by more than 50 percent from post–World War I levels.[16]

In response, governments in the United States, France, and Japan instituted regulations on agricultural production and prices. The 1933 Agricultural Adjustment Act (AAA) in the United States, the 1933 Rice Control Law in Japan, and the creation in 1936 of the Office national interprofessionel du blé in France sought to lift and stabilize prices for the major farm commodities.[17] The transition to commodity regulation was far from seamless, with resistance to government policy from both elements of the farm sector as well as the agricultural trades (such as processors). Yet by the end of World War II, farmers generally accepted government intervention and, as the political basis for farm subsidies grew stronger, depression-era policies evolved into the complex system of government subsidies that formed the core of the agricultural welfare state in each country.

Government subsidies helped underwrite a profound transformation in agriculture in the decades after World War II. With the higher, more stable incomes afforded by price supports and government loans, farmers increased capital expenditures on new technologies such as hybrid seeds, machinery, and chemicals. Government regulations rewarded specialization and intensive farming practices that increased production—the more farmers produced, the more support they received from the government. As a result, yields quickly increased and a new, "industrialized" agriculture became the dominant form of organization in the sector.[18]

In the United States, inputs of machinery such as tractors more than doubled between 1930 and 1970. Over the same period, applications of agricultural chemicals such as pesticides increased tenfold. And with the development of hybrid seeds, corn yields (output per unit of land) more than tripled.[19] In Japan, agricultural output also increased as a result of higher capital expenditures on machinery and greater consumption of fertilizers and pesticides.[20] The transformation of French agriculture after World War II was even more profound. Government subsidies contributed

[16] Ibid., 237–47; U.S. Bureau of the Census, *Historical Statistics*, 511; INSEE, *Annuaire Statistique de la France, 1966*, 102; Ogura, *Can Japanese Agriculture Survive?* 698.

[17] Benedict, *Farm Policies of the United States*; Tracy, *Government and Agriculture in Western Europe*, 168; Ogura, *Can Japanese Agriculture Survive?* 186.

[18] Berlan, "The Historical Roots of the Present Agricultural Crisis"; Kloppenburg, *First the Seed*.

[19] Calculated by author from data in Cochrane, *The Development of American Agriculture*, 128, 130–31.

[20] Half of this increase came from the purchase of machinery and implements. In the ten years between 1955 and 1965 alone, the number of hand tractors in operation rose from 89,000 to 2.5 million. Hayami, *A Century of Agricultural Growth in Japan*, 55, 105, 230.

TABLE 1.1

French Farms and Land in Farms by Size Classification, 1955–1995

Size Classification	Farms (1,000) 1955	Farms (1,000) 1995	Growth Rate[b] 1955–1995	Percent of Land in 1995
Less than 10 hectares[a]	1,299	270	−3.9	3.2
10 to 35 hectares	831	189	−3.6	14.1
35 to 50 hectares	83	77	−0.2	11.4
50 to 100 hectares	75	128	1.3	31.7
More than 100 hectares	20	70	3.2	39.5

[a]1 hectare = 2.47 acres.

[b]Growth rate = $\exp\left[\dfrac{\log (Y_{1995} / Y_{1995})}{40}\right] - 1$, where Y is the number of farms.

Source: INSEE, *1998 Annuaire Statistique de la France*, 1998, 500.

to impressive productivity growth during "les trente glorieuses."[21] Wheat yields nearly tripled between 1945 and 1975 as applications of agricultural chemicals and machinery rose dramatically. By the early 1970s, France had become an agricultural powerhouse, transformed from a net importer of food into the second leading agricultural exporter in the world after the United States.[22]

But the heavy use of industrial inputs transformed agriculture in fundamental ways. Many farmers, unable to afford the high capital costs of intensive production, left agriculture. In the United States, the proportion of the male labor force employed in agriculture declined from over 15 percent in 1950 to less than 5 percent in 1980. Agricultural decline was even more dramatic in France and Japan, where between 30 and 40 percent of the male labor force was in agriculture in 1950. By 1980, the agricultural share of the labor force in both countries plunged to less than 10 percent. Agricultural decline continued, and by the late 1990s farmers constituted less than 5 percent of the workforce in all three countries.[23]

Those farmers who remained worked large enough farms to afford the high production costs of modern agriculture.[24] Particularly in France and the United States, farm size increased and agricultural land became con-

[21] "The thirty glorious years."

[22] Mitchell, *International Historical Statistics*, 215, 270–71. Between 1946 and 1970, the number of tractors in operation increased from just under twenty-seven thousand to nearly one million (an increase of 3600 percent). Fertilizer consumption increased 500 percent between 1950 and 1980. Roudié, *La France*, 93, 96, 115, 121; Hervieu, *Les Agriculteurs*, 38.

[23] For labor force data, see FAO, *Population: Long-Term Series (Decennial)*.

[24] Pugliese, "Agriculture and the New Division of Labor"; Kim and Curry, "Fordism," 61–80; Buttel and LaRamee, "The 'Disappearing Middle,' " 151–69.

TABLE 1.2
Percentage of U.S. Farms, Land, and Government
Payments by Size Classification, 1997

Size Classification	Farms	Land	Government Payments
Less than 50 acres	30.0	1.2	1.8
50 to 179 acres	31.0	6.6	8.0
180 to 499 acres	21.1	1.3	18.9
500 to 999 acres	9.2	13.1	22.9
More than 1,000 acres	9.2	66.1	48.4

Source: USDA, 1997 Census of Agriculture, 96–97, 102–3.

centrated in the hands of fewer producers, a change that is illustrated in tables 1.1 and 1.2. In France, the decline in agriculture between 1955 and 1995 clearly came at the expense of the smallest farms, which decreased at a rate of almost 4 percent per year. Over this period, the number of large farms actually grew, and by 1995 these large farms controlled 70 percent of agricultural land. In the United States, as indicated in table 1.2, less than 10 percent of farms controlled two-thirds of all agricultural land in 1997 and received nearly half of all government payments.[25] For those unable to earn enough from agriculture, many turned to part-time employment in nonagricultural occupations. Particularly in Japan, the vast majority of farmers today earn most of their income from nonagricultural pursuits.[26]

Intensive agriculture had other negative consequences as well, ranging from environmental degradation caused by heavy pesticide use to inflated consumer food prices due to government price-support policies. In addition, government commitments to support farm prices resulted in stocks of surplus commodities held at public expense and large budgetary outlays during times of low market prices. In the United States, expenditures for farm subsidies doubled in real terms between 1980 and 1986, while unlimited price supports nearly bankrupted the European Community during the 1980s.[27] Finally, increased trade in agricultural commodities during the 1970s and 1980s highlighted the international consequences of domestic policies. This was the case both for exporting nations like the United States, where production control programs reduced export

[25] Although the average U.S. farm is much larger than in France, the United States contains roughly thirteen times the agricultural land area. Consequently, the size classifications employed in tables 1.1 and 1.2 permit rough comparisons. Table 1.2 should also dispel any notions that the U.S. farm sector is composed exclusively of mammoth farms.

[26] Moore, Japanese Agriculture.

[27] On U.S. outlays, see Office of Management and Budget, Historical Tables. On the EC, see Moyer and Josling, Agricultural Policy Reform, 24–27.

earnings, and for importing nations like Japan, where import protection for agriculture led to trade conflicts with the United States.[28]

The high cost of farm subsidies in both economic and political terms created pressures for retrenchment of the agricultural welfare state. In the 1990s, governments tried to balance farmers' political demands with consumer and environmental concerns, fiscal constraints, and international pressure for farm trade liberalization. The United States steadily reduced farm subsidies through the first half of the 1990s and, as described, passed a major revision of farm programs in 1996. The European Community (EC) enacted moderate reforms of the Common Agricultural Policy (CAP) in the late 1980s and early 1990s that momentarily relieved financial pressures and partially replaced market supports that lift prices with more transparent direct payments to producers. Finally, in Japan the government worked to rein in agricultural expenditures in the 1980s and partially deregulated the domestic rice market in the 1990s.[29]

In sum, a longitudinal perspective reveals a secular trend in U.S., French, and Japanese agricultural policy. During the nineteenth century, government policies were largely promotional; they built railroads, distributed lands to settlers, and established agricultural research facilities in an attempt to promote the commercial development of agriculture. In the 1930s governments intervened in agricultural markets in response to the Great Depression as policy objectives concentrated on the stabilization of farm incomes. After World War II, lavish subsidies contributed to the intensification of production and helped farmers invest in tractors, fertilizers, and other inputs that raised productivity. But capital-intensive agriculture forced many to leave farming and produced a number of negative public policy externalities. Fiscal constraints, environmental worries, high consumer prices, and farm trade conflicts shaped policy objectives in the 1990s as retrenchment became the focus of agricultural policy debates.

This secular policy trend suggests that any observed cross-national differences in interest group power or government capacity is not due solely to differences in the economic structure of agriculture in each country. Governments in the United States, France, and Japan confronted roughly similar policy constraints at roughly the same time. In addition, the transformation of agricultural production after World War II diminished the importance of land and labor—factors that contributed to the distinctive character of agriculture in each country—in favor of capital-intensive inputs. French agriculture, for example, increasingly resembles that in the United States: both countries possess export-oriented farm sectors where

---

[28] Johnson, *World Agriculture in Disarray.*
[29] For a fuller discussion see chapter 5.

the majority of land and production is concentrated in the hands of a relatively small stratum of highly productive, capital-intensive farms. Important structural differences exist. But the similarity in policy developments over time—and increasingly the similarity in agricultural production itself—cautions against the view that high subsidies in France and Japan protect an autarkic peasant economy or that low subsidies in the United States reflect the dominance of corporate agriculture.

Rather, the secular policy trend in agriculture provides the basis for a cross-sectional study of institutions, interest groups, and government capacity. Each phase in the development of agricultural policy—the promotion of commercial agriculture, the introduction of market intervention, the creation of a mature subsidy regime, and contemporary efforts at retrenchment—presents a distinct policy task that requires different relations between the government and farmers.

The sequence of policy change also shapes the path of institutional development. And because institutions structure relations between the government and farmers, the resulting pattern of institutional development influences government capacity. Institutions suited to the task of promotion may prove maladapted to market intervention. Farm subsidies may require a relationship between the government and farmers—and a corresponding set of institutions—which makes retrenchment exceedingly difficult. But policy feedback can be positive as well. Poor regulators may become precocious reformers as new policy tasks transform institutional liabilities into assets.

INTEREST GROUPS AND AGRICULTURAL POLICY:
A CROSS-SECTIONAL PERSPECTIVE

As E. E. Schattschneider wrote, "New policies create a new politics."[30] This observation underlies all cross-sectional studies and has spawned numerous attempts to develop a public policy typology. Lowi, in one of the earliest attempts at taxonomy, described three policy types or "arenas of power": distributive, regulatory, and redistributive. Distributive politics, such as the classic rivers and harbors bill, operate through reciprocity and logrolling. Regulatory politics, according to Lowi, display characteristics of pluralist interest group conflict.[31]

As various critics have pointed out, Lowi's categories suffered from analytical ambiguity; he failed to delineate clearly the boundaries between

---

[30] Schattschneider, *Politics, Pressures, and the Tariff*, 288.
[31] Lowi, "American Business."

different categories of his typology.[32] Nevertheless, a policy typology can provide a useful heuristic to examine changes over time in the relationship between interest group power and policy capacity in agriculture. Recall that Lowi formulated his typology in order to account for *longitudinal* variation in trade politics between publication of Schattschneider's *Politics, Pressures, and the Tariff* in 1935 and the work by Bauer, Pool, and Dexter published in 1964. According to Lowi, it is the shift from distributive to regulatory trade politics that explains why Bauer, Pool, and Dexter reached such different conclusions than Schattschneider about the role of interest groups in congressional trade politics. As Hayes put it, "Interest groups could be seen as highly influential in certain kinds of issues, while remaining largely irrelevant for others."[33] Similarly in agriculture, secular changes in policy imply different varieties of interest group participation in the farm policy process.

In another attempt at classification, James Q. Wilson proposed a fourfold typology of interest group activity in politics according to the concentration or diffusion of policy costs and benefits. Wilson described four "political situations" that arise from different combinations of his two variables: majoritarian politics (diffuse costs and benefits), interest group politics (concentrated costs and benefits), client politics (concentrated benefits/diffuse costs), and entrepreneurial politics (concentrated costs/diffuse benefits).[34]

There are some useful parallels between Wilson's categories and the secular trend in agricultural policy described in the previous section. For instance, nineteenth-century promotional policies resembled *majoritarian politics*. The costs and benefits of research facilities, land distribution schemes, and railway construction were distributed widely among a largely rural population. Wilson suggests that interest groups will play a small role in majoritarian politics because no group "can expect to capture a disproportionate share of the benefits or avoid a disproportionate share of the burdens."[35] Instead, "the major organization that becomes involved in issues of this type is the political party that seeks out and endorses programs with distributed benefits."[36] In fact, nineteenth-century agricultural promotion, such as the Homestead Act in the United States, was an

---

[32] Hayes, "The Semi-sovereign Pressure Groups," 138.

[33] Ibid.

[34] Wilson, "The Politics of Regulation"; for other fourfold typologies, see Salisbury, "The Analysis of Public Policy," and Salisbury and Heinz, "A Theory of Policy Analysis." Salisbury and Heinz even apply their modified typology to U.S. agricultural policy.

[35] Wilson, "The Politics of Regulation," 367.

[36] Wilson, *Political Organizations*, 333.

important component of party political competition and did take place in a relatively underdeveloped interest group environment.[37]

By the time governments contemplated market intervention in response to the Great Depression, the interest group environment in agriculture was more fully developed. Moreover, the decision to impose production controls and administered prices carried both concentrated costs and benefits. Wilson calls this *interest group* politics. As he explains, "A subsidy or regulation will often benefit a relatively small group at the expense of another comparable small group. Each side has a strong incentive to organize and exercise political influence."[38] In the 1930s, interest group conflict over market intervention often pitted agricultural organizations against business associations. Market intervention, for example, offered discrete benefits to farmers but also imposed concentrated costs on processors and distributors who paid for intervention either through direct taxation (as in the United States under the first AAA) or indirectly through higher input costs or regulations that circumscribed business activity. Similarly, regulation fueled conflicts between producers of various commodities (such as grain and livestock) whose policy interests diverged.[39]

After World War II, some of the initial struggles over market intervention receded, and a mature subsidy regime developed in agriculture.[40] And as farm sector employment steadily declined, the benefits of subsidy programs became concentrated in the hands of fewer producers. At the same time, the costs of farm subsidies became more widely distributed among taxpayers and consumers. This distribution of costs and benefits produces what Wilson calls *client politics*. According to Wilson, "When the benefits of a prospective policy are concentrated, . . . some small, easily organized group will benefit and thus has a powerful incentive to organize and lobby; [when] the costs of the benefit are distributed at a low per capita rate over a large number of people, . . . they have little incentive to organize in opposition."[41] The economic theory of regulation is clearly recognizable in the logic of client politics and the asymmetry in organizational incentives that follows from group size, concentrated benefits, and diffuse costs.

The opposite asymmetric distribution—concentrated costs and diffuse benefits—resembles the politics of retrenchment. As Pierson writes, "Cutbacks generally impose immediate pain on specific groups, usually in return for diffuse, long-term, and uncertain benefits."[42] Because reductions

[37] See chapter 2.
[38] Wilson, "The Politics of Regulation," 367.
[39] See chapter 3.
[40] See chapter 4.
[41] Wilson, "The Politics of Regulation," 369.
[42] Pierson, *Dismantling the Welfare State?* 18.

in agricultural subsidies impose clear and immediate costs on farmers, agricultural interests are likely to organize in opposition to retrenchment. In contrast, with only the diffuse and distant promise of lower taxes or prices, obstacles to collective action will likely impede groups in favor of lower subsidies. As Pierson himself remarks, "Dairy farmers whose livelihood depends on government subsidies have far more reason to organize than the consumers who may pay a few cents more at the store."[43] As a result, most politicians will avoid retrenchment as a political issue for fear of reprisal from the subsidized industry. This produces a status quo bias in policy.[44]

To overcome the status quo bias that arises from asymmetric costs and benefits, policy change "requires the efforts of a skilled entrepreneur who can mobilize latent public sentiment."[45] Wilson calls this *entrepreneurial politics*. The figure of the political entrepreneur is a common one in political science. For example, entrepreneurs figure prominently in John Kingdon's work on policy change. Significantly, Kingdon remarks on the important roles played by policy entrepreneurs such as Ted Kennedy in the promotion of airline deregulation as a political issue.[46] Derthick and Quirk reached a similar conclusion on the importance of entrepreneurs in their work on deregulation.[47] Deregulation, like retrenchment, entails concentrated costs and diffuse benefits.

Although a Wilsonian typology helps delineate varieties of interest group politics in agriculture, it tells us very little about the relationship between interest group power and government capacity. What role do interest groups play in government pursuits of policy objectives? In cases of retrenchment, as Pierson argues, powerful interest groups diminish government capacity to cut subsidies. But do powerful interest groups enhance government capacity in other types of policy?

Consider, for instance, the task at the core of the agricultural welfare state—government intervention in agricultural production and prices. Government regulations attempt to redress market imperfections in agriculture.[48] But production controls and price supports must overcome a

[43] Ibid.

[44] On concentrated costs, diffuse benefits, and the status quo bias, see Weaver, "The Politics of Blame Avoidance."

[45] Wilson, "The Politics of Regulation," 370.

[46] Kingdon, *Agendas, Alternatives, and Public Policies*, 11.

[47] Derthick and Quirk, *The Politics of Deregulation*.

[48] Farm commodities are inelastic with respect to demand and supply. That is, both the consumption and the production of food are relatively insensitive to price. As a result, small changes in production can produce large swings in price, while the asset and factor specificity of agricultural inputs (plus constraints such as the growing cycle) prevent farmers from adjusting production to meet demand. In an unregulated market, agriculture is subject to

profound collective dilemma in agriculture. The farm sector is typically composed of thousands of individual producers. Come harvest time, each farmer rushes his produce to market, which creates a market glut and a decline in price. Collectively, farmers have an interest to cooperate; together they can lift prices by limiting production or marketing their crops over several months. However, the temptation to free ride is very high, and an individual farmer can reap windfall profits from defection—selling more than his prescribed amount or unloading his crop earlier than his prescribed time. Of course, defections undermine the efficacy of government production controls and administered prices. Moreover, the large number of individual producers makes monitoring compliance very costly.[49]

According to John Keeler, corporatist partnerships between the government and farm organizations are a particularly attractive solution to this collective dilemma in agriculture and the technical complexity of monitoring regulatory compliance.[50] In Graham Wilson's formulation, under corporatism, "interest groups, licensed, recognized or encouraged by the state, enjoy the right to represent their sector of society and . . . work in partnership with the government in both the formulation and implementation of policy."[51] In agriculture, *sectoral* corporatism hinges on the designation of a peak association—such as state-subsidized farmer cooperatives—as an official partner in the administration of government programs.[52] The corporatist client guarantees compliance with government regulations in exchange for resources from the government such as influence over policy, direct cash subsidies, or some other set of benefits that advance its own organizational interests.[53] At least in the case of market intervention, the corporatist literature suggests that government capacity may be enhanced by the presence of a powerful peak association of farmers working closely with the government in policy formation and implementation.

In other words, the relationship between interest group power and government capacity will vary over the course of agricultural welfare state development. Figure 1.1 attempts to illustrate this relationship as a product of two variables borrowed from Keeler's discussion of agricultural

---

boom and bust cycles that leave farm incomes highly unstable and agricultural investment exceptionally risky. Schultz, *The Economic Organization of Agriculture*, 175–94.

[49] For discussion of this collective dilemma in agricultural policy, see Hamilton, *From New Day to New Deal.*

[50] Keeler, *The Politics of Neocorporatism*, 256–58.

[51] Wilson, *Interest Groups*, 22.

[52] The term *sectoral* is meant to distinguish corporatism in a single sector from economy-wide corporatist arrangements. See Cawson, "Introduction: Varieties of Corporatism."

[53] Keeler, *The Politics of Neocorporatism*, 14–15.

Government need for a client to implement policy

	Low	High
Low	1. Promotion *Majoritarian/party* (DB/DC) 1860s–1910s	2. Market intervention *Interest group* (CB/CC) 1920s–1940s
High	4. Retrenchment *Entrepreneurial* (DB/CC) 1970s–1990s	3. Mature subsidy regime *Client* (CB/DC) 1950s–1960s

Relative organizational capacity in agriculture

Figure 1.1. Historical Development of the Agricultural Welfare State
Key: DB = diffuse benefits; DC = diffuse costs; CB = concentrated benefits; CC = concentrated costs.
  Sources: Adapted from Keeler, *The Politics of Neocorporatism*, and Wilson, "The Politics of Regulation."

corporatism and Wilson's typology of public policy. The horizontal axis in figure 1.1 is the government's need for a client to implement policy effectively.[54] Whereas the technical complexity of market intervention and subsidy provision in agriculture requires such a client, this is not the case for promotional policies such as the creation of research facilities or the distribution of land. Nor is it the case for retrenchment when governments want to *reduce* intervention, often over the objections of a powerful client.

The vertical axis in figure 1.1 is the relative organizational capacity of agricultural interest groups. As described previously, a corporatist client must be able to mobilize and discipline its members in line with government policy goals such as the enforcement of production controls or administered prices. This is difficult, however, because of the atomistic character of the farm sector and the temptation to defect from collective arrangements. Under what conditions, then, are farm groups likely to overcome this collective dilemma?

[54] Ibid., 256–59.

As Wilson argued, groups are more likely to overcome obstacles to collective action when the costs or benefits of a policy proposal are concentrated rather than diffuse. Since we are interested in the conditions that produce an *agricultural* client rather than some other economic group, *relative* organizational capacity in agriculture will be higher when the distribution of costs and benefits is asymmetric—concentrated for agricultural groups and diffuse for other interests such as businesses or consumers.[55] Both a mature subsidy regime and struggles over retrenchment display this asymmetry in costs and benefits. Note as well that this asymmetry occurs at a time of rapid decline in farm-sector employment (roughly 1950s through 1990s), a factor that contributes further to high relative organizational capacity in agriculture. Thus, if interest group power is a function of relative organizational capacity, then farm organizations will exercise the most (relative) power under a mature subsidy regime and during retrenchment.

In sum, figure 1.1 combines both cross-sectional and longitudinal analyses of agricultural policy. Moving clockwise from the upper left quadrant of the figure, one can trace the development of the agricultural welfare state from the late nineteenth century to the present. When mapped on to a cross-sectional analysis, it is clear that the relative power of agricultural organizations does not always correspond to the degree of government need for an agricultural client. Government capacity, other things being equal, will vary as a result.

Although agricultural promotion occurs in a relatively underdeveloped interest group environment, government need for a client to achieve promotional goals is low. The wide distribution of promotional costs and benefits resembles the majoritarian policies described by Wilson. With the shift to market intervention, the technical complexity of policy increases, as does the need for an agricultural client to help implement government programs. However, during the initial period of market intervention, organizational capacity in agriculture *relative to other interests* remains low as the concentration of both costs and benefits produce interest group conflicts over policy between groups of farmers or between farmers and other economic groups in society. With the shift to a mature regulatory regime, the distribution of costs and benefits becomes asymmetric, and farm groups develop the organizational capacity necessary to play the

---

[55] I emphasize relative capacity because if both costs and benefits are concentrated, then farm groups would have no particular organizational advantage over other interests in the policy process. Rather than a corporatist partnership between the government and agriculture, we would expect pluralist conflict over policy or interest group politics in Wilson's terms.

client role. Finally, in the shift to retrenchment, the government no longer needs (or desires) a client, but the organizational advantages enjoyed by agricultural groups remain. The concentrated costs of retrenchment proposals with the promise of only distant and diffuse benefits will reduce the likelihood of policy change in the absence of an entrepreneurial politician able to mobilize public support as Wilson suggests.

But interest group power in agriculture is not simply a function of the distribution of costs and benefits. It is also a function of institutions and government resources that underwrite the cost of organizational maintenance and provide exclusive access to the policy process. Examination of institutional effects on interest group power (and government capacity) requires variation in government structures while holding policy tasks constant. That is, we must examine agricultural policy from a comparative perspective.

AGRICULTURAL POLICY IN COMPARATIVE PERSPECTIVE: THE ROLE OF INSTITUTIONS

In order to explore the effect of institutions on interest group power and government capacity, I compare agricultural policy in the United States, France, and Japan. I chose these three countries because early comparative work on institutions juxtaposed the fragmented and permeable American state with countries like France and Japan, where centralized institutions and strong executives supposedly insulated officials from political pressure by interest groups.

When we place American agriculture in a comparative context, these distinctions between "strong" and "weak" break down. Particularly in matters of retrenchment, institutions in France and Japan did not provide bureaucrats or politicians with autonomy from agricultural interests, but rather *solidified* the influence of farm organizations over the direction of agricultural policy. In fact, agricultural politics in France and Japan often display precisely those characteristics—agency capture and policy sclerosis—we are supposed to find in decentralized political systems such as that of the United States. These comparative experiences with agriculture caution against the view that centralized authority always guarantees government capacity.

More recent studies of comparative institutions moved beyond the blunt instrument of the weak-strong state continuum. For instance, Weaver and Rockman show that the exclusive focus on the organization of executive and legislative power—parliamentary versus presidential systems—misses a host of important institutional variants that influence government capabilities. These include unified versus divided governments in presidential systems or the prevalence of coalitional, party government, and single-party-dominant-regimes in parliamentary systems. In addition, Weaver and Rockman direct our attention to institutional influences wholly unrelated to parliamentary or presidential systems such as federalism, the power of an independent judiciary, or the autonomy of bureaucrats.[56]

In the case of agriculture, we can extend the domain of relevant institutions even further. The development and design of agricultural bureaucracies, the definition and scope of departmental jurisdictions, and the location of decision-making authority in the agricultural policy process are examples of sectoral (or agriculture-specific) institutions that influence capabilities. Agricultural policy is also shaped by the structure of interest representation. Whether farmers are organized into a single peak association or divided among regional, ideological, and commodity groupings influences the relationship between producers, the politicians who represent them, and the bureaucracies responsible for the administration of policy.

Weaver and Rockman also point out that institutions are not uniformly "strong" or "weak." In their words, "the effects of specific institutional arrangements . . . are neither uniform or unidirectional."[57] Instead, institutional capabilities vary according to the objectives governments pursue. When government objectives change, so do the institutional requirements of policy. As we shall see in the case of agriculture, institutional assets can become liabilities and vice versa.

The literature on distributive politics, for example, associates decentralized institutions—such as congressional committees—with higher spending on "pork-barrel" projects.[58] Decentralization in this case refers to the number of participants and decision-making units in the policy process. In distributive politics, where decisions are the product of universal logrolling (i.e., everyone agrees to support everyone else's project), decentralized institutions will produce higher expenditures. In contrast, institutions that centralize spending authority operate as instruments of austerity by turning a positive-sum logroll among multiple participants into a single, negative-sum decision on resource allocation.[59]

Many promotional policies in agriculture, in fact, share characteristics of the distributive pork barrel.[60] Therefore, fragmented or decentralized

[56] In particular, see Weaver and Rockman, "Assessing the Effects of Institutions"; Weaver and Rockman, "When and How Do Institutions Matter?"

[57] Weaver and Rockman, "When and How Do Institutions Matter?" 454. This point is more fully developed in Pierson, *Dismantling the Welfare State?*

[58] Stewart, "Budget Reform as Strategic Legislative Action," 296.

[59] Ibid., 294–97.

[60] In fact, Lowi used nineteenth-century land policies to exemplify distributive politics. Lowi, "American Business," 690.

institutions might facilitate promotional policies such as land distribution schemes or the creation of an agricultural research system. As I describe in chapter 2, American institutions were particularly suited to the task of agricultural promotion. The power of individual states under federalism, the capacity of politicians to distribute federal funds through a decentralized appropriations process in Congress, and a regionally based party system fueled the growth of agricultural expenditures and encouraged the development of a decentralized, location-specific system of research facilities. In contrast, the centralization of political institutions in France and Japan limited the capacity of politicians to channel government resources toward the farm sector.

Promotional policies also resemble "majoritarian politics," as I described in the previous section. According to Wilson, one important characteristic of majoritarian politics is that political parties rather than interest groups play the predominant role in policy advocacy. A comparison of nineteenth-century agricultural policy, therefore, must take into account differences in the structure of political competition, such as the relative maturity of the party system in each country. In the United States, a regionally based, patronage-driven party system was already in place by the mid–nineteenth century. In contrast, the first mass-based political party in France was not established until 1901.[61] In Japan, party politics remained in its infancy until well into the twentieth century.

Differences in the relative maturity of party politics had important consequences for the development of administrative capacities and farm organizations during the nineteenth century. In the United States, where the agricultural bureaucracy developed as an outgrowth of patronage politics, administrative authority was divided among various executive departments and levels of government. At the same time, the regional basis of party competition stymied nineteenth-century attempts to construct a national farm organization in the United States. In clear contrast, the relative underdevelopment of party politics in France and Japan led to the development of a centralized agricultural bureaucracy and the creation of state-sponsored farm organizations engaged in national politics and policy debates. Created in order to attract the political loyalties of farmers, agriculture ministries and farm organizations operated in lieu of formal political parties in France and Japan.

The institutional consequences of agricultural promotion influenced the transition to market intervention in the 1920s and 1930s. As described in the previous section, the implementation of production controls and price supports required the assistance of a willing interest group client

---

[61] Hazareesingh, *Political Traditions in Modern France*, 47.

in a way promotion had not. Due to the symmetric distribution of costs and benefits, I suggested that—*other things being equal*—the relative organizational capacity of agricultural groups would be low. However, governments influence the interest group environment through the provision of resources that underwrite the costs of organizational creation and maintenance.[62] Governments also shape interest group politics through the provision of privileged access to the policy process.

As I describe in chapter 3, the capacity to manipulate the interest group environment made the transition to market intervention easier in France and Japan than in the United States. In France and Japan, the legacy of state-sponsored farm organizations led to the creation of corporatist relations in agriculture. In the 1920s and 1930s, agricultural cooperatives became the official government agent for the regulation of rice production and distribution in Japan. Meanwhile, in France, specialty producer groups organized around single crops such as wine and wheat performed critical regulatory functions on behalf of the government. In both countries, centralized bureaucracies made it possible to provide agricultural clients privileged access to the policy process. In the United States, the government tried to develop a policy partnership with the American Farm Bureau Federation. But with responsibility for policy divided among various administrative units and rival farm organizations contesting Farm Bureau dominance, a close policy partnership in agriculture never fully developed. Policy capacity suffered as a result: efforts in the United States to raise and stabilize agricultural prices and control production were less effective than in France or Japan.

In other words, institutions made the shift from interest group politics to client politics (a shift from cell 2 to cell 3 in figure 1.1) difficult in the United States. Even after World War II, interest group conflicts between various farm organizations foiled efforts by both political parties to establish a clientelistic relationship with farmers. Proposals to lift prices for one set of commodities threatened the profits of producers of other products. Institutions transformed these economic differences between producers into partisan battle lines and hampered the development of clientele relations in agriculture. In France and Japan, on the other hand, corporatist relations between farmers and the government became the basis for a political alliance that linked peak agricultural organizations to electorally dominant conservative parties. In both countries, farmers become a core political constituency to an extent not found in the United States.

Not surprisingly, a legacy of clientele relations between farmers and the government makes retrenchment particularly difficult in France and Japan.

---

[62] Walker, "The Origins and Maintenance of Interest Groups."

The concentrated cost of subsidy cuts and the long history of market intervention in agriculture give farmers both an organizational and a political advantage in retrenchment battles with the government. As Pierson would predict, retrenchment is unlikely unless politicians can diffuse accountability for unpopular decisions. Following Wilson, successful retrenchment will also require the efforts of a skilled entrepreneur. But how do institutions shape retrenchment politics?

As in the case of promotion, U.S. institutions would seem to offer distinct advantages in matters of retrenchment. Separated powers, federalism, bicameralism, and congressional committees diffuse authority throughout the political system; this helps the individual politician minimize political losses for unpopular decisions. In contrast, the concentration of agricultural policy authority within Japan and France (and in the institutions of the European Community) focuses accountability for farm policy decisions. This makes retrenchment a riskier political enterprise.[63]

Second, U.S. institutions promote entrepreneurial behavior. The candidate-centered nature of elections, a product of electoral rules and relatively weak political parties, encourages politicians to pursue new issues that might pay large political dividends. Ted Kennedy, in his advocacy of deregulation in the 1970s, is emblematic. As Derthick and Quirk conclude, deregulation "was attributable to properties of the political system. . . . fragmentation and competitive leadership did not prevent action, but rather prodded sometimes reluctant leaders to act more boldly."[64] In contrast, the one-party-dominant parliamentary system in Japan and the strong-executive, semi-presidential system in Fifth Republic France provide the individual legislator with fewer opportunities for entrepreneurial activity.

More important, U.S. institutions facilitate entrepreneurial success. Baumgartner and Jones show how the capacity to shift the location of policy authority from one "policy venue" to another can produce dramatic policy change. Because the location of policy authority, or policy venue, "carries with it a decisional bias," Baumgartner and Jones argue that "When the venue of a public policy changes, . . . those who previously dominated the policy process may find themselves in the minority, and erstwhile losers may be transformed into winners."[65] Retrenchment entrepreneurs, by shifting policy authority away from institutions dominated by agricultural interests, can increase the likelihood of success.

---

[63] Weaver, "The Politics of Blame Avoidance"; Pierson, *Dismantling the Welfare State?*
[64] Derthick and Quirk, *The Politics of Deregulation*, 252–57.
[65] Baumgartner and Jones, "Agenda Dynamics and Policy Subsystems," 1047.

U.S. institutions multiply these opportunities for venue change. For example, Baumgartner and Jones describe how "federalism creates a great number of distinct and partially autonomous venues of policy action." Similarly, "Congress provides one of the most important elements in creating the system of positive feedback, potential instability, and reversals in policy outcomes," in particular through jurisdictional competition among committees.[66] In clear contrast, the concentration of policy authority in Japan and France (and the EU) creates jurisdictional monopolies in agriculture that severely restrict opportunities for venue change.

Finally, U.S. institutions represent diffuse interests in the policy process. This also facilitates retrenchment. Becker argued that increased inefficiencies in the provision of subsidies—deadweight losses, in the language of economists—stimulate lobbying activity by groups that pay for subsidies (in agriculture, consumers and taxpayers) and discourage lobbying by groups that receive subsidies (farmers).[67] When these conditions hold, a lower level of subsidy—agricultural retrenchment—will maximize political support. Politicians will cut subsidies when, in Peltzman's words, "deregulation benefits some part of the *relevant coalition*."[68]

But membership in the "relevant coalition" is a function of access to the policy process. In the United States, the location of policy authority in Congress rather than the executive, periodic reapportionment on the basis of population, and reforms that diminished the policy autonomy of committees provided ample access for representatives of the taxpayers and consumers who pay for agricultural subsidies. In France and Japan, on the other hand, institutions generally exclude such groups from the agricultural policy process. Overrepresentation of rural voters means that retrenchment may not maximize political support, despite rising inefficiencies of subsidy programs.

As I examine in chapter 5, U.S. institutions did make retrenchment easier in various ways. Beginning in the 1970s, congressional scrutiny of farm programs increased in response to the high program costs, inflated food prices, massive surpluses, and environmental damage caused by price supports and other policies. While consumer groups, environmental organizations, and other critics of farm programs became more active in congressional farm politics, urban and suburban members of the House of Representatives found agricultural retrenchment an attractive political issue. The congressional budget process, meanwhile, made cuts

---

[66] Baumgartner and Jones, *Agendas and Instability in American Politics*, 193, 216.

[67] Becker, "A Theory of Competition among Pressure Groups," 381.

[68] Peltzman, "The Economic Theory of Regulation after a Decade of Deregulation," 38; emphasis added.

in agricultural expenditures possible in two ways: budget reconciliation offered retrenchment advocates an alternative policy venue in agriculture and helped farm-state politicians deflect blame for unpopular subsidy cuts.

In France and Japan, institutions made retrenchment much more difficult. Critics of farm subsidies, such as consumers and even business groups, enjoyed little access to the agricultural policy process. With opportunities for venue change much more limited in the institutional context of French and Japanese farm policy, advocates of the status quo could often block retrenchment or significantly dilute its impact. International pressures for farm trade liberalization did present opportunities for venue change and a pretense to diminish blame for unpopular retrenchment decisions. But even when politicians did execute subsidy cuts, they often faced political reprisals at the polls. All told, these factors contributed to a less impressive retrenchment record than in the United States.

The comparative study of agricultural policy in the United States, France, and Japan yields two interesting conclusions abut the relationship between institutions, interest group power, and government capacity. First, U.S. institutions did not guarantee farm groups any particular advantages in the agricultural policy process. The regional basis of nineteenth-century party politics, the inability to create a corporatist partnership in the 1930s, and the postwar conflicts over agricultural policy presented obstacles to farm group influence. In France and Japan, on the other hand, a centralized administration and state-sponsored farm organizations, the corporatist implementation of policy, and the political integration of farmers into conservative politics did produce clientele relations in agriculture.

Second, the effects of these institutional differences on policy were variable. Decentralized institutions facilitated agricultural promotion and retrenchment; centralized institutions eased the transition to market intervention and the creation of an agricultural client. When policy tasks change, so do the assets and liabilities of institutions and government capabilities to achieve policy goals.

IS AGRICULTURE A SPECIAL CASE?

An alternative to the institutional argument presented in the preceding is that agriculture is a special case in the politics of some advanced industrial countries. The persistence of the agricultural welfare state in France and Japan is due not only to government structures but also to the cultural resonance farming retains in the political life of those nations. The rapid urbanization of the United States and the dominance of economic liberalism, some would argue, have caused reverence for agrarian life—as well as the agricultural welfare state—to wither and die.[69]

To be sure, agriculture holds a special place in French political culture. The nineteenth-century peasant was viewed as a guarantor of social harmony who balanced the dangerous radicalism of the cities. During the "thirty glorious years" after World War II, the farmer was viewed as a national champion whose "green petrol" brought the country wealth and prominence in the world economy. In the late twentieth century, the French farmer is seen as a steward of the countryside who protects rural France from the encroachment of urban industrial blight. Agricultural policy, according to some observers, provides a kind of public good. This justifies continued support for farmers, despite the rising cost of subsidies.[70]

The cultural resonance of agriculture is very strong in Japan as well. The cultivation of rice is a central feature of Shinto creation myths, and the emperor still plants a small rice paddy each year as a symbol of national well-being.[71] For many Japanese, urban and rural alike, the ceremonies and traditions surrounding rice cultivation hark back to a simpler, preindustrial time when individuals were closely tied to their communities through reciprocity and mutual dependence. Farmers embody these values.[72] As in France, then, agricultural policy in Japan is viewed as a public good that serves the entire political community rather than the particular interests of a small group of producers.

Some argue that agriculture does not carry the same cultural significance in the United States as it does in France or Japan. Americans view agriculture in purely economic terms; farmers should be exposed to the same competitive pressures as other sectors of the economy. Although the family farmer was once highly esteemed, some argue that the corporate takeover of agriculture and the negative environmental consequences of intensive crop and livestock production have discredited the agrarian myth in the United States. Agricultural policy in the United States, unlike in France or Japan, is viewed not as public good but as a set of programs designed for special interests. As we have seen, for many observers the agricultural policy process exemplified "the private expropriation of public authority."[73]

However, to attribute differences in policy to cultural attributes overlooks an American agrarian tradition that also equates agriculture with

[69] For a recent application to U.S. and EU agricultural policy, see Skogstad, "Ideas, Paradigms and Institutions."

[70] Rogers, "Farming Visions," 5, 31.

[71] Moore, *Japanese Agriculture*.

[72] Smith, "Letter from Tokyo," 108.

[73] Lowi, *The End of Liberalism*, 67.

core political values and national well-being.[74] The Jeffersonian ideal that "those who labor in the earth are the chosen people of God" still holds sway in American political culture. During the 1980s, when farmers endured their worst farm crisis since the 1930s, the collective response of the country was Farm Aid. Public opinion data provide further evidence of agricultural exceptionalism in the United States. Forty-eight percent of respondents to a 1994 survey believed that "the government should protect family farmers."[75] And despite charges that corporate interests control farming, politicians from rural areas still invoke the image of the "family farmer" as a small, independent producer worthy of special protection from economic forces. This was clearly evident in 1998 and 1999, when Congress voted billions of extra dollars in government assistance to compensate farmers for low prices.[76]

In this respect, farming is accorded a special place in all industrialized democracies. Some scholars attribute this prominence to the fact that the agricultural mode of production, particularly the predominance of unpaid family labor, is perceived as virtuous by the larger industrialized community.[77] This begs the question: Why have French and Japanese farmers retained their special status in politics and policy to a greater degree than Farmers in the United States? It may be more helpful to restate this not as a question of culture but as one about the effects of ideas on public policy.[78]

The answer brings us back inevitably to the structure of institutions. As Yee explains, "By regulating the permeability of the policymaking process, institutions influence which ideas gain political access."[79] Agrarianism retains its hold in France and Japan not only because of cultural differences but also because of a particular institutional legacy that magnifies and protects rural power in these countries.[80] As a result of institutions, appeals to an agrarian past—a theme I insist is prevalent in all industrial

---

[74] Danbom describes agrarianism as "the celebration of agriculture and rural life for the positive impact thereof on the individual and society." Danbom, "Romantic Agrarianism," 1.

[75] The *1994 Multi-Investigator Survey* asked respondents whether "the government should protect family farmers by guaranteeing them a minimum price on their crops, or should crop prices be set by the free market." The weighted-response favored the free market alternative 52 percent to 48 percent. Sniderman, Brady and Tetlock, *1994 Multi-Investigator Survey*.

[76] "Congress Disregards Free Market with Farm Bill," *New York Times*, October 16, 1998.

[77] Offer, "Between the Gift and the Market," 464.

[78] See, for example, Hall, "Policy Paradigms, Social Learning, and the State."

[79] Yee, "The Causal Effects of Ideas on Policies," 92.

[80] Skogstad agrees ("Ideas, Paradigms and Institutions," 478–81) but attributes some independent effect to ideas about agriculture. I find it difficult to separate empirically ideas from structural influences.

countries—continue to carry great weight in French and Japanese policy debates. Those who espouse contrary views about agriculture—such as free-market liberals or environmentalists—are generally at the margins of the policy process. In the United States, on the other hand, similar agrarian appeals are made on behalf of farmers, but they must compete with other, rival claimants who enjoy regular access to agricultural policy debates. In recent decades it has become more and more difficult for farmers to be heard in American politics—even in questions of agricultural policy.

CHAPTER 2

Foundations of the Agricultural Welfare State

STUDENTS OF AMERICAN POLITICAL DEVELOPMENT often trace the origins of the modern welfare state back to the decades after the Civil War, when a host of new institutions and policies expanded the role of the federal government in the economy and society. The professional civil service, the independent regulatory commission, and early forms of social welfare policy were all nineteenth-century innovations. Moreover, as students of political development point out, these foundations of the modern welfare state were the products of Gilded Age politics.[1]

The same holds true for the agricultural welfare state. The U.S. Department of Agriculture, the land-grant college system, and the state agricultural experiment stations together formed the foundation for an agricultural bureaucracy that still exists today. All three institutional innovations date from the late nineteenth century. The USDA, created in 1862, was granted cabinet status in 1889. The land-grant college system, funded through grants of public lands to each state for the creation of an agricultural university, also dates from 1862. Finally, the system of state agricultural research facilities, or experiment stations, was created by an act of Congress in 1887.

Like other nineteenth-century institutions, the agricultural bureaucracy bears the distinct mark of Gilded Age political conflicts. At a time when the majority of the working population was engaged in farming, agricultural policies took on an important political component. Public assistance for agriculture was fueled by the politician's search for farm votes.

This political component is brought into relief when one examines the development of an agricultural bureaucracy in France and Japan. As in the United States, agricultural ministries and research facilities in these countries were also nineteenth-century creations, but there were important differences in the structure of early agricultural bureaucracies. Whereas administrative authority in the United States was divided among various departments at both the state and the federal level, responsibility

---

[1] Among others, see Skowronek, *Building a New American State*; Skocpol, *Protecting Soldiers and Mothers*.

for agriculture in France and Japan was unified within a single ministerial portfolio at the national level. Second, Congress defined policy responsibilities for the USDA along narrow, *sectoral* lines. Only matters directly related to agricultural production were within USDA jurisdiction. In France and Japan, policy responsibilities developed along broad, *territorial* lines. Farm ministries not only governed agriculture but also controlled other aspects of the rural economy.

This institutional variation was the product of differences in political competition, specifically the role played by political parties. In the United States, nineteenth-century politics was organized around party competition. Consequently, the patronage needs and electoral prospects of party politicians shaped the development of the agricultural bureaucracy. France and Japan lacked a developed party system at this time, and competition took place between elite factions rather than political parties. Agricultural bureaucracies were created *in lieu of* party organizations; farm ministries were designed not simply to promote agriculture but also to mobilize political support from peasants and landowners.

These characteristics of political competition had a second important consequence. The development of farm organizations in the nineteenth century was similarly influenced by political party development. In the United States, early agricultural associations such as the Grange or the Farmers' Alliance were constrained by the nineteenth-century party system. While farm groups achieved some success in state politics or in narrowly defined agricultural issues, they foundered once the movement directly challenged the established party system. In France and Japan, on the other hand, farm groups were often a creation of government elites and benefited organizationally from public resources. As in the case of agricultural administration, state-supported farm groups carried out important political functions.

Patterns of political competition, the structure of agricultural bureaucracies, and the organizational strength of farm groups provided the institutional setting for a variety of nineteenth-century agricultural policies. Governments in all three countries promoted commercial agriculture through a variety of mechanisms, ranging from the distribution of public lands to the creation of agricultural research facilities. Institutions influenced both the choice of promotional mechanisms and the capacity of governments to effectively channel resources to the farm sector. In some important respects, the fragmented and decentralized institutions of the United States were, in fact, better equipped to promote the commercial development of agriculture than the unitary, centralized institutions of France and Japan.

POLITICAL COMPETITION IN THE UNITED
STATES, FRANCE, AND JAPAN

In the nineteenth century, farmers were an essential ally to anyone in pursuit of political power. In the United States, the two major political parties competed with one another for control of key agricultural areas. In France, leaders of the Third Republic viewed the peasant as the key to political success over the antirepublican aristocracy in the countryside. In Japan, founders of nascent political parties appealed to landowners for political support while the oligarchs who ruled Meiji Japan distributed government resources in an attempt to minimize the popularity of party politicians in rural areas. Agricultural promotion was, at its base, a strategy of political competition.

The United States: The "Party Period" and Political Competition

Following the Civil War, political parties in the United States underwent an important transition. As the factional division among Republicans dissipated after Reconstruction, political professionals replaced ideologues at the top of the party hierarchy. The Democrats, who had retained a presence in key districts of the North throughout the war, took control of the House of Representatives in 1875. The remainder of the century was perhaps the most politically competitive period in American history. Party control of the House changed hands seven times over the next twenty-five years. Conditions of divided government in which different parties controlled the White House and at least one chamber of Congress prevailed 56 percent of the time between 1861 and 1897.[2]

Republicans and Democrats responded to this intense political competition with improved party organization. Morton Keller has referred to this period as the "triumph of organizational politics," when party leaders perfected the political machine capable of delivering votes through the distribution of funds and favors. From the ward to the statehouse, a party hierarchy developed that was capable of mobilizing votes, choosing delegates to political conventions, and filling party slates. At the level of national politics, party professionals such as Roscoe Conkling or Mark Hanna balanced the interests of various state party machines. This was the age of the political fixer, the party boss, the "politico."[3]

[2] Stewart, "Lessons from the Post–Civil War Era"; Kleppner, The Third Electoral System, 16–47; Skowronek, Building a New American State.

[3] Keller, Affairs of State, 238–87, 522–63; McCormick, The Party Period and Public Policy, 143–227; Marcus, Grand Old Party; Josephson, The Politicos; Foner, Reconstruction, 469–88.

Patronage was essential to the operation of the Gilded Age party organization. Although patronage had been an important aspect of American politics since the emergence of mass parties in the Jacksonian era, it reached its apex in the postbellum period, when the expansion of the federal government multiplied the number of public offices. Patronage provided politicians with political resources in two ways. First, politicians used patronage to reward supporters. This percolated downward as each position controlled appointments to other subordinate positions, and so on. Patronage provided parties with internal cohesion; it linked state and local political machines to politicians and party organizations in Washington. Second, patronage was an important reelection resource. Appointees were not just expected to work on their patrons' behalf come election time; they also gave back a portion of their salaries to the party or politicians who appointed them. Assessments on patronage appointees filled party coffers with money for future campaigns.[4]

The patronage needs of political parties also required access to the resources of government. In the 1880s, for example, the decentralization of congressional appropriations helped politicians channel federal funds back home to their districts. Created in 1867, the House Appropriations Committee was designed to defend the Treasury; the committee often reduced federal spending, to the chagrin of representatives in search of government pork. By the late 1870s, critics complained of the committee's seemingly absolute power over budgetary decisions. In 1880, a House revolt against this power resulted in the devolution of authority from the Appropriations Committee to individual authorizing committees, and by 1885, virtually all power over spending decisions was in the hands of the authorizing committees. Stewart refers to these changes as a process of "expansionary fragmentation": institutional changes that decentralized authority in order to promote increased federal spending. The House Agriculture Committee was one of the first committees to gain control over its own appropriations in 1880. Not surprisingly, the annual budget of the Department of Agriculture increased soon thereafter.[5]

The growth of party organization in the late nineteenth century and the devolution of the congressional appropriations process served the same purpose: they both afforded politicians with the resources necessary for reelection. Through the patronage system, parties provided candidates with money and the access to political appointments necessary to mobilize

[4] Lowi, "Party, Policy and Constitution"; Shefter, "Party, Bureaucracy and Political Change"; White, *The Republican Era.*

[5] Brady, *Critical Elections and Congressional Policy Making,* 125–28; Stewart, "Does Structure Matter?" 585–605; Stewart, "Budget Reform as Strategic Legislative Action," 303–7; Kursman, "Structure and Policy Shifts," 31–37.

voters. Decentralized appropriations allowed individual politicians to channel government resources to their districts. Aside from their political value, these reelection resources helped promote commercial agriculture in the United States.

France: The Consolidation of Republican Rule

The defeat of French forces at Sedan and the abdication of Napoleon III in 1870 began the transition toward the parliamentary democracy of the Third Republic. Over the next decade, splintered factions on the Left and Right competed with each other for control of the new regime. By 1879, a Center-Left coalition controlled Parliament. Led by men such as Jules Ferry and Leon Gambetta, this "Opportunist Republican" coalition derived its electoral support from the *nouvelles couches sociales* (new social strata): provincial manufacturers (textiles, silk, sugar refiners), petit bourgeois merchants, and farmers.[6]

Merchants and farmers of provincial France were particularly important to the success of the Center-Left. For republican leaders such as Gambetta, Ferry, and Méline, the allegiance of these voters was critical for the Republic to succeed over the rural aristocracy on the Right and the urban proletariat on the Left.[7] And with the advent of universal suffrage in the last years of the Second Empire, 67 percent of the French electorate was now rural. Malapportionment further magnified the political value of the peasant vote. Senate representation, for example, was particularly skewed toward rural France. The constitution of 1875 stipulated indirect election by a college composed of deputies, local administrative officials (the *conseillers-généraux* and the *conseillers d'arrondissement*), and members of the municipal councils (usually the mayor). Because the vast majority of Senate electors came from rural areas, the Senate heavily reflected the interests of the countryside.[8] Thus, for the Center-Left to control the national government, republican leaders would have to secure the political allegiance of the peasantry. As Ferry insisted, "The Republic will be a Republic of peasants or it will not be."[9]

---

[6] Chapman, *The Third Republic of France*, 1–74, 160–202; Goguel, *La Politique des partis*, 44–55.

[7] Elwitt, *The Making of the Third Republic*, 53–56; Agulhon, *The French Republic*, 11–112; Agulhon, "Les Paysans dans la vie politique," 371–81.

[8] Barral, "Agrarisme de gauche et agrarisme de droite," 244; Chapman, *The Third Republic*, 260–61.

[9] Barral, "Agrarisme de gauche et agrarisme de droite," 247.

This task was complicated, however, by the organizational weakness of French parties in the 1870s. Republican leaders did not exercise great control over the selection of candidates; instead, candidates selected their party affiliations. This problem was exacerbated by electoral rules. Under the two-ballot system, a large number of candidates with loose party affiliations often participated in the first round of voting. Second, single-member constituencies, as opposed to departmental lists of candidates selected by the parties, placed emphasis on local reputation and personal resources rather than endorsements and assistance from party officials.[10] As a result, the Chamber of Deputies tended to reflect the geographic diversity of rural political attachments. This favored republicans in the East, Paris Basin, and upper Massif Central; however, parts of the West, Brittany, and lower Massif Central remained conservative strongholds.[11] Once elected, moreover, deputies enjoyed relative independence from party organizations in how they voted and in their selection of parliamentary groups with which to affiliate. This independence and lack of party discipline meant there was a tenuous link between Parliament and the ostensible party leaders who constituted the cabinet. In fact, the Third Republic was plagued by ministerial instability. Between 1876 and 1914, forty-six governments were formed; forty of these lasted less than six months.[12]

To overcome the organizational weakness of political parties and secure the loyalty of peasant voters, republican leaders utilized the institutions of local government. Ironically, the political value of local administration was the product of imperial France. Central state authority radiated from Paris through a system of administration in which each department, canton, and commune was headed by a prefect, subprefect, and mayor responsible to the minister of the interior. In addition to their administrative and police duties, prefects and mayors during the Second Empire designated official candidates for local elections, presided over balloting, and controlled various forms of local patronage such as the appointment of inspectors, tax collectors, and postmen.[13]

---

[10] Under the two-ballot system, if no candidate received an absolute majority in the first round of voting, another round of voting was carried out in which a plurality sufficed. Usually negotiations among candidates between the two votes would result in the withdrawal of weaker candidates. Gambetta strongly urged adoption of list voting (*scrutin des listes*) rather than single-member constituencies (*scrutin des arrondissements*). Notwithstanding the brief experimentation with list voting in the early 1880s, single-member constituencies were the norm. See Duverger, *Political Parties*, 45, 324–27.

[11] Siegfried, *Tableau politique*; Goguel, *Géographie des élections françaises*.

[12] Chapman, *The Third Republic*, 70–71, 214–22, 228–32, 287; Agulhon, *The French Republic*, 33–36.

[13] Chapman, *The Prefects and Provincial France*, 45–53.

During the Government of National Defense in the early 1870s, Gambetta ordered the purge of department prefects suspected of Bonapartist sympathies. Their republican replacements provided information on local electoral politics and in some cases instructed mayors (who were appointed by the prefects until the 1880s) to campaign for republican candidates. Even if the prefects and other officials were dedicated bureaucrats *first*, their utility come election time was not overlooked by local deputies, who turned to them for access to patronage and other electorally valuable resources.[14]

In addition, republican leaders opened up local offices to election and increased the authority of elected departmental councils over administrative decisions. Over the next decades, mayors became symbolic representatives of republicanism as local notables were replaced with a new generation of elected officials—doctors, lawyers, petit bourgeois, and, occasionally, farmers. Thus, the administrative system was used in lieu of a formal party organization. As Schmidt notes, "By bringing politics to the periphery, decentralization effectively enfranchised . . . the middle-income peasants and the shopkeepers, at the expense of the aristocracy on the one hand, and the urban proletariat on the other."[15]

In France, politicians were acutely aware of the value of rural votes, but they lacked party organizations capable of mobilizing support. As a remedy, politicians turned to the network of local administrative officials, such as the mayors. In addition, republican leaders created new institutions that could mobilize political support in lieu of a party organization. Agricultural policy, as Jobert and Muller describe, "was a central strategy in the competition between the new rural elite and the conservative elite that traditionally dominated the countryside."[16] Both the establishment of an agricultural bureaucracy and early national farm organizations were components of this central strategy—political creations designed to secure the electoral support of the French peasantry.

Japan: Competition and Compromise among Political Elites

Mass-based political parties did not exist in nineteenth-century Japan; the franchise was limited to those who paid the most in taxes—a fraction of the population. Instead, political competition consisted of a factional

[14] Elwitt, *The Making of the Third Republic*, 59–75.

[15] Schmidt, *Democratizing France*, 51–52, 55–61. Following the law of March 28, 1882, mayors were elected by a municipal council. Agulhon, "Attitudes politiques," 504–9; Halévy, *Le Fin des notables*.

[16] Jobert and Muller, *L'état en action*, 83.

struggle between elites who had distinguished themselves during the restoration of Emperor Meiji in 1868. These elites came from four regional clans, or *han*: Satsuma, Choshu, Hizen, and Tosa. As the Satsuma and Choshu clans consolidated their hold on the government at the expense of others, a rift emerged among the oligarchs.[17]

It was out of this factional rivalry that the first political parties emerged. After efforts to challenge Satsuma-Choshu dominance through violence or coup had failed, members of the lesser clans turned to politics as the only remaining option. In 1874, Itagaki Taisuki, a leader of the Tosa *han*, left the government and organized a political club, the Patriotic Society. The number of political societies quickly spread, and in 1881 Itagaki established the Jiyuto (Liberal Party). Composed mainly of lower-rank samurai and wealthy landowners opposed to the onerous 3 percent tax on land, the Jiyuto called upon the emperor to draft a constitution.

Meanwhile, Okuma Shigenobu, a member of the Hizen *han*, circulated a proposal for a British-style parliament but was quickly purged from the government. Removed from the responsibilities of office, Okuma established a political party of his own with several faithful bureaucrats in 1881. The Kaishinto (Progressive Party) distinguished itself from the Jiyuto's rural orientation by drawing its support from the new class of urban industrialists.[18]

When the government finally did draft a constitution in 1889, its structure reflected this competition between the oligarchs in power and the political losers who established parties to challenge Satsuma-Choshu supremacy. The constitution established a Diet consisting of an upper House of Peers and a lower House of Representatives. Although the legislative branch was not given control over the cabinet (the power of selection and dismissal of government officials resided in the emperor), government budgets did require Diet approval, a source of significant leverage. However, it was the Privy Council, established in 1888 to oversee the drafting of the constitution, that became the true seat of oligarchic power. As the highest advisory group to the emperor, it allowed the oligarchs to influence most important decisions such as the selection of cabinet members, legislation, and imperial orders.[19]

When the first Diet sat in 1890, it became immediately apparent that the oligarchs' attempt to contain the influence of party politicians had backfired: under the Meiji constitution, party politicians now bargained

[17] Beasley, "Meiji Political Institutions," 645; Scalapino, *Democracy and the Party Movement*, 40–62; Iwasaki, *The Working Forces in Japanese Politics*, 16.

[18] Akita, *Foundations of Constitutional Government*, 15–57; Scalapino, *Democracy and the Party Movement*, 43–46, 57–58, 65–67; Iwasaki, *The Working Forces in Japanese Politics*, 87–88

[19] Ramseyer and Rosenbluth, *The Politics of Oligarchy*, 31.

from a position of strength, the House of Representatives. The political parties that controlled the House after 1890 used their veto over the annual budget to obstruct government action. In response, the government either dissolved the Diet (which forced parties to undergo an expensive election), restricted political freedoms (which hampered the operation of parties), or attempted to sway Diet members with promises of government largesse. But pork-barrel politics became difficult to sustain after 1895, when colonial forays in Asia created a revenue pinch for the government. In order to overcome parliamentary obstruction of government budgets, the oligarchs made greater concessions to the party politicians, such as higher salaries for Diet members, greater political freedoms, and, eventually, cabinet positions and prefectural governorships for party members.[20]

The competition between party politicians and oligarchs had important ramifications for the development of agricultural institutions in Japan. Landowners were the most important political group in Meiji Japan. Electoral rules limited the franchise to taxpayers, of which landowners were the principal contributors. In addition, district boundaries were drawn in a manner that overrepresented rural areas. An 1898 survey of the three-hundred member Diet reported 168 landowners or farmers, compared with only 42 engaged in industry and commerce. Moreover, the 3 percent tax on land was the principal source of tax revenue for the government; land-tax receipts accounted for 60 percent of all government revenue in 1895.[21] Because the landowners were politically and fiscally important, party politicians and oligarchs vied for their support. While the parties adopted a position against the land tax, the oligarchs seized upon agricultural promotion as a device to win the support of landowners and contain the popularity of party politicians.

In conclusion, a crucial difference between nineteenth-century politics in the United States as compared with France and Japan was the existence of a developed party system. The structure of political competition and, in particular, the strength of the party system had two important consequences for institutional development. At the level of agricultural institutions, nineteenth-century politics in the United States, France, and Japan shaped the development of agencies responsible for the administration of agricultural policies. At the level of interest representation, party politics influenced the structure and development of agricultural organizations.

[20] Ibid., 42–43; Fraser, Mason, and Mitchell, *Japan's Early Parliaments*, 8, 20–21.
[21] Ramseyer and Rosenbluth, *The Politics of Oligarchy*, 42; Scalapino, *Democracy and the Party Movement*, 114, 254–55. Between 1886 and 1890, the land tax averaged 66.9 percent of total government revenues. This proportion was steadily reduced. Between 126 and 1930, the land tax accounted for only 5.9 percent of government revenues. For figures see Ogura, *Can Japanese Agriculture Survive?* 675.

INSTITUTIONAL FOUNDATIONS I:
AGRICULTURAL ADMINISTRATION

As a device to promote the commercial development of agriculture, governments in the United States, France, and Japan established new departments and ministries responsible for the administration of agricultural policy. But newly created agricultural bureaucracies reflected the dominant political cleavages in each country. In the United States, the Department of Agriculture and the system of land-grant colleges were the outcome of a complicated regional logroll designed to balance the interests of eastern and western factions in the Republican Party. In France, the creation of an agricultural ministry helped secure republican political support in the rural periphery. In Japan, oligarchs created an agricultural bureaucracy as a bulwark against further political encroachments from party politicians. Characteristics of political competition influenced institutional design. In the United States, political decentralization led to a fragmented administrative system. In France and Japan, the metropolitan focus of politics in Paris or Tokyo concentrated bureaucratic tasks within a single ministerial portfolio.

The United States: Creation and Growth
of a Fractured Bureaucracy

During the Civil War, Congress passed legislation that created an independent department of agriculture and provided states with land grants for agricultural colleges. Over the next fifty years, the USDA and the land-grant colleges grew, but coordination often proved elusive; both the department and the colleges maintained independence from other bureaucratic entities with agricultural concerns. This independence and lack of coordination were often caused by rivalries between political parties, between individual politicians, and between federal and state officials.

Such rivalries were clearly evident when Congress created the Department of Agriculture and the land-grant colleges in the spring of 1862. Justin Morrill of Vermont introduced a bill that promised each state a portion of the public domain for the construction of agricultural colleges.[22] With land grants based on the size of congressional delegations (thirty thousand acres for each member), the bill found its most ardent support among representatives of the land-poor, populous eastern states.[23]

---

[22] *Congressional Globe*, 37th Cong., 2d sess., 2187.
[23] Gates, *Agriculture and the Civil War*, 262.

Senators and representatives of the western "public-lands states," how-ever, were concerned that the Morrill bill would surrender vast tracts of land—nearly entire states in some cases—to eastern speculators.[24] Timo-thy Howe of Wisconsin argued the proposal would make "the whole West but little more than a province of New York."[25] Others feared the Morrill bill would inhibit passage of homestead and railroad legislation, both dear to the hearts of western delegations.[26] In the words of Iowa Republi-can James Harlan, who sponsored homestead legislation in the Senate, land grants "may be procured by land speculators, . . . thus retarding settlements and improvements."[27] Opposition was so strong in the House that Morrill failed to get his bill out of committee.[28]

As the weeks progressed, these conflicts between East and West came under the influence of election-year politics. In 1862, the Republican Party remained an amalgam of various interests: former Whigs, free-soil Democrats, nativist Know-Nothings, and staunch abolitionists. In order to cast the widest net possible—particularly in the critical states such as Illinois, Indiana, and Pennsylvania—the Republican platform of 1860 balanced pronouncements against slavery with discrete economic propos-als. The Chicago convention adopted planks in support of the tariff, homestead legislation, and construction of a Pacific railway.[29] As the Re-publican majority in Congress approached the election of 1862, enact-ment of the Chicago platform, and in particular homestead legislation, was deemed essential to electoral success in the fall. In the words of Leo-nard Curry, "The position of the Republican Party in the Middle West was . . . entirely too shaky to permit that party's political campaigners to go before the electorate without a homestead act on the statute books."[30]

When the Republican leadership pushed homestead legislation through Congress in May, western opposition to the Morrill bill softened. To quote Senator Pomeroy of Kansas, "They [eastern members] have just

[24] On the sectional aspect of this debate, see Bensel, *Yankee Leviathan*, 69, 73–76.

[25] James Lane of Kansas, who led the opposition to the bill in the Senate, feared that "Land scrip . . . will go into the hands of some speculator in the city of New York." *Congressional Globe*, 37th Cong., 2d sess., 2248–49, 2275, 2626.

[26] Ibid., 2329, 2395. Both measures were deemed essential to the economic development of the West. Homestead legislation, it was believed, would entice settlers, while a transconti-nental railroad would provide links to commercial opportunities in the East. Another possi-ble reason for western support of homestead legislation is power in Congress. The 1862 election followed reapportionment in which the West gained more than twenty seats in the House of Representatives.

[27] Ibid.

[28] Curry, *Blueprint for Modern America*, 104, 109.

[29] For the text of the 1860 Republican Party platform, see Johnson and Porter, *National Party Platforms*, 31–33.

[30] Curry, *Blueprint for Modern America*, 108.

voted almost unanimously for the homestead bill, putting the lands out of their own reach forever. . . . [Therefore,] the old states . . . should have at least thirty thousand acres for each of their Senators and Representatives."[31] Eased by this sectional logroll—colleges in exchange for homesteads—the Morrill bill passed the House on June 17, 1862.[32]

Meanwhile, a separate constituency pressed for a federal department of agriculture.[33] Charles Calvert, founder of the Maryland Agricultural College and a member of the House Agriculture Committee, believed "farmers ought to be as weighty in politics as any other class."[34] To achieve this goal, Calvert championed for the creation of an independent department of agriculture with cabinet-level status. Opponents of the Calvert plan argued that an independent department was nothing more than a patronage ploy.[35] In 1852, Stephen Douglas warned members of the United States Agricultural Society that an agriculture department "would soon become, like all other offices of the government, a place for politicians."[36]

As a compromise, Lafayette Foster of Connecticut proposed a substitute bill that would create a bureau of agriculture within the Department of the Interior. This made administrative sense because the Patent Office, which employed a clerk for agricultural matters, was already located in the Department of Interior.[37] Lane of Indiana, who supported the Foster bill, argued that a cabinet-level agriculture department as envisioned by Calvert would "break up a well established system of the government, by which all inferior divisions are subordinate to and under direct control of . . . one of the departments."[38]

Nevertheless, supporters and opponents agreed that there was a symbolic currency to an independent department. Again quoting Calvert, "Until . . . a representative [of the farmer] takes his seat in the Cabinet,

[31] *Congressional Globe*, 37th Cong., 2d sess., 2249.

[32] Curry, *Blueprint for Modern America*, 114; Simon, "The Politics of the Morrill Act," 106–7. House opposition was also bought off with promises of a canal between Chicago and the Mississippi River. When the Illinois canal bill died in the House, its chief proponent, Elihu Washburne, confessed, "I was surprised when I saw the gentleman from Vermont [Morrill], after we of the West had generously come forward and voted for his measure, slaughtering us in the West, slaughtering the farmers of my own State." *Congressional Globe*, 37th Cong., 2d sess., 2625–34, 3058–59.

[33] An agricultural bureau within the Patent Office had existed since the 1840s. The movement for an independent department began shortly thereafter.

[34] *Journal of the United States Agricultural Society* 1, no. 1 (1852): 17.

[35] Ross, "The United States Department of Agriculture," 132.

[36] Douglas, Calvert, and other prominent individuals were members of the United States Agricultural Society. *Journal of the United States Agricultural Society* 1, no. 1 (1852): 14.

[37] *Congressional Globe*, 37th Cong., 2d sess., 1752, 1756.

[38] Ibid.

the hope . . . that the Government will regard agriculture as its chief bulwark . . . is fallacious."[39] John Hale of New Hampshire, who opposed the
department plan, insisted, "The great anxiety to have agriculture elevated
to a department . . . does not come from the men . . . that lean upon their
plow handles; but . . . from the men who want [farmers] to . . . vote for
them at the ballot box."[40] The 1862, report of the House Agriculture
Committee summed up the issue most succinctly when it reported that
farmers "are numerous, they are worthy, [and] they have votes."[41] Congress faced two alternatives; one was administratively expedient, the
other politically efficacious. In the end, a compromise bill passed Congress that created an unprecedented administrative entity: an independent
department *without* cabinet status. One historian remarked, "Such an
anomalous makeshift in the Federal system was confusing to contempo-
raries and has remained so to later students of government."[42]

In the early days after its creation, the USDA resembled precisely what
its opponents feared—another patronage haven. Commissioners and secretaries fielded constant inquiries for employment from individuals who
had been active in state agricultural societies or party politics. The first
commissioner of agriculture, Isaac Newton, lacked any formal scientific
training, but he was well connected to the Republican Party in Pennsylvania and was a close friend of the Lincolns. Most commissioners and secretaries displayed similar political talents; many served as members of Congress before their appointments to head the department. James "Tama
Jim" Wilson, whose sixteen-year tenure as USDA secretary is longer than
that of any other cabinet member in U.S. history, was chairman of the
House Agriculture Committee before his appointment in 1897. In the
words of President William Howard Taft, Wilson "knew politics and was
a good politician. He was familiar with the ways of the Senate and the
House . . . and knew how to lay the business of his Department before
legislative committees."[43] In the context of Gilded Age politics, leaders of
the Department of Agriculture had to be astute in the workings of patronage and congressional relations.[44]

As a result, the new department focused most of its efforts on activities
deemed electorally beneficial by members of Congress. One popular activity was the distribution of free seeds. Most of the department budget in
these early years was spent on seeds and reports mailed to voters by mem-

---

[39] Calvert quoted in True, *A History of Agricultural Experimentation*, 38.
[40] *Congressional Globe*, 37th cong., 2d sess., 2015–16.
[41] Ibid., 856, 1756, 1916.
[42] Instead of a secretary, a commissioner headed the agriculture department. Ross, "The
United States Department of Agriculture," 133.
[43] Baker et al., *Century of Service*, 40–42.
[44] Ross, "The United States Department of Agriculture," 133–39.

bers of Congress using the franking privilege (usually with the name of the representative conveniently printed on the package).[45] Although some USDA Secretaries opposed the practice, Congress would not forego the political value of seed distribution. When Secretary Julius Morton (1893–1897) refused to spend the seed appropriation, Congress passed a joint resolution that effectively forced him to spend the money.[46] As Alan Marcus points out, "The [agriculture] department served congressmen two ways. Its existence permitted them the pretense of acknowledging . . . farmers' demands, while they rewarded the political faithful and fueled their reelection campaigns." Despite the fact that many seeds were of little practical value, the Office of Congressional Seed Distribution was not abolished until 1923.[47]

For the most part, however, the political value of department activities guaranteed a steady flow of government resources that helped the Department of Agriculture grow quickly. Pressure on Congress from commissioners of agriculture and farm groups such as the Grange led to the department's elevation to cabinet status in 1889. After it was placed on an equal footing with the Interior Department, jurisdictional rivalries surfaced between these two federal departments involved in natural resource policy. As one former USDA bureaucrat wrote, "The work of the Interior Department and that of the Department of Agriculture touches and overlaps at so many points that it is sometimes difficult for Congress and the department heads properly to determine their respective spheres."[48] For example, questions of irrigation simultaneously engaged the Bureau of Reclamation, the Land Office, and the Geological Survey of the Department of Interior, as well as the Forest Service, the Bureau of Soils, and the Weather Bureau of the Department of Agriculture, not to mention the U.S. Army Corps of Engineers. In 1910, competition between Secretary of the Interior Richard Ballinger and USDA Chief Forester Gifford Pinchot over administration of the national forests erupted into "one of the pivotal administrative controversies of modern American state development."[49] This conflict over sales of public forestlands ended with Pinchot's dismissal, Ballinger's resignation, and Taft's presidency in shambles.

Policy coordination was not much better within the USDA. Administrative units were divided according to scientific disciplines. Before its reorganization in 1901, the department contained separate divisions for pomology (study of fruit trees), agrostology (study of grasses), microscopy (use

[45] True, A History of Agricultural Experimentation, 47.

[46] Baker et al., Century of Service, 34, 105–6.

[47] Marcus, Agricultural Science and the Quest for Legitimacy, 147.

[48] Wanlass, The United States Department of Agriculture, 53.

[49] Skowronek, Building a New American State, 190–91; Gaus and Wolcott, Public Administration and the United States Department of Agriculture, 28.

of microscopes), ornithology and mammology (study of birds and mammals), as well as chemistry, entomology, statistics, and weather. Although many of these divisions shared overlapping interests, there was little coordination between them. The Bureaus of Chemistry, Entomology, and Plant Industry, for example, simultaneously carried out research on pesticides. When the federal government began inspections of live animals, food, plants, and drugs in the late nineteenth century, these tasks were handled independently by the Bureaus of Animal Industry, Chemistry, and Plant Industry with little or no departmental coordination.[50]

Meanwhile, the land-grant colleges developed along their own trajectory. Due to the ambiguity of the Morrill Act, state legislatures exercised considerable leeway in the structure and operation of schools.[51] In an effort to improve the research capacity and image of the land-grant colleges, Commissioner of Agriculture George Loring asked Seaman Knapp of the Iowa Agricultural College to draft a proposal for a system of agricultural experiment stations. Knapp, who submitted his plan to a convention of land-grant college administrators in 1882, envisioned a system of experiment stations that would operate "under the general control of the . . . agricultural colleges." Knapp insisted that "the general character of the work and of the experiments to be performed at each station shall be determined by the Commissioner of Agriculture." This federal guidance would "systemize their [the stations'] work throughout the United States and will avoid too much repetition of experiments at different stations."[52] Here was an attempt to create a research network that linked state and federal institutions under the guidance of the commissioner in Washington.

The Knapp proposal was introduced in Congress in 1883. However, the proposed role of the USDA raised immediate objections. Certain college administrators voiced objections to the apparent subordination of the stations to the federal department. While Knapp's plan languished in committee, a substitute bill, recommended favorably by the House Agriculture Committee, placed the new experiment stations under the control of state governments. Stations would be directly affiliated with existing agricultural colleges and would submit annual reports directly to each state government. The bill even went so far as to emphasize that nothing "shall be construed to authorize [the] Commissioner to control or direct the work or management of any such station."[53]

---

[50] True, *A History of Agricultural Experimentation*, 41–66; Baker et al., *Century of Service*, 14–62.

[51] Marcus, *Agricultural Science and the Quest for Legitimacy*, 128ff.

[52] Knapp quoted in True, *A History of Agricultural Experimentation*, 122.

[53] True, "History of the Hatch Experiment Station Act," 96.

The elimination of USDA oversight, however, concerned agricultural groups, which feared that the colleges would exercise too much control over the stations and orient their research away from practical subjects. Influential members of the Grange, Commissioner of Agriculture Norman Colman, and critics of the land-grant colleges such as Senator John C. Spooner of Wisconsin successfully pushed for amendments that allowed state governments to use funds for the support of stations not affiliated with any college or university.[54] In the end, the 1887 Hatch Act bore little resemblance to the system of agricultural research envisioned by Knapp. Although the act created a system of experiment stations for agricultural research, neither the USDA nor the land-grant colleges exercised much control over their operation.

In the twenty-five years after the Hatch Act, the land-grant colleges, experiment stations, and USDA remained uneasy partners in agricultural research; each viewed the other suspiciously and guarded jurisdictions vigilantly. The sentiments of state officials were summed up by Eugene Davenport, dean of the Illinois Agricultural College: "[The USDA] violated every distinction that ought to obtain as demarking the legitimate and proper fields of its effort. . . . [It] has interested itself in purely local questions . . . to a degree which no other branch of the federal service has ever attempted."[55] However, as mentioned previously, USDA activities were popular in Congress, especially research projects that channeled appropriations to local constituencies. Unable to attack federal involvement directly, college and experiment station administrators lobbied Congress for increased appropriations of their own. In 1906, for example, Congress passed the Adams Act, which doubled the annual appropriation of the state experiment stations. In the words of one historian, the Adams Act was "a strategic victory for the [experiment] stations in a continuing conflict with the Department of Agriculture."[56]

In sum, the creation of an agricultural bureaucracy was the product of two distinct political bargains—one between the land-poor East and the land-rich West, the other between political entrepreneurs in search of farm votes and those critical of patronage politics. These bargains prevented the development of a unified agricultural administration. The creation of the USDA and its elevation to cabinet status placed the department in conflict with other agencies, notably the Department of Interior, over natural resource policy. At the same time, the land-grant colleges and agricultural experiment stations in each state used their congressional

---

[54] Ibid., 102; Marcus, *Agricultural Science and the Quest for Legitimacy*, 200–215.

[55] Davenport, "The Relations between the Federal Department of Agriculture and the Agricultural Colleges," 121–33.

[56] Rosenberg, "The Adams Act," 5.

connections to secure greater appropriations without being subordinated or crowded out of agricultural administration by the federal department. The agricultural bureaucracy grew in a fractured manner, the product of competition between the USDA, the land-grant colleges, and other federal departments for appropriations and jurisdictions ultimately controlled by Congress.

France: Agricultural Administration in the "Ministry of Rural Affairs"

The creation of a national agricultural bureaucracy was a key element in the republican strategy to consolidate the Third Republic. Gambetta and others insisted that the peasants must look to the state for guidance in agricultural matters rather than to the local notables who had taken the lead in agricultural improvement schemes for most of the nineteenth century. In 1880, Gambetta wrote, "The Republic . . . will not sacrifice the interests of the rural democracy to a coterie of nobles and lords. The rural populations no longer need a privileged group to intervene between [farmers] and the government. They will address themselves directly to the state."[57] In order to consummate this relationship between farmers and the state, Gambetta envisioned a ministry exclusively devoted to the needs and concerns of rural France.[58]

During the Second Empire and the early Third Republic, the Ministry of Agriculture and Commerce handled agricultural matters. On his first day in office as prime minister (November 14, 1881), Gambetta issued a decree that created a ministry devoted solely to agricultural affairs. According to Gambetta, the new Ministry of Agriculture would give farmers "the special representation in the councils of government they deserve."[59] Although Gambetta circumvented parliamentary jurisdiction over the number and content of ministries, it was difficult for opponents to vote against the interests of the farmer. As one member of the opposition noted, the creation of two distinct ministries was not justified on administrative grounds but because of the "magnitude of the interests that it [the new ministry] represents."[60]

Soon after the creation of the Ministry of Agriculture, the Gambetta government reorganized the administration of rural policy. In addition to questions of agriculture, the new ministry was also responsible for the

[57] Gambetta quoted in Cépède and Weill, *L'Agriculture*, 65.
[58] Jobert and Muller, *L'état en action*, 81.
[59] Gambetta quoted in Cusson, *Origines et évolution du Ministère de l'agriculture*, 94.
[60] Senator Fresnau quoted in ibid., 117.

administration of forest and water resources, as well as matters of irrigation, reclamation, and road maintenance, previously controlled by the Ministry of Public Works. This reorganization presented some administrative problems because it required the minister of agriculture to extend his authority over the technical corps of engineers trained in the *hautes écoles*.[61]

The history of the Service hydraulique, responsible for irrigation and reclamation, illustrates the administrative problems experienced, by the new ministry. Transferred from the Ministry of Public Works to Agriculture in 1881, the Service hydraulique was composed of engineers from the technical corps, the Ponts et Chaussées, whose principle occupation was the construction of bridges, railroads, and other public works. Although taken from graduates of the prestigious École polytechnique, the members of the Service hydraulique were not formally trained in agricultural matters. As a government report complained in 1903, "[the Service] has not met the hopes . . . for which it was created. . . . in particular, it remains closed to agricultural ideas and influences and . . . despite its high scientific and technical value, does not possess the special agricultural knowledge that is necessary."[62]

Finally, the early governments of the Third Republic expanded the system of agricultural instruction and administration. Within each department, a *professeur d'agriculture* oversaw demonstration and extension work. Like the public school teacher, the function of the *professeur d'agriculture* was to promote republican attachments in the countryside. According to Augé-Laribé, "Agricultural bureaucrats . . . devoted to republican and democratic ideas thought that the services they provided to farmers would provoke . . . gratitude toward the Republic."[63]

These administrative developments illustrate how nineteenth-century political competition influenced the structure of the French agricultural bureaucracy. In his effort to create a republican peasantry, Gambetta brought several administrative tasks associated with rural France under the control of a single portfolio. That is, Gambetta designed the new Ministry of Agriculture according to *territorial* considerations rather than *sectoral* ones as in the United States. In order to consolidate political control over the countryside, Gambetta essentially created an "Interior Ministry for Rural France" that performed functions in the villages and communes that other ministries handled in the cities and towns. Unlike

[61] Cépède and Weill, *L'Agriculture*, 107–215; Blanc-Gonnet, *La Réforme des services extérieurs*, 28–31; Cusson, *Origines et évolution du Ministère de l'agriculture*, 148–54.

[62] Quoted in Cépède and Weill, *L'Agriculture*, 221–22. See also Blanc-Gonnet, *La Réforme des service extérieurs*, 32–34; Cusson, *Origines et évolution du Ministère de l'agriculture*, 131–63.

[63] Augé-Laribé, *Syndicats et coopératives agricoles*, 37.

in the United States, where responsibility for agriculture—as a distinct economic sector—was separated from other aspects of natural resource policy, agricultural administration in France concentrated most government functions relating to the rural economy (agriculture, forests, water, etc.) in one ministry.[64]

Japan: Toward an Administration-Association Nexus

The creation of prefectural and municipal governments under central state authority in 1871 required a cadre of bureaucrats to assume the responsibilities of administration. Initially, Japanese oligarchs chose officials of the new regime according to social networks and kinship ties; members of the Satsuma and Choshu clans received the plum positions in the bureaucracy. However, as a strategy to insulate the bureaucracy from possible infiltration by party politics, the oligarchs instituted a rigid selection process that drew the top students of elite universities into the civil service through a rigorous examination system. By the 1890s, the Japanese bureaucracy had evolved into a highly trained cadre of civil servants. In addition, a relatively predictable pattern of advancement and promotion within individual ministries produced a high degree of bureaucratic specialization and commitment to agency priorities.[65]

Agricultural administration benefited from this bureaucratic development. Initially, administrative tasks for agriculture were divided between various agencies and periodically shuffled between the Ministry of Civil Affairs, the Ministry of Finance, and the Ministry of Home Affairs. In 1880, however, Okuma Shigenobu and Ito Hirobumi pressed for the creation of a Ministry of Agricultural and Commercial Affairs (MACA), arguing that this would unify economic policy in a single ministry, rationalize expenditures, and more effectively promote agriculture and industry. The new Ministry of Agriculture and Commercial Affairs, created in 1881, brought essentially all questions of agricultural administration under one roof.[66]

From the beginning, the orientation of the Bureau of Agricultural Affairs in the new ministry was toward increases in productivity through the application of Western science and the development of local resources. This orientation can be traced to the efforts of early MACA bureaucrats

---

[64] Vaugelas, "Le Ministère de l'agriculture," 253–54, 261.

[65] Silberman, "The Bureaucratic State in Japan," 226–57; Silberman, "Bureaucratic Development and the Structure of Decision-Making in Japan," 347–62.

[66] Ogura, *Can Japanese Agriculture Survive?* 355–57.

such as Maeda Masana. Using recruits from the Komaba Agricultural School of the Tokyo Imperial University (founded in 1877), Maeda established the Itinerant Instructor System in 1885. These young officials were sent throughout the country to popularize various farming techniques practiced successfully in other areas of Japan and encourage the adoption of new seed varieties.[67]

The rise of party politics after 1890, however, soon enmeshed the agricultural bureaucracy in the competition between oligarchs and party politicians. Rural-based parties in the Diet called for a downward revision of the land tax even as the revenue needs of the Meiji government grew larger. Caught between electoral and fiscal pressures, the government tried to appease landowners with greater resources for agricultural research and extension. In 1893, an experimental farm on the grounds of Minister of Agriculture and Commerce Mutsu Munemitsu's villa in Tokyo became the National Agricultural Experiment Station. At the same time, six regional branch stations and several prefectural stations were established as well.[68]

In 1898, the issue of the land tax once again came before the Diet, and again the scope of agricultural administration expanded. That year, the founders of Japan's two political parties, Itagaki and Okuma, briefly formed a government under a unified party label, the Kenseito. When this union failed, the oligarch Yamagata took control of the government. Exploiting the rift between the parliamentary parties, Yamagata bribed members of the chiefly rural faction (the Jiyuto) with cash bounties for every government bill passed by the Diet. Through this tactic, Yamagata secured an increase in the land tax; the following year, the Diet passed several important agricultural measures, including the construction of experiment stations in each prefecture, the regulation of fertilizers sold by urban merchants, and the creation of landowner associations for land-improvement projects.[69]

[67] Ogura, *Agricultural Development in Modern Japan*, 302; Hayami, *A Century of Agricultural Growth in Japan*, 49–51. On Maeda Masana, see Ogura, *Can Japanese Agriculture Survive?* 70–75, and Havens, *Farm and Nation in Modern Japan*, 60–63. An excellent study of promotion efforts in the Saga plain is Francks, *Technology and Agricultural Development in Pre-war Japan*, 77–79, 150–56.

[68] Hayami and Yamada, "Agricultural Research Organization in Economic Development," 237–39. On the connection between pressure for tax relief and agricultural promotion, see Hayami, *A Century of Agricultural Growth in Japan*, 51, and Ogura, *Can Japanese Agriculture Survive?* 83. In addition to these research-oriented policies, the Diet passed legislation in 1896 that created two banks, the Industrial and Agricultural Bank and Japan Hypothec Bank, for agricultural investment loans.

[69] On Yamagata's tactics, see Scalapino, *Democracy and the Party Movement*, 176–79. On the legislation, see Hayami, *A Century of Agricultural Growth in Japan*, 52.

In sum, the creation of an agricultural bureaucracy was an instrument of political competition in all three countries. In the United States, the decision to create a Department of Agriculture took place in the context of a federalist political structure and a developed party system. In contrast, French and Japanese agricultural ministries emerged from a unitary political structure and a nascent party system. This difference shaped agricultural administration. The USDA, forced to carve a niche within a decentralized network of patronage, defined its jurisdiction narrowly and competed with other sources of administrative authority at the state and the national level. The French Ministry of Agriculture and the Japanese Ministry of Agriculture and Commercial Affairs, designed to *create* channels of patronage where few yet existed, defined their jurisdictions broadly and encountered relatively less bureaucratic competition, particularly within the central government.

INSTITUTIONAL FOUNDATIONS II: PRODUCER GROUPS

With the spread of commercial agriculture in the nineteenth century, farmers established a host of cooperatives, mutual aid societies, improvement associations, and other groups. Often these organizations promoted the adoption of new farming techniques, offered credit, insurance, and other services to its members, or improved prices through cooperative marketing.

In the United States, a former government employee, Oliver H. Kelley, organized the Grange in the mid-1870s. Although the Grange grew quickly, it never met Kelley's expectations for a national farm organization affiliated in some way with the federal government. Instead, the focus of Grange activity remained local; state chapters were highly suspicious of efforts by national leaders to focus the attention of the organization on activities in Washington. In less than two decades, the Grange receded from the forefront of farmer organizations. In the 1880s and 1890s, the Farmers' Alliance encountered similar organizational hurdles. Mobilized around the issues of antitrust legislation and railroad regulation, its leaders divided over the question of political action and eventually failed in their bid to establish an agrarian party in American politics. Not until World War I did a national agricultural organization finally emerge in the United States.

In contrast, national agricultural organizations were firmly established in France and Japan by the end of the nineteenth century. Like agricultural ministries, producer groups were an instrument of political competition. In France, republican leaders promoted mutual aid societies as a counterorganization to the antirepublican agricultural societies established during the Second Empire. In Japan, oligarchs created quasi-public farmer cooperatives to maintain landowner loyalty in the countryside. Because of their political function, farmer societies in France and Japan received direct government subsidies critical for organizational growth and maintenance.

The United States: Producers and the Limits of Party Politics

Although farmers were involved in politics through a variety of societies, organizations, and fledgling political parties, the experiences of the Order of the Patrons of Husbandry (commonly known as the Grange) and the Farmers' Alliance best illustrate the problems farm groups encountered during the late nineteenth century. The origins, rise, and decline of these organizations reveal how the structure of nineteenth-century political competition shaped the successes and failures of farmer associations.

The Grange began as a collection of government employees in Washington, D.C. Oliver H. Kelley, upon his return from a tour of the South as a clerk for the USDA in 1867, set forth to establish an organization dedicated to the promotion of agriculture and the interests of farmers.[70] Kelley envisioned an organization that would be an adjunct to the Department of Agriculture. Local granges would be organized into state chapters represented at an annual convention of the National Grange. This "grand level of the organizations will be an auxiliary to the department of agriculture," Kelley wrote. In association with the department, the Grange would help collect statistics, market crops, test new machinery, and generally "increase the products of the earth by increasing the knowledge of the producer." Kelley predicted that, "through the power of this Order, Congress will appropriate a million . . . dollars annually for the Department of Agriculture," adding that "hardly any member of Congress would wish to vote against appropriations that would be called for by the department."[71]

Following the organization of the first grange in Washington, Kelley embarked on a personal mission to establish local and state chapters throughout the country. At first, success was slow; Kelley's work languished for several years. By the early 1870s, however, economic depression and

---

[70] Kelley, *Origin and Progress*, 17; Buck, *The Granger Movement*, 40–42. Of the seven founding members who established the first grange in Washington, D.C., only one was directly engaged in agriculture. The remaining six, including Kelley, were government clerks from the USDA, the Post Office, and the Treasury Department.

[71] Kelley, *Origins and Progress*, 19, 44.

discontent in the Upper Midwest over railroads and grain traders raised farmer interest in the Grange. Again quoting Kelley, "The wind blows out west about monopolies. The people are waking up, and the farmers will see the advantage of a permanent organization like the Patrons."[72]

Once Kelley and other organizers recognized the currency of the monopoly issue, the number of local granges mushroomed. In 1871, there were 132 granges distributed among the eleven states of the Midwest and the Great Plains. At the organization's peak in early 1875, these states registered over twelve thousand local granges. Growth was rapid in the southern states as well. Only five granges had been formed by 1871; four years later there were more than eight thousand. At its peak in 1875, the membership of the National Grange exceeded 750,000 men and women.[73] What began as an initiative of government clerks in Washington had grown into a nationwide movement of farmers less than a decade after the Civil War.[74]

However, the rapid growth of many local granges exceeded the capacity of the national leadership to effectively coordinate the organization's activities. The antimonopoly sentiment that contributed to the proliferation of local chapters produced hostility toward all concentrations of authority, including that of the National Grange. When the dues from newly established granges filled the treasury of the headquarters in Washington, local and state chapters accused the National Grange of misusing funds. As Buck writes, "The average farmer . . . looked upon the National Grange not as a means of helping him in local affairs, but as a combination of monopolists . . . who forced him to pay a royalty." This hostility limited the ability of Grange leaders to coordinate or expand the organization's activities. Leaders of the National Grange complained that "their powers were far too contracted to enable them to proceed in the execution of measures for the benefit of the Order." Despite this plea, state delegates reduced the powers of the National Grange and distributed the treasury surplus among them. Kelley's vision for a hierarchical organization of farmers devolved into a radically decentralized association of local and state chapters fearful of any national control.[75]

Decentralized and autonomous state chapters, however, had their advantages. In state politics, granges endorsed candidates who supported

[72] Ibid., 249.

[73] For membership statistics, see Buck, *The Granger Movement*, 52–69.

[74] In 1875, the national convention was held in Charleston, South Carolina. Buck writes that this meeting "was probably the first national convention of importance held in the southern states since the war." Ibid., 282.

[75] Buck, *The Agrarian Crusade*, 62; National Grange Executive Committee, *Proceedings of the Sixth Session of the National Grange*, 1874, 21, 31; see also Buck, *The Granger Movement*, 71.

railroad regulation, public improvements, and other issues approved by the state grange. Occasionally, grange conventions were held in the state capital while the legislature was in session. Under such circumstances, "it was a bold legislator who, in the presence of his farmer constituents, would vote against the measures they approved."[76] Similar tactics were employed in national politics. Proceedings of the National Grange often included resolutions directing state and local granges to petition Congress and pressure representatives on a variety of legislative issues. The Grange was seminal in the elevation of the USDA to cabinet status in 1889.[77]

However, cabinet status for the USDA was a unique case because farmers and agricultural organizations were virtually unanimous in favor of elevation. Usually, the federal structure of the Grange and the distribution of the movement across many areas of the country made concerted political action unwieldy, if not impossible. For example, the tariff issue cut across regional and commodity lines. Efforts by southern state granges to introduce resolutions calling for the reduction of duties were opposed by delegates from the Midwestern granges who feared competition from Canadian wheat. As Buck's assessment of the Patrons' political activity points out, "The deciding factor . . . was generally the financial interest of the individual grangers, and when these differed . . . it was impossible to bring any effective influence on Congress."[78]

Put differently, federalism and the party system defined the scope of Grange political activity. In the case of agricultural administration, the narrow jurisdiction of the USDA reflected the efforts of politicians such as Charles Calvert to find a niche within the developed patronage system. Similarly for the Grange, national political success was limited to narrow sectoral issues. In questions of agricultural promotion such as the elevation of the USDA, agricultural education, and "more or less technical agricultural subjects, . . . the Patrons of Husbandry were looked upon as representing [farmers]." As a result, "their petitions for legislation . . . were likely to receive favorable consideration." On the other hand, "When it was a question of legislation of more general interests, such as the regulation of corporations, . . . the Patrons found their resolutions of no result." Broader regulatory issues, such as the tariff or railroad regulation, either crosscut regional lines among the Grange membership (itself magnified by the federal structure of the Patrons) or confronted more powerful forces in nineteenth-century party politics. Farm leaders had limited resources with which to effectively compete. Although the Grange

[76] Buck, *Agrarian Crusade*, 52.

[77] True, *A History of Agricultural Experimentation*, 176; Baker et al., *Century of Service*, 27–30.

[78] Buck, *The Granger Movement*, 114–17.

had votes, they could not overcome the distribution of railroad passes to politicians or large campaign contributions made by corporations.[79]

In sum, the decentralization of Grange organization and the autonomy of state chapters produced political successes and failures for the Patrons of Husbandry. In the language of group theory, we see in the history of the Grange the tension between the advantages of a wide geographic distribution, on the one hand, and the disadvantages of large groups, on the other.[80] Federalism and the system of geographic representation in Congress rewarded geographically diffuse organizations like the Grange because significant policy questions were decided in state houses. In addition, a large number of congressional districts possessed local granges. On the downside, the advantages of diffusion could be reaped only when there was consensus and coordination, and when political action did not directly challenge other prominent interests in party politics, such as railroads. As we have seen, this was a difficult task for a national leadership with little power and a suspicious rank and file. In the 1880s, political immobilism and widespread financial failure of Granger purchasing cooperatives led to a precipitous decline in membership.[81]

The organizational limits imposed by the nineteenth-century party system are even better illustrated by the history of the Farmers' Alliance. Like the Grange, the Farmers' Alliance attracted members who were united in their criticism of railroads, corporate power, and other characteristics of the American political economy that placed farmers in a precarious economic position. As hard times continued for many farmers through the 1880s, Alliance membership swelled rapidly. An innovative system of traveling lecturers spread the organization's message and attracted new members. At the same time, these activists used the lectures to promote economic cooperation among producers. In Texas, North Carolina, and other southern states, Alliance leaders convinced farmers to join cotton and tobacco cooperatives that allowed producers to store their crops,

[79] Ibid., 102–3. For a fuller discussion of the obstacles farm organizers faced due to Gilded Age party politics, see Clemens, *The People's Lobby*, 84, 95, 145–56.

[80] Olson argued that small, geographically concentrated groups are the most effective lobbies. Small size helps groups overcome the free-rider problem, while geographic concentration lowers organizational costs through easier communication, surveillance, and so on. Pincus, on the other hand, argued that geographically diffuse (deconcentrated) groups benefit from the placement of constituents in a large number of electoral districts. This, in turn, lowers the costs of reaching a compromise between legislators. Olson, *The Logic of Collective Action*; Pincus, "Pressure Groups and the Pattern of Tariffs." See also Schonhardt-Bailey, "Lessons in Lobbying for Free Trade," 37–58.

[81] Dues-paying members declined from over 800,000 in 1875 to fewer than 150,000 in 1880. See Tontz, "Memberships of General Farmers' Organizations," 147.

market directly to manufacturers, and secure credit without recourse to the exploitative crop lien system.[82]

The success of these "Alliance Exchanges" was an impressive achievement, but as the farm economy worsened, dues payments declined and many of the cooperatives went bankrupt. As Goodwyn describes, "Farmers simply lacked the capital to make large-scale cooperatives workable."[83] With the failure of the cooperatives, Charles Macune, one of the Alliance's founders from Texas, conceived of a radical plan that would achieve through government intervention what the farmers, privately, could not. According to the "subtreasury plan" envisioned by Macune, the federal government would establish a publicly financed system of cooperatives that would permit farmers to store crops, secure loans, and effectively create a system of currency based on agricultural commodities rather than specie.[84]

However, the recourse to government action envisioned by the subtreasury plan inevitably raised the issue of political action, a question that deeply divided the Alliance leadership. Macune and others were reticent about political involvement; cooperatives, they hoped, could improve the economic condition of farmers without recourse to politics. Other Alliance leaders, however, advocated direct political action and, in some cases, a third-party challenge to the dominant political system.[85]

When the subtreasury plan failed to make headway in the Republican Congress, the advocates of political action gained the upper hand. In 1890, Alliance leaders instructed the network of lecturers to mobilize a political campaign to elect pro-Alliance candidates in the next election. Although more than forty candidates sympathetic to Alliance views won congressional seats in 1890, once elected many proved more conservative than expected—particularly on the subtreasury plan. Convinced that Alliance goals could not be achieved through the two major parties, advocates of a third-party movement gathered in Omaha in 1892 and nominated James Weaver of Iowa to stand as the Populist candidate for president in the fall election. Although impressive by third-party standards, Weaver failed to overcome sectional antipathies and polled poorly in the South. Votes for southern Populist candidates increased in 1894, but hopes for a viable third party steadily waned. In 1896, the Populists swung their support behind Bryan and a fusion ticket with the Democratic Party. But in a campaign dominated by the silver issue, Bryan's defeat in

---

[82] Hicks, *The Populist Revolt*, 96–152; Goodwyn, *Democratic Promise*, 110–53.

[83] Goodwyn, *Democratic Promise*, 169.

[84] Sanders, *Roots of Reform*, chap. 4; Goodwyn, *Democratic Promise*, 152–67.

[85] Goodwyn, *Democratic Promise*, 169–76.

1896 was the high-water mark of Populist influence in electoral politics and, in Elisabeth Clemens' words, "discredited independent agrarian politics as a viable organizational strategy."[86]

The failure of the Populists as a social movement is often attributed to the decision of its leaders to enter the political fray.[87] Although politics may have diluted or debased the Populists' radical critique of finance capitalism, we can put the failure of the Alliance in more starkly institutional terms. In the words of Lawrence Goodwyn, reformers faced "the unhappy fact that the sectional memories of the American people . . . divided millions of farmers and laborers into two parties." Populist efforts to create a party of farmers encountered strong sectional antipathies. "For a new party to bring Northerners and Southerners together, these sectional memories had to be overcome."[88] This was a daunting task, as Elizabeth Sanders reminds us: "Farmers struggled to run the gauntlet of the two-party system, and lost many of their troops along the way." More specifically, the Populists (and Grange for that matter) confronted "single-member districts, territorial elections, . . . [and] the powerful socio-historical divide of the Civil War."[89] In 1890, reformers in the West tried to work within the Republican Party, while reformers in the South tried to influence Democratic Party candidates. When this strategy failed, Populists tried to field third-party candidates in the 1892 and 1894 elections but found that economic cleavages between producers and finance capital could not overcome the dominant party and sectional cleavages between North and South.

As John Mark Hansen concludes in his study of twentieth-century agricultural organizations, "Lobbies compete with political parties for the allegiances of political leaders." Extending Hansen's analysis backward to the nineteenth century, farm lobbies faced a competitive disadvantage vis-à-vis the party system. As a result, as Elisabeth Clemens argues, "to invent a politics of interest required disassembling—at least in part—the politics of party."[90] In France and Japan, the opposite was true: because political parties were weak, farm organizations enjoyed a competitive advantage vis-à-vis parties and became important players in national politics. In fact, political leaders in both countries often *created* farm organizations in order to perform those functions beyond the capacity of the existing party structure.

[86] Clemens, *The People's Lobby*, 160; Hicks, *The Populist Revolt*, 238–73, 321–79; Goodwyn, *Democratic Promise*, 213–74.

[87] See, for example, Schwartz, *Radical Protest and Social Structure*; Palmer, *Man over Money*.

[88] Goodwyn, *Democratic Promise*, 651 n. 39.

[89] Sanders, *Roots of Reform*, chap. 4; Clemens, *The People's Lobby*, 156–61.

[90] Hansen, *Gaining Access*, 223; Clemens, *The People's Lobby*, 3.

France: The Producer in Politics

Like the creation of an independent Ministry of Agriculture, the development of farm groups in the late nineteenth century reflected the same struggle for republican control of rural France. Agricultural syndicates—organizations for the purchase of farm inputs, rural credit, and crop insurance—were the result of direct and indirect state action designed to bolster republican political success in the countryside.

Associations held an ambiguous position in France. The Jacobins frowned upon intermediary groups as an example of "particular interests" that undermined the general will. During the nineteenth century, the authoritarian regimes of Louis Philippe and Napoleon III outlawed many forms of association because of their perceived threat to central state authority.[91]

This changed under the Third Republic. In 1884, the Waldeck-Rousseau law legalized associations "for the defense of economic interests, industrial, commercial, and agricultural." The 1884 legislation had an important influence on agricultural organization in France. During the Second Empire, rural aristocrats formed a number of agricultural societies, schools, and experimental farms designed to promote technological developments in agriculture. In 1861, Edouard Lecouteaux, editor of the *Journal d'Agriculture Pratique*, established the Société des agriculteurs de la France (SAF). Composed mainly of rural *notables* and agricultural scientists, the organization grew steadily over the next two decades. After passage of the associations law in 1884, leaders of the SAF began promoting agricultural syndicates throughout France. Although made possible by the republican expansion of political rights, the syndical movement was a reaction against the perceived encroachments of a hostile state. As one member of the SAF claimed, syndicates were needed to "combat the army of 400,000 state bureaucrats who distort statistics and . . . increase taxes." In 1886, conservative farm leaders brought together the newly established agricultural syndicates under an umbrella organization, the Union centrale des syndicats agricole.[92]

In response to the success of these early syndicates, republican leaders created their own countryside associations. In 1880, Leon Gambetta—the same man responsible for the Ministry of Agriculture—founded the Société nationale d'encouragement à l'agriculture. Intended as a direct challenge to the antirepublican SAF, the new organization enjoyed government patronage and close relations with the republican state. In Paris,

---

[91] Hazareesingh, *Political Traditions in Modern France*, 209–13.

[92] Barral, *Les Agrariens*, 80; Prugnaud, *Les Étapes du syndicalisme agricole*, 22, 25; Augé-Laribé, *La Politique agricole*, 135.

the president of the Société nationale was often drawn from the higher echelons of the republican leadership. Prugnaud called the Société nationale "a breeding ground of . . . future ministers of agriculture."[93] Republican leaders in Paris, for example, directed prefects and subprefects to help organize local branches. Another republican creation, the secular public teacher, also encouraged farmers to form syndicates as a way to improve agricultural output. Departmental professors of agriculture and local extension officials, in their efforts to "consolidate the Republic . . . and defend against reaction," were instrumental in the establishment of farm organizations in several departments.[94]

State support was particularly important in the creation of a nationwide system of farm credit mutual societies and other forms of cooperative ventures. A caucus of three hundred rural (mostly republican) deputies created in 1885 pushed through several laws at the end of the nineteenth century that expanded the range of legal services agricultural syndicates could offer. Syndical provision of credit and insurance to farmers, of course, offered selective incentives useful for attracting new members. Legislation also provided subsidies and secured financial support from the Bank of France that guaranteed the financial viability of the syndicates. A law passed in 1906 offered long-term loans without interest to cooperatives and mutuals. Underwritten by government funds, syndical banks and mutuals proliferated. In the first decade of the twentieth century, the number of local branches for agricultural credit jumped from 87 to 3,150. In 1910, republican farm leaders consolidated the credit, insurance, and cooperative societies into the Fédération nationale de la mutualité et de la coopération agricoles.[95]

On issues such as the tariff, republican politicians and agricultural leaders forged a powerful marriage of "iron and wheat." During parliamentary elections in 1889, farm leaders joined with the Association de l'industrie française in a campaign to elect protectionist deputies. Their efforts produced a protectionist caucus in the Chamber that numbered between three and four hundred deputies of various ideological stripes. After passage of the general tariff increase of 1892 (the Méline Tariff), these ad hoc political alliances between agrarians and industrialists became more formal. The republican Société nationale joined with the antirepublican Société des agriculteurs and the Association de l'industrie to form a powerful protectionist organization, the Association de l'industrie et de l'agriculture Française. With republican notable Jules Méline as president, this

---

[93] Prugnaud, *Les Étapes du syndicalisme agricole*, 94.

[94] Barral, *Les Agrariens*, 113–16; Cleary, *Peasants, Politicians, and Producers*, 94.

[95] Barral, *Les Agrariens*, 81, 96, 122, 127; Augé-Laribé, *Syndicats et coopératives agricoles*, 39.

union "signaled to all the new ties binding the economic leaders of industry and agriculture . . . [as] the most inclusive and most powerful organization of industrialists and growers in France."[96]

Agricultural organizations in Third Republic France operated as instruments of political competition and maintained a strong presence in national politics. Political elites secured subsidies for newly created farm organizations and brokered alliances with other economic interests in ways that augmented agricultural influence in national politics. With many of the resources necessary for organizational maintenance provided by the state, producer groups in France flourished in ways their American counterparts could not.[97]

Japan: Agricultural Associations and Cooperatives

It is difficult to separate a discussion of farm organizations in Japan from the development of agricultural administration. Soon after the creation of the Ministry of Agriculture and Commercial Affairs (MACA) in 1881, government officials established a network of organizations designed to extend the reaches of agricultural administration and help in efforts to raise productivity. Shinagawa Yajiro, a member of the hard-line Yamagata faction, established the Agricultural Society of Japan in 1881 when he was the vice minister of MACA. Patterned after the Royal Agricultural Society of England, the society published statistics and organized fairs and demonstrations. Toward the end of the decade, ministry bureaucrats and Agricultural Society members began a movement for the creation of a nationwide network of associations. In 1889, a report published by a group of agricultural scientists in the ministry recommended that "the systematic organization of agricultural associations is the best way for agricultural progress." Over the next two years, legislation was drafted to create a national agricultural organization with subordinate associations in each prefecture and village.[98]

Meanwhile, similar developments occurred in the area of agricultural cooperatives. Cooperatives for credit and marketing were established by landowners in the first decades after the restoration. The agricultural depression of the 1880s, however, fueled the movement. The leading proponents of agricultural cooperatives were Shinagawa (again) and Hirata To-

[96] Lebovics, *The Alliance of Iron and Wheat*, 126; Smith, *Tariff Reform in France*, 197–210; Golob, *The Méline Tariff*.

[97] On the government provision of resources, see Walker, "The Origins and Maintenance of Interest Groups."

[98] Ogura, *Can Japanese Agriculture Survive?* 302–4. On Shinagawa, see Havens, *Farm and Nation in Modern Japan*, 64–65.

suke, a high-ranking bureaucrat in the Legislation Bureau, who as a member of the Yamagata faction eventually became Lord Keeper of the Privy Seal. Together, Shinagawa and Hirata drafted a law that promised government subsidies to new cooperatives. Introduced in the House of Peers in 1891, the law failed to pass the Diet.[99]

As the century came to an end, the twin movements for cooperatives and a nationwide system of agricultural associations dovetailed. As described earlier, bargains between the oligarchs and political parties over the land-tax revision in 1898 led to the enactment of several agricultural measures. Among these were the Agricultural Association Law, passed in 1899, and the Industrial Cooperative Law, passed in 1900. The Agricultural Association Law granted subsidies of 150,000 yen per year to the National Agricultural Society, a national body of associations created in 1894. The Industrial Cooperative Law established rules for the formation and operation of credit, purchasing, marketing, and production cooperatives.[100]

In the decade after this legislation, the associations and cooperatives developed into hierarchical organizations in which the government played a significant role in administrative oversight. Cooperatives reaped the benefit of government measures that exempted them from income taxes and provided low-cost loans. As the number of cooperatives grew throughout Japan (from 21 in 1900 to 3,363 in 1907), Hirata and the director of the Agricultural Affairs Bureau, Sako Tsuneaki, established the Central Association of Industrial Cooperatives in 1905. In 1909, the Central Association was reorganized into a national federation of prefectural and local branches with Hirata as president. Most of the directors of the reorganized association were bureaucrats from the MACA. More important, the prefectural governors appointed by the minister of home affairs became presidents of their respective prefectural cooperative unions.[101]

The agricultural associations went through a transformation similar to that of the cooperatives. Through the efforts of association president Kano Hisayoshi (who was also vice president of the Central Association for Industrial Cooperatives and member of the House of Peers), legislation passed by the Diet in 1905 made membership in the association compulsory. The law also designated prefectural governors and county and village heads as the leaders of the agricultural association in their respective jurisdiction. To quote Ogura, "The Association on one hand became an official organization to carry out the Government's agricultural extension while on the other hand it became an organization through which landowners were able to voice their interests."[102]

[99] Ogura, *Can Japanese Agriculture Survive?* 266.
[100] Ogura, *Agricultural Development in Modern Japan,* 248–53.
[101] Ogura, *Can Japanese Agriculture Survive?* 270.
[102] Ogura, *Agricultural Development in Modern Japan,* 304.

For the agricultural cooperatives and associations, the boundaries between business, public administration, agricultural research, and politics gradually blurred. By World War I, almost every village in Japan contained both a cooperative and an agricultural association. Usually, the same individuals simultaneously occupied leadership positions in both organizations. Because these leaders were always government officials as well, the central government authority weighed heavily on the operations of the agricultural bodies. In the case of the Imperial Agricultural Association, government officials exercised control over the establishment of associations, the dismissal of directors, oversight of decisions taken by the association, and the ability to suspend operations or order dissolution.[103]

Of course, the creation of this administrative-association nexus fit well with the larger political strategy of the oligarchs. Fearful of political party encroachment, hard-liners like Shinagawa, Hirata, and other members of the Yamagata faction pressed for local institutions that could "purify" rural society and halt the advance of social disintegration. As one MACA official wrote in 1905, "We cannot help but fear that the small-scale farmer . . . will lose [his] energy . . . listening instead in vain to the empty theories of demagogues. . . . it is urgent to prevent . . . [this] social crisis through . . . the cooperative." In more straightforward political terms, the union of local administration and semipublic agricultural institutions extended oligarch control precisely where the parties appeared most dangerous, at the grass roots.[104]

In sum, governments in Japan and France subsidized the cost of organizational creation and maintenance for producer organizations in the nineteenth century. In the United States, where the government did not directly provide resources, associations like the Grange or the Farmers' Alliance were weaker and short-lived. The reason for this difference was largely political. Agricultural organizations in France and Japan furthered the goals of political elites. Like the creation of an agricultural bureaucracy, these early farm organizations were designed to consolidate political control over a largely rural electorate.

In the United States, organized parties structured political competition in ways that limited the growth of early farm organizations. As the experience of the Grange demonstrated, success was possible only when the organization pursued narrowly sectoral issues such as agricultural education or funding for the USDA. In these cases, the Grange successfully presented itself as the representative of farmers' interests. When the

[103] Ibid., 250.

[104] Yanagita Kunio quoted in Ogura, *Can Japanese Agriculture Survive?* 271. Najita writes that the Yamagata faction "dominated influential semi-bureaucratic organizations such as the agricultural associations (nokai) and industrial cooperatives (sangyo kumiai)." Najita, *Hara Kei*, 48.

Grange addressed questions of the larger rural political economy, it suffered from factional dissent and insufficient political resources compared with the industrial interests closely connected with party leaders.

The Farmers' Alliance is an even clearer case of the limits imposed by the party system. The subtreasury plan was essentially a publicly funded system of agricultural credit and cooperatives—not much different from the kinds of state-supported systems established in France and Japan. Unable to convince Congress to pass the plan, Alliance leaders entered politics. But they found that economic cleavages between farmers and finance capital were not powerful enough to overcome the dominant sectional cleavage between northern Republicans and southern Democrats. This left Populist leaders with only a third-party option to achieve their policy goals, an option that ultimately failed in political terms.

POLITICAL COMPETITION AND AGRICULTURAL PROMOTION

As we have seen, differences between federalist and unitary systems, as well as the relative strength of political parties, shaped the content of promotional policies in the United States, France, and Japan. When politicians in the United States distributed land to settlers or created agricultural research facilities, they tended to maximize the distributive qualities of the relevant legislation. For instance, the Morrill Act distributed land according to the size of congressional delegations—thirty thousand acres of public land for each representative and senator. Promotional policies were designed so that each state delegation could channel a portion of the government resources dedicated to agriculture back to its home district. But party competition also produced a fractured agricultural bureaucracy and prevented the emergence of a viable national farm organization.

In France and Japan, promotional policies fulfilled different political motives. Rather than grease a political machine, French and Japanese elites worked to create a machine where one did not yet exist. Credit, research, and other promotional policies created institutions linking peasants and republican leaders in France and landowners and oligarchs in Japan. The institutional consequences are clear. By the end of the nineteenth century, France and Japan possessed a centralized agricultural bureaucracy and a national organization of farmers.

But what was the impact of institutions on nineteenth-century government capacity? There is some evidence that efforts to promote the development of commercial agriculture in the United States benefited from institutional fragmentation. Federalism, the separation of powers, and bureaucratic rivalries among agencies multiplied the opportunities for individual politicians to channel resources to rural constituents. Jurisdic-

TABLE 2.1

Real Growth Rates for Ministry or Department of Agriculture Expenditures
During the First Three Decades of Existence[a]

Country (year established)	Decade 1	Decade 2	Decade 3	30 Years
United States (1962)	10.3	10.4	19.1	13.2
France (1881)	5.3	2.2	2.4	3.3
Japan (1881)	1.5	13.4	14.8	9.7

[a]Growth rate $= \exp\left[\frac{\log (Y_t / Y_{t-years})}{years}\right] - 1$, where Y is the five-year average of agricultural expenditures in constant national currencies for the period beginning at year t and years is 10 or 30.

Sources: USDA, Annual Reports of the Department of Agriculture, 1914, 212; INSEE, Annuaire statistique de la France: Résumé rétrospectif, 1966, 491; Yamada, "Changes in Output and in Conventional and Nonconventional Inputs in Japanese Agriculture since 1880," 390.

tional jealousies between agricultural bureaucracies at the federal and state levels increased promotional expenditures rather than retarded them. Agricultural research benefited from the multiplication of colleges and experiment stations at the state level. In addition, the decentralization of the congressional budget process during the 1880s—what Charles Stewart refers to as *expansionary fragmentation*—increased the flow of financial resources available for agricultural promotion.[105]

Table 2.1 compares real growth rates for agricultural expenditures in the United States, France, and Japan at equivalent periods in the history of each department or ministry. In the first ten years after the creation of the USDA, expenditures for the department grew at an annual rate of 10.3 percent.[106] Expenditures in the ten years after the creation of the French Ministry of Agriculture and the Japanese MACA grew at a much slower rate of 5.3 percent and 1.5 percent, respectively.

Growth rates for the USDA in the second decade after its creation (1872–1882) remained unchanged, while expenditure growth for the French ministry slowed down between 1891 and 1901. Meanwhile, Japanese expenditures grew much more rapidly—13.4 percent on an annualized basis—during the 1891–1901 period. Significantly, this period in Japanese history corresponds to a time of intensified competition between oligarchs and party politicians after creation of the Diet in 1890. Efforts to woo landowners' political support boosted agricultural expenditures: the 1893 Agricultural Experiment Station Law created a nationwide research system, the 1899 Arable Land Consolidation Law provided funding

[105] Stewart, "Budget Reform as Strategic Legislative Action," 303–7.

[106] Because I used five-year averages, the 10.3 percent growth rate actually refers to the increase in expenditures between 1862–1866 and 1872–1876.

for irrigation and drainage, and the 1899 Agricultural Association Law and 1900 Industrial Cooperative Law subsidized producer groups. Most of the expenditure growth during the third decade of the MACA (roughly, 1901–1911) came from increases in funding for land improvement projects. Increased expenditures for these projects, usually executed through the system of local cooperatives and associations, correspond to legislation passed in 1909 and 1910 that reorganized state-sponsored producer groups into a hierarchical structure under close government supervision.[107]

After steady growth during the first two decades of the USDA's existence, department expenditures grew quickly between 1881 and 1891. Increases in the agricultural budget during this period correspond to the devolution of the appropriations process in Congress. As described earlier, the House Agriculture Committee was one of the first authorizing committees to gain control over appropriations in 1880. Judging from table 2.1, the USDA reaped clear benefits as expenditures increased at an annual rate of 19.1 percent over the next ten years.

In the first thirty years after governments in each country established an agricultural ministry or department, expenditures grew more quickly in the United States (13.2 percent), than in either France (3.3 percent) or Japan (9.7 percent). The annual growth rate for USDA expenditures partly reflects the effects of deflation—the real value of the dollar was half as much in 1890 as in 1865. But even in nominal terms, perhaps a more significant measure from the point of view of politicians, USDA budgets grew at the impressive rate of 10.5 percent per year between 1862 and 1892. Again, the pace and timing of expenditure increases for agriculture in the United States suggest that the decentralized appropriations process in Congress facilitated access to the government resources necessary for agricultural promotion. Moreover, figures for the United States do not include state-level expenditures for agriculture that also contributed positively to nineteenth-century agricultural promotion.

Second, agricultural research policy also benefited from institutional competition between Congress, federal agencies, and the states. Conditions of agricultural production vary geographically according to "physical, biological, and socioeconomic environments." As a result, agricultural economists argue that "agricultural research must be conducted and the results analyzed, tested, interpreted, and applied within a relatively decentralized system."[108] As I have described, intense jurisdictional rivalries gave rise to a decentralized system of research institutions in the United States. For example, efforts in 1887 to create a unified experiment

---

[107] Yamada, "Changes in Output," 390. On the 1909 and 1910 legislation, see Ogura, *Can Japanese Agriculture Survive?* 270, 815.

[108] Hayami and Ruttan, *Agricultural Development*, 422–23.

station system in which the USDA could dictate the research agenda were rebuffed by the representatives of agricultural college interests in Congress. Instead, under the Hatch Act experiment stations received a large degree of autonomy over research questions; the USDA exercised little guidance.

Although an unintended consequence of federalism and party politics, the geographic distribution of research facilities across the United States resulted in a decentralized, "location-specific" system of research institutions rather than a system in which the research agenda was dictated in a top-down fashion from a central point of administration. Competition between state and federal agencies produced a diffuse and decentralized system well suited to the geographic variation in crops, climates, and markets across the United States.[109]

In contrast, French agricultural research institutions developed slowly or not at all. Confident that rural votes were secure so long as high tariffs prevailed, French governments before World War I spent few resources on agricultural research. Although professors of agriculture were assigned to each department, the central administration paid only their salary and offered no subsidies for research. One agriculture ministry official wrote to these departmental officials in an 1885 circular, "I hope it will be easy . . . to find, free of charge, [someone] who is disposed to offer several parcels of land for [crop] demonstrations." French extension officials lacked the political or economic resources to create an effective research network.[110] National institutions, such as the Institut agronomique, also lacked adequate resources. In 1908, Jules Méline complained that the national agricultural research institute had deplorable laboratory facilities. Moreover, of the small number of students who actually graduated from the institute (only eighty-seven in 1913), most became ministry bureaucrats rather than extension workers. Finally, without any system to adapt research findings to local conditions, most farmers viewed the work of agricultural scientists as abstract investigations with no practical application to farming. According to Michel Augé-Laribé, agricultural research and extension in France were "the regrettable failure of agricultural policy."[111] Similarly, Jobert and Muller remark on "the staggering gap between the discourse of the state about agriculture and the weakness of the means devoted to it."[112]

---

[109] For an interesting parallel, Colleen Dunlavy, in her study of railroad diffusion during the nineteenth century, argued that the fiscal autonomy of U.S. states and localities under federalism facilitated railroad construction. Dunlavy, "Political Structure, State Policy, and Industrial Change."

[110] Augé-Laribé, *La Politique agricole*, 124–31.

[111] Ibid., 128; Leveau, "L'Enseignement et la vulgarisation agricoles," 269–80.

[112] Jobert and Muller, *L'état en action*, 81.

The development of research institutions proceeded more favorably in Japan, but it was not until the 1920s that a network of national and prefectural experiment stations achieved success in areas such as rice breeding. Before then, "the resources allocated to activities for agricultural research and development were very meager." Hayami reports that the entire staff of the national and prefectural stations numbered only forty-five researchers and technicians in 1899. Although this number increased with the Law for State Subsidy of Prefectural Agricultural Experiment Stations, passed that year, it remained the case that "experiments were always handicapped by insufficient facilities and logistical support. Under such conditions it was only possible to conduct simple field experiments. . . . Facilities, personnel, and, above all, the state of knowledge did not permit conducting research beyond simple tests and demonstrations." In sum, Hayami and Yamada conclude that "there was gross underinvestment in agricultural research."[113]

CONCLUSION

In an age when the population of the United States was largely rural, agricultural policies were an important political resource. As we have seen, nineteenth-century political competition had important institutional consequences. Constrained by federalism and party politics, advocates of an agriculture department in the United States created a fractured system of agricultural administration and research. At the same time, efforts to establish a farm organization closely tied to the government did not succeed. Yet in the context of nineteenth-century agricultural promotion, these institutional attributes were not a liability. Instead, U.S. institutions fueled the growth of agricultural expenditures and the development of a research system adaptable to local problems. Although France and Japan possessed centralized bureaucracies and state-supported farm groups, this resulted in a less flexible research apparatus. Moreover, agricultural expenditures in both countries grew more slowly than in the United States.

But government capacity is not transferable across policy types. When the economic conditions of agriculture changed after World War I, each country experienced a reversal of institutional fortunes. Agricultural bureaucrats and farm organizations took on new roles in the context of market regulation. As I examine in the next chapter, institutions in France and Japan were well suited to the task of regulating markets. Agricultural

---

[113] Hayami, *A Century of Agricultural Growth in Japan*, 52; Hayami and Yamada, "Agricultural Research Organization in Economic Development," 248.

officials took control over the new policy domain of price supports and drew upon national farm organizations for assistance in the implementation of new policies.

In the United States, policy makers tried and failed to establish the kind of partnership with farm organizations that developed in France and Japan. Congressional dominance of policy, jurisdictional rivalries between agencies, and a pluralistic interest group environment—institutional characteristics beneficial in the context of promotion—hampered efforts to regulate agricultural markets.

CHAPTER 3

The Challenge of Market Intervention

As I examined in the previous chapter, the government promotion of commercial agriculture during the nineteenth century left an important institutional legacy. Both the design and structure of agricultural bureaucracies and the development of early farm organizations were products of political competition among elites. Agricultural institutions were shaped by the characteristics of the larger political milieu.

Differences in the structure of political competition produced distinct institutional outcomes in the United States, France, and Japan. Federalism and the regional basis of party competition in the United States resulted in a decentralized system of agricultural administration. Politicians used the network of land-grant colleges and experiment stations to distribute party favors across individual state delegations in Congress. Meanwhile, the regional basis of party politics also inhibited the development of a national farm organization. Leaders of the Grange and the Farmers' Alliance found it difficult to overcome sectional antipathies or to directly challenge powerful interests in Gilded Age party politics. In France and Japan, on the other hand, the lack of a developed party system opened up institutional possibilities as both countries developed state-supported farm organizations and a centralized system of agricultural administration by the turn of the century.

Institutional differences influenced government capacity. In the United States, the placement of research institutions in each state, although motivated by party politics, ensured that local needs and conditions would determine research priorities. Decentralized institutions proved beneficial in the context of agricultural promotion. In France and Japan, on the other hand, centralized institutions retarded the distribution of government resources from the center to the periphery. Agricultural expenditures and research facilities critical for the promotion of commercial farming grew slowly.

Government policies in all three countries continued to focus on the promotion of commercial agriculture through the boom years of the early twentieth century and World War I. With the end of the war, however, demand for farm commodities slackened. The recovery of European agriculture and increased competition on export markets produced a glut of farm products on world markets. Prices fell during the 1920s, and farmers who expanded production during the boom suffered tremendous economic losses. By the 1930s, farmers in the United States, France, and Japan were in the grip of a deep depression. Farm policy in all three countries was at a crossroads: under conditions of chronic surplus, promotional programs that increased production and productivity only contributed to the decline of agricultural income.

As I will examine in this chapter, governments in all three countries attempted to remedy the problem of surplus and low prices through a variety of new policy mechanisms such as production controls, price supports, and other regulatory measures. However, as the economic conditions of agriculture changed, so did the institutional requirements of agricultural policy. The depression of the 1920s and 1930s precipitated a reversal of institutional fortunes. The decentralization of institutions in the United States, beneficial in the context of promotion, hampered efforts to regulate agricultural markets. Meanwhile, government elites in France and Japan found that institutions designed for agricultural promotion were more easily adapted to new regulatory tasks.

NEW DEAL HISTORIOGRAPHY
AND AGRICULTURAL REGULATION

The inauguration of federal commodity programs in the United States has been used to illustrate a variety of social science approaches to the study of institutions, interest group power, and government capacity. The diversity and often-conflicting nature of these studies deserves brief attention before I examine policy developments in greater detail. In fact, the debate sheds light on how the agricultural crisis of the 1930s transformed the institutional requirements of policy.[1]

Social science treatments of New Deal agricultural policies usually fall into one of two categories. One group of scholars has emphasized how American farm programs of this period reflected the dominant class or group interests within the agricultural sector. In this "society-centered" view, policies are determined through a struggle among organized interests; the state is a passive arena within which this struggle takes place. In Grant McConnell's well-known study, for example, he argues that the conservative leaders of the American Farm Bureau Federation exercised their considerable political influence to defeat policy proposals—such as assistance programs for tenant farmers—deemed contrary to the interests

---

[1] By making the variety of approaches to New Deal agricultural policies explicit, I hope to introduce an account that explains some of the variance in this historiography. See Lustick, "History, Historiography, and Political Science," 605–18.

of Farm Bureau members. Indeed, as McConnell and others point out, government benefits distributed through federal farm programs became concentrated in the hands of a relatively small stratum of affluent farmers.[2]

Critical of the near-exclusive attention paid to interest groups, other scholars have emphasized the role of government administrators and bureaucratic politics in New Deal farm programs. According to this view, relatively autonomous bureaucrats formulated policies apart from societal interests such as farm groups. In the most forceful articulation of this argument, Kenneth Finegold and Theda Skocpol refer to the U.S. Department of Agriculture as "an island of state strength" in a sea of institutional weakness. Skocpol and Finegold argue that linkages between the USDA and the land-grant colleges supplied the federal government with a cadre of well-trained economists who developed New Deal agricultural programs and imposed them on a generally recalcitrant farm population. Like others who use "state-centered" approaches, Finegold and Skocpol focus on the attempts by government officials to promote their policy preferences or extend the institutional reach of the USDA over natural resource policy.[3]

Debates between these opposing views of New Deal agricultural policy often center on the identity and intentions of the actors involved in the critical stages of policy formation. Such determinations, however, are always problematic. Many academic economists trained in the land-grant system who worked in government during the New Deal also maintained close relations with farm organizations over the course of their careers. Economists and administrators within the USDA played a central role in the development of New Deal agricultural policy, but in many instances farm organizations were consulted about their policy preferences as well. Because of this intermingling, it is possible to make a case for both arguments.

What keeps these approaches consistently at loggerheads is a failure to understand how the regulation of agricultural markets transformed relations between farmers and the government. These new relations required institutional arrangements that simultaneously increased government intervention in the economy *and* incorporated farm groups into the policy process. The failure to grasp these new institutional requirements is particularly a shortcoming for Finegold and Skocpol, since they place

[2] McConnell, *The Decline of Agrarian Democracy*; Lowi, *The End of Liberalism*; Campbell, *The Farm Bureau and the New Deal*; Young, "The Origins of New Deal Agricultural Policy"; Gilbert and Howe, "Beyond 'State vs. Society.' "

[3] Finegold and Skocpol, *State and Party in America's New Deal*; Skocpol and Finegold, "State Capacity and Economic Intervention in the Early New Deal"; Hooks, "From an Autonomous to a Captured State Agency"; Saloutos, *The American Farmer and the New Deal*; Kirkendall, *Social Scientists and Farm Politics*.

government structure and political development at the center of their analysis. Through their use of definitional boundaries between state and society as an analytical point of departure, Finegold and Skocpol, like other scholars of institutions, have not paid adequate attention to the boundary itself.[4]

The Corporatist Challenge of Agricultural Regulation

Intervention in the operation of agricultural markets after World War I redefined the relationship between farmers and the government; regulation changed the boundary between state and society. Agricultural bureaucrats, for instance, faced new challenges. For the first time, the success or failure of policy depended on the actions of millions of independent farmers. The adjustment of production at the farm level required adequate surveillance of planting and harvest, as well as the capacity to sanction violators of production control programs. Government-mandated prices for basic commodities failed unless agents of the state controlled distribution networks and public officials possessed the authority to punish individuals who bought and sold products in the underground economy. Without the active participation of farmers—through either voluntary or coercive means—government programs would certainly fail. The administrative challenge of agricultural policy in the 1920s and 1930s illustrated Samuel Beer's observation that "the greater degree of detailed technical control the government seeks to exert over interests, the greater must be their degree of consent and active participation."[5]

As I explore in this chapter, governments in the United States, France, and Japan seized upon *corporatist* arrangements as a strategy to forge these new links between producers and the state. As John Keeler argues, the distinctive features of agriculture just described make corporatism a particularly attractive solution to the challenge of regulation. Through such partnerships, bureaucrats gained critical assistance from farm organizations in the implementation of government programs. In addition, corporatism had distinct advantages as a political strategy both for the government and for farm organizations. By designating an official representative of farmers as an agent of government policy, politicians could allay fears that regulations on production were a statist encroachment on private property. Subsidies for cooperatives and other associations were justified as measures designed to rationalize production and marketing, rather than subject the business of agriculture to heavy-handed officials.

[4] For a fuller critique, see Mitchell, "The Limits of the State."
[5] Beer, *Britain against itself*, 14.

At the same time, producers gained access to and influence in the creation of policies that affected them directly. In accepting the role of a corporatist client, farm groups could use influence over policy as an incentive to attract membership or as a means to achieve a competitive advantage over rival organizations.[6]

Although such arrangements were politically and administratively expedient, the capacity of governments in the United States, France, and Japan to establish a corporatist partnership was shaped by two institutional factors, the agricultural bureaucracy and farm organizations. Corporatism required capable administration and a willing client. As I examine later, these institutional prerequisites did exist in France and Japan. But in the United States, corporatist arrangements failed to take hold in agricultural policy despite the efforts of bureaucrats in the USDA and the leaders of the major farm organization in the country, the American Farm Bureau Federation.

Institutional Legacies and the Corporatist Challenge

In France and Japan, the legacy of agricultural promotion left government officials with a centralized administrative apparatus and a system of state-supported farm organizations. When the farm economy soured in the 1920s, bureaucrats empowered these state-sponsored associations to police farmers and act as a partner with the government in the regulation of markets. In Japan, close ties between the agricultural cooperatives and the state paved the way for a government monopoly of food production and distribution executed largely through peak farm organizations. In France, no sectorwide corporatism existed before World War II, but producer groups in wheat and wine both became corporatist clients in the regulation of these two critical commodities.

In the United States, government officials tried to enlist agricultural organizations in the struggle against low farm prices. During the depression, Congress appropriated millions of dollars to encourage the formation of marketing cooperatives that could regulate the flow of commodities on to the market. Through the work of government extension agents, the American Farm Bureau Federation emerged as the largest agricultural organization in the United States and a likely candidate to become a cor-

[6] Keeler, *The Politics of Neocorporatism*. Keeler argues that the institutional prerequisites for corporatism did not arise until the Fifth Republic. I argue that although no sectorwide corporatism existed in the Third Republic, corporatist arrangements did emerge in critical commodities like wheat and wine. For an application of the corporatist literature to U.S. agriculture, see Hamilton, "Building the Associative State," 207–18.

poratist client in the implementation of agricultural policy. Yet by the 1940s, relations between the Department of Agriculture and the Farm Bureau were openly hostile.

Agricultural corporatism failed to develop in the United States because neither bureaucrats nor producers possessed the institutional requirements for a stable policy partnership. Although the Department of Agriculture created a network of officials that extended throughout the country, divisions over policy in Washington led to the fragmentation of administration across several agencies. Despite growth in Farm Bureau membership, other rival farm organizations continually challenged the Farm Bureau for dominance in the policy process throughout the New Deal. Farm Bureau failure to secure organizational dominance confirmed Salisbury's observation that "peak interest group associations in the United States have great difficulty achieving enough comprehensiveness of membership . . . to represent their respective sectors in the political process."[7] Lacking both a united bureaucracy and a dominant farm group, government officials found the corporatist path to agricultural policy foreclosed.

Institutional differences had important policy consequences. Unable to forge a corporatist partnership, officials in the USDA found their alternatives limited. Farm programs operated through bargains with individual farmers rather than farm organizations. Efforts to reallocate market power away from merchants or to raise the conditions of tenants and sharecroppers failed. Worst of all, government policies did not effectively support or stabilize commodity prices. Where corporatist arrangements did exist, as in Japan and, to a limited degree, in France, the records of government policies appear brighter.

JAPAN: RICE AND REGULATION

Agricultural promotion in Japan during the nineteenth century produced an administrative-association nexus that joined the agricultural bureaucracy to a network of local associations and cooperatives. These quasi-public farm organizations served as instruments of agricultural bureaucrats as well as a conduit through which rural interests influenced government policy. Given this institutional legacy, it is not surprising that government responses to the agricultural crisis of the 1920s and 1930s relied heavily on the system of agricultural cooperatives and associations created decades earlier. Of the three countries, it is in Japan that the instruments

---

[7] Salisbury, "Why No Corporatism in America?" 214. For a similar conclusion, see Wilson, "Why Is There No Corporatism in the United States?"

of agricultural regulation most closely resemble the corporatist ideal type of a single, peak association joined with a state bureaucracy as partners in the regulation of farm products.

Even though the Japanese government could draw upon existing institutions for the purpose of regulation, control over domestic commodity markets was difficult nonetheless. Particularly in the case of rice, the most important agricultural commodity in Japan, government regulations ran directly counter to the interests of merchants, futures traders, and Japanese investors in Korea and Taiwan. The ability to subordinate these economic interests to the agricultural policy agenda tested the strength of the administrative-association nexus in the 1920s and 1930s. Yet, as we will see, the government managed to implement price controls, import restrictions, and other regulatory measures over the opposition of these groups. Through government intervention, interest group conflict gave way to clientele relations as the link between agricultural cooperatives and the government grew closer. When the entire agricultural sector came under the monopoly control of government administrators and farm organizations in the 1940s, the division between state and state client was indistinguishable.

The commercial development of Japanese agriculture during the late nineteenth and early twentieth centuries was accompanied by great volatility in domestic rice prices. Newly established regional rice markets fueled an active business in speculation and futures trading. Rice merchants profited from the daily movements of rice prices, and collusion among rice dealers created artificial swings in prices. Widespread tenant farming further contributed to price instability. In the early decades of the twentieth century, tenants farmed 45 percent of all agricultural land, and fully 70 percent of all farm households rented at least some land. For paddy fields, rent was usually paid in kind; farmers turned over a portion of their crop to the landlord and most of what remained was sold on the market to pay for seeds, fertilizers, and other inputs. Whereas landlords could spread out the marketing of their crop over the year, tenants usually sold their rice immediately to generate cash for debt repayment. As a result, a glut of rice entered the market in the months of November, December, and January, driving the price downward. For many unfortunate tenants, it was necessary to purchase rice later in the year at a higher price in order to feed the family.[8]

The effects of commodity speculation and the seasonal rhythms of rice prices were magnified in years when crops were exceptionally good or bad. Between 1914 and 1920, in fact, farmers suffered a succession of

---

[8] Donnelly, "Political Management of Japan's Rice Economy," 187–90; Tobata, *Control of the Price of Rice*, 7–8; Waswo, *Japanese Landlords*.

erratic growing seasons that resulted in a particularly volatile rice market. Between 1913 and 1915, several bumper crops pushed down nominal prices by nearly 40 percent. However, fortunes changed rapidly. Tight grain markets in Europe and a series of poor harvests in 1917 and 1918 depleted domestic rice stocks. Combined with speculation by rice merchants and an inefficient distribution system, these events caused rice prices to more than double in just two years. In July 1918, riots spread throughout the country as protesters burned the houses of rice merchants and demanded government action to halt the rise in rice prices. By 1920, price trends reversed again as large harvests and worldwide recession following the end of World War I caused rice prices to drop more than 50 percent in 1920.[9]

The volatility in the domestic rice market—and the social unrest that followed—forced the government to consider regulation. Yet the appropriate form or purpose of intervention remained unclear. Although drastic changes in the price of rice hurt urban consumers and farmers alike, the interests of these groups with respect to policy were quite different. Consumers and employers demanded protection from upside price swings that increased the cost of living. Of course, high prices benefited farmers, and particularly landowners, who collected land rents in rice. These rural interests demanded protection from downside price declines that cut directly into income and made agricultural investments unprofitable. Finally, a third group—the rice merchants who profited from market speculation—opposed any government intervention in rice prices.

This diversity of interests placed the political parties in a difficult position. When the Terauchi government fell as a result of the rice riots in 1918, Hara Takashi, president of the majority Seiyukai Party, became prime minister and formed the first true party cabinet in Japanese history. Although agrarian interests remained predominant in the Diet and the Seiyukai Party, urban concerns and the opinions of Japanese business leaders could not be ignored either. During consideration of rice regulation, rural demands for price supports were tempered by government fears of urban unrest precipitated by high rice prices.[10]

Under the terms of the Rice Law passed in March 1921, the government created a 200 million yen fund to purchase and sell rice, ostensibly to smooth out seasonal fluctuations in supply. Although the government recognized the necessity to "adjust the supply and demand of rice," the text of the new law omitted any reference to prices. It remained ambiguous whether the new law was for the protection of food security (i.e., release

---

[9] Bank of Japan, *Economic Statistics of Japan*, 115; On the rice riots, see Lewis, *Rioters and Citizens*, 1–81.

[10] On the Hara ministry, see Scalapino, *Democracy and the Party Movement*, 210–21.

rice stocks in lean years) or as a device for price supports (i.e., purchase rice stocks in bountiful years). This ambiguity, however, provided Diet politicians with sufficient cover from both urban and rural interests.[11]

Although the 1921 Rice Law was a tentative foray in market intervention, the institutional consequences of the law would prove critical for future rice regulation.[12] The government entrusted administration of the Rice Law to the newly created Rice Bureau within the Ministry of Agriculture and Commerce (MAC). Officials in the Rice Bureau soon established prefectural offices to oversee government rice transactions at the local level. This expansion of administrative duties in the regulation of rice energized arguments for the establishment of a separate agricultural ministry. Members of the Imperial Agricultural Association, Dietmen, and officials in the Bureau of Agricultural Affairs argued that the responsibilities of the minister of agriculture and commerce were too broad and privileged commercial demands for low food prices over the interests of agriculture. Persistent lobbying by rural interests in the Diet, heightened by the deteriorating economic situation of farmers, finally resulted in the creation of the Ministry of Agriculture and Forestry (MAF) in 1925.[13]

The Rice Law also gave a boost to agricultural cooperatives. Even if the government was unsure about market intervention, public subsidization of the cooperative movement remained a popular policy alternative. The 1921 law required that government purchases of rice be executed through agricultural cooperatives rather than on the open market. A series of measures intended to strengthen the economic position of agricultural cooperatives in the farm sector followed. A revision of the Industrial Cooperative Association Law united the federations of credit, purchasing, and marketing cooperatives into a single, national federation. In 1923, the government established the Central Bank for Industrial Cooperative Associations, which greatly increased the availability of financing for cooperative activities.[14]

Meanwhile, the system of local improvement organizations under the leadership of the Imperial Agricultural Association (IAA) received similar encouragement. Amendments to the Agricultural Association Law in 1922 gave the IAA responsibility for the mediation of disputes between tenants and landlords over rents, leases, and other matters. In addition,

---

[11] Tobata, *Control of the Price of Rice*, 22–23; Donnelly, "Political Management of Japan's Rice Economy," 164–67.

[12] Rice purchases by the government amounted to 923,000 *koku* (1 koku = 60 kg) in the first year of the Rice Law, a mere 1.5 percent of total production. Tobata, *Control of the Price of Rice*, 46.

[13] Ogura, *Can Japanese Agriculture Survive?* 358–62.

[14] Donnelly, "Political Management of Japan's Rice Economy," 192; Ogura, *Agricultural Development in Modern Japan*, 254.

the government doubled the size of its annual subsidy to the organization. According to Takahashi Korekiyo, finance minister in the Hara cabinet, the prime minister initially opposed the increased subsidy on fiscal grounds. However, "because of party interest," Hara approved the subsidy increase nonetheless.[15] In sum, leaders of agricultural organizations in Japan drew power not only from their role in the policy process (as the conduit through which rice supplies were managed and tenancy disputes resolved) but also as players in party politics—particularly through the rural-based Seiyukai.

As the rural economy worsened in the late 1920s and early 1930s, leaders of the IAA and the agricultural cooperatives used their administrative and political connections to secure greater government control over the vagaries of the rice market. After a sharp decline in rice prices in 1929, the IAA and a group of rural backbenchers in the Diet demanded that the government revise the Rice Law. In response, a blue-ribbon committee composed of bureaucrats, Diet members, and representatives from industrial and agricultural organizations recommended a system of government-mandated prices coupled with subsidies for rice storage. Under the revision codified by imperial ordinance in 1931, government intervention in the rice market would occur within a range of maximum and minimum prices set at the beginning of each marketing season. Reflecting the mix of industrial and agricultural interests on the committee, this dual price system tried to strike a balance between the interests of producers and consumers.[16] By bringing the issue of prices directly into policy, however, the 1931 revision opened the possibility of a system of government price supports.

In the meantime, the crisis in the rural economy grew acute. Rice imports from Korea and Taiwan added to record harvests in 1931. Rice prices dropped as a result, and farm income declined by 50 percent. As the situation in rural Japan grew dire, observers blamed the growing political instability on the farm crisis.[17] In response to the deepening depression, leaders of the agricultural organizations renewed their calls for government action.

[15] Ogura, *Agricultural Development in Modern Japan*, 250–51; Takahashi quoted by Harada Kumao, "Farmers Demand Subsidies" (November 18, 1933), *The Saionji-Harada Memoirs*, 740–46.

[16] Tobata, *Control of the Price of Rice*, 32–34.

[17] On May 15, 1932, several young military cadets attempted a coup d'état. Although unsuccessful, the rebels killed a prominent leader, Inukai Tsuyoshi. At their trial, the rebels claimed their actions were intended to remedy the plight of the farmers. See, for example, "Farmers Plight in 1931 Depicted at May 15 Trial," *Japan Times and Mail*, October 6, 1933. On the deteriorating economic conditions, see "1931 Loss on Farms was yen 16.51 per Tan," *Trans Pacific* (hereafter *TP*), April 14, 1932; "Market Conditions of Agricultural Products in Japan," *Monthly Circular*, no. 149 (March 1936): 12–13; Donnelly, "Political Management of Japan's Rice Economy," 195–201.

In the summer of 1932, the cabinet convened a special session of the Diet to consider debt forgiveness, public works projects, and other rural relief measures. Unsatisfied by the government plans, three hundred farmers assembled at the prime minister's residence in July to demand greater aid. One month later, at the national convention of the IAA, twenty-five hundred farmers, officials from the Ministry of Agriculture, and one hundred Diet members from rural districts called for the abolition of the Rice Law and its replacement with a system of unlimited government purchases. In addition, the IAA and its allies demanded government control of colonial imports to stem the tide of Korean and Taiwanese rice.[18]

Through the fall of 1932, debate in the Diet over farm relief was acrimonious. Both major political parties, the Seiyukai and the Minseito, were hopelessly factionalized, and the subject of rural relief only exacerbated the divisions. The cabinet, headed by a nonparty prime minister, favored fiscal restraint and opposed a major overhaul of the Rice Law. The Minseito also opposed scrapping current rice legislation. The majority Seiyukai, because it was a primarily rural party (and in an effort to regain control of the government), advocated the demands of the IAA for unlimited government purchases of rice and rural debt relief at a sum well above the government proposal. In September 1932, the Seiyukai successfully defeated the government rice reform plan in the Diet, prompting the government to negotiate with the Seiyukai over a suitable relief alternative.[19]

In the compromise that evolved, the Seiyukai secured higher relief funds than initially offered by the government. In exchange, the Seiyukai accepted the government plan for rice legislation. Government purchases of rice to boost prices would be unlimited and at prices calculated according to the cost of production as demanded by the IAA and rural backbenchers. This in effect created a dual pricing structure for rice, with separate government prices for producers and consumers. In the realm of colonial rice imports, the government refused to impose strict controls but agreed to purchase colonial rice at certain times of the year to regulate supplies. This agreement, struck in September 1932, became the basis for the new Rice Control Law passed by the Diet in March 1933.[20]

---

[18] "Farmers Appeal Directly to Throne," *TP*, June 9, 1932; "Plan Public Works to Assist Farmers," *TP*, June 23, 1932; "Impatient Farmers Chide Government," *TP*, July 14, 1932; "Farmers Assemble at Premier's Home," *TP*, July 28, 1932; "Farm Group Asks Concrete Relief," *TP*, August 18, 1932; "Farmers Demands Reveal Discontent," *TP*, September 1, 1932.

[19] "Ranks of Seiyukai Split over Relief," *TP*, August 18, 1932; "Politicians Secure Government Relief," *TP*, August 25, 1932; "Seiyukai Forcing Views on Cabinet," *TP*, September 1, 1932.

[20] "Cabinet Rice Plan Wins as Diet Ends," *TP*, September 8, 1932; "Rice Control Act Drafted for Diet," *Japan Times and Mail*, February 17, 1933; Tobata, *Control of the Price of Rice*, 43–44.

As in the 1920s, the development of price support programs during the 1930s strengthened the position of agricultural cooperatives and associations in the rice economy. Many of the farm relief funds appropriated in 1932, for example, were distributed through local associations. Meanwhile, the government guaranteed the financial liability of each cooperative with public funds. In 1933, the leaders of the cooperative movement, in conjunction with officials from the Ministry of Agriculture, outlined a five-year expansion plan that pledged to establish a cooperative in every village or town. Government subsidies and loans funded the construction of cooperative rice warehouses used for official purchases and sales of rice. Even efforts to calculate the level of price support for rice required the government to elicit cost-of-production data from the agricultural associations. In these ways, the quasi-public system of agricultural organizations was intimately tied to the evolving regulatory framework for farm products.[21]

But the new rice regulations engendered conflict with other, rival economic interests. Market intervention entailed both concentrated costs and concentrated benefits. The most directly threatened group was understandably the rice merchants. Government controls on maximum and minimum prices limited the range of speculative price movements. More important, government purchases and sales through cooperatives cut directly into the business of rice merchants and wholesalers. The Japan Chamber of Commerce and Industry quickly voiced its opposition to government regulations on rice markets. "Great privileges are given to cooperative societies in connection with farm relief. . . . [T]he interest of these societies is being rapidly promoted, while that of medium sized and small businessmen . . . [is] neglected. . . . [T]his protection of cooperative societies will destroy the commercial and industrial interests. . . . Businessmen and industrialists must oppose co-operative societies."[22] Answering the call, merchants and traders of the Tokyo Rice and Produce Exchange formed an opposition movement against proposed government regulations. Unable to prevent passage of the new regulations, members of the Japan Chamber of Commerce and Industry began an anticooperative campaign in the Diet to prevent further encroachments on private business.[23]

---

[21] "For Relief of Farmers," *Japan Times and Mail*, March 16, 1933; "Emergency Loans Ready for Farms," *TP*, June 2, 1932; "More Cooperatives Planned for Farms," *TP*, July 28, 1932; Ogura, *Agricultural Development*, 254–55.

[22] Statement by Japan Chamber of Commerce and Industry, translated in *TP*, October 26, 1933, 21.

[23] *TP*, October 26, 1933, 21; "Produce Exchanges Fight Monopoly," *TP*, September 22, 1932.

Another group, the Japanese who invested in Korean and Taiwanese land projects, also opposed regulations, particularly plans to restrict colonial imports of rice. During the 1920s, these investors received subsidies for research, irrigation, and other promotional projects. With the help of subsidies, colonial exports of rice increased dramatically, and by the 1930s rice exports were a major component of the Taiwanese and Korean economies. But gluts of rice imports from the colonies added to the downward pressure on prices in Japan. Aware that their livelihood would be threatened by market regulation, landowner associations in the colonies joined business leaders in Japan in opposition to the IAA and the cooperatives.[24]

At first, colonial investors and rice merchants resisted government regulations with varying degrees of success. Speculation and hoarding continued on the rice exchanges despite government policies that set maximum and minimum prices. Meanwhile, the IAA and the Ministry of Agriculture offered a plan in 1933 to cut rice production in Korea and Taiwan. Arguing that the plan threatened Japanese food security, colonial investors used their connections in the Ministry of Overseas Affairs to defeat the proposal.[25]

By the late 1930s, however, the capacity of colonial investors and merchants to resist regulatory encroachments dwindled considerably. In 1935, the Ministry of Agriculture ceased all promotional measures in Korea and Taiwan. Credit facilities were removed, irrigation projects terminated, and other forms of investment suddenly withdrawn. In 1936, the Rice Autonomous Storage Law initiated a system of supply controls that assigned mandatory storage quotas to rice districts on the mainland *and* in the colonies. Designed to hold rice from the market during seasonal peaks in supply, these measures achieved moderate success as rice imports from Korea and Taiwan declined by one-third between 1933 and 1938.[26]

Merchants suffered a more dramatic decline under the government policies of the late 1930s. Through tax breaks and subsidies for warehouse construction, cooperatives were able to compete directly with private concerns in rice collection and distribution. Between 1932 and 1938, the volume of rice handled by cooperatives more than tripled. Over the same period, the volume of futures transactions—an important source of income for rice dealers—dropped more than 75 percent. In 1939, the Diet passed the Rice Distribution Control Law, which outlawed all futures transactions. The government reduced the number of commodity ex-

[24] Tobata, *Control of the Price of Rice*, 27, 31.

[25] "Rice Restricting Plan Approved by Conference," *Japan Times and Mail*, September 22, 1933; "Give Up Plan to Reduce Area Now Planted in Rice," *Japan Times and Mail*, October 10, 1933.

[26] Johnston, *Japanese Food Management*, 268; Ogura, *Agricultural Development in Modern Japan*, 195.

changes from seventeen to a mere two and created a new government corporation, the Japan Rice Company, to supervise rice purchases between cooperatives and producers.[27]

As the country moved toward a war economy, the links between the Ministry of Agriculture and the farm organizations grew closer. Under wartime regulations, cooperatives executed critical functions of food collection and distribution. The 1940 Regulations for Rice Control required the mandatory delivery of rice from producers directly to cooperatives or agricultural associations. The cooperatives and associations were, in turn, responsible for distribution to consumers. In describing these controls, the *Monthly Circular* of the Mitsubishi Economic Research Bureau remarked, "Cooperatives have thus become ... mere Government agents."[28] In fact, the cooperatives had forged a corporatist partnership with the government. Cooperatives assisted in the implementation of policy and, in exchange, gained critical leverage over private merchants in the provision of food and other agricultural materials.

In addition, bureaucrats within the Ministry of Agriculture and Forestry (MAF) used the corporatist relationship with cooperatives to expand their jurisdiction over economic policies and defend encroachments from other hostile ministries. In 1939, MAF bureaucrats successfully resisted efforts to place the portfolios for the Ministry of Agriculture and the Ministry of Commerce and Industry (MCI) in the hands of a single minister, Godo Takuo. MAF also secured key victories in jurisdictional battles with its old rival, the MCI.[29] In 1939, the MCI announced regulations on the distribution of critical inputs such as petroleum and fertilizers. Control over these inputs was to be executed through an association of merchants under ministry tutelage. Arguing that farmers who depended on these items would suffer great injustice at the hands of merchants and their allies in the MCI, MAF bureaucrats demanded that fertilizers and petroleum be distributed to farmers through the agricultural cooperatives, not the merchant associations. The government endorsed this sectoral division of labor among the ministries, and the cooperatives subsequently added agricultural inputs to their growing list of regulatory responsibilities.[30]

[27] Donnelly, "Political Management of Japan's Rice Economy," 233; "Development of Government Control," *Monthly Circular*, no. 183 (January 1939): 33; "Changes in the Mechanism of Rice Distribution," *Monthly Circular*, no. 206 (December 1940): 8; "Rice Speculation to Be Restricted," *TP*, August 17, 1939; "Japan, Facing Rice Shortage, Debates Stricter Controls," Ogura, *For Eastern Survey*, April 10, 1940, 95; *Agricultural Development in Modern Japan*, 226.

[28] "Changes in the Mechanism of Rice Distribution," 9.

[29] Recall that the MCI and MAF were formerly two halves of a single ministry. See "Japanese Agriculture under War Pressure" *For Eastern Survey*, June 5, 1940, 135–39.

[30] See "Four Farm Groups Appealing to Abe," *TP*, October 12, 1939; "Two Ministries Differ on Farm Aid Plans," *TP*, August 17, 1939; "Ministries Agree on Price Control," *TP*,

By the time of the Pacific War, government control of the Japanese economy was pervasive. In 1942, the government codified the growing number of complex regulations under the Food Control Law. The new law regulated the prices, production, and distribution of all staple foods. MAF officials in the Agricultural Administration Bureau, in conjunction with leaders of the local agricultural associations, dictated the selection of rice varieties, the time of planting, the distribution of inputs such as fertilizers, and the assignment of production quotas to each farmer. The Food Management Bureau, also under MAF jurisdiction, controlled staple food collection through local Food Offices. Production quotas for rice and other staple foods assigned by the Food Offices, in turn, were collected by the cooperatives, which transported their stocks to a government corporation that sold directly to consumers under a strict rationing system.[31]

As the government completed its system of monopoly control over the production and distribution of food, farmer organizations in Japan became indistinguishable from the mechanisms of state authority. In 1943, agricultural associations and cooperatives were amalgamated into a single system of national, prefectural, and village farm organizations. All farmers and landowners were required to join. As stipulated by the Agricultural Organizations Law, the new system of rural organizations would operate "in perfect compliance with national policy."[32] By accepting the role of a corporatist client—a policy partnership in which agricultural leaders gained access to policy and generous organizational assistance from the state—the IAA and the National Federation of Agricultural Cooperatives lost all capacity to operate independently from government bureaucrats. Only after the defeat of the Japanese state at the hands of a foreign army did agricultural organizations gain a measure of equality and, in some cases, ascendancy in their policy dealings with the government.

FRANCE: FROM POSTWAR RECONSTRUCTION TO REGULATION

As in Japan, political elites in France turned to farm organizations for assistance in the regulation of agricultural markets. This delegation of public power to private associations was the only legitimate policy solution in the eyes of a rural elite suspicious of central state authority. More so than in Japan, agricultural leaders in France viewed corporatism as a strategy to uplift the rural economy without statist intervention. This

---

August 24, 1939; "Japanese Agriculture under War Pressure," [135–39. After World War II, government control over these items was devolved to the cooperatives, resulting in a financial windfall.

[31] Johnston, *Japanese Food Management*, 177–98.

[32] Article 58, Agricultural Organizations Law, translated in ibid., 181.

strategy depended heavily on the strength of a new cadre of local extension agents and the leaders of commodity-specific farm organizations who advocated a technocratic approach to agricultural policy.

World War I had a devastating effect on French agriculture. Hesitation about enacting controls over prices and supplies left the government unprepared for a prolonged conflict. Invading German armies occupied some of the most productive farmland in France, between Paris and the Belgian frontier, causing a profound food crisis. Although Parliament empowered the government to requisition supplies, control prices, and stimulate production, officials achieved only limited success. Efforts to increase production or direct the flow of supplies encountered numerous obstacles in the departments. At war's end, many fields were in ruin, and more than 10 percent of the active agricultural population was dead.[33]

The wartime devastation of French agriculture and the failure of government policies exposed the weaknesses of agricultural administration. Ministerial capacity to direct policy on the ground remained circumscribed. Rival corps of officials, engineers, and educators competed with one another for policy predominance. Relations between local officials and prefects were sometimes strained, and access to basic information such as production quantities was inadequate. The government had failed to take an agricultural census since 1902.[34] French failure to support an army in the field was blamed on inadequate agricultural administration.

In light of this experience, government strategies for the postwar reconstruction of French agriculture focused on the creation of new and improved technical services in the departments. Plans to create a departmental extension service patterned after those in Germany and Austria quickly gained support. In 1918, the government established a new agricultural service corps, the Corps du génie rural (rural management), and provided it with a broad grant of authority. Placed on a level with the prestigious Ponts et chausées (bridges and roads), the new corps was given the responsibility for a variety of tasks in rural France such as the drainage of swamps, *remembrement* (consolidation of landholdings), the construction of rural roads, and rural electrification. In 1919, the government created special Offices agricole in each department to oversee the implementation of the new modernization policies carried out by the Génie rural and supervise the distribution of government subsidies. In 1921, the government reorganized the national agricultural research facility, the Institut national du recherche agronomique, to train new agronomists and improve the state of agricultural research.[35]

---

[33] Barral, *Les Agrariens*, 180.

[34] For an example of the problems of information, see Augé-Laribé, *La Politique agricole*, 142.

[35] Cépède and Weill, *L'Agriculture*, 222–24, 311–27.

The postwar emphasis on agricultural research and extension created a new cadre of agronomists, engineers, and other technical experts who worked to modernize French farming. Within each department, the government assigned a *directeur des service agricole* who, acting as an agricultural "prefect," coordinated the provision of government services to the French peasant. One measure of government success during the interwar period is the rapid electrification of rural communes. In 1919, only 7,500, less than 25 percent, of the more than 38,000 communes in France had electricity. By 1927, electricity reached more than 18,000 communes, and by 1937, 95 percent of French communes possessed electricity.[36]

The expansion and rationalization of agricultural administration in the departments was not universally welcomed. For the conservative, rural right, government involvement in agriculture threatened a creeping socialism that would erode rural society. As Suzanne Berger documented in Brittany, conservatives feared that "once the conditions of peasant life became the subject of political decisions and bureaucratic regulation, the autonomy of the rural world would be destroyed."[37] As one conservative commentator noted in 1922, "There isn't an industry that lends itself less to regulations . . . than agriculture. It needs to live in the full sun of liberty."[38] In their search for a way to preserve this autonomy, conservative elites in the countryside turned to agricultural syndicates and an alternative vision of a rural political economy in which the agricultural profession rather than the state supplied services and assistance to farmers. In 1900, there were 2,069 syndical unions with a membership of 512,000. By 1929, according to the national agricultural census, the number of syndicates had grown to 15,000, with a membership of 1.5 million.[39]

Aware of the political consequences at stake, republican leaders boosted subsidies for agricultural syndicates as well. Throughout the 1920s, this competition between the conservative Right and the republican Center-Left fueled the spread of farm organizations in France. Agricultural officials at the local level, such as the *professeurs d'agriculture* and the engineers in the Génie rural, helped establish and run local cooperatives. Writing in 1926, Augé-Laribé noted that "it is not uncommon for the director of the services agricoles in the department to serve as the secretary . . . of the departmental farm union."[40] Meanwhile, government policies, such as the Law of 12 March 1920, expanded the legal range of commercial opportunities for cooperatives. That same year, the govern-

---

[36] Barral, *Les Agrariens*, 210.

[37] Berger, *Peasants against Politics*, 53.

[38] M. Chéron quoted in Barral, *Les Agrariens*, 210.

[39] Cleary, *Peasants, Politicians, and Producers*, 36–38; Prugnaud, *Les Étapes du syndicalisme agricole*, 30–40; Barral, *Les Agrariens*, 107–9.

[40] Augé-Laribé, *Syndicats et coopératives agricoles*, 39–40.

ment consolidated the national agricultural credit system under the Caisse nationale du crédit agricole, thus increasing the availability of agricultural credit and sparking the creation of new agricultural cooperatives.[41]

The French government also created a new organization, the Chambres d'agriculture, in 1924. A quasi-public organization of farmers funded by property taxes, the Chambres were to perform two functions: promote better technical skills in agriculture and serve as the official representative of farm interests before the government.[42] The creation of the Chambres marks an important transition in French agricultural organizations. Like the efforts by the state to create a new administrative corps, agricultural organizations in post–World War I France embraced the goal of modernization and technological development. A new generation of farm leaders eschewed the ideological conflicts of the past and instead established technocratic societies dedicated to the promotion of mechanization, seed selection, and other techniques that increased production and productivity. In 1919, for example, members of the conservative Société des agriculteurs de France and the republican Société nationale d'encouragement à l'agriculture established the nonpartisan Confédération nationale des associations agricole (CNAA). The CNAA participated in high-level consultations with the government, such as the Conseil national économique. But this effort to create a single representative of farmers ultimately failed to overcome the heterogeneity of agricultural interests.[43]

Whereas umbrella organizations foundered upon political, social, and economic divisions among farmers, specialist producer associations flourished during the 1920s. The first such association was established in 1907, when wine producers in the Midi founded the Confédération générale des vignerons du Midi (CGV). After World War I, farmers who had trained in the new agricultural schools organized other producer associations for wheat (Association générale des producteurs de blé; AGPB) and sugar beets (Confédération générale des planteurs de betterave; CGB). Producer associations tended to develop in commodities where crop production displayed regional concentration. Unencumbered by the diversity of interests in general associations, organizations such as the AGPB promoted technical advances in farming and offered an alternative to the ideological divisions between conservative and republican farm associations.[44]

---

[41] Boussard, *Les Agriculteurs et la république*, 49–52; Ministère de l'agriculture, *Cent ans de Ministère de l'agriculture*, 80–81.

[42] Cleary, *Peasants, Politicians, and Producers*, 52–53; Prugnaud, *Les Étapes du syndicalisme agricole*, 118–19.

[43] Augé-Laribé, *La politique agricole*, 441–43 (Augé-Laribé served as the secretary-general of the organization); Rouveroux, "La Représentation professionnelle de l'agriculture," 73–74.

[44] Roussillon, *L'Association générale des producteurs du blé*.

It was the network of local offices and producer associations created after World War I that carried out government responses to the agricultural depression of the interwar period. When prices of commodities such as wheat and wine declined as a result of oversupply, institutions designed to increase agricultural productivity gradually became instruments of government control over prices and production.

Of course, this transition was far from seamless. Initial responses to the agricultural crisis centered on border measures such as tariffs. The government reinstated protectionist policies it had suspended during and after the war because of food shortages. Although the government raised duties on almost every agricultural product and instituted a complex system of import quotas, border measures failed to remedy the problem of low prices for two reasons. First, domestic production, by itself, outstripped consumption. Even with fewer imports, the problem of surplus remained. Second, in two critical commodities, wheat and wine, French farmers faced considerable competition from North African imports that entered metropolitan France duty-free.[45]

Even as the economic crisis deepened, direct government intervention into agricultural markets remained unpalatable to many conservative politicians and farm organizations. Opposition to government intervention was not motivated by an unwavering liberal faith in the operation of markets but rather by a preference for self-regulation (*autogestion*) in which farmers themselves had the authority to enforce controls on production and prices.[46] In order to allay fears of state encroachment, the government pursued ways to incorporate producers into the formation and implementation of policy. But unlike the sectorwide corporatism found in Japan, agricultural corporatism in France was commodity-specific.

In the wine sector, for example, the delegation of some public functions to producer groups began with the wine crisis of 1905. In the midst of chronic overproduction and low prices, the Clemenceau government instituted quality control regulations. Because many attributed the drop in prices to a glut of cheap wine on the market, the "antifraud" laws passed in 1905 aimed to prevent the use of sugar in winemaking so as to reduce output and raise prices. Enforcement of the new laws, however, required agents who could inspect vineyards and test wine for sugar content. In the Midi, members of the CGV took it upon themselves to deputize agents for this task. The role of the CGV in the enforcement of various regulations was soon well established, and in 1912 the government placed the CGV antifraud agents under the direct authority of the Ministry of Agri-

---

[45] Tracy, *Government and Agriculture in Western Europe*, 165.
[46] Elbow, *French Corporative Theory*.

culture. The new organization, an adjunct of the Ministry of Agriculture, was renamed the Service de la répression des fraudes.[47]

When overproduction drove down the price of wine again in the late 1920s, government responses to the wine crisis reflected the influence of the CGV and the close relationship between winegrowers and the state. The Statut du vin, a complex set of regulations passed in 1931, tried to lift wine prices through a variety of mechanisms such as stronger enforcement of the *appellations d'origine du controlée* (an official designation of high-quality wine types) and government prohibitions against cultivation of certain high-yielding grape varieties. In addition to these *quality* controls, the government also instituted, for the first time, *quantity* controls. Regulations stipulated that winegrowers cease irrigation after July 15 to reduce yield, pull up old vines, and pay a progressive tax on overproduction. In addition, the government could block part of the harvest on the vineyard, in essence, imposing a marketing quota on producers. Finally, if overproduction persisted, the government had the authority to purchase excess stocks from producers and distill the surplus wine into alcohol that was then mixed with gasoline and used for fuel.[48]

The interest of the major wine organization, the CGV, was well represented during consideration of the new law. Deputies from the Midi, an area of France economically dependent on the vine, organized a legislative bloc to defend the interests of winegrowers in Parliament. The leader of this bloc, as well as the chairman of the parliamentary committee responsible for drafting the new law, was Edouard Barthe. Barthe hailed from the department of the Héurault, which contained more hectares of vines than any other department in France at the time.[49] Under his influence, the Statut du vin addressed the demands of winegrowers for government assistance, as well as the fears that an interventionist, or *dirigiste*, agricultural policy eventually would regulate all facets of production. To critics in the Chamber of Deputies, the new law was clearly pro-producer and ignored the rights of consumers of cheap wine (a French staple). For Frédéric Brunet, a socialist deputy from Paris who opposed the law, this pro-producer orientation was due to the influence of the wine associations. In Brunet's words, "Is it not the case that the winegrowers give us an example of a perfect union when it is a matter of defending their interests?" According to Charles Warner, Brunet's assessment was largely correct.

[47] Warner, *The Winegrowers of France*, 41–51.

[48] For the text of the Statut du vin, see *Journal Officiel*, July 5, 1931, 7283–84. For a description of the legislation, see Morel, "L'Économie dirigée."

[49] Barral calls Barthe the "wine deputy." In fact, Barthe was instrumental in the creation of the Commission de boissons (Beverage Commission), which he led. Barral, *Les Agrariens*, 213, 227–28.

"In general the *Statut* conformed to the recommendations of the CGV and the other winegrowing associations."[50]

The new Statut reinforced the role of the CGV and other associations in the implementation of policy. Article 3 instructed the minister of agriculture to establish a commission composed of "syndicates and associations of wine producers" to determine the level of compensation for winegrowers who reduce their acreage of vines under the new law. Agents of the Service de la répression des fraudes participated in the enforcement of the new law, sometimes in tandem with other government agencies. An amendment to the Statut in 1934 increased the powers of these agents in order to facilitate more accurate assessments of the harvest. In other aspects of implementation, such as the varieties of grapes that could be planted and the exact date irrigation would be stopped, the service agricole decided in conjunction with local winegrowers.[51]

In the case of wheat, initial efforts at price stabilization also promoted cooperative marketing as a solution to the crisis. Legislation passed in 1930 offered government subsidies to producers who signed storage contracts with cooperatives and syndicates. Despite the formation of many new cooperatives, volatility in the wheat market continued nonetheless. Cooperatives that paid farmers an advance price for their harvest suffered profound losses as the market price continued to drop through the early 1930s. In an attempt to remedy the situation, the government increased subsidies to cooperatives in 1933 and purchased excess stocks of wheat, which were subsequently "denatured" (a process that renders wheat unfit for human consumption). Although initially an unwilling client, the association of wheat producers, the AGPB, eventually became a partner in policy. For example, the AGPB published bulletins that helped leaders of new cooperatives set up business. After 1933, cooperatives assumed responsibility for wheat denaturation while the AGPB began a campaign to promote the use of denatured wheat for animal feed.[52]

As government policy evolved, so did the participation of wheat growers in the formation and implementation of market controls. In July 1933, facing the prospect of a record harvest, the government legislated a minimum price for wheat. In some areas, cooperatives designated their own inspection agents to enforce the new law in a manner reminiscent of the winegrowers in the Midi. In addition, leaders of the AGPB supplied the government with information on the successes and failures of the

[50] Journal Officiel, Débats parlementaires, Chambre des Deputés, June 10, 1931, 2941–43; Warner, *The Winegrowers of France*, 109.

[51] Journal Officiel, July 5, 1931, 7284; *Journal Officiel*, December 25, 1934, 12701.

[52] Noly, "Le Role des coopératives," 19–27; *Archives nationale*, F10 2170, Fédération regionale des associations agricole du Centre, "Table analytique des lois, décrets et arrêtés concernant le blé," 2.

minimum-price policy in various regions and offered suggestions on possible improvements; subsequent revisions of the law incorporated some of these recommendations. Despite these efforts, however, a black market for wheat quickly developed that undercut the efficacy of government policies. By 1934, the minimum price policy was an acknowledged failure, and the AGPB, along with many others, advocated the return to market prices. In December, legislation abolished the minimum price policy and, instead, instituted a program of acreage reduction and export promotion.[53]

In 1936, elections radically reconfigured national politics in France and elevated a socialist coalition to power. The Popular Front, as the coalition was known, enacted a host of economic legislation in a variety of sectors. In agriculture, legislation passed in August 1936 created the Office national interprofessional du blé (ONIB), a public body composed of government officials, wheat producers, members of the grain trades, and consumer cooperatives. Under the new law, ONIB could fix prices for wheat and control all grain exports and imports. During consideration of the *projet du loi*, deputies criticized previous measures for failing to incorporate farm organizations in policy. As one deputy remarked, "For this project to succeed, it must have the approval of the mass of farmers, and must be established in direct collaboration with them."[54]

Indeed, agricultural cooperatives became the fulcrum for the new legislation. Unlike earlier efforts to control prices, the 1936 law *required* producers to deliver all wheat to officially designated agricultural cooperatives or, in special circumstances, government-approved wheat merchants. Although efforts to completely outlaw the grain trade failed to pass the Senate, the Law of August 15 abolished futures trading and subjected wheat merchants to strict regulations. In order to buy and sell grain, merchants required approval from departmental committees composed mainly of farmers.[55]

As in Japan, government policies gave cooperatives an advantage over their commercial rivals. As instruments of governmental authority in the regulation of production, producer organizations tried to improve the position of farmers in the circuits of exchange. In the words of an early ONIB publication, "Confronted by the large trusts that dominate the wheat market, it is necessary that the state [*pouvoirs publics*] help producers organize their profession. The movement of cooperatives, unions, and

[53] Noly, "Le Role des coopératives," 26, 32–52; Tracy, *Government and Agriculture in Western Europe*, 167–68.

[54] Journal Officiel, July 3, 1936, 1729.

[55] Cleary, *Peasants, Politicians, and Producers*, 85–86; Tracy, *Government and Agriculture in Western Europe*, 168.

mutuals has united . . . hundreds of thousands of farmers; but the agricultural organizations cannot, without the intervention of the law, liberate production and consumption from the grip of speculators." Corporatism, in other words, would reallocate market power in the farm sector away from merchants and toward producers.[56]

For its part, the Bank of France financed the government purchases of wheat executed through the cooperatives; this assured the continued liquidity of the cooperatives. In addition, the government embarked on a massive campaign to establish enough cooperatives and grain silos to handle the wheat harvest. Government agencies such as the Corps du génie rural and the Directeurs des services agricoles led the efforts to complete the physical infrastructure required for the new regulations. Within a year after the creation of the Office du blé, the number of wheat cooperatives increased from 750 to 1,205. Local agricultural officials also inspected wheat crops to assure quality standards and designated which cooperatives were "official" collection stations for the harvest.[57]

At first, the AGPB opposed the Office du blé. The capacity of agricultural administrators to designate "official" cooperatives appeared as the first step toward complete state control of production. But supporters of the new law argued that the Office du blé provided farmers with representation in the decision process. Of the fifty-two members on the national council responsible for price decisions, thirty were representatives of producer associations, compared with nine from commerce and 9 from industry. Farmers also held the majority of seats at the local level, where producers worked closely with agents of the offices agricoles in the inspection of fraud and the establishment of new cooperatives. Thus, despite initial reservations, a leader of the AGPB would admit in 1939 that "the Office du blé has been accepted with satisfaction in the peasant world."[58] Indeed, the ONIB was one of the few policy innovations of the Popular Front to survive beyond the short life of the fragile coalition.

The evolution of regulations on wheat production and prices illustrates, as in the case of wine, how producer associations established during the 1920s became integral to government policy formation and implementation in the 1930s. The increasingly technical nature of agricultural policy and the political limitations on government intervention placed cooperatives and other producer associations in a strategic position. These associations not only amplified the voice of farmers in politics but also supplied government administrators with information, assistance, and political cover in the implementation of agricultural policy. The agricultural bureaucracy also adapted to the new tasks of production and price control.

---

[56] Archives nationale, F10 2170, Miscellaneous ONIB publication, August 1936.
[57] de Bresson, *L'Office du blé*; Noly, *Le Role des coopératives*, 76.
[58] Barral, *Les Agrariens*, 253.

Government agencies such as the Corps du génie rural and the Offices agricoles became responsible for the oversight of new regulations on production, prices, and marketing. Although initially established to increase agricultural production, these agencies became instruments for agricultural regulation in the 1930s.

When the Third Republic fell in 1940, the technocratic leaders of cooperatives and producer associations brought their corporatist vision to Vichy agricultural policy. Through the influence of these farm leaders, the Pétain government created the Corporation paysanne, a sectorwide federation of local, regional, and national farm unions responsible for the regulation of markets, the provision of credit, technical instruction, and a variety of other activities.[59] By 1943, however, the effort to create a self-regulating peasant organization became little more than an instrument of the German occupation for the requisition of agricultural supplies from French farmers. Ironically, the persistent fear that government intervention would ultimately lead to socialism resulted in the creation of institutions that paved the way for more rigid state controls of production and prices during the war.

UNITED STATES: THE FAILURE OF CORPORATISM

In France and Japan, government responses to the agricultural depression relied heavily on policy partnerships between farm organizations and agricultural bureaucracies. With few major obstacles, institutions in both countries adapted to new regulatory tasks. Government subsidies financed the growth and maintenance of farm organizations and promoted close links between farmers and the state. These links were critical to the success of regulations that required government surveillance of production, prices, and exchange.

In the United States, farmers and bureaucrats also attempted to forge a policy partnership with one another. The rise of the Extension Service and the county agent after 1914 extended the influence of the USDA throughout the rural United States. In addition to their work as technical advisers in agriculture, the county agents organized farmers into local associations called *farm bureaus*. By 1919, these associations joined to form the American Farm Bureau Federation (AFBF), which quickly became the largest farm organization in the United States.

As in France and Japan, officials in the USDA turned to these state-sponsored farm organizations for solutions to the economic crisis of the 1920s. Through the early 1930s, the USDA and the Farm Bureau worked closely

---

[59] Boussard, *Vichy et la Corporation paysanne*, 32.

together in agricultural policy matters. However, the corporatist relationship between farmers and the government quickly broke down under the weight of administrative fragmentation and challenges by rival farm organizations. By World War II, officials in the USDA and the major farm groups were deeply divided over policy. Although farmers and bureaucrats embraced a corporatist solution to the farm crisis, institutional limitations stunted the development of a stable policy partnership in U.S. agriculture

The March toward Corporatism, 1914–1929

Although historically plagued by bureaucratic infighting, several USDA secretaries streamlined the structure of agricultural administration during and after World War I. Departmental reorganization under Secretary David Houston improved the coordination of USDA activities and expanded the resources of the Office of the Secretary. The traditional research focus of the USDA shifted away from the natural sciences such as biology and chemistry and embraced a new concern for economics and sociology. The Office of Markets and the Rural Organization Service, both created in 1913, studied questions of marketing, production, and trade. The creation of the Bureau of Crop Estimates in 1914 increased department resources for the collection and analysis of statistics. In 1922, these offices concerned with farm economics and statistics were unified under the new Bureau of Agricultural Economics (BAE). Staffed by prominent agricultural economists from the land-grant colleges, the BAE "performed important general-staff services for the Secretary and the Department." Through its research and publications, the BAE quickly became a center of policy expertise and coordination in the department.[60]

Simultaneously, the department expanded its presence in the field. During the first decade of the twentieth century, the USDA sent technical advisers throughout the southern United States. Initially intended to instruct farmers about defenses against the boll weevil epidemic, this demonstration work led to calls for a nationwide extension system. Under pressure from the USDA, agricultural colleges, and farm organizations, in 1914 Congress passed the Smith-Lever Act, which appropriated federal funds for the placement of extension agents in each rural county, to be administered jointly by the agricultural colleges and the USDA. In addition, the Smith-Lever Act required that all extension programs meet the approval of the secretary of agriculture. With the creation of the Office on States

---

[60] Gaus and Wolcott, *Public Administration and the United States Department of Agriculture*, 33–38, 47–54; Huffman and Evenson, *Science for Agriculture*, 31–32.

Relations to coordinate these activities, the USDA enjoyed greater control over the direction and scope of research at the state and local level.[61]

The number of county agents expanded rapidly during World War I. Under the Emergency Food Production Act of 1917, the Extension Service administered programs designed to increase the production of food, conserve resources, and perform other tasks deemed necessary for the mobilization effort. Within a year, the number of extension agents at work in the states increased from 2,500 to 6,215. The percentage of rural counties serviced by an extension agent increased from 47 percent to 80 percent over the same period.[62]

County agents organized farmers into local committees, or farm bureaus, to help coordinate programs and disseminate technical information. As the number of county farm bureaus increased, leaders in Illinois, New York, and several other states established statewide federations. In 1919, members of nine state chapters formed the American Farm Bureau Federation (AFBF) and employed a lobbyist, Gray Silver, to represent the organization in Washington, D.C. Meanwhile, public encouragement of farm bureaus continued. Where county agents did not yet exist, state legislatures occasionally required farmers to organize farm bureaus as a prerequisite for extension service appropriations.[63]

From the beginning, therefore, county agents enjoyed close relations with their local farm bureau. Often, the dues collected from bureau members helped pay the county agent's salary. Agents, in turn, became financially dependent on these local associations. Meanwhile, USDA officials in Washington praised the new network of county agents and endorsed a close advisory relationship between the farm bureaus and the Extension Service. In the words of C. B. Smith, an official in the States Relations Service, the agency responsible for the Extension Service, "The county farm bureau is not just another farmers' organizations. It is essentially a new public institution."[64] The Farm Bureau occupied an ambiguous position between a private interest lobby and a public service organization. This ambiguity, coupled with fiscal resources from the state, helped it grow as an organization.[65]

Just as the Farm Bureau became a national force in agricultural politics and policy, prices for many farm products dropped sharply. Corn prices fell from $1.50 per bushel in 1919 to $.54 per bushel in 1921. Wheat

[61] True, *A History of Agricultural Extension Work*, 101–42.

[62] Ibid., 200–202.

[63] Kile, *The Farm Bureau through Three Decades*, 35–57; Campbell, *The Farm Bureau and the New Deal*, 5–13; Hansen, *Gaining Access*, 31–61; Clemens, *The People's Lobby*, 168.

[64] Smith quoted in True, *A History of Agricultural Extension Work*, 167.

[65] Ibid., 152–65.

tumbled from $2.18 to $.92 per bushel between 1919 and 1923.[66] As the crisis worsened, calls increased for government action to prop up prices. One plan, developed by George Peek and Hugh Johnson, consisted of government price supports for agricultural commodities. In an effort to keep commodity prices on a par with the prices farmers paid for industrial inputs, Peek and Johnson proposed that the government purchase farm products off of the open market and sell (dump) the surplus commodities on the world market at prevailing prices. The losses incurred (the difference between world and domestic prices) would be paid by farmers according to the amount they produced. In this way, farmers would have an incentive to cut production.[67]

In 1924, Senator Charles McNary and Representative Gilbert Haugen introduced the central elements of the Peek-Johnson plan in Congress. For the next four years, the McNary-Haugen bill was debated. Although it was popular in the wheat states of the Midwest and Great Plains, cotton producers in the South opposed the export dumping components of the bill. Lacking southern support in Congress, advocates of the McNary-Haugen bill failed to secure passage of the plan in 1924 and again in 1926. But when the price of cotton fell the following year, southern delegations swung in support of the plan, and the McNary-Haugen bill passed the House and Senate. Despite this victory in Congress, supporters of the McNary-Haugen bill could not override two vetoes by Calvin Coolidge in 1927 and 1928.[68] Opponents of the McNary-Haugen plan, including President Coolidge, criticized the idea that a new bureaucratic entity was needed to regulate the farm economy.

For a Republican Party wary of direct government intervention, cooperative marketing was embraced as an alternative solution to the farm crisis. Congress passed a variety of legislation in the 1920s intended to promote agricultural cooperatives. The 1922 Capper-Volsted Act, for example, exempted agricultural cooperatives from prosecution under antitrust law and relieved cooperatives from income tax liabilities. In 1923, the Agricultural Credit Act offered government loans to agricultural cooperatives. Legislation in 1926 appropriated funds for research and pro-

[66] USDA, *Yearbook of Agriculture, 1926*, 818, 845.

[67] Peek and Johnson argued that the prices received by farmers for their products should keep pace with the prices farmers paid for industrial inputs. In the years before World War I, this ratio between agricultural and nonagricultural commodities was roughly equal—a condition referred to as *parity*. After 1921, agricultural prices failed to keep pace with the cost of production, prompting Peek, Johnson, and others to campaign for a return to "parity" through government-supported prices. Fite, *George N. Peek and the Fight for Farm Parity*; Hansen, *Gaining Access*, 39–40.

[68] Hansen, *Gaining Access*, 45–66; Black, "The McNary-Haugen Movement," 405–27; Benedict, *Farm Policies of the United States*, 212–29.

motion of agricultural cooperatives and established a Division of Cooperative Marketing in the BAE.[69]

Leaders of cooperatives and their allies within the Coolidge administration insisted that farmer organizations, in conjunction with the technical advisory institutions already in place, could solve the problem of low prices. In his first veto message of McNary-Haugen, President Coolidge stated, "It is axiomatic that progress is made through building on the good foundations that already exist. . . . The bill under consideration throws this aside. . . . It says in effect that all the agricultural scientists and all the thinking farmers of the last 50 years are wrong."[70] In order to utilize the "good foundations that exist," the Coolidge administration and Secretary of Agriculture William Jardine proposed a system of stabilization corporations that could link farmer cooperatives in a rational marketing network.

Jardine's approach to the farm crisis carried the distinct mark of Secretary of Commerce Herbert Hoover. As leader of the wartime Food Administration, Hoover oversaw production and conservation efforts through close collaboration with associations of processors, railroads, and other business organizations. As secretary of commerce, Hoover expanded on his wartime experiences and developed an approach to public policy based on cooperative efforts between scientifically trained government experts and private organizations. Such "associationalism" avoided the twin evils of politicized policy making and bureaucratic encroachments on personal freedom. After the death of Secretary of Agriculture Henry C. Wallace in 1924 (a McNary-Haugen proponent), Hoover secured the appointment of his protégé, William Jardine, who promptly purged the USDA of McNary-Haugen supporters.[71]

As a candidate for president in 1928, Hoover pledged to call a special session of Congress to address the persistent problems of the farm economy. Soon after his inauguration, President Hoover fulfilled his promise and proposed legislation that closely resembled the Jardine plan of 1927. A federal farm board capitalized at $500 million would promote farmer-owned cooperatives and establish stabilization corporations that could smooth price fluctuations through purchases and sales. In his message to the special session, Hoover praised the agricultural cooperative movement: "The most progressive movement in all agriculture has been the

[69] Benedict, *Form Policies of the United States*, 184, 198; Saloutos, *The American Farmer and the New Deal*, 19–20; Hoffman and Libecap, "Institutional Choice and the Development of U.S. Agricultural Policies."

[70] For the text of Coolidge's veto message, see *Congressional Record*, 69th Cong., 2d sess., 4771–76.

[71] Hawley, "Herbert Hoover, the Commerce Secretariat and the Vision of an 'Associative State,' 1921–1928," 117–37.

upbuilding of the farmer's own marketing organizations. . . . all proposals for governmental assistance should originate with such organizations." Only through the promotion of "farmer-owned and farmer-controlled agencies," Hoover insisted, can the nation end the farm crisis without "bureaucratic and governmental domination."[72] After several months of wrangling and a last-ditch effort by the McNary-Haugenites, the Agricultural Marketing Act established the Federal Farm Board in June 1929.

Herbert Hoover's "associationalism" and the enthusiasm for agricultural cooperatives resembled the position of many French producers and politicians. Farmers and government officials in both countries recognized the need for policy innovation, yet they remained apprehensive of direct state intervention. Policy proposals that empowered farmers to regulate themselves were the most politically viable solutions to the agricultural crisis.

Corporatism I: The Federal Farm Board

Proponents of the Federal Farm Board claimed the farm crisis could be solved through a system of rational marketing executed through farmer cooperatives. The Farm Board, as envisioned, would build upon the organizational advances made in cooperative marketing during the 1920s and exploit the network of agricultural advisers in rural counties. Aided by government loans, farmers established hundreds of new cooperatives in 1930 and 1931. According to data furnished by the Farm Board, twelve thousand cooperatives were in operation in 1932, with a membership of three million farmers. In some commodities such as dairy, fruits, and vegetables, cooperatives handled between 50 and 75 percent of all commercial sales.[73]

Next to its role as promoter of cooperatives, the Federal Farm Board established national marketing agencies for grains, livestock, wool, and cotton. The Farmers National Grain Corporation, for example, established a central board of directors that consisted of representatives from farmer elevator associations, sales agencies, and other cooperatives. With a capital stock of $10 million, the Farmers National Grain Corporation offered advance payments to farmers who delivered their crop to the local cooperative. Once the crops were in storage, the cooperative could release

---

[72] Hoover, "Message to the Special Session of the Congress on Farm Relief, Tariff and Certain Emergency Measures," April 16, 1929, *Public Papers of the Presidents of the United States, Herbert Hoover, 1929*, 78.

[73] Federal Farm Board, *Second Annual Report* (1931), 3; Federal Farm Board, *Third Annual Report* (1932), 12.

them more slowly on to the market, thereby smoothing out seasonal price fluctuations. In addition, the national agency purchased grain futures on commodity markets to stabilize prices. Finally, the Farm Board created a Grain Stabilization Corporation to absorb market surpluses through direct purchases.[74]

These agencies were created in the midst of the October 1929 stock market crash and the subsequent upheaval in the nonfarm economy. Leaders of the marketing agencies for wheat and cotton spent most of their energy on market stabilization. Huge stocks of wheat and cotton fell into agency hands; losses suffered from advance loans to farmers quickly outpaced Farm Board resources. By 1931, the Farm Board was an acknowledged failure.

The problems of the Federal Farm Board and the marketing agencies revealed that the institutional developments of the 1920s, although significant, were not adequate to the task of corporatist policy coordination. Farm Board administration was hopelessly fragmented. Work assignments fell along commodity lines, and there was insufficient coordination between administrative units or adequate oversight by those responsible for overall policy. Congress, with the blessing of Secretary of Agriculture Arthur Hyde, separated administration of the Federal Farm Board from the USDA and transferred the Office of Cooperative Marketing from the department to the new board. Mordecai Ezekial, a Farm Board administrator who later served in the Agricultural Adjustment Administration, complained about "overlaps and conflicts" between the board and the department in the administration of policy.[75] Although the Farm Board had authority under the Agricultural Marketing Act to use the research and extension resources of the USDA and the state agricultural colleges, Farm Board leaders complained that "the resources of those institutions are insufficient to meet certain highly important needs." The Federal Farm Board revisited pitfalls experienced earlier in the history of the USDA: divided authority, bureaucratic rivalry, and an absence of coordination.[76]

Nor did coordination prove any easier among cooperative associations and farm organizations that were supposed to lead the new "farmer-owned,

[74] Federal Farm Board, *Third Annual Report* (1932), 2; Benedict, *Farm Policies of the United States*, 258–63; Saloutos and Hicks, *Agricultural Discontent in the Middle West*, 412–19.

[75] Columbia Oral History Project, Reminiscences of Mordecai Ezekial, 85; Saloutos, *The American Farmer and the New Deal*, 30.

[76] Federal Farm Board, *Second Annual Report* (1931), 75; *Congressional Record*, 71st Cong., 1st sess., April 19, 1929, 170; Committee on Agriculture, House of Representatives, *Hearing before the Committee on Agriculture, House of Representatives*, "Agricultural Relief," 71st Cong., 1st sess., Serial A-Part 7, April 2, 1929, 624ff.

farmer-controlled" marketing system. At first, the general farm organizations, in particular the American Farm Bureau Federation, actively supported the Farm Board. When members of the grain trade denounced the Hoover administration and the Farm Board, AFBF president Sam Thompson (who was appointed to the Federal Farm Board in March 1931) dispatched circulars to each county affiliate so that the "full force of the Farm Bureau [can] be mobilized." Even after farmers began to question the utility of Farm Board programs, AFBF leaders warned against the hazards of "playing into the hands of our enemies."[77]

Despite this early support, the membership of the national farm organizations quickly divided over Farm Board policies. As cooperative-held surpluses multiplied, Farm Board leaders realized that current stabilization programs were not enough. Government officials toured the country in an effort to convince farmers that price declines could only be reversed through acreage reduction programs. However, convincing farmers to cut acreage proved difficult. As the Farm Board described in 1931, "The individualistic character of the American farmer is the reason why appeals for uniform reduction in acreage have not been successful."[78]

More specifically, the effort at voluntary acreage reduction exposed regional divisions within farm organizations that quickly undermined the unity displayed during the Farm Board's first year. Producers of spring wheat opposed plans for acreage reduction that neglected winter wheat farmers. Efforts to establish the National Livestock Marketing Association pitted larger cattle operations against smaller ones. As opposition to Farm Board policies mounted, state chapters of various farm organizations openly opposed the positions of national leaders. The Minnesota Farm Bureau joined milk and livestock cooperatives in opposition to a Farm Board plan for a dairy herd reduction, despite open support for the plan by the national AFBF leadership. State chapters of the Farmers' Union divided into pro– and anti–Farm Board factions. When C. E. Huff, a pro–Farm Board president of the Farmers' Union, lost his bid for reelection, several state chapters bolted from the organization and appointed Huff as their representative before the government. In 1931, a meeting in Chicago of farm organizations from Corn Belt states similarly turned acrimonious after passage of a resolution that condemned Hoover and the Farm Board. Pro–Farm Board chapters of the AFBF, Farmers' Union, and other farm groups left the meeting and established a breakaway organization.[79]

---

[77] "The Truth about the Wheat Situation," *Federal Farm Board Press Release*, July 21, 1931, 7; Saloutos and Hicks, *Agricultural Discontent in the Middle West*, 412–13; Kile, *The Farm Bureau through Three Decades*, 163–66.

[78] Federal Farm Board, *Second Annual Report* (1931), 57.

[79] Saloutos and Hicks, *Agricultural Discontent in the Middle West*, 419–33.

Economic circumstances probably doomed the Farm Board, but the disintegration of the cooperative solution revealed important institutional shortcomings. Although leaders of national farm organizations supported the Farm Board and tried to help implement government policies, they lacked sufficient power over state chapters. At the same time, the separation of the Farm Board from the USDA deprived administrators of adequate resources and created coordination problems. Neither the capacity of agricultural administration nor the organization of farmers was sufficient to formulate and implement national policy along the corporatist lines envisioned by Hoover and his supporters.

Corporatism II: The Agricultural Adjustment Act

The failure of the Federal Farm Board proved to be an important lesson both for bureaucrats in the Department of Agriculture and for leaders of farm organizations such as the AFBF. Over the next few years, economists in the USDA refined their policy proposals for acreage reduction programs. Meanwhile, farm leaders examined ways to strengthen their organization and smooth over differences between producers of different commodities and regions. Between 1932 and the first years of the New Deal, farmers and bureaucrats renewed their efforts to create a viable policy partnership in agriculture.

Officials in the USDA learned that cooperative marketing could not, by itself, solve the agricultural crisis. Although it was clear that production controls were necessary, the halfhearted effort by the Farm Board to promote voluntary acreage reductions failed miserably. Under a new plan championed by Milburn L. Wilson of Montana State University, the government would assign individual acreage allotments to each farmer based on historic production levels. Farmers who sold crops produced on allotted acres received a government-supported price; amounts sold above allotments received the world price. Through the use of allotments, farmers had an incentive to limit production, and the government would gain better control over the market in its efforts to adjust production with consumption.[80]

The domestic allotment plan potentially solved a problem identified by the administrators of the Federal Farm Board. In the eyes of Farm Board economist Mordecai Ezekial, attempts to control prices through cooperatives failed because they lifted prices for everybody, including nonmembers. Without universal compliance, "those who are not members of the cooperative can go ahead and produce more and benefit more than the

---

[80] Rowley, *M. L. Wilson and the Campaign for Domestic Allotment.*

members do and don't share the cost." In other words, without incentives or sanctions, the free-rider problem quickly erodes the benefits of cooperative marketing. Noting this problem, Ezekial, Wilson, and other agricultural economists looked for policy solutions that operated through individual rather than collective incentives. Wilson's plan addressed the free-rider problem because only program participants (i.e., only those farmers who grew on allotted acres) would receive higher prices for their products. Program participation and policy efficacy would increase as a result.[81]

In 1932, Wilson's domestic allotment plan caught the attention of Roosevelt adviser Rexford Tugwell. Together, Tugwell and Wilson drafted Roosevelt's major farm policy speech of the 1932 presidential campaign, and soon after Roosevelt's election, work began on drafting agricultural legislation. Passed in May 1933, the Agricultural Adjustment Act (AAA) encompassed the basic principles of the domestic allotment plan. Farmers who cut production in line with government-assigned allotments received federal payments. Program participation was voluntary, but only those who cut acreage were eligible for government supports.[82]

In administrative terms, the new AAA avoided earlier pitfalls and concentrated authority in the office of the secretary of agriculture. Giving the secretary power to implement the AAA as he saw fit reflected the emergency circumstances confronted by Congress; there simply was not enough time to enumerate USDA powers under the new law. On the other hand, the experience of the Farm Board illustrated the dangers that can arise when policy authority is divided between the USDA and an independent agency. Through the lobbying of Ezekial, Wilson, and others, the new Agricultural Adjustment Administration became part of the USDA. This angered the head of the Agricultural Adjustment Administration, George Peek, who claimed that FDR had promised him an independent agency like the National Recovery Administration.[83] Conflicts of authority quickly arose between Peek and Secretary of Agriculture Henry A. Wallace over policy and personnel. Wallace held firm, and by December 1933 Peek resigned from his position as head.[84]

Secretary Wallace also displayed resolve in his decision to use the Extension Service for policy implementation. Many within the service wanted

[81] Columbia Oral History Project, *Reminiscences of Mordecai Ezekial*, 27, 57, 77. The lesson of individual versus collective solutions to the farm problem is emphasized in Hamilton, *From New Day to New Deal*.

[82] Columbia Oral History Project, *Reminiscences of Mordecai Ezekial*, 56.

[83] Columbia Oral History Project, *Reminiscences of Chester C. Davis*, 280–81.

[84] Columbia Oral History Project, *Reminiscences of Mordecai Ezekial*, 84–85; see also the testimony of Frederic Lee, Committee on Agriculture, House of Representatives, *Hearing before the Committee on Agriculture, House of Representatives*, "Agricultural Adjustment Program," 72d Cong., 2d sess., Serial M, 39–51; Saloutos, *The American Farmer and the New Deal*, 54–57.

to retain the educational orientation of the county agents. Others, particularly state extension officials, feared the new regulatory tasks envisioned by the AAA would overtax their resources. Through the considerable effort and influence of M. L. Wilson, Wallace placed local responsibility for the AAA in the hands of the county agent. State directors of agricultural extension were named administrators of the AAA. In both Washington and the field, Wallace and his allies made a concerted effort to concentrate policy authority within the USDA.[85]

But the successful implementation of production controls also required the active participation of farmers. Soon after passage of the AAA, county agents organized local committees of farmers to assign acreage allotments and monitor compliance. Farmer participation, it was argued, improved the chances of policy success. Describing the creation of farmer committees in 1933, a report by the Agricultural Adjustment Administration explained that "only farmers themselves possessed the experience and information which were indispensable to successful development and operation of a program." Moreover, collaboration made political sense. "This course was politically expedient," the report continued; "it is extremely important as a means of retaining public confidence . . . that particular actions are taken in accordance with the recommendations of farmers and their accredited leaders."[86] Herein lies the corporatist bargain: farmer participation afforded the USDA with policy assistance and political cover. In exchange, the corporatist client gains influence over policy and monopoly representation of agricultural interests. After 1933, the Farm Bureau played the client role.

The lessons of the Federal Farm Board were not lost on the leaders of the AFBF, which approached the AAA as an opportunity for organizational dominance in the farm sector. As the presidential election of 1932 approached, AFBF president Edward O'Neal made a concerted effort to bring together leaders of the big three farm organizations—the AFBF, the Farmers' Union, and the National Grange—in the hopes that solidarity could increase farm influence in the presidential contest. A cotton farmer from Alabama, O'Neal also possessed a unique capacity to bridge regional differences between Midwestern and southern interests. Thanks to O'Neal, a January 1932 farm conference produced a unified policy statement enumerating the policy concerns of the nation's three largest farm organizations, the Farm Bureau, Farmers' Union and the National Grange.

Because of this leadership, O'Neal and the Farm Bureau secured a privileged position in dealings with the Roosevelt administration. Between the election in November and the inauguration in March, O'Neal partici-

---

[85] Saloutos, *The American Farmer and the New Deal*, 47–49.
[86] AAA, *Agricultural Adjustment, 1937–1938*, 217.

pated in several meetings, some of which he chaired, between farm leaders and Roosevelt aides to discuss farm policy. By the time plans for the AAA were unveiled in Congress, O'Neal could confidently report to the Farm Bureau rank and file that Roosevelt had followed the farmers' demands.[87]

The actual degree of Farm Bureau influence in the formation of the AAA is not as important as the appearance these consultations created. For Ed O'Neal, a policy partnership with the FDR administration was a key element in his strategy to build the Farm Bureau organization. When the economy worsened in the late 1920s and early 1930s, Farm Bureau membership declined. Between 1930 and 1933, the Farm Bureau lost nearly half of its members. In the South alone, membership fell by 70 percent.[88] With the production of AAA program commodities concentrated in the very states where Farm Bureau membership was in greatest decline, O'Neal and other leaders of the AFBF eyed government acreage-control programs as an opportunity to build their organization. A corporatist partnership with the USDA was a ticket to organizational dominance.

Accordingly, the Farm Bureau welcomed Wallace's decision in 1933 to use the Extension Service for local implementation of the AAA. As already mentioned, the Farm Bureau was very much the product of the Extension Service. In several states, particularly in the Midwest, connections between the two remained quite close.[89] Farm Bureau leaders were enthusiastic about the prospect of county committees organized for the administration of production control programs. As the administrative report for 1935 observed, "The organization of more than 3 million contract signers constitutes . . . the greatest opportunity in the history of the Farm Bureau to strengthen its organization."[90] The Farm Bureau leadership quickly developed a strategy to organize AAA production control committees into county chapters of the AFBF.

In October 1933, O'Neal suggested that "farmers themselves share a responsibility in speeding up the AAA program," adding that "only through the cooperation of farmers can progress be swift and sure."[91] Circulars from the national office asked that each state farm bureau call

[87] Campbell, *The Farm Bureau and the New Deal*, 44–67

[88] Tontz, "Memberships of General Farmers' Organizations," 147. On the importance of political action for organizational maintenance, see Hansen, "The Political Economy of Group Membership," 83–88.

[89] Writing in 1931, Extension Service director C. W. Warburton acknowledged that "the aid . . . of the Farm Bureau locals is invaluable in increasing the influence" of the county agents. C. W. Warburton, "Organization as an Aid to Extension Teaching," *Bureau Farmer*, February 1931, 4.

[90] AFBF, "Administrative Report," June 5–6, 1935, quoted in Campbell, *The Farm Bureau and the New Deal*, 88.

[91] "Clear the Road," *Bureau Farmer*, October 1933, 3.

meetings with its respective extension service officials to draw up names of possible state-level administrators of the AAA. County farm bureaus, in conjunction with the local agent, were instructed to assess the number of farmers likely to sign production control contracts and report their findings to the state and national organizations as well as to Secretary Wallace, of the USDA. According to Kile, many local farm bureaus "literally took over this job of getting local AAA committees organized and mobilizing farmer support and participation."[92]

In the South, where membership was lowest, Farm Bureau organizers approached production control committees with invitations to join the AFBF. Although USDA policy prevented county agents from promoting specific farm organizations, reports surfaced that agents mixed official business, such as distribution of government checks, with recommendations that local farmers join the Farm Bureau. One county agent in Alabama informed farmers that, "for each dollar you invest in Farm Bureau dues, you have received $125 from the government."[93] At the state level, O'Neal enlisted the aid of Extension Service officials from his home state of Alabama to spread the gospel of the Farm Bureau in other southern states. One such friend, L. N. Duncan, used his connections as director of the Alabama Extension Service to make contacts with other southern extension officials. In addition, Duncan released extension service personnel to O'Neal for use in the southern membership drive.[94]

Commemorating the one-year anniversary of the AAA, the AFBF boasted that "the Farm Bureau organization has extended its fullest cooperation to the administration in carrying out [production control] programs."[95] As O'Neal hoped, the New Deal was good for the Farm Bureau. Between 1933 and 1940, AFBF membership more than doubled. In the South, where O'Neal concentrated his efforts to build the organization, Farm Bureau membership increased thirteenfold over the same period.[96] Moreover, the AFBF enjoyed a privileged position as the representative of agricultural interests before the government. As Chester C. Davis, head of the Agricultural Adjustment Administration from 1933 to 1936, recalled, "My associations with the Farm Bureau were closer than any associations with any of the other organizations."[97]

For some commodities, the link between private organizations and program administration was even closer. Efforts by the Farm Board to raise

---

[92] Kile, *The Farm Bureau through Three Decades*, 205.

[93] Block, *The Separation of the Farm Bureau and the Extension Service*, 25.

[94] Campbell, *The Farm Bureau and the New Deal*, 88–92.

[95] "The Farm Bureau's Part," *Bureau Farmer*, April 1934, 12.

[96] Tontz, "Membership of General Farmers' Organizations," 147.

[97] Columbia Oral History Project, *Reminiscences of Chester C. Davis*, 344. Farm Bureau influence was also in ascendance before Congress. See Hansen, *Gaining Access*, 77–87.

prices through cooperative marketing arrangements failed for major field crops such as wheat, as we have seen, but for some commodities, marketing arrangements and price agreements between producer cooperatives and processors met with some success. This was the case in the dairy industry, where, according to a 1931 Federal Farm Board report, "producers have built up organizations which not only are effective marketing agencies but also exert a stabilizing influence on prices and production."[98] Despite this record of success, both dairy cooperatives and milk distributors still faced problems of free riding and destructive price-cutting practices. The prospect of farm legislation in 1933, therefore, presented an opportunity to strengthen these existing arrangements. State sanctions could increase the cost of defection.

With the backing of cooperative leaders, George Peek drafted an amendment to the Agricultural Adjustment bill giving the secretary of agriculture authority to enter into marketing agreements with processors, producers, and cooperatives for the handling of farm products. A licensing provision gave these agreements the power of excludability necessary for enforcement: only cooperatives and licensed distributors had the legal authority to market that product. In dairy, marketing agreements dictated price schedules and trade practices, and also restricted entry by new producers into the milk market. Marketing agreements also governed tobacco and peanuts. In the case of these two commodities, George Peek personally oversaw negotiations between processors and distributors over prices and production quantities.[99]

Cooperatives played a key role in the administration and enforcement of marketing agreements. Cooperatives delivered the farmer's product to distributors and distributed payments to producers. Cooperatives also enforced product standards and quality controls, thus assuming the functions of a corporatist client. Edwin Nourse, describing the role of milk cooperatives in regulation, wrote that "the task of rendering these services and the task of collecting the appropriate service charges on all milk imposed serious difficulty on the newly formed administrative agencies. In cities where there were local branches of the National Dairy Council, this agency was ordinarily designated as the one through which this function was performed."[100] In 1935, dairy cooperatives gained the right to vote in the name of its members, making the producer association the official signatory to the marketing agreements. Dairy cooperatives thus became a major influence in policy making and implementation, and the

[98] Federal Farm Board, *Second Annual Report* (1931), 7.

[99] Nourse, *Marketing Agreements under the AAA*, 13–21; Nourse, Davis, and Black, *Three Years of the Agricultural Adjustment Administration*, 220–25.

[100] Nourse, *Marketing Agreements under the AAA*, 215.

strength of cooperatives as a membership organization increased accordingly. Producers of commodities under marketing agreements did not have the option of exit; they had to join the cooperative to market their products.[101]

The first years of the AAA illustrate how, after the failure of the Federal Farm Board, bureaucrats and producers refined their administrative and organizational skills, respectively. Led by an activist secretary, the USDA retained control over the new regulatory powers created under the Agricultural Adjustment Act. Wallace and his allies shunned efforts to divide and create anew. Existing institutional linkages between Washington, D.C., and the field became the principal medium for regulatory implementation. Meanwhile, leaders of the AFBF similarly exploited the institutional linkages afforded by the county agent. By acting as a willing partner in the enforcement of production controls and as a consensus builder among farm organizations, the AFBF became the largest and most powerful farm organization in the United States. And in commodities such as dairy, tobacco, and peanuts, cooperative associations became official agents of the state in marketing arrangements between producers and processors. Corporatist agriculture had arrived.

Corporatist Failure and Farm Policy, 1936–1943

In 1934, all the elements for a corporatist policy arrangement between farmers and the government appeared to be in place: a dominant bureaucracy, a peak farm organization, and consensus over the goals of government regulation. Over the next several years, however, agricultural corporatism broke down. By 1943, responsibility for wartime food policy resided outside of the USDA, the Farm Bureau lost its preeminent position in Washington, and the lines were drawn for what became the post–World War II debate over farm policy. Unlike in France and Japan, where the war reinforced corporatist arrangements, mobilization fueled a number of centrifugal tendencies in U.S. agricultural policy.

Factional undercurrents were present in the USDA from the beginning of the New Deal. Rural moderates trained in the land-grant college system sat uncomfortably next to urban liberals with no agricultural background. While urban liberals preferred policies that helped the poorest farmers, such as tenants and sharecroppers, the rural moderates directed programs toward the economic mainstream. Liberals complained that the

[101] Young, "The Dairy Industry," 236–58; Nourse et al., *Three Years of the Agricultural Adjustment Administration*, 236–37; Saloutos, *The American Farmer and the New Deal*, 79.

Agricultural Adjustment Administration was merely a tool for big commercial farmers; the moderates viewed their adversaries as "city slickers" foisting revolution in the countryside.[102]

Disagreements over policy objectives also touched upon the relationship between the Farm Bureau and certain government institutions. In the words of Chester Davis, "[Paul] Appleby, [Rexford] Tugwell, [Benham] Baldwin, and the others had contempt for the whole land grant college set up and the county agents, Extension Service, and other established agencies with which we worked so closely. They were doing what they could in little ways to split them off from the activity in the farm program. They definitely thought that the Farm Bureau was playing too large a part in the whole set-up."[103] Tugwell and Appleby were high-ranking officials in the USDA—the former was under secretary of agriculture and the latter served as assistant to the secretary. In short, the departments leadership was divided over the corporatist links between farmers and the government developed during the early New Deal.

Eventually, these ideological differences erupted into open conflicts. In 1935, a dispute over tenants' rights under the cotton code resulted in the infamous "purge" of the AAA. Chester Davis forced the resignation of several USDA lawyers after he discovered that Paul Appleby had issued an important decision while Davis was out of Washington. Facing hostility within the department, Appleby, Tugwell, and others exploited their connections with Roosevelt to create shadow agencies for liberals discouraged by the conservative agenda of the Agricultural Adjustment Administration.

Subsequently, programs designed to help the rural poor or landless resulted in the creation of a new agency either outside the USDA or as a rival to the Agricultural Adjustment Administration within the department. In 1935, for example, Tugwell established the Resettlement Administration (RA) as an independent agency. Eventually incorporated into the Farm Security Administration (FSA), this agency helped farmers remain on the land through loans and other forms of assistance. Although the FSA was technically an action agency within the USDA, conflicts immediately surfaced between it and the administrators of the Extension Service and the Agricultural Adjustment Administration who opposed the orientation of FSA programs toward the rural poor. At the same time, the lending services of the FSA brought it into conflict with the Farm Credit Administration, ostensibly the lead agency for rural credit. Ideological divisions

---

[102] Saloutos, *The American Farmer and the New Deal*, 103–4.
[103] Columbia Oral History Project, *Reminiscences of Chester C. Davis*, 343.

within the USDA resulted in problems of jurisdictional overlap and weakened the administrative unity of New Deal farm policy.[104]

While debates raged over how to help the rural poor, business interests hostile to the New Deal exploited the opportunities presented by an independent judiciary to challenge government intervention in agriculture and other sectors of the economy. The 1936 Supreme Court decision invalidating portions of the AAA created another set of administrative problems.[105] As a stopgap measure, USDA lawyers drafted new legislation that shifted the emphasis of policy from production control to soil conservation. Under the Soil Conservation and Domestic Allotment Act (SCDAA) passed in 1936, farmers who replaced acreage of soil-depleting crops such as corn with soil-conserving crops (grasses, legumes, etc.) received government payments. This subtle change allowed government intervention in agriculture to continue, despite a strict reading of the Constitution. But it also carried important ramifications for program administration. The new emphasis on conservation and land-use planning ignited rivalries with agencies already engaged in conservation projects. The 1936 act failed to spell out the relationship between the Agricultural Adjustment Administration and the Soil Conservation Service (SCS), the Forest Service, or the FSA, all of which operated their own independent conservation programs. Nor did the new law clarify interdepartmental responsibilities between the USDA and the Department of Interior, or between the USDA and independent agencies such as the Rural Electrification Administration and the Tennessee Valley Authority.[106]

The continued search for a long-range agricultural program contributed further to the problem of administrative coordination. In response to the 1937 recession and the dip in farm prices caused by the bumper harvest of that year, Congress passed the Agricultural Adjustment Act of 1938. Designed to strengthen and consolidate federal authority in agriculture, the 1938 AAA gave the secretary three distinct devices for controlling surplus production and raising farm incomes. The system of acreage allotments and direct payments created in 1933 and modified in 1936 paid farmers to cut acreage of the so-called "soil-depleting crops." The 1938 AAA made few changes to the system, but it included directives for the structure and authority of local, county, and state committees of farmers

[104] Saloutos, *The American Farmer and the New Deal*, 113–23.

[105] *Franklin Process Company v. Hoosac Mills*, 1936. The Supreme Court invalidated the tax on processors of agricultural commodities that was used to fund benefit payments received by producers. This effectively ended the production control program as envisioned in the AAA.

[106] Gaus and Wolcott, *Public Administration and the United States Department of Agriculture*, 142–53.

responsible for administrative oversight of the allotment system. Second, the secretary of agriculture could announce marketing quotas that, if approved by two-thirds of producers voting in a referendum, would restrict the amount any individual farmer could actually sell. The 1938 AAA clarified department authority and stipulated penalties for violation of quota limits. Third, the 1938 act broadened the system of government loans executed through the Commodity Credit Corporation (CCC). Created by executive order in 1933, the CCC was initially intended to smooth out price fluctuations through occasional market interventions. Over the next five years, the CCC evolved into a de facto price support mechanism that maintained prices above free-market levels. The 1938 AAA codified this development by setting CCC loan rates for wheat, cotton, corn, and other grains that effectively set a price floor for these commodities.[107]

The increasingly omnibus character of farm policy, with a variety of program and policy instruments for each commodity, produced an acute administrative problem by the late 1930s. The proliferation of action agencies engaged in conservation, price support, marketing, and farm credit resulted in jurisdictional overlap and conflict. The relative unity of farm program administration during the first AAA, with authority concentrated in the USDA and executed through the Extension Service, broke down under the weight of increasing government complexity. In 1936, the head of the Agricultural Adjustment Administration, H. R. Tolley, initiated action to end the Extension Service's role in commodity programs. Tolley's actions precipitated sharp reaction from some state extension directors, and in 1938 officials from the USDA and the Association of Land-Grant Colleges and Universities agreed to clarify administrative roles in agricultural policy. Under the Mount Weather Agreement, the USDA and the colleges would jointly establish state and county land-use planning committees. Committee membership consisted of farmers, representatives from the action agencies engaged in policy (the AAA, SCS, FSA, etc.), as well as Extension Service personnel. The state extension directors would serve as committee chairs, but administrative direction emanated from the USDA. The Bureau of Agricultural Economics was elevated to "a general agricultural program planning and economic research service" that could oversee the coordination of all agricultural programs in the USDA.[108]

---

[107] The CCC offered producers "nonrecourse" loans. Under this scheme, producers borrowed money from the government against their crop. At harvest time, farmers could either pay back the loan or forfeit their crop to the government. This effectively guaranteed a minimum price for the farmer's crop. Benedict, *Farm Policies of the United States*, 377–78, 389.

[108] "Joint Statement by the Association of Land Grant Colleges and Universities and the Department of Agriculture on Building Agricultural Land Use Programs"; see also "Memo-

Although the Mount Weather Agreement tried to rationalize administration, it only institutionalized the division of policy authority that developed over the previous years. Before 1938, the Extension Service was the
only agency with field personnel; federal authority was concentrated in
the hands of the county agent. The Mount Weather Agreement, however,
placed representatives of other agencies on state and county committees.
Farmers subsequently confronted a myriad of agencies in their dealings
with the federal government. The Extension Service, which had served as
the corporatist link between the Farm Bureau and the USDA, was subsequently "outnumbered at both county and state levels by representatives
of the better financed . . . newcomers."[109]

Each of the developments described here—the ideological conflict between liberals and conservatives in the USDA, the growing complexity of
program administration, and the decision by department officials to re-
place the Extension Service as the lead agency at the state and local level—
ultimately touched the relationship between the government and the Farm
Bureau. The mutual embrace that had characterized relations between the
AFBF and the USDA during the early years of the AAA dissolved into an
increasingly antagonistic relationship. By the 1940s, the Farm Bureau was
engaged in a political campaign against programs and policies that either
were contrary to the interests of the membership or that challenged the
organizational supremacy of the AFBF.

The FSA and the land-use planning committees were two early targets.
In both cases, the central role of Congress in farm policy was of critical
importance as the Farm Bureau used the annual appropriations process
to attack programs it opposed. The FSA, for example, helped tenants buy
land, particularly in the South, where it directly threatened the racial and
class divisions beneficial to landowners like Farm Bureau president Ed
O'Neal. Before several congressional committees in 1942 and 1943, the
Farm Bureau attacked the FSA as an unnecessary expenditure that should
be eliminated. Farm Bureau allies in Congress testified that FSA funds
were used to pay poll taxes and for other unauthorized uses. Thanks in
part to continued Farm Bureau criticism, Congress launched a full-scale
inquiry into FSA activities in 1943. New Deal liberals such as Rexford
Tugwell received particularly harsh treatment as red-baiting conservatives
criticized "communistic resettlement projects . . . [that] followed the Rus-
sian pattern of collective farming . . . in violation of the traditional land

randum Describing Departmental Organization." Both documents can be found in Gaus
and Wolcott, *Public Administration and the United States Department of Agriculture*, 463–
75.

[109] Block, *The Separation of the Farm Bureau and the Extension Service*, 23; Benedict,
Farm Policies of the United States, 394–95.

policies of America." The Agricultural Appropriations Act of 1944 froze the loan activities of the AAA and began the liquidation of rural resettlement projects.[110]

Land-use planning committees presented a more immediate challenge to Farm Bureau influence as it undermined the position of the Extension Service in the local administration of commodity programs. Farm Bureau leaders feared that the USDA would use the planning committees to create a rival, government-sponsored farm organization. Unhappy with the outcome of the Mount Weather Agreement, the Farm Bureau offered a USDA reorganization plan of its own in 1941. The plan placed the bulk of administrative authority within the Extension Service and a nonpartisan planning committee chosen by the state extension director in consultation with farm organizations. The secretary of agriculture would lose much of his power, as would the administrators of action agencies such as the FSA and the SCS. Although the reorganization plan failed to find allies in Congress, the Farm Bureau successfully lobbied for the elimination of planning committee appropriations in 1943. As Campbell writes, "The county land-use planning program was buried, . . . and there is no doubt that the AFBF was the chief undertaker."[111]

Liberal opponents of the Farm Bureau responded in kind. Beginning in the early 1940s, officials in the USDA cultivated relations with other, rival farm organizations. In particular, the National Farmers' Union, which enjoyed close ties to organized labor and the liberal wing of the Democratic Party, emerged as a willing partner in attacks against the Farm Bureau. In Congress, the Farmers' Union lobbied in favor of the FSA and other policies opposed by the Farm Bureau. More important, the Farmers' Union attacked the Farm Bureau–Extension Service relationship and lobbied Congress to force a statutory separation. Separation, of course, would cut directly into the source of the Farm Bureau's competitive advantage. Many in the USDA favored statutory separation, including Secretary of Agriculture Claude Wickard, who issued thinly veiled criticisms of the Farm Bureau's "unique" relationship to the county agent. In 1941, Wickard distributed a departmental memorandum that prohibited any USDA employee from aiding with membership campaigns for, or holding office in, any general farm organization.[112] By the early 1940s, a clear

[110] Committee on Agriculture, House of Representatives, *Activities of the Farm Security Administration*, House Report 1430, 78th Cong., 2d sess., May 6, 1944, 2, 12; Block, *The Separation of the Farm Bureau and the Extension Service*, 38.

[111] Block, *The Separation of the Farm Burea and the Extension Service*, 35–36, 44; Campbell, *The Farm Bureau and the New Deal*, 177.

[112] Block, *The Separation of the Farm Bureau and the Extension Service*, 44; Campbell, *The Farm Bureau and the New Deal*, 171.

schism emerged in the USDA between officials who embraced the goals of the National Farmers' Union and those who favored a continued alliance between the AFBF and the Extension Service in the states and counties.

United States entry into World War II only exacerbated the problems of the previous five years. During war mobilization, Roosevelt divided policy authority over food and agriculture among several wartime agencies. While the Office of Price Administration (OPA) struggled to keep food prices in control, the War Production Board governed production and distribution programs. In March 1943 the USDA lost all responsibility for food programs when Roosevelt transferred production and rationing policies to the newly created War Food Administration. Confusion reigned as the various agencies operated largely independent of each other. As *Kiplinger's Washington Newsletter* observed of government food policies, "What's lacking is management, coordination, [and] direction."[113]

Meanwhile, conflicts emerged over pricing and production of agricultural commodities. Heightened wartime demand in the United States and abroad boosted farm prices in 1942 and 1943. But rising prices placed the Roosevelt administration in a difficult position. Government economists feared that higher food prices would cause inflation, wage pressures, and labor unrest. On the other hand, price controls on farm goods might discourage farmers from increasing production, which was needed for the war effort. As a solution, Roosevelt and the OPA lowered prices on commodities and made up the difference with production subsidies.

The introduction of producer subsidies divided the agricultural community. The Farm Bureau, many farm-state members of Congress, and the rural moderates in the USDA opposed the use of subsidies. The Roosevelt administration, the National Farmers' Union, and urban liberals in the department favored them. In an argument that became increasingly common during the 1940s, the Farm Bureau and its allies charged that government agricultural policies favored labor interests within the Democratic Party. In the end, wartime price and production policies settled into a compromise. The government continued subsidies and price controls but guaranteed farmers high price supports and crop loans for the first two years after the war. As I will describe in the next chapter, this conflict over wartime production measures drew the lines for what became the postwar struggle between the Farm Bureau and the Farmers' Union over price supports policies.[114]

[113] *Kiplinger's Washington Newsletter*, June 26, 1943; Benedict, *Farm Policies of the United States*, 402–30.

[114] Wilcox, *The Farmer in the Second World War*, 243–63.

From Corporatism to Pluralism

In less than ten years, the policy partnership between the Farm Bureau and the USDA dissolved completely. The agricultural bureaucracy divided into hostile camps, with two rival farm organizations competing for access to and influence in departmental decisions. Consensus over farm policy goals broke down. Contrary to treatments of the USDA as a bastion of administrative capacity, ideological divisions quickly reduced the department to a loose collection of action agencies engaged in their own pet programs and perennially confronted by a hostile state and county Extension Service. Contrary to treatments of the USDA as a tool of conservative farmers, Farm Bureau dominance was challenged vigorously in the late 1930s by the Farmers' Union, the Roosevelt administration, and the Democratic Party. Although the Farm Bureau continued to wield influence, it was a far cry from the early 1930s, when the AFBF was a corporatist client of the USDA. By the 1940s, its role as the undisputed peak organization of farmers was under direct challenge by the Farmers' Union.

Corporatist agriculture broke down because neither the Farm Bureau nor the USDA could guarantee each other a stable policy partnership. The reasons for this instability were largely institutional. Various interests exploited the apparatus of the state to destabilize the corporatist relationship between farmers and the government. Businesses, such as food processors, used the courts to challenge the constitutionality of the AAA and protect industrial interests in the food production chain. Liberal "New Dealers" used the presidency to create independent agencies within the executive branch that challenged USDA policy authority. The Farm Bureau used the congressional appropriations process to undercut policy initiatives it opposed. The Farmers' Union used partisan politics and the promise of a farmer-labor alliance to attack the Farm Bureau–Extension Service relationship. Although it took decades to build, agricultural corporatism was short-lived in the United States.

As agricultural corporatism withered, farm policies and political institutions embraced the diversity of agricultural interests in the United States. As I will explain in the next chapter, farm politics was reduced to its lowest common denominator—individual commodities. Increasingly, politicians and bureaucrats tailored institutions and programs according to the interests of wheat growers, corn growers, and so forth. The House and Senate agriculture committees divided into commodity-specific subcommittees, and specialty commodity organizations superseded the general farm organizations in dealings with Congress. With the corporatist avenue foreclosed, farmers, politicians, and bureaucrats adapted to the realities of pluralist policy making in agriculture.

POLICY CONSEQUENCES

What were the practical policy effects of institutional differences in matters of market intervention? In France and Japan, close ties between cooperatives and government officials made possible such policy instruments as state monopolies and legislated prices. In the United States, institutional impediments foreclosed certain policy alternatives. The Federal Farm Board, a solution built around cooperatives and farmer-controlled marketing boards, failed to stem the farm crisis. This failure, moreover, influenced the development of New Deal policies. For bulk commodities such as wheat, cotton, and corn, government production-control programs targeted the individual farmer rather than collectivities. Enrollment in acreage allotment and price support loan programs remained at the discretion of the individual farmer. Most farm programs were in reality a contract between the producer and the government. Even when the secretary of agriculture announced marketing quotas for a given commodity, implementation required the assent of a majority of farmers voting in a referendum. Except for a few commodities such as dairy, intermediate organizations did not play a key role in policy implementation.

Institutions also shaped the capacity of government officials to reallocate market power in the farm sector. In Japan, cooperatives, with the considerable assistance of allies in the Ministry of Agriculture, displaced merchants in markets for commodities and agricultural inputs. In France, commercial interests retained their position in the wheat market, but the use of government licenses and subsidies gave cooperatives a distinct advantage over their commercial rivals in the collection and distribution of wheat. Government regulations in France and Japan also transformed tenant-landlord relations. In France, the Corporation paysanne regulated lease rights and mandated compensation for tenant farmers who made improvements on rented land. In Japan, the government strictly controlled land rents and abolished the payment of rent-in-kind. Although intended to maximize the production and collection of rice for the war effort, regulations on rent effectively undermined the position of landlords in the rural economy.[115] In contrast, institutions in the United States made the reallocation of market power much more difficult. Programs designed to help tenants and sharecroppers became mired in political conflicts and were vulnerable to the congressional appropriations process where conservative interests effectively removed funding for liberal programs. The independent judiciary, meanwhile, allowed processors and merchants to defend their interests against regulatory encroachments.

---

[115] Wright, *Rural Revolution in France*; Ogura, *Agricultural Development in Modern Japan*, 114, 139, 140, 143.

Admittedly, most policy makers in the United States never intended to alter the structure of agriculture in any radical manner. The avowed purpose of regulation was to support and stabilize prices and bring production in closer line with demand. But comparative price data from this period indicate that the United States achieved only mild success in price support policy.

Figure 3.1 compares the index of nominal annual prices for select commodities using 1925 as the base year. I compare nominal prices because government efforts and farmer expectations focused on actual market prices.[116] The choice of commodities reflects both economic and policy significance of each crop. Wheat and rice were at the center of policy efforts in France and Japan, respectively, and were the most widely produced crop as well. In the United States, corn acreage far exceeded wheat, but corn was used largely as feed for on-farm livestock production. As a cash crop, therefore, wheat was more important than corn or cotton. Moreover, the effort to control wheat production through the domestic allotment plan was at the heart of the first AAA. From a policy perspective, then, wheat is the most appropriate choice for a discussion of U.S. regulatory capacity in agriculture during the 1930s.

As indicated in figure 3.1, prices declined in all three countries during the late 1920s and early 1930s. In Japan, prices recovered around 1931 when the government instituted a minimum price for rice; prices increased monotonically after the 1933 Rice Control Law, which authorized unlimited government purchases of rice. In France, the decline in wheat prices continued into the mid-1930s but increased rapidly after 1936, when the government instituted a system of official prices administered by the Office du blé. Finally, in the United States, wheat prices suffered a sharp decline through 1932. A modest price recovery did occur during the early years of the AAA, thanks in large part to a severe drought in 1934 and 1936. Evaluating the early years of the wheat program and its effect on production and prices, economists Nourse, Davis, and Black concluded, "Nature was primarily responsible."[117] In fact, wheat prices dropped sharply following the bumper crop of 1937 and remained at around 50 percent of their 1925 levels.

Table 3.1 examines the U.S. wheat situation more closely and gives some indication of why the United States was less successful in its effort to lift prices. As indicated, the area planted in wheat actually increased after passage of the AAA in 1933, decreased slightly the following year,

---

[116] In real terms, price declines in the early 1930s were not as severe due to deflation, while price increases in the late 1930s were not as great due to inflation.

[117] Nourse, Davis, and Black, *Three Years of the Agricultural Adjustment Administration*, 125.

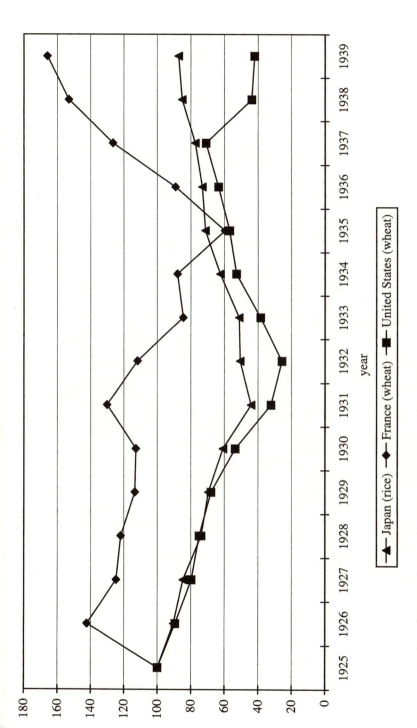

Figure 3.1 Index of Nominal Annual Prices, 1925–1939 (1925 = 100)
Sources: INSEE, *Annuaire Statistique de la France,* various years; Bank of Japan, *Economic Statistics of Japan,* various years; USDA, *Yearbook of Agriculture,* various years.

TABLE 3.1
U.S. Wheat Area and Production, 1930–1940

Year	Area (million acres) Planted	Harvested	Production (million bushels)
1930	67.6	62.6	886.5
1931	66.5	57.7	941.5
1932	66.3	57.9	756.3
1933	69.0	49.4	552.2
1934	64.1	43.3	526.1
1935	69.6	51.3	628.2
1936	74.0	49.1	629.9
1937	80.8	64.2	873.9
1938	79.0	69.2	919.9
1939	62.8	52.7	741.2
1940	61.8	53.3	814.6

Source: USDA, Track Records: United States Crop Production.

and then increased rapidly again thereafter, despite efforts to control production through acreage allotments. In 1933 and 1934, the area of wheat harvested and total wheat production did decline, but this outcome is due almost entirely to the drought of those years. As Benedict and Stine concluded, "All in all, the wheat program of the 1933–1936 period seems not to have had any large effect on the wheat situation generally. . . . The very small outputs of 1933–1935 were due almost wholly to drought." Acreage, both planted and harvested, increased to record levels in 1937 and 1938 as "the mere announcement of [reduction] goals . . . had little effect since there was no way of forcing farmers to abide by them."[118] As a result, production increased substantially with the return to more favorable growing conditions. The 1938 AAA did attempt to rectify this problem of enforcement and gave the secretary of agriculture added powers to penalize noncompliant farmers. Acreage declined in 1939, although it still remained above government targets. In sum, efforts to lift prices failed, in part, because the regulation of production through acreage allotments never achieved its stated goal.

CONCLUSION

The agricultural depression of the 1920s and 1930s presented governments in the United States, France, and Japan with an administrative challenge. What bureaucratic mechanism would uplift farm income without

[118] Benedict and Stine, The Agricultural Commodity Programs, 109–10, 130.

heavy-handed government intervention? A close relation between bureaucracies and farm organizations—agricultural corporatism—was seized upon by political elites as an effective response to the economic crisis of the 1920s and 1930s. By designating an official representative of agricultural interests with policy responsibilities, bureaucrats could disguise regulation as a benign attempt to rectify market inefficiencies.

In order to forge a corporatist relationship, bureaucrats required two things: a well-equipped administrative apparatus and a willing client capable of functioning as a partner in policy formation and implementation. Unless these institutional preconditions were met, sectoral bargains between farmers and the state would disintegrate into conflict or fall prey to the interference of interests, such as merchants, who stood to lose from agricultural regulations. As we have seen, each country faced the corporatist challenge of the 1920s and 1930s with a different set of institutions inherited from the early years of farm policy.

In Japan, the system of agricultural associations and cooperatives created in the late nineteenth and early twentieth centuries provided a strong foundation for agricultural corporatism. In response to the farm crisis, agricultural officials and leaders of cooperatives seized the opportunity to strengthen their respective positions in policy. The Ministry of Agriculture and Forestry gained independence from the Ministry of Commerce, and the cooperatives secured greater financial guarantees from the government. Together, cooperatives and the MAF formed the institutional basis for a state monopoly of agriculture in the 1940s.

Cooperatives played an important role in French policy as well, but the pattern of institutional development resulted in a less comprehensive corporatist arrangement. After World War I, the agricultural bureaucracy expanded at the local level, and government funds promoted further development of rural organizations such as specialist producer associations. In wheat and wine, commodity groups became central to the regulation of production and prices during the 1930s. Corporatist doctrine was particularly well suited to the task of regulation in rural France, where conservative fears of central government interference were rampant. However, the most effective policy partnerships developed in those commodities where strong, technocratic associations of farmers were already in place.

When the depression hit the United States, many of the institutional requirements for agricultural corporatism appeared to exist. During the 1920s, the American Farm Bureau Federation, with government support, became the largest agricultural organization in the United States. Over the same period, the U.S. Department of Agriculture grew into an immense bureaucracy with personnel and field offices throughout the country. As president, Herbert Hoover embraced producer associations in his plan for rural relief, the Federal Farm Board. Yet corporatism did not develop.

Despite the power of the Farm Bureau, rival agricultural organizations retained allies in the USDA and continued to influence policy decisions. As for the Department of Agriculture, ideological divisions between top administrators led to a bleeding of power as evidenced by the rise of independent agencies responsible for different facets of policy. Under these conditions, a stable partnership between the Farm Bureau and the USDA could not materialize.

After World War II, the legitimacy of government intervention largely accepted, the political opportunities from agricultural subsidies became clearer. Farm organizations involved in the policy process not only guaranteed efficient administration but also supplied critical votes. As I examine in the next chapter, the experiences of the 1930s greatly influenced the policies and politics of agriculture after World War II. Politicians who wanted to reap the electoral benefits of agricultural subsidies confronted an institutional and policy setting born out of the prewar economic crisis. In France and Japan, agricultural corporatism evolved into clientelistic relations between peak agricultural associations and conservative political parties. Meanwhile, in the United States, conflicts between parties, farm groups, and producers of various commodities prevented the emergence of a similar alliance between American farmers and either political party. Political conflicts, fueled by institutions, diminished the capacity of farmers to control the agricultural policy agenda in the United States.

CHAPTER 4

The Postwar Development
of the Agricultural Welfare State

THE INAUGURATION OF AGRICULTURAL PRICE SUPPORT POLICIES during the 1930s presented governments in the United States, France, and Japan with an administrative challenge. How could policy makers legitimately extend the authority of the state in order to regulate the behavior of thousands of individual producers? Governments in each country seized upon corporatist arrangements with farmers as one solution to the administrative challenge of regulation. By giving producer groups the authority to formulate and implement policy, bureaucrats could improve their chances of regulatory success, as well as defuse criticisms of government intervention in the farm economy.

With the end of World War II and government intervention in agriculture largely accepted, politicians and producers increasingly recognized the political opportunity of farm subsidies. With a sizable portion of the population still on the farm, agricultural policy became an important component of postwar politics in each country. As governments searched for a long-term agricultural program suitable for the needs of a peacetime economy, political parties in the United States, France, and Japan used the issue of subsidies as an electoral strategy at the ballot box.

Accordingly, the institutional demands of agricultural policy changed slightly. In addition to implementation concerns, policy makers also addressed political needs. To derive the electoral benefits from commodity programs, politicians needed institutional arrangements that fostered political links with farmers. Agricultural organizations that participated in the formation and implementation of policy could also serve as an effective mobilizer of votes for political parties. In practical terms, the administrative (implementation) and political (electoral) demands of regulation could be fulfilled by the same set of institutions. Put differently, government capacity for effective regulation also paid handsome political dividends.

In this chapter I examine the politics of the agricultural welfare state in the postwar period. As we shall see, the relationship between farmers and politicians established during the 1930s shaped the postwar politics of agriculture in each country. In France and Japan, corporatist relations between farmers and the government became the basis for a powerful political alliance after the war that joined peak agricultural associations and conservative political parties. In the United States, on the other hand, prewar conflicts over policy among rival farm groups, political parties, and producers of various commodities foiled efforts to create a lasting political alliance after the war.

These political differences shaped the postwar evolution of policy. In Japan, farm leaders and rural politicians used generous subsidies and pork-barrel projects to forge an alliance between the Central Union of Agricultural Cooperatives (Nokyo) and the Liberal Democratic Party. On the strength of this alliance, postwar agricultural policy strengthened Nokyo's position in the farm economy and gave LDP politicians near-exclusive control over the provision of government benefits to rural Japan. In France, the agricultural welfare state combined structural aids to agriculture with price supports administered through the Common Agricultural Policy of the European Economic Community. This complex mix of policies enabled the peak farm organization in France to balance the interests of its diverse membership and help the Gaullists consolidate the institutional developments of the Fifth Republic.

In the United States, conflicts between farm groups, political parties, and producers of various commodities left policy fluid and unstable through the first two decades after the war. In the 1960s, Congress finally settled on a system of direct government payments made available on a voluntary basis to those producers who complied with acreage restrictions. Wrapped into omnibus legislation passed every four or five years, the policies of the late 1960s and early 1970s lessened partisan strife over agriculture but also opened the farm policy process to greater participation by the representatives of nonagricultural interests. Unlike in France and Japan, the U.S. agricultural welfare state developed without farmers becoming a core constituency of either political party.

THE UNITED STATES

Ironically, the declining political influence of farmers became evident at a time when most political scientists thought agricultural regulation exemplified the capture of public policies by private interests. According to Grant McConnell and Theodore Lowi, the balkanization of the federal government into discrete policy niches concentrated power in the hands of those groups with a vested interest in the outcomes of policy decisions. Within the congressional committee or subcommittee, beyond the gaze of public attention, only actors who stood to gain directly from government policy exercised influence. As a result, regulations invariably benefited the regulated.[1]

---

[1] McConnell, *The Decline of Agrarian Democracy*; Lowi, *The End of Liberalism*.

Not all students of U.S. agriculture have agreed with the views of McConnell and Lowi. As Graham Wilson argued in his 1977 study, agriculture was not the product of consensus politics among farm leaders, rural representatives, and bureaucrats within the USDA.[2] Rather, agricultural policy in the United States after World War II was the source of bitter partisan conflict. As I emphasize in this chapter, conflicts were manifested through institutions. Separated powers, a regionally based party system, and the lack of a single, geographically diverse farm organization limited political possibilities and perpetuated conflicts over policy alternatives. Because of institutions, neither side in the farm policy debate could enact its agricultural program as political opponents maintained at least some degree of access to the policy process. By exploiting institutional opportunities such as divided government, rival party politicians impeded their opponents' efforts to establish ties with farmers on the basis of a coherent agricultural program.

In other words, the suppression of interest group conflict and the development of clientele politics in agriculture proved to be exceptionally difficult in the context of U.S. political institutions. As I will describe, proposals to lift prices for wheat and cotton threatened the profits of corn and livestock producers.[3] More important, institutions transformed these economic differences between producers into ideological and political battle lines. In the 1960s, producers and their representatives eventually overcame these conflicts as the devolution of agricultural representation to commodity-specific groups and the shift from mandatory production controls to voluntary direct payments placed farm policy on a bipartisan footing. But by then, it was too late. By the 1970s, demographic changes meant that passage of farm legislation required bargains with urban and suburban representatives who pushed a new set of concerns on the policy agenda.

Toward a Farmer-Labor Alliance:
The Democratic Party and the Brannan Plan

The lines of debate in the postwar struggle over agriculture were drawn well before the end of the war in 1945. Agricultural legislation passed in 1942 required that most regulated commodities receive high support

[2] The conflict-ridden nature of post-World War II U.S. farm policy was a prominent theme in Graham Wilson's comparative study of agriculture in the United States and Britain. This study concurs with Wilson's conclusions that the sort of interest group capture identified by Lowi was, in fact, very difficult to achieve in the context of U.S. institutions. See Wilson, *Special Interests and Policymaking*, 158–59.

[3] In other words, both the costs and the benefits of policy were concentrated. See chapter 1.

prices for two years following the end of hostilities.[4] Farmers and policy makers remembered the boom and bust cycle after World War I; the 1942 legislation, known as the Steagall Amendment, was intended to prevent a similar occurrence.[5]

As the two-year adjustment period came to an end, differences emerged among farmers over the appropriate direction for long-term agricultural policy in the United States. Cotton, wheat, and rice farmers preferred the continuation of high, fixed supports under the Steagall Amendment. Producers of these commodities confronted an uncertain economic environment, and they were willing to accept production controls in exchange for guaranteed prices. Corn and livestock farmers, on the other hand, expected increased demand for meat from affluent postwar consumers. These farmers preferred to avoid production controls and, instead, favored a system of flexible price supports inversely related to supply. As supplies increased, price supports would decline and encourage farmers to shift production out of surplus crops.[6]

The geographic concentration of crop production and the regional basis of party competition translated these economic differences among farmers into a partisan battle over agricultural policy. Cotton, wheat, and tobacco farmers were concentrated in the Democratic South and the northern tier of the Great Plains. Corn and hog producers were located mainly in the Republican Midwest. As policy opinions sharpened in agricultural debates, so did the divisions between the two largest farm organizations. In December 1947, the Farm Bureau experienced a bitter leadership struggle over the price support issue. Delegates from the South and Plains (advocates of fixed supports) waged an unsuccessful campaign against the election of Allan Kline, an Iowa hog producer (and an advocate of flexible supports). Kline's election divided the rank and file and swung the Farm Bureau leadership behind flexible price supports. Meanwhile, the smaller National Farmers' Union (NFU)—its membership concentrated in the wheat regions of the Great Plains—pressed for high, fixed supports. Reflecting the regional basis of party competition, this rivalry between the NFU and the Farm Bureau turned increasingly partisan: while the NFU lobbied for Democratic farm proposals, the Farm Bureau became a staunch supporter of Republican efforts to reduce government intervention through flexible price supports.[7]

---

[4] These were basic commodities (corn, wheat, cotton, rice, tobacco, and peanuts), as well as any farm product that the government deemed necessary for the war effort.

[5] Wilcox, *The Farmer in the Second World War*, 243–46.

[6] Matusow, *Farm Policies and Politics in the Truman Years*, 136.

[7] Various political scientists have remarked on the commodity basis of constituency interests in farm policy. See, for example, ibid., 137–39; Hansen, *Gaining Access*, 113–15; Jones, "Representation in Congress"; Heinz, "The Political Impasse in Farm Support Legislation," 957; Wilson, *Special Interests and Policymaking*; Mayhew, *Party Loyalty among Congressmen*.

In early 1948, the Republican-controlled Congress debated the issue of fixed versus flexible supports. In the Senate, the Committee on Agriculture and Forestry, chaired by George Aiken of Vermont, embraced a sliding scale of flexible supports. On the House side, however, Agriculture Committee chairman Clifford Hope of Kansas introduced a bill to continue supports at 90 percent of parity for another two years. Democrats were equally divided. The Truman administration supported the Senate bill because the urban, liberal wing of the Democratic Party believed flexible supports would lower food prices for consumers and foster a more rational adjustment in agricultural production.[8] Southern Democrats, however, supported the House bill and fixed supports. After a conference committee split the difference between the House and Senate farm bills, the Hope-Aiken Act passed in the summer of 1948 extended price supports at 90 percent of parity for two years, after which the sliding scale of flexible supports in the Aiken bill would go into effect.[9]

The Hope-Aiken Act was passed in the midst of a healthy farm economy, but as the fall presidential campaign approached, this postwar prosperity wavered. With the European food situation less dire and forecasters predicting record harvests of corn, wheat, and other crops, grain prices in the United States declined. With the downturn in the farm economy, the Truman administration changed its strategy and unequivocally opposed flexible supports. During the 1948 campaign, Truman and Secretary of Agriculture Charles Brannan warned voters in farm states of the Midwest that a Republican victory in November would mark the end of government price supports. The Democratic strategy succeeded: Truman won a surprising victory over Dewey, and the Democrats regained control of both houses of Congress. Democratic successes were particularly notable in the Midwest. Truman won in Iowa, Wisconsin, and Ohio—states that voted Republican in 1944. In the Senate, Democrats picked up GOP seats in several farm states such as Minnesota, Illinois, and Iowa. In the House, more than thirty seats in rural districts of the Midwest changed from Republican to Democratic. In election postmortems, Washington pundits attributed Truman's success to the farm vote. Rural lawmakers, moreover, saw the election as a clear repudiation of flexible price supports and the Hope-Aiken Act.[10]

---

[8] Liberals also liked flexible supports because they fit within a Keynesian economic framework. In other words, farm surpluses were due to underconsumption rather than overproduction. Flexible supports, coupled with consumer subsidies for the underprivileged, were more appropriate for an economic policy of full employment. See Matusow, *Farm Policies and Politics in the Truman Years*, 116–17.

[9] Hansen, *Gaining Access*, 115; Matusow, *Farm Policies and Politics in the Truman Years*, 140–44.

[10] Hansen, *Gaining Access*, 116–19.

The political windfall of 1948 set the stage for a new round of debates on agricultural policy. This time, however, the Truman administration embarked upon a bold policy direction that, if successful, would bring together farmers and labor unions in a powerful electoral coalition under the Democratic Party banner. In April 1949, Secretary of Agriculture Charles Brannan unveiled his plan for agricultural policy. The Brannan Plan, as it was called, would eliminate price supports, allow prices for agricultural commodities to settle at market-clearing levels, and offer farmers direct support payments to augment farm income.[11]

From a partisan perspective, it was a masterful stroke. By scrapping the debate over fixed versus flexible supports, Brannan potentially eliminated the source of conflict among farmers over price supports and production controls. At the same time, direct income payments rather than market intervention would shift the cost of policy from consumers to taxpayers, lower food prices, and cement a Democratic farmer-labor alliance at the ballot box. "[The] farm plan is full of 1950 election politics," Kiplinger advised businessmen. "[The] Democratic aim . . . [is to] win the 1950 elections with labor and farmers." As another political observer noted, "If the Democrats get it through, they are in for life."[12]

The partisan maneuverings began soon after Brannan announced his proposal. In April 1949, the chairman of the Democratic National Committee publicly endorsed the Brannan Plan. As Reo Christenson remarks, "From that point on, the Brannan proposals were clearly labeled 'Democratic,' with all the advantages and liabilities pertaining thereto."[13] Two months later, at a Democratic Party rally in Des Moines, Iowa, the vice president, leading congressional Democrats, Farmers' Union leaders, and the head of the Congress of Industrial Organizations Political Action Committee (CIO-PAC) stood on the dais and promised that the Brannan Plan would bring victory in 1950 congressional elections.[14]

Republicans and their allies in the Farm Bureau balked at the partisan turn in agricultural policy and pledged to oppose the Brannan Plan in Congress.[15] The first indication of trouble came in the summer of 1949,

[11] Christenson, *The Brannan Plan*, 3.

[12] *Kiplinger's Washington Letter*, September 3, 1949; *New York Times*, April 24, 1949, E9; *Kiplinger's Washington Letter*, June 18, 1949; "Brannan Statement on Farm Plan Creates Sensation," *Official Newsletter of the American Farm Bureau Federation*, April 11, 1949, 1; Christenson, *The Brannan Plan*, 143–44

[13] Christenson, *The Brannan Plan*, 153.

[14] Matusow, *Farm Policies and Politics in the Truman Years*, 199–200; "Fight on Production Payments," *Wallace's Farmer*, May 7, 1949, 589; "I'm Waiting to See, Say Farmers," *Wallace's Farmer*, July 2, 1949, 802.

[15] "Calls Brannan Plan Price Fixing," *Official Newsletter of the American Farm Bureau Federation*, May 9, 1949, 4; "Washington from the Inside," *The Nation's Agriculture* [Farm Bureau publication], June 1949, 5; Matusow, *Farm Policies and Politics in the Truman Years*, 201.

when Democrat Albert Gore of Tennessee introduced a one-year extension of high, fixed supports. Southern Democrats bolted and, joined by Republicans eager to defeat the partisan aspirations of Brannan and the Truman administration, passed the Gore bill in the House. Meanwhile, in the Senate, administration allies proved no more adept at holding Democratic factions together. Agriculture and Forestry Committee chairman Elmer Thomas failed to report the Brannan Plan out of his committee. Instead, Clinton Anderson, a freshman senator and former agriculture secretary under Truman, drafted a slightly more flexible variant of the Gore proposal. The conference report passed by Congress in October continued price supports at 90 percent parity through 1950, with a provision for flexible supports beginning in 1952. The Brannan Plan was a dead letter.

Throughout the doomed legislative campaign in 1949, the Farm Bureau led the charge against Brannan and the Truman administration. According to one farm journal, "The Farm Bureau is given credit for helping to line up enough Republican and Southern Democratic votes to put over the Gore bill."[16] Celebrating the defeat of the Brannan Plan, a Farm Bureau newsletter proclaimed, "Agriculture has rebuffed those who would place the national farm program on a partisan political basis."[17]

Congressional support for the Brannan Plan proved so elusive, in part, because the administration lacked a strong organizational ally that could rally farmers behind the plan and defuse attacks from the Farm Bureau. The National Farmers' Union had the greatest entrée of any major farm organization in the Truman administration; NFU president James Patton and Secretary Brannan were old friends from Colorado. Although Patton and the Farmers' Union threw its weight wholeheartedly behind the administration, its strength was limited geographically to the Great Plains. Patton's liberal advocacy in race and tenancy issues, moreover, rendered the organization a nonentity in the South.[18] Another potential ally was the network of county farmer committees in the Production and Marketing Administration (PMA). These local committees (formerly part of the Agricultural Adjustment Administration) were responsible for implementing government programs throughout the country. Although PMA committees in the Midwest promoted the virtues of the Brannan Plan in 1949, the federal government prohibited any overtly "political" activities by the local committees.[19]

---

[16] "Congress in Snarl on Farm Bill," *Wallace's Farmer*, August 6, 1949, 886.

[17] "Washington from the Inside," *The Nation's Agriculture*, September 1949, 6; *Kiplinger's Washington Letter*, July 23, 1949. On the legislative maneuvers, Christenson, *The Brannan Plan*, 159–64; Matusow, *Farm Policies and Politics in the Truman Years*, 209–17.

[18] Crampton, *The National Farmers Union*, 47–52, 174. After his tenure as secretary of agriculture, Charles Brannan became general counsel for the National Farmers' Union.

[19] Christenson, *The Brannan Plan*, 128–42.

In sum, Brannan's attempt to create a political alliance between farmers, labor, and the Democratic Party failed for three reasons. First, the separation of powers protected congressional prerogatives in farm policy matters. Congress could effectively ignore the Brannan Plan. Second, party politics, in particular southern hostility toward the Brannan Plan, made it difficult to hold together congressional Democrats during the legislative process. Third, Brannan and Truman did not have a strong organizational ally that could help wage political battles for the administration. This institutional context made the creation of a farmer-labor alliance an impossible task.

Conservative Backlash: Ezra Taft Benson and the Farm Bureau

In 1950, Brannan again tried to secure congressional support for his farm program. With sagging prices for most farm products, Democratic leaders hoped they could blame the poor farm economy on Republicans and win soundly in 1950 congressional races. The outbreak of the Korean War, however, reversed the decline in prices as demand shot up for agricultural commodities. As the economic circumstances changed, talk of the Brannan Plan quietly slipped away.[20]

The Korean War proved to be only a temporary hiatus in the problem of overproduction and stagnant prices for farm products. At war's end, the problems that plagued lawmakers in the late 1940s returned. Carryover stocks of wheat reached a record high, while net farm income dropped by $2.5 billion between 1952 and 1954.[21] As these problems spread throughout the farm economy, the government renewed its search for a long-term agricultural program.

Following his victory over Stevenson in the 1952 presidential election, Eisenhower appointed Ezra Taft Benson as secretary of agriculture. Benson, a devout free-market liberal, made his approach to policy clear in a 1953 press conference, stating that "farmers should not be placed in a position of working for government bounty rather than producing for a free market."[22] In 1954, Benson and Eisenhower sent Congress draft legislation calling for a flexible support system that divided farm-state lawmakers and agricultural organizations along familiar lines. But the political alignment in Washington made adoption of flexible supports

---

[20] *Kiplinger's Washington Newsletter*, October 1, 1949; Cochrane and Ryan, *American Farm Policy*, 29–31.

[21] Cochrane and Ryan, *American Farm Policy*, 32.

[22] Ezra Taft Benson, "General Statement on Agricultural Policy," February 5, 1953, quoted in ibid., 90.

more likely. The Eisenhower administration enjoyed the benefit of Republican majorities in both houses of Congress, as well as the unflagging support of the Farm Bureau leadership, whose views on agricultural policy matched Benson's perfectly. With some minor horse trading, the 1954 Agriculture Act enacted a system of flexible supports. Farm journals called the 1954 act "a clear-cut Benson–Farm Bureau Victory." As Mississippi Democrat Jamie Whitten, the ranking minority member on the Agriculture Subcommittee of the House Appropriations Committee, told Farm Bureau President Allan Kline, "You are now in control, as I see it, of the Department of Agriculture."[23]

The Farmers' Union, much of its access to the USDA now gone, assumed the role of spoiler previously played by the Farm Bureau. Aided by Democratic allies in Congress, the Farmers' Union renewed its attacks on the relationship between agents of the Extension Service and county chapters of the Farm Bureau. In several key states, such as Illinois and Iowa, Extension Service agents still received substantial financial assistance from local Farm Bureaus. In exchange, critics charged, county agents promoted Farm Bureau membership and supplied critical staff and organizational resources. After the defeat of the Brannan Plan, leaders of the Farmers' Union stepped up efforts to force an official separation of the Farm Bureau and the Extension Service. When Benson and the USDA wholeheartedly embraced the Farm Bureau's policy demands, the campaign for statutory separation from the Extension Service took on added importance. Throughout 1953 and 1954, the Farmers' Union waged a publicity campaign against the Farm Bureau in states where Extension Service ties were closest.[24]

Meanwhile, Benson's activities as secretary further sharpened partisan battle lines in agriculture. During Eisenhower's first term, Benson reorganized the department, augmented the power of the secretary, and weakened elements in the agriculture bureaucracy friendly to the policy goals of the Democrats and the National Farmers' Union. For example, Benson abolished the Bureau of Agricultural Economics—long viewed by conservatives as a bastion of liberal planning. Benson also created a new layer of patronage appointments between himself and the various action agencies in his department to improve control over policy implementation. At the state and county level, "the Republican administration set out to neutralize the Democratic proclivities" of USDA personnel responsible

[23] Schapsmeier and Schapsmeier, *Ezra Taft Benson*, 71–88; Hansen, *Gaining Access*, 131; Subcommittee on Agriculture, House Appropriations Committee, House of Representatives, *Hearings on Department of Agriculture Appropriations for 1954*, 83d Cong., 1st sess., 1953, 420.

[24] Block, *The Separation of the Farm Bureau and the Extension Service*, 135–201.

for the distribution of government checks and other tasks. According to Charles Hardin, congressional Republicans and national GOP leaders pressed Benson to use "the farm support agencies . . . as instruments for strengthening the Republican Party."[25] In response, Benson recommended that appropriations for the Soil Conservation Service be cut in half, while funds for the Extension Service increased. Farm Bureau leaders, who feared that the local SCS committees would spawn a rival farm organization, warmly endorsed Benson's recommendations.[26] Although the House Committee on Appropriations voted to cut spending for research and extension, the measure was reversed on the House floor, and the Extension Service secured an additional $8.3 million for fiscal year 1955.[27]

With the Farm Bureau and the Extension Service legally tied together in several states, the outcome of the 1954 appropriations battle only fueled Democratic criticisms of Benson, the Farm Bureau, and the USDA. When the Democrats regained control of Congress in the 1954 midterm elections, Farm Bureau leaders, as well as Secretary Benson, soon realized that the Farm Bureau–Extension Service relationship threatened the larger policy goals of the AFBF, the USDA, and the Republican Party. Afraid that the new Democratic Congress would reverse the policy gains of the last two years, Secretary Benson issued Memorandum No. 1368 just weeks after the November congressional elections. The memorandum prohibited all employees of the USDA from accepting office space or contributions from farm organizations, or recommending that department duties be carried out through particular farm organization, or soliciting membership, directly or indirectly, on behalf of any farm organization.[28] In the context of divided government, the Farm Bureau–Extension Service relationship had become a political liability that forced Benson to advocate their separation in order to preserve his large policy agenda.

Despite the tactical retreat, Benson did not abandon his advocacy of Farm Bureau goals. As Eisenhower approached reelection, the administration renewed its efforts to secure GOP support from farmers. Fearful that

[25] Hardin, "The Republican Department of Agriculture," 213–19, 223–26; Schapsmeier and Schapsmeier, *Ezra Taft Benson*, 41–54. In late 1954, Benson was rated as the worst at "political cooperation" with congressional Republicans who wanted administration policies and political appointments to further partisan goals. *Kiplinger's Washington Newsletter*, December 11, 1954.

[26] Hardin, *The Politics of Agriculture*, chap. 3. Hardin's book, critical of the Farm Bureau–Extension Service relationship, helped focus public attention on the issue and added to the growing appearance of impropriety in the exercise of Farm Bureau power. See Block, *The Separation of the Farm Bureau and the Extension Service*, 200.

[27] Block, *The Separation of the Farm Bureau and the Extension Service*, 209–13.

[28] Ibid., 215.

economic problems in the Midwest would cause farmers to desert the Republicans, USDA officials and the White House searched for a policy program that could win votes in the Corn Belt. Producers in this region were fickle in partisan attachment, and, more important, they dominated the Farm Bureau leadership in the 1950s. Accordingly, the Eisenhower administration introduced a new land retirement program to tackle surpluses of corn, wheat, and cotton. The "Soil Bank," like the soil conservation programs of the New Deal, would pay farmers a premium to take land out of production for a designated period.[29]

On its face the new program seemed benign, but Democratic critics argued that Benson and the Eisenhower administration implemented the new Soil Bank provisions in a partisan manner. Although producers of all basic crops were eligible for payments, corn producers could remove much less acreage and still receive benefits. As a consequence, the electorally valuable corn producers of the Midwest received 69 percent of all Soil Bank payments during the first year of its operation. Congressional Democrats pointed to other cases of partisan favoritism as well. For example, eligibility for government crop loans was usually tied to compliance with acreage allotments and other programs. In 1956, however, the USDA offered corn producers a special noncompliers loan rate twenty-five cents per bushel below the rate received by farmers who abided by acreage restrictions. This effectively gave corn producers an incentive to produce as much as they liked and still receive government supports.[30]

But just as the Democrats tried in vain to solidify farm support with the Brannan Plan, the Republicans ultimately failed in their partisan bid to secure votes through a partnership with the Farm Bureau. Democrats criticized the USDA for excessive partisanship in policy administration and, aided by the National Farmers' Union, lambasted Republican policies in 1956 congressional races. As agricultural prices declined in the face of an ever-mounting surplus, Ezra Taft Benson became the whipping boy of Democratic Party hopefuls. Republican farm policies played poorly in Midwestern House and Senate contests, despite efforts "not to tag [the GOP farm program] as the 'Benson Plan.' "[31] GOP strongholds in South Dakota, Kansas, Iowa, and Missouri went Democratic for the first time in decades. In the 1958 midterms, Democratic success continued, particularly in the Corn Belt. Of the fourteen new Senate Democrats, five were from the Midwest. Democrats scored resounding victories in House races

[29] Schapsmeier and Schapsmeier, *Ezra Taft Benson*, 154–55.

[30] Hansen, *Gaining Access*, 133.

[31] *Kiplinger's Washington Letter*, January 14, 1956; Schapsmeier and Schapsmeier, *Ezra Taft Benson*, chap. 8.

as well. By the time Ezra Taft Benson stepped down as secretary of agriculture, Democrats had doubled their numbers among Midwestern congressional delegations. Republican efforts to solidify farm support at the polls clearly failed.[32]

Between the battle over the Brannan Plan in the late 1940s and the attacks on Ezra Taft Benson in the 1950s, the roles of the general farm organizations in agricultural politics reversed. While Truman was in power, the Farmers' Union enjoyed privileged access to the executive through its ties with Democratic Party elites. During this period the Farm Bureau maintained influence in Congress, where it successfully derailed administration policies such as the Brannan Plan. Once Eisenhower came to power, the opposite conditions held. In the words of one NFU official, "As the Union's influence went down in the administration, it went up in Congress."[33] While Benson and the Farm Bureau worked closely on policy matters, the Farmers' Union retained its influence via the Democratic Congress, where it successfully attacked the Farm Bureau–Extension Service relationship and pushed through a high, fixed support bill ultimately vetoed by Eisenhower in 1955. In response, Farm Bureau leaders issued red-baiting attacks on congressional Democrats. On the eve of the 1958 elections, AFBF president Charles Shuman told Farm Bureau members, "Congress has recently adjourned after a long session during which the trend toward socialism remained virtually unchecked."[34] Throughout the 1950s, agricultural policy was mired in partisan conflict between the Farm Bureau and the Farmers' Union, between Republicans and Democrats, and between the White House and Congress.

The persistence of these conflicts illustrates how institutions impeded the political goals of both major farm organizations and party leaders in Washington. During both Democratic and Republican administrations, political losers used the separation of powers, the circumstances of divided government, and the lack of a single, geographically diverse farm organization to prevent their opponents from gaining control over agricultural policy. Neither the Farm Bureau nor the Farmers' Union ever completely lost access to the policy process, and both used Congress and the circumstances of divided party control as a base from which to attack executive policy and the privileged access of rival farm organizations. As a result, neither political party secured electoral dominance among farmers with a catchall policy program. As Kiplinger observed in 1958, "Farm state congressmen . . . can't get . . . a bill through Congress. . . . The Farm

[32] On Midwestern backlash against Benson, see Gilpatrick, "Price Support Policy and the Midwest Farm Vote," 319–35; Hansen, *Gaining Access*, 139–43.

[33] Crampton, *The National Farmers Union*, 174.

[34] "Measure Your Candidates," *The Nation's Agriculture*, October 1958, 7.

Bloc in the old days always stood together. Now it has internal quarrels, so . . . [there is] a stalemate."[35] Because of institutional shortcomings, farm politics and policy remained deadlocked.

The Democrats Try Again: The Freeman Plan

Throughout the partisan recriminations of the 1950s, the problems of agriculture continued to grow—literally. Increases in the use of capital-intensive inputs such as hybrid seeds, agricultural chemicals, and machinery raised crop yields (output per acre). In turn, higher yields rendered acreage reduction programs a less and less effective way to control production. When the Democrats captured the White House in 1960, John F. Kennedy inherited a farm economy in which agricultural income was stagnant and carryover stocks of government-supported commodities were at all-time highs. Kennedy's election, however, did little to break the deadlock in agricultural policy. The battles of the previous decade had drawn sharp lines between the parties. As the standard-bearer of the Democrats, candidate Kennedy promised to raise farm income and cut program costs through a combination of high price supports and mandatory production controls.[36]

In March 1961, Kennedy introduced a long-range program for agriculture drafted by the new secretary of agriculture, Orville Freeman. The administration bill embraced marketing quotas rather than acreage allotments as the chief instrument to control output. Quotas would cut quantities sold rather than acres harvested and, therefore, overcome the problem of higher yields. Freeman also proposed a number of institutional changes in the administration of farm programs. In essence, the draft bill gave responsibility for policy to the executive and the secretary of agriculture, who, in conjunction with producer groups of various crops, would draft rules on marketing quotas and price supports. If the rules governing each crop were approved by two-thirds of farmers voting in a referendum, Congress would have sixty days to veto them before they became law.[37]

Clearly the new law, if enacted, would significantly reduce the role of Congress in agricultural policy. Secretary of Agriculture Freeman claimed that with the shift in policy authority, "Congress would be relieved of the onerous burden of. . .a multitude of separate proposals, commodity by commodity, season after season, under countless and

---

[35] *Kiplinger's Washington Letter*, February 1, 1958.
[36] Cochrane and Ryan, *American Farm Policy*, 40.
[37] Hadwiger and Talbot, *Pressures and Protests*, 18–19, 48–51.

fragmented pressures."[38] Democrats on the House Agriculture Committee as well as representatives of specialist producer groups such as the National Association of Wheat Growers (NAWG) agreed. As NAWG president Carl Bruns argued, "This bill, provides a constructive departure from the past when, because of political expediency, . . . legislation resulted in patching and repatching worn-out programs."[39] The Freeman Plan was a clear attempt to remove agriculture from the partisan wrangling in Congress and place it almost exclusively within the ambit of a Democratic-controlled USDA. At the same time, Freeman's proposal to devolve authority to a number of commodity organizations was the last attempt to create a sectorwide corporatist partnership in American agriculture.

Predictably, Republicans and the Farm Bureau opposed the effort to remove agricultural policy from congressional politics. Charles Hoeven, ranking Republican on the Agriculture Committee, was "greatly disturbed about the usurpation of legislative authority by the executive branch." Charles Shuman of the Farm Bureau, prone to hyperbole, argued, "This legislation . . . would make the Secretary of Agriculture . . . the most powerful agricultural man outside of the Iron Curtain."[40] Republicans and the Farm Bureau charged further that the secretary could easily transform the system of farmer committees responsible for policy formulation into a powerful political machine in national elections. But just as during the 1949 battle over the Brannan Plan, southern Democrats wavered, and the House Agriculture Committee ditched the Kennedy administration program. In July 1961, Congress passed a substitute farm bill. The Agricultural Act of 1961 abandoned the marketing quota provisions and, instead, enacted one-year, voluntary acreage-reduction programs for feed grains and wheat.[41]

The following year, the Kennedy administration again proposed mandatory production controls on wheat, feed grains, and dairy. The forces in agriculture aligned in the same manner they had for the past decade. Although the plan was supported by most Democrats and the National Farmers' Union, the Republicans stood solidly against it, and enough southern Democrats expressed dissatisfaction to stall the administration bill in committee. Once again, the Farm Bureau led the charge against production controls. In order to pass a bill before the 1962 midterm elections, the Kennedy administration jettisoned whole portions of its pro-

[38] Committee on Agriculture, House of Representatives, *Hearings before the House Agriculture Committee,* "Agricultural Act of 1961," 87th Cong., 1st sess., Serial E, 1961, 42.

[39] Ibid., 366.

[40] Ibid., 49, 271.

[41] *Congressional Quarterly Weekly Report,* April 28, 1961, 714; *Congressional Quarterly Almanac,* 1961, 104–18; Hadwiger and Talbot, *Pressures and Protests,* 60–66.

gram. The 1962 Food and Agriculture Act removed the mandatory control provisions for dairy and feed grains but retained them for wheat.[42] Before the system of strict production controls went into effect, however, the 1962 act offered wheat farmers the chance to vote on the plan in a referendum. After the Farm Bureau waged an intense public relations campaign urging farmers to vote no in the referendum, wheat farmers rejected the mandatory control program in May 1963.[43] It was a resounding defeat for the Kennedy administration.

Finding Common Ground: The New Politics of Agriculture

Kennedy and Freeman learned the same bitter lesson as Truman and Brannan in 1949 and Eisenhower and Benson in 1956: partisan aspirations for agriculture were impossible without congressional acquiescence, party unity, and a dominant farm organization supportive of administration policies. Subsequent legislative efforts would have to solve these impediments to policy making. In short, politicians had to adapt farm programs to the institutional constraints of agricultural policy in the United States.

Movement toward this end began in late 1963. Conditions in the wheat sector were becoming so critical that members of both parties realized that some program was needed for the 1964 crop. As Secretary Freeman of the USDA remarked, "It is clear . . . that the Congress is more receptive to a wheat program than it would have been last spring."[44] The question was, what kind of program? The events of the previous two years narrowed the scope of policy alternatives considerably.

Earlier, in 1961, Congress had passed an emergency bill to deal with a critical situation in the corn and feed grains sector. To cut production, the 1961 law offered participants price supports plus a direct payment if they cut between 20 and 50 percent of their acreage. The program was completely voluntary, but farmers who chose not to enroll received nothing. Surprisingly, the program was a success. In the Food and Agricultural Act of 1962, the voluntary feed grains program was continued, but the price

[42] *Congressional Quarterly Almanac*, 1962, 94–124; Cochrane and Ryan, *American Farm Policy*, 42, 80; Hadwiger and Talbot, *Pressures and Protests*, chaps. 7–10.

[43] "Supply Management Faces Test in Wheat Referendum," *Congressional Quarterly Weekly Report*, May 17, 1963, 756–58; "Wheat Farmers Reject Kennedy Control Plan," *Congressional Quarterly Weekly Report*, May 24, 1963, 795–96. As Hansen describes, "Through a skillful exploitation of typically low turnout, the American Farm Bureau Federation had a engineered a dramatic setback for the Kennedy administration farm program." Hansen, *Gaining Access*, 150; Hadwiger and Talbot, *Pressures and Protests*, chap. 11.

[44] "President Johnson to Offer Wheat Control Bill," *Wall Street Journal*, December 11, 1963, 7.

support rate was dropped to world levels, with the difference made up with a direct payment. As Cochrane points out, the combination of support prices at world levels and direct income payments "had important implications. It permitted export crops to move into international markets without subsidy; it provided a mechanism for holding down prices to the domestic consumer; and it provided a means for supporting producers' incomes." It was, in essence, a voluntary version of the Brannan Plan.[45]

The remarkable success of the feed grains program convinced Democratic lawmakers that farmers who had rejected mandatory controls might accept a voluntary acreage-reduction program patterned after the one for corn. In 1963, Representative George McGovern introduced a voluntary wheat program that drew immediate support from Plains State Republicans on the House Agriculture Committee. However, the bill still faced an uphill battle in Congress. To secure passage of the voluntary wheat plan, Democratic leaders added a cotton provision that swung southern delegations behind the bill. In addition, Lyndon Johnson personally lobbied twenty-five or thirty wavering Democrats to hold the party line. Finally, and most important, President Johnson supported efforts by urban, liberal Democrats to link passage of the farm bill with a vote on permanent food stamp legislation on the House floor. The now famous urban-rural logroll was critical to the passage of the 1964 act and marked a new turn in the politics of agriculture.[46]

In 1965, Congress incorporated the accomplishments of the previous year into a new omnibus farm bill. For field crops such as wheat, cotton, and corn, the 1965 bill reaffirmed the principle of voluntary production adjustment and direct payments. At the same time, commodities such as dairy, sugar, tobacco, and peanuts retained their traditional dependence on marketing quotas and price supports. And as in 1964, urban support for the farm bill was critical, this time in exchange for rural votes on the repeal of Section 14(b) of the Taft-Hartley Act. The 1965 Food and Agriculture Act also authorized commodity programs for four years and gave the secretary of agriculture discretionary authority to adjust program provisions along with changes in the farm economy.[47]

Unlike the debate over delegation in 1961, now it was the farm-state lawmakers themselves who favored a multiyear agriculture bill. The USDA initially proposed a two-year life span for the commodity titles of the farm bill, but the House Agriculture Committee insisted on a four-

---

[45] Cochrane and Ryan, *American Farm Policy*, 81; Hadwiger and Talbot, *Pressures and Protests*, 46–48.

[46] *Congressional Quarterly Almanac*, 1964, 98; Hansen, *Gaining Access*, 152–53, 171–72.

[47] Cochrane and Ryan, *American Farm Policy*, 81–82, 162–63; Hansen, *Gaining Access*, 154, 172.

year authorization. Rural members were concerned about the new politics of agriculture: declining rural representation in Congress, rising program costs, and increased influence of urban representatives in farm policy decisions prompted a shift in attitudes on the House Agriculture Committee. As one farm leader told the committee, "We are concerned that other people would begin to write our agricultural policies other than this committee and the farmers. . . . [N]ow is the time to work out the best program possible and to get a longer extension than just two years." Representative Bob Dole of Kansas, one of nineteen Republicans to vote for the 1965 act, agreed: "There is no question . . . that the farm representation is a very minor group in the Congress. . . . [T]here could be more protection with a longer range program."[48]

In the Food and Agriculture Act of 1965, Congress adapted farm policy to the institutional realities of U.S. agricultural politics. Unable to unite farm programs with party politics, debates over policy were reduced to their lowest common denominator: individual commodities. Congress learned the hard way that comprehensive proposals advocated in party platforms and championed by general farm organizations—high supports, the Brannan Plan, flexible supports, mandatory controls—only exacerbated tensions between parties, regions, and producers of various commodities.

The policy process in agriculture reflected these changes. By the time Congress passed the 1965 act, specialty commodity organizations rather than the general farm organizations increasingly became ascendant in the representation of agricultural interests.[49] Although efforts by commodity organizations to assume a larger role in farm policy began in the late 1950s, commodity groups could not always overcome partisan conflicts and forge a cooperative logroll.[50] Once voluntary programs introduced a new bipartisanship in farm policy, commodity representation flourished. By virtue of their relatively homogeneous membership, commodity groups could present the Agriculture Committees with a clear and unified view toward policy in a manner that the general farm organizations could not.[51]

[48] Committee on Agriculture, House of Representatives, *Hearings before the House Agriculture Committee, Subcommittee on Livestock and Feed Grains and Subcommittee on Wheat,* "Wheat and Feed Grains," 89th Cong., 1st sess., Serial J, 1965, 152–63; 202–9.

[49] The increasing compartmentalization of farm policy in committee subcommittees was identified earlier in the decade by Jones, "Representation in Congress," 258–67.

[50] In 1957, the National Conference of Commodity Organizations brought sixteen groups together in a loose federation of producer groups. Hoping to occupy a pragmatic, middle ground between the Farm Bureau and the Farmers' Union, the NCCO proved short-lived. Hansen, *Gaining Access,* 174–75.

[51] Ibid.

Put differently, from the perspective of agricultural interests, farm policy alternatives in the 1940s and 1950s were zero-sum. High price supports and mandatory acreage controls, as favored by producers of most field crops (except feed grains), raised input prices for producers of livestock. With both the costs and the benefits of agricultural subsidies concentrated among producers of different commodities, interest group conflicts routinely foiled partisan aspirations to establish electoral links with farmers. The 1965 act instead embraced a less ambitious set of goals. Voluntary programs designed for individual commodities transformed farm policy into positive-sum terms. Direct payments for one set of producers did not threaten the profitability of other commodities. Instead, policy costs were subsequently distributed widely among taxpayers. This dampened partisan conflicts over policy and ushered in a new politics of agriculture where specialized commodity groups rather than general farm organizations took the lead in the representation of agricultural interests before the government.

The political change in agricultural policy after 1965 is illustrated in figure 4.1. An analysis of roll call votes on agricultural measures in the House of Representatives between 1945 and 1980 indicates that partisanship declined after the policy shift of the mid-1960s. Figure 4.1 utilizes two common measures of party conflict. The mean party difference, indicated by the line graph, measures the absolute value of the difference in the proportion of each party voting in the affirmative and is computed on a scale of one hundred.[52] The percentage of party votes, indicated by the bar graph, measures the proportion of votes in which a majority of one party voted against the majority of the other party. Together, the percentage of party votes and the mean party difference illustrate, respectively, the frequency and intensity of party conflict.[53]

Between 1945 and 1964, as described earlier, both parties tried unsuccessfully to secure farm votes through agricultural programs. Partisan conflict over agricultural policy was frequent and intense during this period. As indicated in figure 4.1, party votes accounted for more than half of all agricultural votes during the 1945–1964 period. The mean party difference on agricultural roll calls between 1945 and 1964 was 43.7. As Wilson pointed out in his 1977 study, the recurrent partisan conflict over agriculture challenges the view espoused by capture theorists that farm policy was the product of consensus politics among farm leaders and their representatives on the House and Senate Agriculture Committees.[54]

[52] For instance, if 100 percent of Democrats vote in favor and 0 percent of Republicans vote in favor (i.e., 100 percent against), then the mean party difference is 100 (100 − 0).

[53] The data set for figure 4.1 excludes consensual votes, that is, votes with majorities of 90 percent or more. Rohde, *Parties and Leaders in the Postreform House*, 8–9, 200.

[54] Wilson, *Special Interests and Policymaking*, 139.

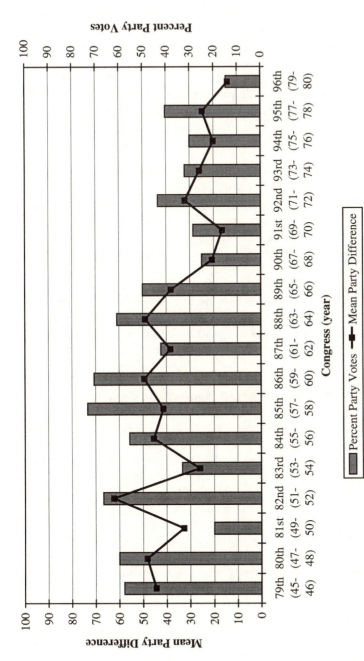

Figure 4.1 Mean Party Difference and Party Votes in Agriculture, 1945–1980
Note: N = 445, consensual votes excluded.
Source: Congressional Quarterly, *Congressional Quarterly Almanac,* various years.

Notice, however, that partisanship declined considerably after the failed wheat referendum in 1963 and the successful passage of a wheat-cotton bill in 1964. Both the mean party difference and the percentage of party votes decreased during the remainder of the 1960s and remained at low levels through the 1970s. Between 1965 and 1980, party votes accounted for only a third of all votes on agriculture. For the 1965 to 1980 period, the mean party difference on agricultural roll call votes was much lower as well (24.0). Once Congress removed the source of economic conflict among groups of producers, the partisan conflict over policy abated.[55]

The policy developments of the 1960s established three pillars of the agricultural welfare state. First, the financial burden of farm policy rested predominantly on the taxpayer, rather than the consumer. Second, commodity prices dropped to world levels, increasing the competitiveness of U.S. agricultural exports abroad. Third, food stamps subsidized increased domestic consumption and provided important political support for agriculture among urban members of Congress. But just as a long-term farm program finally took shape in the United States, the inexorable shift of labor out of agriculture began to have noticeable political consequences. As rural representation in Congress declined, farmers and their representatives were forced into a series of coalitions and compromises with the growing number of urban and suburban representatives in Congress.

Coalition Politics and the U.S. Agricultural Welfare State

Farm legislation in the 1970s reflected a changing political environment in Congress: agriculture was losing its power to control the farm policy agenda. Supreme Court decisions in the 1960s forced states to reapportion House seats more equitably. Following the 1970 census, farm representation in Congress declined from 12 percent to 3 percent of House seats.[56] Meanwhile, congressional reforms centralized authority in the House leadership, increased the power of the House Democratic Caucus, and gave subcommittees greater independence in the legislative process. These reforms weakened the autonomy of individual committees.[57] As a result of these two trends, growing numbers of urban and suburban members of Congress increasingly left their mark on federal farm programs.

[55] It is here where I diverge from Wilson, who sees the conflict over agriculture as one driven by ideological differences. The decline in partisanship after 1965 suggests that constituency interests in policy played a larger role than ideology. Ibid., 132, 148.

[56] McCubbins and Schwartz, "Congress, the Courts, and Public Policy," 388–415; Hansen, *Gaining Access*, 167.

[57] Rohde, *Parties and Leaders in the Postreform House*, 17–39.

When discussion of a new farm bill began in 1970, House Agriculture Committee chairman Bob Poage of Texas decided to consider both farm legislation and food stamps at the same time. Whereas coalition formation around agricultural policy was largely ad hoc in the 1960s, now the deal between rural and urban members was rather explicit.[58] Meanwhile, critics of farm programs proposed to limit the size of federal payments to individuals. These proposals caused consternation among farm organizations. As Hansen documents, "By the time the 1970 Agriculture Act came to the floor, none of the major farm organizations supported it."[59] Despite their protestations, farm groups were unable to prevent Congress passing a $55,000 cap on government payments per crop.[60]

Scrutiny of the costs of federal commodity programs continued with the 1973 Agriculture and Consumer Protection Act. Against the backdrop of high inflation, consumer interests waged a public campaign against federal farm programs. On the first day of hearings for the 1973 farm bill, Senate Agriculture Committee chairman Herman Talmadge informed his colleagues that "drafting new farm legislation this year comes at what is perhaps the poorest possible . . . political moment." Talmadge went on to describe the new, hostile environment surrounding agricultural politics in Congress: "The U.S. House of Representatives has just been redistricted in such a way that the vast majority of its membership is from large cities and their suburbs. Food prices are higher than they have been in some time, and many consumers are angry. The major metropolitan newspapers have begun what appears to be a massive campaign . . . to end the farm program. The President of the United States indicates that he wants the government off the farm."[61] Both agricultural committees in Congress realized the 1973 legislation would have to satisfy a larger constituency beyond only farmers.

The major farm organizations, general and commodity-specific, favored an extension of the 1970 Agriculture Act. But farm-state lawmakers soon ruled out an extension as a possibility. Building public concern over inflation drew attention to the effects of federal commodity programs, and Richard Nixon, in his address to the nation on economic stabilization, promised to veto farm legislation if it contributed to rising food prices.[62] Facing external pressure to reduce the cost of farm programs for consumers, the House Agriculture Committee approved a system of target prices and deficiency payments for the major field crops like cotton,

[58] Ferejohn, "Logrolling in an Institutional Context," 235–37; Barton, "Coalition-Building in the United States House of Representatives," 141–61.

[59] Hansen, *Gaining Access*, 210.

[60] Melcher quoted in *Congressional Quarterly Almanac* 26 (1970): 638.

[61] Talmadge quoted in *Congressional Quarterly Almanac* 29 (1973): 290.

[62] Ibid.

wheat, and corn. Under this scheme, farmers received payment from the government only when market prices fell below the target price. This change linked program payments more closely to market conditions, and under the high commodity prices of the early 1970s farmers received no deficiency payments, bringing farm program costs down considerably. In addition, the 1973 legislation significantly lowered the caps of farm program payments. Over the vigorous opposition of cotton state representatives, Congress changed the limit from $55,000 per individual *per crop* to a flat subsidy ceiling of $20,000 for each farmer.[63]

Perhaps the most dramatic evidence of the new political realities in agriculture came in 1975 when House Agriculture Committee chairman Bob Poage became one of three old guard committee chairs purged by the Democratic Caucus. According to Michael Lyons and Marcia Taylor, "What did trouble many Democratic members about Poage was . . . what they saw as unsympathetic and anachronistic attitudes toward consumers and toward the Food Stamp Program." Poage lost his chairmanship by three votes and would have retained control "had he not antagonized the 75 House Democratic freshman."[64] The purge not only underscored the new institutional environment in the postreform Congress but also exemplified how agricultural policy served a much wider constituency than just farmers.

In fact, during the 1970s farmers ceased to be the principal clientele of the USDA. As indicated in figure 4.2, the share of USDA expenditures devoted to nutrition increased steadily during the 1970s. Accounting for only 11 percent of USDA outlays in 1970, by 1980 nutrition programs consumed 40 percent of the annual budget for the Department of Agriculture. Over the same period, the portion of the USDA budget spent on farm subsidies and agricultural research decreased from 60 percent in 1970 to 25 percent in 1980.

Agricultural policy making in the 1970s revealed that lawmakers depended heavily on urban and suburban politicians in order to secure passage of a farm bill. But the new coalition politics in agriculture took its toll. With each deal made, rural members of Congress incrementally surrendered portions of their autonomy over agricultural policy. In the words of one senior member of the House Agriculture Committee interviewed in the mid-1970s, "It has gotten harder and harder to pass farm bills on the floor, and the committee has had to compromise farther and farther to pick up the votes it needs."[65]

[63] Lyons and Taylor, "Farm Politics in Transition," 139; Bowers, Rasmussen, and Baker, *History of Agricultural Price Support and Adjustment Programs*, 27–31; *Congressional Quarterly Almanac* 29 (1973): 295–307.

[64] Lyons and Taylor, "Farm Politics in Transition," 134.

[65] Ibid., 141.

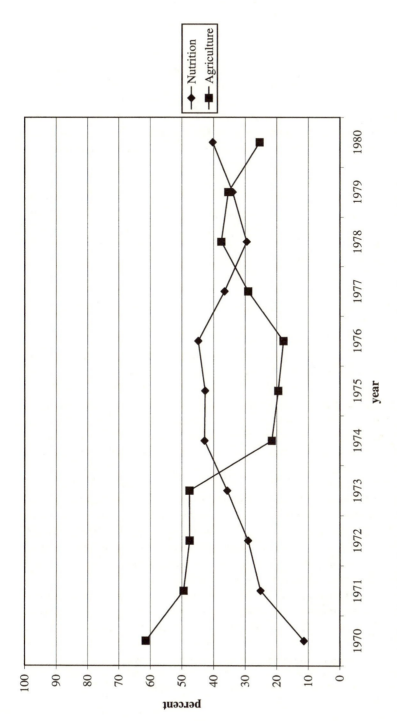

Figure 4.2 Outlays for Agriculture and Nutrition Programs as a Percentage of Total USDA Expenditures, 1970–1980
Source: Office of Management and Budget, *Historical Tables, Budget of the United States Government, Fiscal Year 1999.*

JAPAN

Postwar agricultural policy in Japan evolved within a much different institutional environment than in the United States. Bolstered by a powerful alliance between agricultural cooperatives and conservative politicians, the Japanese agricultural welfare state that emerged in the 1950s and 1960s combined government-controlled markets with generous pork-barrel projects. This policy combination reflected the political basis of agricultural policy in Japan. While the tightly controlled system of rice collection and distribution cemented the role of the cooperatives as the dominant organization in rural Japan, the distribution of government funds through rural pork-barrel projects solidified the electoral dominance of the Liberal Democratic Party, (LDP). This overlap of interests between the LDP and the cooperatives sustained the agricultural welfare state in the face of profound economic and social changes in rural Japan.

The Political and Economic Reconstruction of Rural Japan

The origins of this political alliance between farmers and conservative politicians can be found in the Occupation period. To achieve the twin goals of political democratization and economic reconstruction, officials of the General Headquarters for the Supreme Commander for the Allied Powers (SCAP) pursued two contradictory strategies. In the name of democratization, Occupation authorities *eradicated* existing institutions they believed were responsible for the rise of authoritarianism and replaced them with new forms of social, economic, and political organization. At the same time, however, SCAP often *resurrected* institutions dating from before the war believed to be essential for economic recovery.[66] This contradiction was clearly evident in rural Japan, where Occupation officials oversaw both the complete transformation of land tenure relations and the reconstruction of the wartime cooperative system as the centerpiece of government food control. Together, the land reforms and the rise of a reconstructed Nokyo laid the institutional groundwork for the political power of farmers in postwar Japan.

Next to the Constitution, the postwar land reforms stand as one of the most important innovations of the early Occupation period. Officials in the SCAP, including General MacArthur himself, attributed part of the

---

[66] There is a complex and interesting debate on the tension between the earlier, reforming, and democratic phase of the Occupation and the latter, conservative, or "reverse course" period of the Occupation. See, for example, Ward, "Conclusion," 405–14. On postwar continuity with prewar institutions, see Dower, "The Useful War," 49–70.

rise of authoritarianism in Japan to the system of land tenancy. Although the power of landlords had been weakened by the wartime controls on agricultural production, SCAP officials feared landowners would return to prominence in rural Japan. Because a revived tenancy system could lead to a relapse of authoritarianism or a communist insurgency among landless farmers, SCAP viewed land reforms as critical to the democratization of rural Japan.[67]

In late 1945, bureaucrats in the Ministry of Agriculture submitted a land reform bill to the Diet that abolished rents-in-kind and replaced them with their money equivalent. The bill also stipulated that all land held by absentee landlords and land held by resident landlords in excess of 5 hectares (around 12.5 acres) should be transferred to the current tenants. Finally, a system of local land committees, with equal representation given to landlords and tenants, would oversee the implementation of the reform measures.[68] Arguing that the new law did not go far enough to redistribute farmland, SCAP pressed the Ministry of Agriculture to draft a second land reform law. Passed in October 1946, the second law limited landholdings of all resident landlords to 3 hectares (around 7.5 acres). Land held in excess of this limit would be purchased by the government and sold to tenants.[69]

Once implemented, the second land reform led to a dramatic restructuring of landholdings in rural Japan. At war's end, tenants cultivated 45 percent of arable land. By 1950, tenants cultivated only 10 percent of arable land. In the space of a few short years, the number of farm families that owned 90 percent or more of their land increased from 1.7 million to 3.8 million.[70]

The creation of an agricultural sector composed of small landholders profoundly weakened the socialist farm union movement in Japan. Membership in the unions, which were a product of tenant unrest in the 1930s, climbed to one million farmers after the war amid demands for reforms of the tenancy system. Farm union power, however, was a victim of its own success. As Fukutake argues, "With the completion of the land reform, the Farmers' Unions lost their immediate campaign objective and began to disintegrate."[71] Political divisions between socialists and communists tore the organization apart in the late 1940s, and union membership declined.

[67] Dore, *Land Reform in Japan*, 131–32.

[68] Ibid., 133–35.

[69] Ibid., 137–41; "Rural Land Reform in Japan: Its Legislative Development," *Monthly Circular*, no. 264 (November 1951): 7–11.

[70] Ogura, *Can Japanese Agriculture Survive?* 747–48.

[71] Fukutake, *Japanese Rural Society*, 181.

The reforms, in other words, transformed radical and landless peasants into conservative landowners. Political demands shifted from the redistribution of land to concerns over prices, access to productivity-increasing inputs, and improvements in the quality of rural life. With the reconstruction of the cooperative system by Occupation authorities in the late 1940s, a private organization of farmers transmitted these conservative tendencies into political power.

SCAP officials confronted a rural economy in shambles, and serious food shortages threatened inflation, black markets, and civil unrest. Because economic reconstruction depended on adequate supplies of rice and other staples, Occupation officials continued the wartime food control system. Farmers were required to deliver production quotas to government food agencies. As in the wartime food control system, agricultural cooperatives performed critical functions: cooperatives assigned production quotas to farmers, collected rice at harvest, and delivered farm produce to government food control agencies.[72]

Despite this continuity in function, Occupation authorities did change the legal standing of the cooperatives. During the war, the cooperatives were part of the Imperial Agricultural Association (IAA). As an instrument of government control over agriculture during the war, the IAA was tainted by authoritarianism in the eyes of SCAP officials, and in 1947 Occupation authorities ordered its dissolution. Under the Agricultural Cooperative Association Law passed in December of that year, local cooperatives were reconstituted as a private, voluntary organization. Despite this new legal authority, few practical changes occurred. Critically, the cooperatives retained their central role in the food control system and took over the membership, assets, and operations of their wartime predecessors.[73]

SCAP, in essence, created a private farm organization that possessed tremendous organizational advantages by virtue of its role in government policy. Although farmers could deliver their rice to either cooperatives or licensed rice dealers, the vast majority utilized the cooperatives in which they were now stakeholders. In 1948, over twelve thousand cooperatives received deliveries from roughly 5.5 million farm households. Meanwhile, only 1,718 commercial dealers received official rice deliveries from a mere 214,000 farm households. By 1950, cooperative dominance of the food control system was clear; cooperatives handled 94 percent of staple food collection. This achievement is even more re-

---

[72] Johnston, *Japanese Food Management*, 213–37; Ogura, *Agricultural Development in Modern Japan*, 201–10.

[73] SCAP, Natural Resources Section, *Agricultural Programs in Japan, 1945–51*, 1952, 37; Junnosuke, *Postwar Politics in Japan*, 258–59.

markable when compared with prewar levels of cooperative food deliveries. In 1937, for example, cooperatives handled only a third of official rice deliveries for the government.[74]

As the principal outlet for government-controlled rice, the cooperatives received handling, storage, and transportation fees. In addition, the cooperative banks collected government payments received by producers. These government transfers, in turn, fueled the expansion of cooperative activities in other areas. By 1950, Nokyo handled 47 percent of all fertilizer sales, while 60 percent of farm-sector savings resided in the cooperative's banking arm, Norin Chukin. According to a 1951 SCAP publication, "In most villages, general-purpose cooperatives now provide the primary credit, marketing, purchasing, processing, and other essential services used by farmers." With 90 percent of all farm households represented by at least one cooperative member, the reconstituted cooperative association was the most important organization in rural Japan.[75]

As a *private* organization, however, Nokyo also served as the chief *political* representative of farmers in policy matters. For instance, when agricultural prices declined as a result of the Dodge Line in 1949, the cooperatives took the lead in petitioning the government for rural relief.[76] In 1953, Nokyo pressure in the Diet prompted the cabinet to create a Rice Price Deliberation Council composed of Nokyo representatives, consumer groups, politicians, and academics. Charged with the responsibility to evaluate government price policy, the council provided Nokyo with a forum within which to press for higher prices. Creation of the council in 1953 marked the beginning of the annual struggle over prices that would characterize Japanese agricultural politics in the years to come.[77]

The Creation of a Rural Political Machine

With the end of Occupation in 1952, a myriad of political parties competed for supremacy in Japanese politics. Given the sizable proportion of Japanese workers engaged in agriculture, it is not surprising that those politicians most adept at capturing the political allegiance of farmers and cooperatives gained control of the government. By 1955, the leaders of

[74] Donnelly, "Political Management of Japan's Rice Economy," 347–51; Moore, *Japanese Agriculture*, 141–49.

[75] SCAP, *Agricultural Programs in Japan, 1945–51*, 114–16; Dore, *Land Reform in Japan*, 282–87.

[76] In late 1948, General MacArthur announced a series of deflationary policies known collectively as the *Dodge Line*. SCAP imposed austerity measures on government spending, such as agricultural subsidies, and implemented fiscal policies to halt inflation.

[77] Donnelly, "Political Management of Japan's Rice Economy," 327–30.

the LDP had consummated a political marriage with Nokyo that led to a rapid expansion of the Japanese agricultural welfare state.

Japanese politics in the ten years after World War II was marked by constant maneuverings among factions competing for political ascendancy. In November 1945, leaders of the prewar Seiyukai and Minseito established two conservative parties, the Japan Liberal Party and the Japan Progressive Party. Meanwhile, several members of the prewar and wartime cooperative movement in rural Japan established the Cooperative Party, aligned somewhere on the Center-Right of the political spectrum. On the Left, veterans of the prewar farmer, labor, and socialist movements banded together to the Japan Socialist Party. In addition, several former political prisoners founded the Japan Communist Party in October 1945.[78]

Each of these postwar political parties was little more than a collection of factions. On the Right, divisions fell along personal political affiliations as well as between individuals who had served as former bureaucrats and those who had been active in party politics before the war. On the Left, the Japan Socialist Party was also organized along personal factions, but it suffered more generally from ideological divisions between the left and right wings of the party.[79] Because of factional competition, a problem exacerbated by SCAP-directed purges of prominent politicians for their complicity with the wartime regime, the postwar political parties were weak and fragmented. With no single party able to secure an outright majority, a series of unstable coalition governments ruled Japan through the early 1950s.[80]

It was during this period of profound political instability that the agricultural cooperatives established themselves as an adept political force at the grass roots. According to Junnosuke, "As the largest organization in the countryside, Nokyo possessed the ability to mobilize votes and exhibited its influence in national as well as local elections. There were frequent instances in which the position taken by Nokyo determined the success or failure of a given candidate. Furthermore, Nokyo executives made use of their vote-gathering capacities to enter and win national and local elections."[81] Such effective vote mobilization at the local level is echoed by Ronald Dore, who remarks that "even the mere word, spread around the village, that . . . the Co-operative president . . . 'is for [a given

[78] Junnosuke, *Postwar Politics in Japan*, 73–92.

[79] Ibid., 277–84; Tani, "The Japan Socialist Party before the Mid-1960s," 79–90.

[80] Baerwald, *The Purge of Japanese Leaders under the Occupation*; Junnosuke, *Postwar Politics in Japan*, 92–96, 98–167; Curtis, *The Japanese Way of Politics*, 4–14.

[81] Junnosuke, *Postwar Politics in Japan*, 259.

candidate]' . . . may influence . . . votes."[82] In short, cooperatives became an essential component of every rural politician's reelection constituency.

In order to receive the political support of the local cooperative, however, politicians had to distinguish themselves as advocates of agricultural interests. The surest way to secure the endorsement of Nokyo officials was through government largesse. Funds for paddy reconstruction, irrigation, and other pork-barrel projects carried out through the local cooperative were critical for rural political success.

In the early years after the Occupation, conservative politicians clearly outdistanced their socialist rivals at channeling government resources to rural Japan. Between 1949 and 1953, years of government rule by conservative coalitions, agricultural expenditures increased from 5.9 to 16.6 percent of the national budget. Direct subsidies and grants accounted for 50 percent of the Ministry of Agriculture budget.[83] Hirokawa Kozen, minister of agriculture under the third Yoshida cabinet (1949–1952) used his control over pork-barrel projects to reward political allies. According to Michael Donnelly, "By carefully manipulating the granting of subsidies according to partisan interests, Hirokawa helped create solid party foundations for the Liberals in rural areas."[84] Cooperatives, of course, were major beneficiaries of Hirokawa's largesse. The 1951 Agriculture, Forestry, and Fisheries Cooperative Reconstruction Law, for example, bailed out thousands of cooperatives suffering from the deflationary policies of the Dodge Line. Socialist politicians were either unwilling to engage in pork-barrel politics for ideological reasons or, lacking access to the centers of power, unable to secure government funds for rural constituents.[85]

In exchange for government subsidies, conservative politicians received overwhelming support from rural voters. A 1952 opinion poll reported that 77 percent of farmers favored the two conservative parties over their socialist rivals.[86] By the time the various postwar parties combined in 1955 into the Liberal Democratic Party on the Right and the Japan Socialist Party on the Left, the cooperative associations were a central part of the conservatives' electoral strategy and a main reason for subsequent LDP political success in rural Japan. As the LDP-Nokyo alliance solidified

---

[82] Dore, *Land Reform in Japan*, 415.

[83] Donnelly, "Political Management of Japan's Rice Economy," 406–7.

[84] Ibid., 408.

[85] Ogura, *Can Japanese Agriculture Survive?* 288; Cole, Totten, and Uyehara, *Socialist Parties in Postwar Japan*, 392–93. Tani recounts the rise of former prime minister Tanaka Kakui in Niigata. Although Niigata was a socialist stronghold after World War II, Tanaka established LDP dominance there by proving himself more adept at securing government pork than his socialist rival Miyake Soichi. See Tani, "The Japan Socialist Party before the Mid-1960s," 94.

[86] Flanagan et al., *The Japanese Voter*, 58.

over the next decade, rice price supports rose steadily, as did the subsidies for local public works projects. When disputes over policy arose, they were resolved within the complex policy apparatus of the LDP. As a result, LDP leaders retained control over important policy decisions and provided agricultural programs with political protection—despite profound economic and demographic changes in the farm sector.

The Japanese Agricultural Welfare State

The consolidation of party politics into a two-party system and the electoral dominance of the LDP is referred to by some Japanese scholars as the *1955 System*.[87] Significantly, this year also marks important developments in agricultural policy and politics. In 1955, an amendment to the Food Control Law strengthened the role of Nokyo in the administration of rice policy. It also marked the transition in agricultural politics from a focus on food production and economic recovery to a new politics of income support and parity between agriculture and the industrial sectors of the economy. At the same time, Nokyo solidified its ties with the LDP policy machinery, which emerged as an important locus of decision making and conflict resolution in agricultural matters.

Not every conservative politician embraced the idea of government control over the rice economy or Nokyo's prominence in rural affairs. Kono Ichiro, who served as minister of agriculture in the mid-1950s and again in the early 1960s, was a critic of both the food control system and Nokyo's growing political influence. When Kono first became minister in 1954, he advocated ending the food control system as a device to curb black markets and relieve a major burden on the government budget. However, Kono faced strong opposition from other members in his cabinet, and with elections scheduled a few months later, he was forced to abandon his plan for rice decontrol.[88]

With the decontrol option foreclosed for political reasons, the government explored ways to strengthen the existing rice collection system. Using a plan proposed by Ishii Einosuke, the president of the National Federation of Agricultural Marketing Cooperatives, Kono reluctantly agreed to a new system of rice control whereby farmers would sign advance delivery contracts with their local cooperative.[89] Beginning in 1955, farmers who signed contracts received a 20 percent advance payment, a

---

[87] Junnosuke, "The 1955 System," 34–54.
[88] Donnelly, "Political Management of Japan's Rice Economy," 430, 435–37.
[89] Ibid., 431–34, 437–39; Ogura, *Can Japanese Agriculture Survive?* 206.

signing bonus, and a 15 percent tax break on their payments. The cooperative, in turn, signed a delivery contract with the government and received a similar set of bonuses and advance payments. Farmers could choose how much rice to sell, but with the government still the only official purchaser of rice, the new subscription system offered a package of incentives that made black market sales less attractive to the farmer. Success of the new collection system hinged on the local cooperative, and its introduction in 1955 firmly entrenched Nokyo at the center of the rice economy.[90]

But in a direct challenge to Nokyo's political and economic power, Kono supported a plan in 1956 to create a rival agricultural organization in rural Japan. Five years earlier, the government created a network of local farmer committees responsible for a number of policy functions. Under the plan announced in 1956, the committees would reorganize into a national federation of farmers' associations that would represent agricultural interests before the government, assist in agricultural extension activities, and operate some credit and insurance operations. In effect, the plan would limit Nokyo to certain economic activities and leave political functions such as participation on government advisory boards to the new farmer associations. For Kono, an ambitious politician, the farmers' associations would create a strong electoral machine for the LDP in rural Japan and provide a counterweight to the influence of the massive agricultural bureaucracy.[91]

From the perspective of Nokyo, however, the proposed farmers' association posed a direct challenge to the position currently enjoyed by the cooperatives in the farm economy and electoral politics. According to Dore, the proposal "would have dealt a crippling blow to the cooperative system."[92] Thus, Nokyo waged a bitter campaign against the plan, arguing that the Ministry of Agriculture sought to re-create the wartime system of agricultural associations controlled by the government. In addition, Nokyo political pressure secured the support of LDP members in the Upper House who faced reelection in summer 1956. When the LDP Policy Committee officially denounced the proposal, Kono abandoned his plan. Nokyo success revealed, according to Dore, "that the cooperative organization . . . is able to exert sufficient influence on rural voters to constitute an extremely strong pressure group capable of influencing government policy."[93]

---

[90] *Monthly Circular*, no. 306 (May 1955): 32; *Monthly Circular*, no. 311 (October 1955): 32.

[91] Dore, *Land Reform in Japan*, 425–28.

[92] Ibid., 429.

[93] Ibid., 431.

With Nokyo's position intact and Japan on the verge of sustained industrial growth, the agricultural cooperatives focused increasing political attention on the government price of rice. Debates over prices, however, often centered on how the government calculated a "fair" return and adequate income.[94] During the 1950s, Nokyo demanded higher government prices that reflected increases in rice production costs and provided income parity with rising industrial wages. Under the production cost and income compensation formula announced in 1960, government rice prices included not only the cost of capital goods such as fertilizers but also the cost of unpaid family labor, calculated according to prevailing industrial wages. This change in the production cost formula pegged rice prices to the steadily rising wages paid in manufacturing and other industrial sectors.[95]

When the government enumerated a set of guiding principles for agricultural policy in 1961, the core elements of the new rice calculation method were codified futher. Noting the widening gap in the "livelihood . . . between farming . . . and non-farming people," the preamble of the 1961 Agricultural Basic Law pledged that "it belongs to the responsibility of our nation to enable the farming population to enjoy a . . . livelihood well-balanced with the other strata of the nation." The Basic Law, in turn, provided the statutory basis for the Japanese agricultural welfare state in the 1960s.[96]

Passage of the Basic Law marked the official embrace of income parity as the goal of agricultural policy. During the 1960s, the annual determination of producer prices for rice, the most important contributor to farm income, became the focal point of agricultural policy and politics in Japan. Every spring, government bureaucrats and Nokyo officials squared off over rice prices for the coming year.[97] While cabinet negotiations established a single government price recommendation, Nokyo officials mobilized prefectural and local cooperative associations into a massive political movement. As the Rice Price Deliberation Council considered various proposals, farmers waged a constant campaign of letter writing, petitions, and demonstrations, culminating in large protests in the streets of Tokyo. The number of participants in Nokyo rallies grew steadily from three thousand delegates in 1961 to sixteen thousand in 1966.[98]

[94] Ogura, *Agricultural Development in Modern Japan*, 208.

[95] Ibid.; *Monthly Circular*, no. 333 (August 1957): 27; Donnelly, "Political Management of Japan's Rice Economy," 476–82.

[96] Ogura, *Can Japanese Agriculture Survive?* 446.

[97] For a summary of the rice pricing season, see Donnelly, "Setting the Price of Rice," 161–67.

[98] Ibid., 169, 172, 182.

As Nokyo became more outspoken in its policy demands, the rice issue took on greater political salience for the majority LDP. In 1963, more than two hundred rural LDP backbenchers formed an ad hoc political organization around the rice issue.[99] Outspoken in their demands for higher rice prices, these rural Dietmen often joined Nokyo delegates in street rallies and demonstrations. At the same time, the Rice Council became equally politicized and lost its capacity to mediate among diverse interests. With the Rice Council deadlocked, the LDP leadership emerged as the final arbiter in rice price decision making.[100] Party leaders with expertise in agricultural policy determined the LDP price position within the internal policy apparatus of the party, the Policy Affairs Research Council (PARC). Negotiations between party leaders[101] and government officials followed in which a final price—usually higher than what the government bureaucrats offered but less than what the cooperatives demanded—was formally agreed upon.

As the LDP assumed a larger role in policy matters, politicians and Ministry of Agriculture bureaucrats resisted efforts by the Ministry of Finance to rein in agricultural expenditures. According to John Campbell, LDP influence in budget decisions made it increasingly difficult for Finance officials "to defend micro budgeting decision against penetration by the line ministry–interest group–PARC division alliances." During the early 1960s, Campbell notes, "groups of politicians, now beginning to work closely with spending ministries and clientele groups, continued to press for more and more spending on particularistic programs. . . . the rice subsidy is a case in point."[102] This assessment is borne out by the dramatic rise in agricultural expenditures. Between 1960 and 1970, the general account budget of the Ministry of Agriculture, Forestry, and Fisheries (MAFF) increased in real terms by 267 percent, nearly twice as fast as overall government expenditures.[103]

A large portion of this increase can be attributed to rice support policies. Between 1960 and 1978, the government price for rice more than

[99] Ibid., 172–73.

[100] This transition was marked by the change in the rice-pricing season in 1961. Formerly, the Rice Council was the final step in setting the price of rice. After an acrimonious pricing season in 1961, several council members resigned. The following year, LDP negotiations on prices occurred *after* the Rice Council met, signifying the increased role of party leaders in the pricing process. Ibid., 173–75.

[101] LDP or party leaders included the LDP secretary-general, the chairman of the Policy Affairs Research Council, and the party's Executive Council.

[102] Campbell, *Contemporary Japanese Budget Politics*, 268.

[103] For MAFF expenditures, see Ogura, *Can Japanese Agriculture Survive?* 700, and MAFF, *Statistical Yearbook, 1973*, 580. For overall general account budget and GDP deflator, see IMF, *International Financial Statistics Yearbook, 1990*, 444–45.

doubled, a 38 percent increase in real terms.[104] Under the 1942 Food Control Law still in effect, however, the government maintained a separate consumer price. Beginning in 1963, the government producer price exceeded the consumer price and thereafter failed to keep pace with the rapid increase in producer prices.[105] The gap between producer and consumer prices contributed to a mounting deficit in the food control special account. By 1969, the food control deficit ran upwards of 340 billion yen, a sum equivalent to 40 percent of the annual budget of the Ministry of Agriculture and 5 percent of all government expenditures.[106]

During this expansion of the agricultural welfare state, rural Japan experienced dramatic change. Between 1950 and 1970, agriculture decreased from 40 percent to 15 percent of the total male workforce.[107] Those who remained in agriculture took advantage of the growing opportunities for off-farm employment that followed the spread of manufacturing and other industries to the countryside. By 1970, the majority of farm households in Japan earned most of their income from nonagricultural sources.[108]

Despite this rapid transformation of rural Japan, the agricultural welfare state proved remarkably resistant to change—sustained by the continued reliance of the LDP on farm votes. Throughout the 1970s, more than 80 percent of farmers and fishermen voted for the LDP. And as conservative support decreased among urban voters, LDP reliance on the farm vote became that much greater.[109] Meanwhile, Nokyo continued to play its central role in the rural economy and steadily expanded its business activities in insurance, banking, and other services. When government policy did change, such as modifications of the rice control system or the inauguration of a rice reduction scheme to tackle problems of surplus, Nokyo carefully preserved its prerogatives in the administration of policy.[110] Nokyo political influence also helped producer prices for rice double again between 1970 and 1978.[111]

If the administrative foundation of the Japanese agricultural welfare state was established in the years before World War II, then the political

---

[104] Ogura, *Can Japanese Agriculture Survive?* 706.

[105] Between 1960 and 1968, the producer price grew at an annual rate that was more than twice that of the consumer price. For producer (purchase) and consumer (sales) prices, see, ibid., 706.

[106] Donnelly, "Setting the Price of Rice," 151; Ogura, *Can Japanese Agriculture Survive?* 700, 706.

[107] FAO, *Population: Long-Term Series (Decennial)*.

[108] Ogura, *Can Japanese Agriculture Survive?* 763.

[109] Flanagan et al., *The Japanese Voter*, 80.

[110] George, "Rice Politics in Japan," 13.

[111] Ogura, *Can Japanese Agriculture Survive?* 706.

grounding of farm policy in conservative politics was the principal innovation of the postwar period. Agricultural policies in Japan assured continued political dominance of the conservatives and secured a central position for the cooperatives in the rural economy. As industrialization
changed the economic context of farm policy in the 1970s, critics of the
agricultural welfare state found their paths blocked by institutions that
insulated decision making in the hands of those who benefited directly
from government subsidies and high rice prices.

FRANCE

As in Japan, the institutionalization of agricultural policies in France
rested upon a political alliance between farmers and politicians. But the
evolution of this alliance was far from smooth. As in the United States,
economic characteristics of different producers informed divergent opinions toward farm policy. While the large-scale cash grain farmers in the
Paris Basin called for government supports of agricultural prices, small-
and medium-scale farmers demanded structural assistance to help increase farm size and productivity. Ultimately, agricultural policy embraced both sets of goals even though the underlying tension remained
unresolved. Alongside domestic subsidies for mechanization, land consolidation, and other development programs, farmers received generous
price supports administered through the Common Agricultural Policy
(CAP) of the European Community (EC). Together, development programs and price supports modernized French agriculture, lifted farm income, and ensured the dominance of French farm exports in European
markets.

The resolution of diverse policy objectives within the French agricultural welfare state was made possible by two institutional developments.
First, using the prewar specialist associations and the wartime Corporation paysanne as an institutional foundation, rural leaders created an organizationally dominant farm union in the decade after World War II.
The dominance of the Fédération nationale des syndicats d'exploitants
agricoles (FNSEA) provided the organizational basis for an effective partnership with the government in policy administration, as well as the conduit for an electoral alliance between farmers and the Gaullist majorities
of the 1960s.

Second, the institutional changes of the Fifth Republic elevated the role
of the bureaucracy in farm policy and reinforced both administrative and
political links between the FNSEA and the government. As farmers became a powerful constituency in postwar French politics, the FNSEA
gained leverage over the implementation of government programs in

exchange for political support at the ballot box. By 1970, rural France was a critical constituency for the Right, and a complex, overlapping subsidy package was in place that maintained the tenuous balance between the diverse interests in French agriculture and the policy goals of the government. With the rise of the agricultural welfare state, the process of political integration of the French peasant begun by Gambetta in the 1870s was finally complete.

The Rise of the FNSEA

As World War II came to a close, members of de Gaulle's provisional government contemplated a new farm organization that could help direct the postwar reconstruction of French agriculture. The newly appointed minister of agriculture, Pierre Tanguy-Prigent, envisioned a confederation of farm associations composed of rural credit facilities, agricultural cooperatives, and farm unions that would work closely with the government in the articulation of agricultural policy.[112] In addition, Tanguy, a prominent Socialist leader from Brittany, hoped to establish political ties between French farmers and the Left. In October 1944, he approved a government ordinance that formally dissolved the Corporation paysanne and required that all future agricultural organizations receive the approval of departmental committees appointed by the minister of agriculture. With an effective monopoly on rural organization, Tanguy set the groundwork for a new, state-supported farm group that in many instances simply adopted the local organizations of the Corporation paysanne. In March 1945, at the Congress of Peasant Unity, Tanguy officially proclaimed the Confédération générale d'agriculture (CGA).[113]

Tanguy also created a new national federation of departmental farm unions, the Fédération nationale des syndicats d'exploitants agricole FNSEA. As initially conceived, the FNSEA occupied a subordinate status to the umbrella CGA. According to its bylaws, the FNSEA was to engage in "the representation and defense . . . of the interests of the agricultural profession . . . to the exclusion of all commercial operations." While the FNSEA could gather information and coordinate political activities, the statutes of the organization expressly forbade offering services such as fertilizers, insurance, or other benefits to farmers. Such a device, Tanguy hoped, would ensure that the FNSEA did not overshadow the other orga-

---

[112] Cleary, *Peasants, Politicians, and Producers*, 104–6; Wright, *Rural Revolution in France*, 95–101.

[113] *Journal Officiel*, October 13, 1944, 924–26; Wright, *Rural Revolution in France*, 99; Barral, *Les Agrariens*, 285; Emeri, "La CGA," 289.

nizations within the CGA. More specifically, it helped reinforce socialist dominance within the network of farm organizations.[114]

Although the strategy worked at first, dominance by the Left in agricultural politics proved very short-lived. When Tanguy formed the CGA in 1945, many conservative leaders of the prewar and wartime farm organizations were either discredited or in jail for their complicity with the Vichy regime.[115] But to Tanguy's surprise, farmers voted overwhelmingly for the Right in 1946 elections to the FNSEA national congress; conservative candidates won the majority of seats over their Socialist and Communist Party rivals. The newly elected delegates to the first FNSEA congress chose Eugene Forget, a right-leaning Christian Democrat, and René Blondelle, a staunch conservative from the Paris Basin, as president and secretary-general, respectively. Forget and Blondelle were both prominent in the Corporation paysanne, and with their election the prewar and wartime conservative elite reassumed its position at the top of the farm union movement. According to Boussard, every FNSEA president and secretary-general between 1946 and 1961 served prominently in the Corporation paysanne. Continuity, rather than change, characterized the leadership of the postwar farm union movement in France.[116]

Soon after the 1946 FNSEA elections, René Blondelle quickly consolidated the power of his conservative faction. In particular, Blondelle cleverly utilized prewar agricultural associations, such as the specialist producer groups—to magnify conservative power at the national level. Under FNSEA bylaws, the specialist producer associations such as the AGPB (wheat), CGB (sugar beets), and CGV (wine) enjoyed independent representation at every level of the farm union hierarchy. This effectively doubled the votes of farmers from the wealthy and conservative Paris Basin who enjoyed both geographic *and* commodity representation on the national committees of the FNSEA.[117] When voting on various policy measures, departmental representatives from the Paris Basin often formed a bloc with leaders of the specialist producer groups. With the help of this alliance, Blondelle's faction pushed out the remaining Communists and Socialists from the national bureau of the FNSEA. When Christian Democrat Pierre Pfimlin replaced Tanguy as minister of agriculture in 1947, Pfimlin withdrew state support of the CGA and recognized

[114] FNSEA, *Statutes*, Title III, Article 8; reprinted in Tavernier, *Le Syndicalisme paysan*, 40; Prugnaud, *Les étapes du syndicalisme agricole*, 163–68; Keeler, *The Politics of Neocorporatism*, 38–40.

[115] Boussard, *Vichy et la Corporation paysanne*, 358–60.

[116] Ibid., 366; Wright, *Rural Revolution in France*, 104–6.

[117] Roussillon, *L'Association générale des producteurs de blé*, 39; Cleary, *Peasants, Politicians, and Producers*, 107; Tavernier, *Le Syndicalisme paysan*, 24–31; Emeri, "La CGA," 291.

the FNSEA as the principal representative of the agricultural sector. Lacking a budget and a general staff, the CGA disappeared completely during the 1950s, leaving the FNSEA the single most important farm organization in France.[118] In less than ten years, the prewar agricultural elite regained its prominence and fashioned an organizationally dominant farm union in France.

However, not all farmers shared the politics or policy preferences of the conservative FNSEA leadership. In the late 1950s, a group of young farmers educated in the tradition of social Catholicism became active in the youth auxiliary of the FNSEA, the Cercle national des jeunes agriculteurs (CNJA). Unlike in the FNSEA or the specialist producer associations, the leaders of the CNJA came from modest backgrounds of medium-sized farms in Brittany and the Massif Central. They engaged in mixed-crop and livestock farming rather than specializing in single crops such as wheat or sugar beets. These economic differences influenced the younger generation's attitude toward government policy. Specifically, members of the CNJA opposed the overwhelming focus on agricultural prices. This policy of "prices first" only benefited large producers of grain, sugar beets, and other *grandes cultures* who, because of scale, could take advantage of small price increases. Farmers who produced smaller quantities received only a marginal benefit from higher prices and instead favored policies that modernized their operations through land improvements and mechanization.[119]

For a time, it appeared the reformers in the CNJA would rival the FNSEA in the representation of agricultural interests. At the FNSEA national congress in 1959, leaders of the CNJA called for a structural policy program that emphasized state development aids instead of price supports. Politically, the CNJA emphasis on modernization and economic development sat well with the new Gaullist administrators of the Fifth Republic, and reform leaders soon found themselves included in official meetings with the government. According to Jobert and Muller, CNJA leader Michel Debatisse played an influential role along with Prime Minister Michel Debré in drafting the government's plan for agricultural modernization unveiled in 1960.[120]

Yet rather than form a breakaway union, CNJA leaders rose through the ranks of the FNSEA hierarchy. In 1962, one of the reform leaders, Marcel Bruel, was elected to the critical position of secretary-general at

---

[118] Prugnaud, *Les étapes du syndicalisme*, 199; Wright, *Rural Revolution in France*, 125; Keeler, *The Politics of Neocorporatism*, 42.

[119] Cleary, *Peasants, Politicians, and Producers*, 119–20.

[120] Jobert and Muller, *L'état en action*, 88.

the FNSEA national congress.[121] Critically, the new generation of leaders worked *within* the existing structure of its parent farm union to further the goal of structural policy. And even though reformers occupied top positions in the FNSEA, they never completely displaced the conservative faction of large-scale farmers from the Paris Basin or their allies in the specialist associations. At the same time, old guard conservatives found themselves constrained by the government's promotion of the CNJA program. In order to maintain the image of peasant unity before the government and the political power this afforded, the conservative faction was forced to adopt (or co-opt) at least part of the structural program advocated by the younger generation. Farm leaders of both camps crafted their demands into a delicate balance between government-supported prices and structural improvements.[122]

Why did the young CNJA leaders continue to work through the FNSEA rather than establish an independent organization? The question is particularly interesting when compared with the experience of U.S. farm organizations. In both France and the United States, economic differences between producers informed divergent policy preferences. In the United States, these differences first found expression through two polarized farm organizations aligned on opposite ends of the political spectrum and then through a myriad of commodity-specific producer groups. In France, however, the institutional changes of the Fifth Republic encouraged farm leaders to maintain at least the appearance of unity in order to maximize influence within government circles.

Fifth Republic Institutions and Agricultural Politics

During the 1950s, FNSEA leaders used the weakness of Fourth Republic political institutions to convert organizational strength into political power. With a strong Parliament and weak political parties, government crises and cabinet reshuffles were endemic to the Fourth Republic. Twenty-five governments formed between the general election of 1945 and de Gaulle's return in June 1958.[123] Political instability rewarded agricultural interests. Representing a third of the French population in the 1950s, farmers were an attractive, identifiable bloc of voters.[124]

---

[121] Keeler, *The Politics of Neocorporatism*, 67–68; Bruneteau, *Les Paysans dans l'état*, 40–50; Rémy, "Le Gaullisme et les paysans," 261.

[122] Keeler, *The Politics of Neocorporatism*, 68–69; Coulomb and Nallet, "Les Organisations syndicales agricoles a l'éprouve de l'unité," 388–99.

[123] Williams, *Crisis and Compromise*, 36–39, 66.

[124] Dogan, "La Représentation parlementaire du monde rural," 207.

When a Center-Right coalition (which included an independent peasant party) formed a government in 1951, FNSEA president René Blondelle began an ambitious lobbying campaign on behalf of French farmers. Blondelle organized the Amicale parlementaire agricole (APA), a multi-party farm bloc consisting of 130 deputies who supported the conservative FNSEA in parliamentary matters. Between 1951 and 1956, every minister of agriculture was drawn from the ranks of the APA. The strategy achieved clear policy results. When the government announced its system of agricultural price supports in September 1953, the minister of agriculture granted the FNSEA seats on the bodies responsible for the new market regulations. As Gordon Wright describes the 1953 price support system, "Decisions were taken in close consultation with the farm organizations; indeed the FNSEA later boasted that it had helped draft the marketing decrees."[125]

In 1957, as the French economy suffered from rampant inflation, Blondelle and the FNSEA achieved another policy victory. Nationwide peasant protests combined with intense parliamentary pressure convinced the government to call a special session of Parliament. Under the Law of 18 September 1957 passed during the extraordinary session, the government agreed to index support prices for seven major farm products to inflation. Intervention agencies would shore up the market when commodity prices dropped below the index prices for industrial inputs. Describing the capacity of the FNSEA to extract policy concessions during the Fourth Republic, Wright concluded that "few other interest groups in the state . . . won so many concessions [as farmers]; no other group had participated so directly in the shaping of government policy."[126] The political crisis of 1958, however, led to changes in French government structures that forced a change in FNSEA political strategy.

The postwar history of France is punctuated by the Algerian crisis, de Gaulle's return to power, and the inauguration of the Fifth Republic in 1958. The new constitution replaced proportional representation with a two-ballot, single-member district electoral system that removed smaller parties from the National Assembly. New rules gave the government the power to control the parliamentary agenda, force votes on government-sponsored bills, and limit amendments. In addition, the new constitution reduced the policy domain of Parliament—especially in budgetary matters. These limits on parliamentary power and the expansion of executive

---

[125] Wright, *Rural Revolution in France*, 124; Tracy, *Government and Agriculture in Western Europe*, 222.

[126] Wright, *Rural Revolution in France*, 134, 141; Keeler, *The Politics of Neocorporatism*, 47; Williams, *Crisis and Compromise*, 375; Barral, *Les Agrariens*, 308.

authority in the hands of the president of the Republic ameliorated the government instability characteristic of the Third and Fourth Republics.[127] In the words of Michel Debré, former prime minister and architect of the Fifth Republic, the new constitution was designed to "keep the assembly from infringing on the administration's action."[128] In de Gaulle's hands, these institutions were used to implement sweeping policy programs, at times over parliamentary objections.

Farm leaders eyed these changes somewhat suspiciously. De Gaulle received only 7 percent of the rural vote in the 1958 election, prompting the FNSEA to keep at arm's length from the new government until the general unveiled his plans for agriculture.[129] The farm union leadership was soon disappointed. As part of his larger effort to stabilize the economy, de Gaulle announced in 1958 that agricultural price supports would no longer be indexed to inflation. The FNSEA viewed indexation as the centerpiece of its policy achievements under the Fourth Republic and insisted that income parity between agriculture and industry required high government price supports for farm products. When de Gaulle introduced agricultural legislation two years later, however, it made no mention of price supports. Instead, the government bill embraced structural reform and economic development—the CNJA program—as the goal of agricultural policy. Henceforth, government programs would help medium-sized farms increase revenues through land policies, mechanization, and education.[130]

Outraged by the new direction in government policy, the FNSEA leadership organized demonstrations in thirty-one towns throughout France where farmers demanded a return to indexation. In March 1960, the FNSEA reconvened the APA and convinced a majority of deputies in the National Assembly to approve a resolution calling for a special session of Parliament devoted to the indexation issue. De Gaulle steadfastly opposed the resolution, and the standoff between the president and National Assembly over agriculture was one of the earliest tests for the new constitution. Two days after the vote, de Gaulle made clear his views. In a letter to the National Assembly, de Gaulle announced that he would not convene a special session of Parliament because, in his words, "I do not believe that a meeting of Parliament brought about by 'invitations' of this nature [and] supported by public demonstration . . . conforms to

---

[127] Debré, "The Constitution of 1958," 11–24; Pierce, *French Politics and Political Institutions.* For an analysis of constitutional effects on policy, see Keeler, "Executive Power and Policy-Making Patterns in France," 524–29.

[128] Debré, "The Constitution of 1958," 18.

[129] Rémy, "Le Gaullisme et les paysans," 255–59.

[130] Tavernier, "Le Syndicalisme paysan et la politique agricole," 611–14.

the character of our new institutions."[131] The general had spoken: Parliament would not dictate policy.

In April 1960, the French Parliament began debate on the government's agricultural proposal. Although the National Assembly approved the plan, Senate obstruction delayed passage of a new law. Through three rounds of voting, former FNSEA president René Blondelle—now a Senator—successfully led the opposition to the agriculture bill. Under the new constitution, however, the government could bypass the Senate and call for a definitive vote on the measure in the Assembly. On the fourth round of voting, the Gaullist majority in the National Assembly overrode the Senate veto and passed the Loi d'orientation in late July 1960.[132] The defeat was a bitter lesson for the FNSEA leaders, who learned that their old political tactics were ineffective under the new institutional arrangements of the Fifth Republic. With the increase in executive power, parliamentary pressure no longer secured policy success. As one leader of the CNJA remarked, "It was now better to know two well-placed civil servants than twenty deputies."[133]

The growth of executive power under the Fifth Republic, coupled with the Gaullist emphasis on modernization, carried with it important organizational consequences for French agriculture. Embarking on the new structural program, the government demonstrated its desire for an active partner, like the CNJA, that shared the government's views and could help implement policy on the ground. Although divisions among farmers were obvious, the government encouraged farm leaders to work out differences among themselves and then present a relatively unified position in consultative meetings.[134] As the largest farm organization in France, the FNSEA warmed to this task. Its system of representation—combining departmental representatives, commodity organizations, and an activist youth auxiliary—allowed the FNSEA to give diverse interests expression within the organization yet still present a relatively united front before the government.

[131] De Gaulle, "Lettre à Jacques Chaban-Delmas, Président de l'Assemblée Nationale," March 18, 1960, *Lettres, notes et carnets, Juin 1958–Décembre 1960*, 341–43. Vincent Wright calls the 1960 refusal "an exceptional, yet revealing incident: it demonstrated [de Gaulle's] contempt for an institution to which he had never belonged and to which he attributed many of the errors of the previous regime." Wright, *Government and Politics of France*, 137. See also Tavernier, "Le Syndicalisme paysan," 618, 630–31.

[132] Wright, *Rural Revolution in France*, 166–67. The Loi d'orientation established a set of guidelines for future policies that centered on structural improvements—development aids, land programs, and so on—rather than price supports. Cleary, *Peasants, Politicians, and Producers*, 121.

[133] Quoted in Wright, *Rural Revolution in France*, 162.

[134] Clerc, "FNSEA-CNJA: Les conflicts de l'unité," 342–43.

As Keeler argued, FNSEA status as a corporatist client depended on several factors such as government need for assistance, the organizational capacity of the client, and consensus over policy goals.[135] Another important factor in FNSEA influence, however, was political. French party politics, particularly on the Right, offered substantial gains for a rural electorate unified under the organizational banner of the FNSEA. In the 1960s, the FNSEA discovered that the image of peasant unity, real or imagined, could translate into substantial political influence.

The Gaullist Transformation

In the early 1960s, the FNSEA confronted a government whose commitment to agriculture appeared, at the least, uncertain. For conservative leaders, Gaullist visions of modernization and economic development subordinated farm policy to the larger interests of the French state. Even the young reformers in the CNJA began to question government promises of structural reform; despite passage of the Loi d'orientation in August 1960, progress toward implementation of the government's program was painfully slow. In 1961, violent demonstrations took place in many parts of rural France as farmers protested against low prices and falling incomes.[136]

Amid nationwide protests and upcoming parliamentary elections, the government tried to assuage some of agriculture's demands. In 1961, Prime Minister Michel Debré appointed Edgard Pisani to head the Ministry of Agriculture. Pisani, who brought a reformer's zeal to the job, promptly instituted a reorganization of his ministry in order to improve the delivery of services to rural France. He consolidated the three technical corps responsible for extension and development into a single entity, removed layers of bureaucracy, and clarified jurisdictional conflicts between Agriculture and other ministries.[137] In 1962, Pisani drafted and secured passage of implementing legislation (Loi complementaire) for the property reforms and structural subsidies envisioned in the 1960 Loi d'orientation. That same year, Pisani signed an agreement in Brussels to move forward with a European common market for agricultural products.[138]

Despite Pisani's efforts, relations between farmers and the government did not improve. An austerity program announced in 1964 froze milk

---

[135] This is the core of the argument in Keeler, *The Politics of Neocorporatism.*

[136] Mendras and Tavernier, "Les Manifestations de Juin 1961," 599–600.

[137] Jobert and Muller, *L'état en action*, 91–92.

[138] Keeler, *The Politics of Neocorporatism*, 65; Laligant, *L'Intervention de l'état*, 163; Tavernier, "Le Syndicalisme paysan et la politique agricole," 626–27; Tavernier, "Le Syndicalisme paysan et la cinquième république," 874–77.

prices at 1963 levels. The FNSEA responded with calls for a motion of censure in Parliament and a strike by milk producers in several regions of the country. In 1965, progress toward completion of the Common Agricultural Policy (CAP) stumbled when France withdrew from negotiations over how to finance the community-wide farm program. The so-called empty-chair crisis angered FNSEA leaders, who insisted that the gains from a common market in agriculture outweighed de Gaulle's ambivalence over the power of proposed European institutions. FNSEA vice president Albert Genin believed "the only path of salvation for agriculture . . . is the Common Agricultural Policy." Farm leaders viewed the diplomatic standoff as a catastrophe for French agriculture and as indicative of de Gaulle's contempt for agricultural interests.[139] When Minister of Agriculture Pisani announced that agricultural income in 1965 had declined for the second straight year, farm leaders could point to a series of decisions—from the austerity program to the deadlock in European negotiations—that illustrated how the de Gaulle government consistently subordinated agriculture to other economic and political interests.[140]

As the 1965 presidential election approached, relations between farmers and the government reached their nadir. Conservative elements in the FNSEA demanded that the farm union openly oppose de Gaulle's candidacy. The reform faction of the CNJA, although disappointed with government policies, was uneasy about direct confrontation with de Gaulle. Nevertheless, at the 1965 FNSEA national congress the conservative faction from the Paris Basin, in alliance with the specialist producer groups, outnumbered the reformers and passed a resolution calling upon farmers to actively oppose de Gaulle's presidential campaign.[141]

The FNSEA campaign against de Gaulle in the 1965 presidential election was the critical turning point in postwar relations between the government and organized agriculture. By engaging in party politics, the FNSEA turned an institutional innovation of the Fifth Republic to its advantage. Under the two-ballot system, if no candidate received a majority of votes in the first round, then a runoff would take place between the top two vote recipients. De Gaulle, running in the first presidential election of the Fifth Republic, anticipated a first-round victory, but he re-

<hr />

[139] Genin quoted in *Le Monde*, October 23, 1965, 5; Grant, *The Common Agricultural Policy*, 69; Nugent, *The Government and Politics of the European Community*, 102; Muth, *French Agriculture*, 218.

[140] Tavernier, "Le Syndicalisme paysan et la cinquième république," 880–92; Tracy, *Government and Agriculture in Western Europe*, 263–66. See also *Le Monde*, October 21, 1965, 22.

[141] *Le Monde*, October 23, 1; Jean Delau quoted in Roussillon, *L'Association générale des producteurs de blé*, 128; Tavernier, "Le Syndicalisme paysan et la cinquième république," 905–7.

ceived only 44 percent of the vote. In the months just prior to the election, following the FNSEA declaration against de Gaulle, surveys indicated a sharp decline in rural support for the general, and political analysts agreed that the farm vote had been partly responsible for his "defeat" in the first round. Although de Gaulle won the presidency on the second ballot, the 1965 election revealed that under the two-ballot system French farmers were a vital constituency for any presidential candidate, particularly one on the Right.[142]

In the aftermath of the election, government relations with the FNSEA changed dramatically. Edgar Faure replaced Edgard Pisani as minister of agriculture. Faure, a politico adept at conciliation, backed off considerably from the modernization goal embraced by his predecessor. Faure's job was to soothe tensions with farmers before the upcoming legislative elections, and soon after his appointment as minister, the government issued a series of pronouncements that conformed closely to FNSEA demands.[143] In February, the government announced 130 million francs in development grants for livestock production. In March, it increased the support price for milk 7 percent, prompting the remark from *Le Monde* that the milk price concerned "1.5 million peasant families . . . and 3 million voters."[144] In May, the government rejoined negotiations in Brussels and agreed to financial rules for the CAP. In July, a tax on wheat and barley, levied in 1965 over the protests of the AGPB, was abolished.[145]

With the change in government policy, farmers became steadfast in their support for Gaullist candidates. After a second straight year of growth in agricultural income, 45 percent of farmers supported Gaullist candidates in the 1967 legislative elections. In June 1968, one month after the unrest of May, the Gaullists won an absolute majority of parliamentary seats by polling favorably among farmers. In 1969, farmers again turned out for the Gaullists and elected Georges Pompidou as president of the Republic. With more than half of farmers voting for the Gaullist candidate, agriculture supported Pompidou more than any other economic sector in France. This achievement is put in perspective when we remember that ten years earlier de Gaulle's party polled only 7 percent of the farm vote.[146]

---

[142] Tavernier, "Le Syndicalisme paysan et la cinquième république," 908; Rémy, "Le Gaullisme et les paysans," 266–67; Muth, *French Agriculture*, 232–48.

[143] Barral, *Les Agrariens*, 318; Roussillon, *L'Association générale des producteurs de blé*, 129.

[144] *Le Monde*, March 18, 1966, 20.

[145] Tavernier, "Le Syndicalisme paysan et la cinquième république," 908–9.

[146] Platone, *Les électorats sous la Vème République*, 60; Rémy, "Le Gaullisme et les paysans," 269–72; Boy and Dupoirier, "La Stabilité du vote de droite des agriculteurs," 58.

When the Right became more fragmented in the 1970s, the political importance of the farm vote increased. Partly this was due to the tireless efforts of Jacques Chirac. The founder of the Gaullist party Rassemblement pour la République (RPR), a former prime minister and president of the Republic, Chirac assiduously cultivated the farm vote, particularly through the connections with FNSEA leaders established during his tenure as a popular minister of agriculture from 1972 to 1974. Chirac's endorsement and 49 percent of the farm vote helped Giscard beat Chaban-Delmas in the first round of the 1974 presidential election. Giscard then won a narrow victory over Mitterand with 51 percent of the vote. Agriculture was a critical component of the winning coalition as 72 percent of farmers supported Giscard (following the election, Chirac became prime minister). Similarly, in 1978 parliamentary elections, Coulomb reports that the Right "benefited . . . from the political alliance of farm leaders with J. Chirac." A third of the votes for the combined Right in 1978 came from farm households.[147]

The Agricultural Welfare State in France

As Pierre Coulomb remarks, close ties between farmers and the state in France "follow[ed] the political needs of the government and not the technical demands of managing agricultural production."[148] Through various institutional linkages established in the late 1960s, public officials and farm leaders crafted a set of agricultural policies that served both the political interests of the government and the organizational interests of the FNSEA. With respect to the latter, John Keeler documented how the FNSEA benefited from "exclusive or privileged access to the decision-making centers of the state, . . . power to formulate and implement important aspects of agricultural policy, . . . [and] monetary subsidies . . . [that] served to reinforce FNSEA hegemony."[149]

One reason for eventual FNSEA dominance was the institutional weakness of local agriculture officials. Although intended to improve government provision of services to rural France, the administrative reorganization of the agriculture ministry in the 1960s left a gap at the local level eagerly filled by the FNSEA.[150] Another reason, of course, was political.

---

[147] Coulomb, "La Cogestion: Une nouvelle corporatiste?" 178; Platone, *Les électorats sous la Vème République*, 73.

[148] Coulomb, "La Cogestion: Une nouvelle corporatiste?" 152.

[149] Keeler, *The Politics of Neocorporatism*, 110.

[150] Under the Pisani reorganization, the three technical corps—Génie rural, Eaux et forêts, and Services agricole—were merged into a single corps. In the reorganization, however, the Services agricole—although it was the best equipped corps to provide technical

As I examined in chapter 3, the delegation of policy responsibility to producer associations protected the government from the consequences of unpopular policy decisions. Consequently, nearly all the structural programs instituted during the 1960s made provision for the formal representation of agricultural organizations at the departmental, regional, or national level. According to Keeler, "The power to administer many important aspects of . . . policy was devolved to a network of institutions . . . dominated by the FNSEA."[151]

By statute, departmental leaders of farm organizations sat on the boards of regional agencies responsible for land improvement policies, particularly buying and selling property. In the departments Keeler studied in depth—Aisne, Landes, and Creuse—the president of the regional land agency was either the president or vice president of the departmental branch of the FNSEA. The local offices responsible for the distribution of structural aids also came under FNSEA influence and, according to Keeler, "served more or less as a state-financed adjunct of the staff of the FNSEA's departmental organization." Critical to FNSEA dominance of these local organizations were the departmental Chambers of Agriculture, which combined the functions of a government extension service with those of a representative body for local agricultural interests. Thus, the chambers discharged government subsidies as quasi-public entities, but control of the chambers depended on the elections of delegates in which the FNSEA won the majority of seats. FNSEA control over these representative institutions translated into power over the distribution of subsidies as well as other valuable organizational resources. With chamber personnel usually housed in the same building as the departmental offices of the FNSEA and often carrying out union business, there was, as Keeler concludes, "the de facto fusion of elites, infrastructure, and personnel."[152] Control over the levers of authority at the local level gave the FNSEA benefits and resources that other, rival farm unions clearly lacked.

Complementing this power at the local level was FNSEA representation on national policy-making bodies. According to Keeler, the FNSEA "was given the opportunity to exert considerable influence" within the advisory boards responsible for agricultural development, the distribution of structural subsidies, and the intervention into commodity markets.[153] The

---

assistance to farmers—lost jurisdiction to the more prominent engineers from the Génie rural and Eaux et forêts, who had been trained in the *grandes écoles*. According to Jobert and Muller, this left a significant administrative gap in the departments. Jobert and Muller, *L'état en action*, 92–93.

[151] Keeler, *The Politics of Neocorporatism*, 113.

[152] Ibid., 115–18.

[153] In particular, the FNSEA dominated the Agence nationale pour le développement agricole (ANDA) and the Centre national pour l'aménagement des structures des exploitations agricoles (CNASEA). Ibid., 110–11.

FNSEA participated regularly in highly publicized meetings with government leaders, known as the *conférences annuelles*. During the tenure of Jacques Chirac as minister of agriculture in 1972, these conferences took on greater importance. Meetings were more frequent, and farm union policy demands became more explicitly integrated into government programs. The importance of the *conférences annuelles* continued when Chirac became prime minister in 1974. During this "golden age" of *cogestion* (comanagement) lasting until 1977, the FNSEA influenced Ministry of Agriculture spending priorities and the distribution of subsidies. Although FNSEA influence over spending variously frustrated Finance officials and even bureaucrats within the Ministry of Agriculture itself, the political benefits were clear. According to Coulomb, the *conférences annuelles* "permitted Jacques Chirac to construct an electoral bastion for the future RPR by relying on the FNSEA national leadership."[154]

Finally, at the European level, the Common Agricultural Policy of the European Community reinforced links between the FNSEA and the French executive. The shift of policy authority from Paris to Brussels further weakened the role of Parliament and added a number of new policy tasks to the Ministry of Agriculture, ranging from the negotiation of price support policies to the implementation of EC directives. The CAP, and the growth in executive authority it required, was quite consistent with the institutional perspective of the French Fifth Republic. As Petot observes, "Europe [is] another step on the pedestal which elevates presidential and government authority. . . . The more power is exercised in Brussels, . . . the less it is in the Palais Bourbon [the National Assembly] and the Palais du Luxembourg [the Senate]."[155]

Consequently, the CAP presented the FNSEA with new opportunities to participate in the policy process and help government bureaucrats achieve objectives in the context of European negotiations. While the minister of agriculture pressed French interests in Brussels, the FNSEA lobbied the European Commission and the Council of Ministers through the umbrella European farm organization Comités des organisations professionnelles agricoles (COPA), of which several FNSEA and AGPB leaders were founding members.[156] In sum, the CAP created quasi-corporatist arrangements reminiscent of the pattern of interest group relations found in most of the member states, including France.[157]

---

[154] Coulomb, "Les Conférences annuelles," 159–72.

[155] Petot, "L'Europe, la France, et son président," 325–95.

[156] Neville-Rolfe, *The Politics of Agriculture in the European Community*, 117.

[157] For discussions of agricultural corporatism at the EU level, see Delorme, "L'Emergence d'un corporatisme agro-alimentaire"; and Daugbjerg, "Policy Networks and Agricultural Policy Reforms."

The policies of the French agricultural welfare state reflected the privileged position of the FNSEA in policy deliberations and the diverse interests of the farm union's membership. The long-awaited arrival of a European customs union in 1968 gave the large cash-grain farmers of the Paris Basin a protected and highly lucrative export market for wheat in Germany and the other nations of the EC. The value of French farm exports to the EC increased by 45 percent in real terms between 1970 and 1977.[158] At the same time, the new CAP elevated French farm prices to a level equivalent with the rest of the EC. The monetary benefits of this price increase became immediately apparent. In 1968, the first year of operation for the CAP, France received 78 percent of the monies distributed through the Guarantee Fund of the EC. The French contribution to the fund was only 24 percent of the total, making France the largest net beneficiary from the newly established CAP.[159] In this way, the CAP fulfilled the demands of the conservative faction and the specialist producer groups, voiced since the 1950s, for a policy of "prices first."

Intra-European transfers through the CAP, in turn, loosened up domestic resources in France for the support of an elaborate structural program of agricultural modernization. Government farm expenditures, including CAP subsidies, increased in real terms by 56 percent between 1968 and 1978.[160] During this period, the government offered farmers a range of subsidies designed to increase scale, mechanization, and productivity of small and medium-sized farms. Generous subsidies encouraged older farmers to retire and helped younger farmers just starting out. Tax breaks and grants encouraged farmers to form limited partnerships with each other. Mountainous regions of France were designated as special zones deserving of subsidies to keep farmers on the land. Other programs were used to relocate farmers from overcrowded Brittany to the sparsely populated Massif Central.[161] This overlapping subsidy package fulfilled in large measure the program supported by the CNJA and envisioned in the 1960 Loi d'orientation.

But the policies of the French agricultural welfare state carried a price—a dramatic decline in the number of farmers, low incomes for many small producers, and the economic demise of rural communities throughout France. After 1970, criticisms of FNSEA complicity with government policies responsible for rural depopulation fueled a new dissident union

---

[158] In 1990 francs, French exports to the EEC rose from Fr 25.8 billion to Fr 37.5 billion. INSEE, *Annuaire Statistique de laFrance 1979*, 176.

[159] European Economic Community, *Second General Report* (1969), 169.

[160] Expressed in 1990 francs, government expenditures for agriculture increased from FF69.9 billion to FF109.5 billion. "Dépenses de l'état bénéficiant à l'agriculture," INSEE, *Annuaire Statistique de la France 1979*, 167.

[161] Naylor, *Socio-Structural Policy in French Agriculture*.

movement on the Left. The rise of the Mouvement de défense des exploitants familiaux (MODEF) and the Confédération nationale des syndicats de travailleurs-paysans (CNSTP) forced the government and the FNSEA to downplay the Gaullist preoccupation with agricultural modernization and instead advocate policies that promised to maintain the largest number of farmers on the land. The change partially co-opted the dissidents' message, and despite important victories for MODEF in local elections for the Chamber of Agriculture, ties between the government and the FNSEA strengthened during the 1970s through instruments such as the *conférence annuelle*. Again Chirac, more than any other politician, was responsible for both the shift in rhetoric and the consolidation of the FNSEA's privileged status in the policy process. Even the arrival of a Socialist government in 1981 and an overt attempt to increase the representation of MODEF and other groups in the policy process ultimately failed to upset FNSEA organizational dominance in French agriculture.[162]

The pattern of interest group development in France suggests that sectoral structure, alone, cannot explain differences between the three countries. As in the United States, French agricultural politics in the 1950s and 1960s displayed profound internal divisions. Economic differences between the large-scale producers of the Paris Basin and the medium- and small-scale producers of the south and west informed divergent policy preferences. But unlike in the United States, economic differences in French agriculture did not prevent the emergence of a single, umbrella farm union closely involved in the administration of agricultural policy.

Instead, French political institutions enforced a degree of unity among diverse economic interests within agriculture and encouraged the development of a close relationship between the FNSEA and the government in policy matters and electoral politics. Yet the underlying tensions in French agriculture remain. The agricultural welfare state that evolved out of this institutional environment is an uneasy balance between corporatist policy making and clientele politics, between social and economic goals in farm policy, and between a vision of France as a nation of small family farms and the reality of France as an agricultural export powerhouse.

CONCLUSION: THE POSSIBILITY OF CAPTURE

In France and Japan, the articulation of a long-term agricultural policy after World War II had an important political component. In both countries, farmers became a key constituency of politically dominant, conservative parties precisely at the moment when politicians, producers, and

---

[162] On MODEF and other dissidents, see Hervieu, "Pluralité reconnue, pluralisme contesté," and Lagrave, "Les Gauches syndicales."

bureaucrats were negotiating the boundaries of the agricultural welfare state. Through the alliances formed during the 1950s and 1960s, peak agricultural associations such as the FNSEA in France and Nokyo in Japan secured unparalleled influence in farm policy deliberations. With farmers organized into an electoral bloc by the peak agricultural associations, conservative politicians solidified their dominance over postwar politics in France and Japan.

In contrast, the elaboration of a long-term agricultural policy in the United States *was not* accompanied by an alliance between farm groups and political parties. American farmers as an occupational group did not became a bulwark of the Republican Party; nor, for that matter, did farmers vote consistently for the Democrats (except in the South). Although both parties made significant overtures toward farmers in the years after World War II, attempts by Republicans and Democrats to merge agricultural policy with electoral politics failed miserably. Agricultural policies proved volatile as a result: with each change in party control of national political institutions, farm programs vacillated between alternatives that divided political parties, farm organizations, and producers of different commodities. Agricultural policy was the subject of intense partisan conflict during the first two decades after the war (see figure 4.1).

Partisan conflict over policy in the United States was accompanied by electoral volatility among U.S. farmers. Unlike Japan, where "the most cohesive pattern of broad social sector support for a political party . . . has been that of farmers for the Liberal Democrats," American farmers proved fickle in their partisan attachments.[163] Nor did farmers in the United States become "anchored to the Right" like farmers in France.[164] The regional basis of party competition divided farmers between a relatively solid South and a politically volatile Midwest and West. Writing in 1960, the authors of *The American Voter* noted that in national elections since 1948, "the two-party vote division among farmers outside the South has fluctuated more sharply than . . . any of the other major occupational groupings."[165] Indeed, both Democrats and Republicans tried and failed to establish firm political alliances with farmers after World War II.

Comparative electoral data further illustrate cross-national differences. Table 4.1 includes several summary statistics for the farm vote in lower house elections between 1952 and 1980 in the United States, France, and Japan. Unfortunately, the Japanese election data are rather incomplete, but the link between farmers and the LDP is widely known and uncontroversial. As indicated in the table, the Democratic Party in the United States enjoyed a slim margin of support among farmers over

[163] Flanagan et al., *The Japanese Voter*, 401.
[164] Hervieu, *Les Agriculteurs*, 99
[165] Campbell et al., *The American Voter*, 402.

TABLE 4.1
Stability of Farm Vote in Legislative Elections for Lower Houses, 1952–1980

	N Elections	Mean	Range	Standard Deviation	Coefficient of Variation
United States (Democratic Party)[a]	12	56.05	45.20	13.66	0.24
France (Combined Right)[b]	7	65.29	16.00	5.47	0.08
Japan (Liberal Democratic Party)[c]	6	77.00	12.00	4.00	0.05

[a] Does not include 1954 and 1962 elections.

[b] For France, data begin with the 1956 legislative election and do not include votes for the National Front or other extreme right parties.

[c] The 1952 election data are for combined conservative vote (Jiyuto and Kaishinto); do not include 1953, 1955, 1963, 1969, 1972, and 1979 elections.

Sources: Miller, American National Election Studies Cumulative Data File, 1952–1992; Klatzmann, "Géographie électorale," 48; Platone, *Les Électorats sous la Vème République*, 26, 28, 38–39, 47; Flanagan et al., *The Japanese Voter*, 58–59, 62, 69; Curtis, *The Japanese Way of Politics*, 204–5.

the period in question. But the range of Democratic support varied widely, from a high of 72 percent in 1970 to a low of 25 percent in 1980. In contrast, farm support for the LDP in Japan did not fall below 70 percent during this period; farm support for the combined Right in France stayed above 60 percent after de Gaulle's return in 1958. As indicated by the coefficient of variation (the ratio of the standard deviation to the mean), fluctuations in the farm vote in the United States were three times greater than in France and nearly five times greater than in Japan.

The failure of both political parties in the United States to secure a political alliance with farmers shaped the agricultural welfare state after World War II. Under the pressure of mounting surpluses, politicians and farm leaders abandoned partisan aspirations for agricultural policy in the mid-1960s. Voluntary land-retirement schemes and direct payments to producers replaced mandatory acreage control and price support programs for the major field crops. Omnibus, multiyear legislation replaced annual reauthorizations of individual commodity programs. Representation in Washington by general farm organizations like the Farm Bureau yielded to specialty producer groups, which formed a new, bipartisan logroll among the commodity subcommittees of Congress. The compromises of the 1960s muted partisan conflicts over agriculture but also institutionalized interest group pluralism as agricultural legislation in the 1970s tried to please a wide range of interests.

Contrary to the views of Lowi and McConnell, farm groups *tried and failed* to capture the agricultural policy process. With policy authority centered in Congress and routine conditions of divided government, no single group of farmers could secure privileged access to policy. Regional and commodity conflicts among producers led to the separation of the

Farm Bureau from the Extension Service, a valuable source of organizational strength, and delayed the emergence of a long-term farm program in the United States. By the 1970s, when internecine conflicts finally gave way to a cooperative logroll among commodity groups, it was too late. Reductions in the number of farm-state representatives, mounting criticism of the costs associated with commodity programs, and institutional changes in Congress that reduced the autonomy of committees pushed the concerns of consumers and taxpayers onto the farm policy agenda. In Schattschneider's terms, postwar institutional developments widened the scope of conflict over agricultural programs, a process that assures "the private interests most immediately involved shall not prevail." Capture was impossible where agricultural decisions were the product of either partisan conflict or coalition building among a variety of urban and rural interests. In short, capture required a set of institutions not found in the United States.[166]

In some ways, there is greater evidence for agricultural policy capture in the supposedly "strong" states of France and Japan. The rise of the LDP in Japan and the aggrandizement of executive authority under the Fifth Republic placed policy decisions almost exclusively in the hands of party leaders and agricultural bureaucrats who, together with peak farm organizations, negotiated a mutually beneficial agricultural program. In France, the *conférence annuelle* allowed the FNSEA to establish policy guidelines and influence departmental budgets without either parliamentary scrutiny or Finance Ministry controls over the spending priorities of the Ministry of Agriculture. And with the rise of Chirac and the fragmentation of the Right, the FNSEA exercised an influence in electoral politics above and beyond its dwindling numbers.

Similarly in Japan, agricultural influence sometimes ran contrary to the wishes of government leaders. In 1956, the minister of agriculture tried unsuccessfully to separate Nokyo as a political organization from its role in the administration of policy. Nokyo also blocked government attempts to decontrol rice during the 1950s and in the early 1960s. Instead, the government modified the food control system in ways that increased the role of cooperatives in the rural economy. Meanwhile, efforts by Ministry of Finance bureaucrats to control agricultural expenditures often ran into opposition by Nokyo's allies in the LDP. In agricultural policy at least, centralized institutions did not provide policy makers with autonomy from producer interests.

Institutions determine who has access to policy. In France and Japan, the evolution of postwar agricultural policy concentrated power in the

---

[166] Schattschneider, *The Semisovereign People*, 38. See also Baumgartner and Jones, "Agenda Dynamics and Policy Subsystems."

hands of farm organizations, party leaders, and agricultural policy specialists. In the United States, agricultural policy debates incorporated a variety of interests, many of them critical of government farm supports. As I will examine in the next chapter, these differences in the historical evolution of the agricultural welfare state influenced contemporary struggles over agriculture and the attempt to reduce farm subsidies in the 1980s and 1990s.

CHAPTER 5

The Politics of Agricultural Retrenchment

OVER THE PAST SEVERAL CHAPTERS, I have traced the rise of the agricultural welfare state in the United States, France, and Japan. As we have seen, institutions shaped government capacity for various policy tasks, ranging from the promotion of commercial agriculture in the nineteenth century to the regulation of agricultural markets in the twentieth century. Institutions also influenced agricultural politics. In France and Japan, state-sponsored farm organizations, the corporatist management of regulation, and the incorporation of producers into conservative politics conferred great power on farmers and fueled the expansion of agricultural supports in these countries. In the United States, on the other hand, politicians, bureaucrats, and farmers confronted a fractured administration, partisan wrangling over policy alternatives, and political conflicts among producers of various commodities. Interest group pluralism in the making of farm policy assured decisions on agriculture were the product of coalition and compromise between urban and rural interests in Congress.

The contemporary politics of agriculture reflect these institutional developments. Declining farm-sector employment, mounting stocks of surplus commodities, and increasing international trade in farm products prompted critics both in and outside government to call for the retrenchment of farm subsidies. But because institutional effects vary according to the types of policies governments pursue, efforts to dismantle portions of the agricultural welfare state presented policy makers with a new set of tasks and, consequently, a new array of institutional assets and liabilities.

Whereas the regulation of agricultural production and prices benefited from a close policy partnership between farm organizations and the government, retrenchment required policy makers to sever these ties. Whereas market intervention flourished in institutions that insulated policy decisions from external influences and restricted access to a select few, retrenchment benefited from overlapping policy jurisdictions and a pluralistic interest group environment. Whereas electoral alliances between farm organizations and political parties fueled the development of a mature subsidy regime, clientele relations made the reduction of farm subsidies politically difficult. In other words, differences in the historical development of the agricultural welfare state shaped the capacity to reduce farm subsidies in the United States, France, and Japan.

THE POLITICS OF RETRENCHMENT

Gary Becker, in his theory of competition among interest groups, argued that the social cost of subsidies influences lobbying capacity. According to Becker, higher costs *encourage* lobbying by taxed groups and *discourage* lobbying by subsidized groups.[1] Politicians will respond to this change in political pressure by adjusting the policy mix of subsidies and taxes. According to Peltzman, lower subsidies will maximize political support for reelection-seeking politicians, other things being equal, "as long as deregulation benefits some part of the relevant coalition."[2] In the case of agriculture, the rising cost of farm subsidies will stimulate political pressure by taxpayers, consumers, and so on, possibly leading to retrenchment and deregulation.

In fact, political pressure for farm subsidy retrenchment did increase with the rising cost of the agricultural welfare state in the 1970s and 1980s. Specifically, the budgetary cost of price support programs increased as low farm prices and excess supplies raised public expenditures for export subsidies, price support payments, and other government aids. In the European Community, the cost of price support policies doubled in real terms between 1974 and 1984, while export subsidies increased at an annual rate of 13.5 percent over the period.[3] In the United States, expenditures for the Commodity Credit Corporation grew by more than 20 percent per year in real terms between 1976 and 1986.[4] In Japan, real agricultural expenditures increased by 60 percent during the 1970s.[5] Fiscal pressures became an important component of agricultural politics in Europe, the United States, and Japan.

Price support policies also sparked trade conflicts over agriculture. In order to maintain high domestic prices for agricultural products, governments restricted access to cheaper imports through quotas or tariffs, and

[1] Specifically, Becker is concerned with policy costs that do not benefit the subsidized group (i.e., expenses of surplus disposal or environmental damage in the case of agriculture). These costs are known as *deadweight losses*. If deadweight losses increase from zero to $0.50, then the amount of subsidy provided by a $1.00 tax decreases from $1.00 to $0.50. For taxpayers, rising deadweight losses reduce the adverse effects of a tax cut on the amount of available revenue: the loss of revenue from a $1.00 tax cut decreases from $1.00 to $0.50. This encourages lobbying by taxpayers for lower taxes. For subsidized groups, rising deadweight losses increase the cost of lobbying as the tax increase required for a $1.00 subsidy increase rises from $1.00 to $2.00. This discourages lobbying by subsidized groups for higher subsidies. Becker, "A Theory of Competition among Pressure Groups," 381.

[2] Peltzman, "The Economic Theory of Regulation after a Decade of Deregulation," 38.

[3] Commission of the European Communities, *The Agricultural Situation in the Community*, various years.

[4] USDA, *Historical Budget Outlays, 1962–1996*.

[5] Moore, *Japanese Agriculture*, 162.

subsidized exports in order to shift excess production on to world markets. In the initial decades after World War II, when farmers produced almost exclusively for national markets, countries could effectively "export" the cost of domestic price adjustment with tariffs and subsidies. At the behest of the United States, in fact, the General Agreement on Tariffs and Trade (GATT) included exemptions from international trade law for farm trade barriers used in conjunction with domestic price support policies.[6]

The U.S. position changed with the dramatic rise in agricultural trade during the 1970s. The value of U.S. farm exports increased 150 percent in real terms between 1970 and 1980.[7] With the help of export subsidies, French farm exports doubled between 1970 and 1980, a decade in which France became the second-leading exporter of farm products after the United States.[8] Facing increased competition in world markets, the United States became a forceful proponent of farm trade liberalization. The inauguration of the Uruguay Round in 1986 pushed agriculture to the top of the multilateral trade agenda, but disagreement over export subsidies and market access delayed conclusion of the round until 1994.[9] The impasse over agriculture resulted in threats by the United States in farm trade disputes with the EC and Japan. The threat of retaliation highlighted the cost of agricultural protection for other sectors of the economy and contributed to domestic pressures for farm subsidy retrenchment in Europe and Japan.

Finally, environmental activists linked government policies that encourage heavy input use to the destruction of wetlands and groundwater contamination from pesticide runoff and concentrated livestock populations. In the early 1990s, environmental and consumer concerns merged to include food-borne diseases, the health effects of pesticides, and new food technologies such as genetically modified organisms.[10] Because of the link between agriculture and environmental risks, environmental groups pressed for reductions in the subsidies that encouraged intensive production practices.

Thus, the rising cost of farm subsidies for taxpayers (due to higher government expenditures on agriculture), producers of manufactured goods threatened by trade retaliation, and environmentalists and consumers concerned about agricultural production practices can increase political pressure for agricultural retrenchment. But retrenchment advocates still confront significant political hurdles to any changes in policy.

---

[6] Cohn, "The Changing Role of the United States," 21–22.

[7] FAO, *Trade Indices.*

[8] Ibid.

[9] Cohn, "The Changing Role of the United States."

[10] Potter, *Against the Grain*; Grant, "Biotechnology."

Experiences in agriculture support the argument by Paul Pierson that "retrenchment is a distinctive and difficult political enterprise."[11] As discussed in chapter 1, retrenchment is characterized by an asymmetric distribution of costs and benefits. In Pierson's words, it imposes "immediate pain on specific groups, usually in return for diffuse, long-term, and uncertain benefits."[12] In the case of agriculture, subsidy cuts impose an immediate and identifiable cost on farmers, while the benefits of agricultural retrenchment, such as lower taxes, better relations with trading partners, or a cleaner environment, are distant and diffuse. Because this asymmetry creates a clear organizational advantage for groups threatened by retrenchment, farmers will likely overcome collective action problems and "inflict political retribution for . . . visible assaults on programs they favor."[13] When risk-averse politicians calculate the political costs and benefits of retrenchment, they will likely support the status quo and oppose cuts in subsidies.

In his work on retrenchment, Pierson draws substantially on the concept of "blame avoidance" developed by R. Kent Weaver.[14] Blame avoidance is a rational response to the asymmetric distribution of costs and benefits. Concentrated policy effects, such as subsidy cuts, are more visible than diffuse ones, such as lower taxes, that might result from retrenchment. The negativity bias in constituency evaluations of politicians compounds the effects of this asymmetry. According to Weaver, "Voters are more sensitive to what has [been] done *to* them than to what has been done *for* them."[15] In the context of retrenchment, as Pierson shows, blame-avoidance strategies include the use of side payments to buy off potential opposition to policy change, the selective distribution of pain and gain in order to divide those interests opposed to retrenchment, and the use of policy mechanisms that obfuscate or hide the true cost of retrenchment proposals.[16]

Unless politicians can employ these strategies and minimize the risk of political retribution, it is unlikely that they will advocate retrenchment. This suggests a status quo bias in policies with concentrated costs and

[11] Pierson, *Dismantling the Welfare State?* 1.

[12] Ibid., 17–19.

[13] Ibid., 161. Some may question whether "better relations with trading partners" is a diffuse benefit. Although retaliatory measures against a specific product are a concentrated cost, in general the benefits of agricultural trade liberalization, or more generally the completion of a multilateral trade agreement, are widely diffused across countries, producers of nonfarm products, and consumers. The costs of farm trade liberalization are, however, concentrated among producers.

[14] Weaver, "The Politics of Blame Avoidance."

[15] Ibid., 373–75; emphasis in the original.

[16] Pierson, *Dismantling the Welfare State?* 19–24.

diffuse benefits. According to Weaver, "Because costs and benefits are perceived asymmetrically, policymakers fear that new policies will not win them as much support as dismantling the old ones will lose. They are thus afraid to dismantle policies."[17]

As I described in chapter 1, however, asymmetric costs and benefits might also produce what James Q. Wilson called *entrepreneurial politics*, when leaders "mobilize latent public sentiment" in favor of policy change.[18] Political entrepreneurs are attracted by the potential gains of a policy decision that has widespread public appeal despite its concentrated costs. Oran Young, in his work on international negotiations, provides a useful definition of entrepreneurial leaders as "agenda setters shaping the form in which issues are presented . . . [and] popularizers drawing attention to the issues at stake." In the case of agriculture, political entrepreneurs can promote retrenchment by highlighting the costs of agricultural policies for nonfarm groups in society, just as Ted Kennedy promoted airline deregulation by highlighting the cost of regulations for consumers. Significantly, "the role of entrepreneur . . . will prove more appealing to individuals who are risk takers than to those who are risk averse."[19] In other words, the same high-risk policies that encourage blame-avoiding behavior (retrenchment, concentrated costs/diffuse benefits) might also attract political entrepreneurs.

But the presence of an entrepreneurial leader who will promote agricultural retrenchment as a political issue is often insufficient to facilitate policy change. Institutions, by design, restrict the introduction of certain issues into policy debates through agenda control and other instruments.[20] Consequently, advocates of policy change also try to influence *which* institutions have authority over policy. Baumgartner and Jones refer to this institutional location of decision authority as the policy venue. Because a particular policy venue may be inherently biased toward the status quo, entrepreneurs often look for opportunities to shift the location of policy authority toward a more hospitable venue.[21]

The opportunity for strategic venue change of this kind is particularly important in cases of retrenchment. Quoting Pierson again, the principal obstacle to retrenchment is opposition by well-placed client groups "who can inflict political retribution for visible assaults on programs they favor."[22] For Baumgartner and Jones, the force of issue redefinition and venue change in policy innovation lies precisely in the capacity to shift

[17] Ibid., 394.
[18] Wilson, "The Politics of Regulation," 370.
[19] Young, "Political Leadership and Regime Formation," 288, 293–96.
[20] Shepsle, "Institutional Arrangements."
[21] Baumgartner and Jones, *Agendas and Instability in American Politics*, 31.
[22] Pierson, *Dismantling the Welfare State?* 161.

the location of policy authority away from institutions dominated by those groups that benefit from the status quo. Here Baumgartner and Jones borrow from the work of Schattschneider, who argued that expansion of conflict over policy (a variety of venue change) assures "the private interests most immediately involved shall not prevail."[23]

Retrenchment, as Pierson argues, is a distinct and difficult political enterprise. The concentrated cost of subsidy reductions and the diffuse benefits from lower taxes or food prices make agricultural retrenchment a risky endeavor. Politicians will not support retrenchment as a policy option unless they can minimize the risk of political retribution by farmers through successful blame-avoidance strategies. For the political entrepreneur, however, lower farm subsidies may hold the promise of large political rewards. For these politicians, retrenchment success depends on the capacity to shift the location of agricultural policy decisions to a venue more favorable toward retrenchment.

INSTITUTIONS AND RETRENCHMENT

Institutions fundamentally influence the success of blame-avoidance strategies as well as opportunities for entrepreneurial behavior and venue change. It is easier to avoid blame when institutions divide authority and diffuse responsibility for policy decisions. Both the likelihood of entrepreneurial behavior and its chances of success benefit from institutions that promote individualism among politicians and provide opportunities for venue change in the policy process. Finally, whether the rising cost of farm subsidies does shift the political calculus in favor of retrenchment, as Becker suggests, will depend on institutions and the representation of interests in the policy process.

In this section, I discuss the politics of retrenchment with reference to three levels of institutions: macro political institutions, characteristics of the agricultural policy process, and the structure of interest representation. Macro political institutions include the structure of executive and legislative authority, electoral rules, and the party system. The agricultural policy process includes rules and procedures specific to agriculture such as the farm bill cycle in the United States or the annual pricing process in Japan. Finally, the structure of interest representation includes the role of farm organizations in the policy process, farmers' position in national politics, and the degree of access enjoyed by nonproducer interests in agricultural matters.

[23] Schattschneider, *The Semisovereign People*, 38.

Macro Institutions

Institutions that divide authority diffuse accountability for policy decisions. In contrast, institutions that concentrate authority focus accountability. Consequently, blame avoidance will be more difficult in a parliamentary system (i.e., Japan) or even a semipresidentialist system with a strong executive (i.e., France) than in a political system where power is shared among government branches as in the United States.[24] These same characteristics of macro political institutions also shape opportunities for venue change. Federalism, the separation of powers, bicameralism, and congressional committees create multiple centers of policy authority and facilitate venue change.[25]

Meanwhile, characteristics of the party system in the United States encourage entrepreneurial behavior among politicians. Political parties in the United States play a comparatively small role in electoral competition; individual members of Congress are largely responsible for their own electoral success. Members of Congress enjoy substantial staff resources, which allows greater provision of constituency services and permits individual policy analysis on a wide range of issues. These qualities have prompted some congressional scholars to describe Congress as a collection of "small businesses" or "member enterprises."[26] The individualistic structure of electoral competition in Congress encourages politicians to seek new issues, while abundant staff resources make issue shopping possible.

In France and Japan, the parliamentary system and the partisan structure of electoral competition create an institutional constraint on both entrepreneurial and blame-avoidance behavior. As Weaver notes, "Party discipline seriously constrains the blame-avoiding options for legislators."[27] In Japan, for example, the party apparatus of the LDP is a critical component of career advancement, since membership on PARC committees and the various "policy tribes," or *zoku*, organized around specific policy domains, serve as important springboards to higher positions in the party.[28] Under such constraints, entrepreneurial issue definition holds much less promise as an electoral strategy.

Finally, electoral laws shape the relative political influence of farmers, a factor that partly determines the risks and benefits of retrenchment decisions. Where farmers are overrepresented, their capacity to inflict political

[24] Weaver, "The Politics of Blame Avoidance," 391.

[25] Baumgartner and Jones, *Agendas and Instability in American Politics*, especially chaps. 10 and 11.

[26] Loomis, "The Congressional Office as a Small Business"; Salisbury and Shepsle, "U.S. Congressmen as Enterprise"; Browne, *Cultivating Congress*, 9.

[27] Weaver, "The Politics of Blame Avoidance," 391.

[28] Kohno, "Rational Foundations"; Curtis, *The Japanese Way of Politics*, 114.

TABLE 5.1

Agricultural Representation in National Legislatures (Lower House only)

	"Agricultural" Districts[a]	Number of Seats in the Chamber	Percentage "Agricultural"	Percent Employed Nationally in Agriculture
France (1990)	105	555	18.9	5.5
Japan (1998)	102	500	20.4	4.8
United States (1994)	14	435	3.2	2.8

[a] Districts with populations > 10% employed in agriculture.

Sources: Hervieu, *Les Agriculteurs*, 98; George-Mulgan, *The Politics of Agriculture in Japan*, table 5.20; U.S. Bureau of the Census, *Congressional Districts of the U.S. 104th Congress*; FAO, *Population: Annual Time-Series*.

retribution for retrenchment decisions is enhanced. Table 5.1 reports the number of districts in lower houses with sizable agricultural constituencies. Using 10 percent as a benchmark, the table reveals how electoral rules overrepresent agricultural interests in France and Japan.[29] In the United States, on the other hand, reapportionment and redistricting every ten years have steadily reduced the number of House districts with a significant agricultural constituency. Unlike in France and Japan, the number of "agricultural" districts in the United States closely approximates the proportion employed nationally in agriculture. Even the House Agriculture Committee, for example, reflects this steady decline in agricultural representation. In 1999 (106th Congress), the median district represented on the House Agriculture Committee had just under 5 percent of its population employed in agriculture. This is vastly different than the House Agriculture Committee Charles Jones studied in the late 1950s, when virtually all of the committee's members represented "pure" farm districts.[30]

We see the same pattern in upper houses. In Japan, more than half of upper house seats in 1995 represented districts with 10 percent of the population on farms; more than a fifth of seats represented districts with 20 percent of the population on farms.[31] In France, the system of indirect elections for the Senate benefits agriculture, since the mayors of small rural communes are influential members of the departmental electoral colleges that choose French senators. Hervieu estimates that around a third of French mayors in 1989 were active or retired farmers.[32] Meanwhile, in the United States Senate, the supposed bastion of agricultural

---

[29] Under the new electoral system in Japan, there are three hundred single-member districts and two hundred districts selected by proportional representation.

[30] Jones, "Representation in Congress."

[31] George-Mulgan, "Electoral Determinants of Agrarian Power," 880.

[32] Hervieu, *Les Agriculteurs*, 98–99.

interests, only two states have an agricultural population greater than 10 percent—North and South Dakota. By this measure, then, only 4 percent of Senate seats are "agricultural."[33]

The Agricultural Policy Process

In Japan, those with a direct political or economic interest in agriculture tend to dominate policy; agricultural decisions are largely isolated from external influences. Decisions ranging from the government purchase price of rice to annual expenditures on public works take place through negotiation among high-ranking LDP officials with agricultural expertise (members of the agriculture *zoku*), bureaucrats from the Ministry of Agriculture, Forestry, and Fisheries, (MAFF) and Ministry of Finance officials.[34] In addition, LDP backbenchers from rural districts and leaders of Japan's agricultural cooperatives, Nokyo, press their case for higher prices and subsidies. The result is a highly compartmentalized process. Muramatsu's concept of "patterned pluralism" in Japanese politics accurately describes the segmentation of agricultural policy into a rigid and distinct policy domain.[35]

In the case of France, a large portion of policy decisions now occurs in Brussels. Under the Common Agricultural Policy, final authority over intervention prices (the level at which the EU—formerly the EC—purchases commodities in order to support prices) rests with the Council of Ministers, which consists of the agriculture ministers from each member nation. However, the common practice of unanimity in council decisions often gives each member an effective veto over CAP decisions—an element of EU farm policy France is more than willing to exploit.[36]

The council acts on the recommendations of the agricultural directorate of the European Commission, DG-VI, which exercises tight control over farm policy and enjoys special privileges that set agriculture apart from the rest of EU business. Indeed, thirty years after the CAP began, analysts observe that "agricultural policy still remains remarkably insulated."[37]

---

[33] U.S. Bureau of the Census, *Congressional Districts of the U.S., 104th Congress.*

[34] Donnelly, "Conflict over Government Authority and Markets," 351; George, "Rice Politics in Japan"; Eisuke, "The Japanese Politico-Economic System," 73. *Zoku* membership is reserved for party members who have served in important positions related to their chosen policy areas such as parliamentary vice minister or PARC division chairman. See Schoppa, "Zoku Power and LDP Power," 79–106.

[35] Muramatsu, "Patterned Pluralism under Challenge," 50–71.

[36] In fact, the Agriculture council votes more than any other council in the EU. Grant reports that of 114 legislative acts adopted between December 1993 and March 1995, 75 percent received unanimous votes. Grant, *The Common Agricultural Policy*, 173.

[37] Ibid., 148.

For instance, DG-VI is the only directorate with the authority to negotiate international agreements, a task normally reserved for the External Affairs Directorate (DG-I). Other directorates with concerns in agriculture such as Environment (DG-XI) or Health and Consumer Protection (DG-XXIV) have little access to or influence in agricultural decisions.[38]

Agricultural administration in France mirrors the insulated and compartmentalized character of decision making at the European level. For example, the Ministry of Agriculture contains its own specialists on EU law that free it from dependence on the Foreign Ministry or the interministerial council responsible for EU affairs. As one observer noted, "The sectoral ministry with the most experience of dealing with the EC [EU] has taken the greatest steps to reinforce its autonomy" within the French government.[39]

In sum, responsibility for agriculture in Japan, France, and the EU is concentrated within well-defined policy jurisdictions. As a result, policy makers enjoy near-monopoly control over agricultural policy decisions; this control focuses accountability and diminishes opportunities for effective venue change.

In contrast, agricultural policy jurisdictions in the United States are an object of contestation and competition.[40] For example, congressional farm legislation typically covers a wide range of programs and policies, including nutrition programs (i.e., food stamps), conservation provisions, rural development, and agricultural trade programs, as well as traditional income supports. As a result, omnibus farm legislation involves a large number of congressional committees that compete for jurisdiction over aspects of agricultural policy.

Data on congressional hearings clearly illustrate this jurisdictional competition over agriculture. Using data from the Policy Agendas Project, table 5.2 reports the number of House committees holding hearings on agriculture between 1947 and 1994.[41] Since 1971, the number of House committees involved in agriculture has increased. Put differently, jurisdictional clarity *decreased* in agriculture at a time when congressional reforms diminished committee autonomy. This decline in jurisdictional clarity is further illustrated by a Herfindahl concentration index of agricultural hearings. This index measures the degree to which jurisdiction over ag-

---

[38] Keeler, "Agricultural Power in the European Community," 127–49; Grant, *The Common Agricultural Policy*, 158; Ritson, "The CAP and the Consumer," 242.

[39] Menon, "French-EU Policy Making," 10.

[40] Baumgartner, Jones, and MacLeod, "Policymaking, Jurisdictional Ambiguity, and the Legislative Process."

[41] Frank Baumgartner and Bryan Jones produced a comprehensive data set of congressional committee hearings held between 1947 and 1994. They coded each hearing according to topic as well as the committee and subcommittee in which the hearing was held. Baumgartner and Jones, *Congressional Hearings Dataset*.

TABLE 5.2
Agricultural Policy Jurisdictions in the U.S. House of Representatives, 1947–1994

Years	Average Number of Communities Holding Hearings on Agriculture	Index of Jurisdictional Clarity (overlap)
1947–1952	8.0	44.7
1953–1958	6.7	55.0
1959–1964	6.0	56.3
1965–1970	4.3	54.1
1971–1976	7.0	53.4
1977–1982	7.7	49.8
1983–1988	11.7	35.7
1989–1994	9.3	42.3

Source: Baumgartner and Jones, Congressional Hearings Dataset.

ricultural matters is concentrated in one or more committees. As indicated, the clarity index declined after 1970, indicating an increase in the jurisdictional overlap among committees involved in agriculture.[42]

In sum, the agricultural policy process in the United States takes place in an institutional environment characterized by jurisdictional overlap and competition. As a result, blame (or credit) is shared among a large number of actors, and ample opportunities exist for strategic venue change. In addition, as Baumgartner and Jones emphasize, the determination of policy venue determines the character of interests involved in a given policy domain. Jurisdictional overlap in U.S. agricultural policy provides ample opportunities for consumers, taxpayers, and other diffuse interests to participate in the policy process. Indeed, as Browne found in his study of the 1985 farm bill, only 23 percent of the most active organizations were producer groups.[43]

The Structure of Interest Representation

The organization of agricultural interests and the relationship between farm associations and the government determine who has access to policy. Following the work by William Coleman and others, as well as the path of institutional development traced in the previous chapters, we can contrast the corporatist structure of interest representation in French and Japanese

---

[42] Overlap as a measure of jurisdictional clarity is calculated by taking the Herfindahl index of the proportion of agricultural hearings conducted by each committee holding hearings on agriculture. Baumgartner, Jones, and MacLeod, "Policymaking, Jurisdictional Ambiguity, and the Legislative Process," 5–8.

[43] Browne, Private Interests, Public Policy, and American Agriculture, 30.

agriculture with the essentially pluralist structure in the United States.[44] Whereas single peak associations of farmers in France and Japan came to play a key role in policy formation and implementation, a myriad of farm organizations competed with one another for access and influence in the United States.

In Japan, virtually all farmers are members of the cooperative association, Nokyo. As we have seen, Nokyo played a central role in the public management of the rice economy after World War II. Government subsidies ultimately found their way back into the cooperative bank, Norin Chukin, in the form of deposits by Nokyo members. These assets, in turn, fueled the expansion of cooperative activities into other sectors such as insurance.[45] Although George-Mulgan rejects the corporatist label in the strict sense of the term, she acknowledges that "Nokyo approximates most closely the concept of a sector-wide authoritative spokesperson."[46]

Similarly, the peak agricultural association in France, the Fédération nationale des syndicats d'exploitants agricoles (FNSEA), enjoys a privileged place in policy deliberations.[47] In addition, the FNSEA exercises control over the implementation of policy and distribution of public resources at the local level. As Keeler documented, the FNSEA shares many of the characteristics of a corporatist client in the formation and implementation of agricultural policy.[48] Unlike in Japan, however, the FNSEA must compete for membership with rival farm unions on the Left such as MODEF and the Confédération paysanne. In addition, specialist producer groups such as the AGPB (wheat) and the national Chamber of Agriculture, consisting of representatives elected by farmers in each department, also participate in policy.

Although some observers challenge the applicability of the corporatist label, the FNSEA does play the dominant role in French agricultural politics.[49] The annual FNSEA national congress, for example, remains an important date on the political calendar for politicians on both the Left and Right. Meanwhile, rival farm unions MODEF and the Confédération pay-

---

[44] Coleman, Skogstad, and Atkinson, "Paradigm Shifts and Policy Networks"; Coleman, Atkinson, and Montpetit, "Against the Odds." For an application of the policy networks literature to EU agriculture, see Daugbjerg, "Policy Networks and Agricultural Policy Reforms." For a general comparison of corporatism and pluralism, see Van Waarden, "Dimensions and Types of Policy Networks."

[45] Bullock, "Nokyo"; George, "The Politics of Interest Representation in the Japanese Diet," 506–28; Moore, *Japanese Agriculture.*

[46] George-Mulgan, *The Politics of Agriculture in Japan,* 137.

[47] Coulomb, "Les Conférences annuelles."

[48] Keeler, *The Politics of Neocorporatism in France,* 113.

[49] Culpepper, "Organisational Competition and the Neo-corporatist Fallacy in French Agriculture," 301–13.

sanne have only recently made small inroads in competition with the FNSEA. For instance, the FNSEA holds the majority of seats within the departmental Chambers of Agriculture.[50] And although the AGPB will issue separate policy statements, conduct its own meetings with the government, and occasionally disagree openly with the FNSEA, the wheat growers and other specialist associations enjoy formal representation on the executive council of the FNSEA.[51] Membership in the FNSEA and the specialist producer groups is more complimentary than competitive, as illustrated by the current president of the FNSEA Luc Guyau, himself a past president of the AGPB.

The contrast with the United States is stark. As described in the previous chapters, U.S. agricultural interest groups developed in a highly fractured manner. Regional divisions among producers prevented the emergence of a single peak farm association that could achieve and maintain organizational dominance through collusive relations with the state. The closest equivalent to a peak agricultural association in the United States is the American Farm Bureau Federation (AFBF). However, even at its apex of influence after World War II, the Farm Bureau faced competition from the National Farmers' Union. In the 1950s, political conflicts over agriculture eventually led to the official separation of the Farm Bureau from the Extension Service, a source of organizational advantage in competition for members. By the 1960s, the role of both national farm organizations declined as interest representation devolved to commodity-specific producer groups.[52]

Avoiding blame for unpopular subsidy cuts should be easier when farmers are represented by competitive membership organizations and are limited to ad hoc lobbying pressure rather than a corporatist bargaining process. As Coleman, Atkinson, and Montpetit observe, "When interest groups are highly fragmented . . . they are less able to defend programs than those that are vertically integrated and engaged in corporatist network."[53] A corporatist policy network, on the other hand, is a "tight, closed, highly integrated and highly institutionalized network in which membership is very restricted."[54] Under corporatist arrangements, farm organizations enjoy structural advantages over other interests in the policy process that militate against retrenchment. As Daugbjerg sums

---

[50] Hervieu, *Les Agriculteurs*, 81, 87.

[51] Roussillon, *L'Association générale des producteurs du blé*, 54–57.

[52] Wilson, "Why Is There No Corporatism in the United States?"; Jones, "Representation in Congress," 358–67.

[53] Coleman, Atkinson, and Montpetit, "Against the Odds," 455.

[54] Daugbjerg, "Policy Networks and Agricultural Policy Reforms," 128.

up, "In cohesive networks, groups subject to reform have structural power which they can use to oppose reform attempts."[55]

The policy networks literature reveals how the structure of interest representation in the policy process shapes agricultural influence. But as Keeler and others point out, the "power potential" of farmers is also a function of political factors.[56] As I examined in the previous chapter, corporatist relations in the formation and execution of agricultural policy in France and Japan are reinforced by partisan links between farm organizations and national political parties.

Nokyo, for example, is the largest single voluntary association in Japan and is an important mobilizer of rural votes for LDP candidates. As one study of Japanese voting concluded, "The most cohesive pattern of . . . support for a political party in Japan has been that of farmers for the Liberal Democrats."[57] Long-standing political links between the LDP, Nokyo, and rural voters translate into formidable agricultural influence within the Diet that far exceeds the numerical strength of Japanese farmers. Combining biographical data with sample surveys, George-Mulgan found that more than 40 percent of Diet members in both houses had "some connection, whether central or peripheral, to agricultural interests and agricultural policy issues" throughout the 1990s. The vast majority of these "agricultural" politicians come from the LDP.[58]

French farmers also enjoy political links with conservative politicians. Political scientist Bertrand Hervieu describes "an agricultural electorate anchored to the Right." Farmer support for conservative candidates averaged 66 percent during the 1980s—not including votes for the National Front. President Jacques Chirac and the Gaullist RPR Party enjoy particularly close ties to conservative farmers and the FNSEA; Chirac's association with agriculture dates back to his tenure as a popular minister of agriculture from 1972 to 1974.[59]

---

[55] Ibid., 130.

[56] Keeler, "Agricultural Power in the European Community;" Coleman, "Assessing the Changing Political Influence of Farmers."

[57] Flanagan et al., *The Japanese Voter*, 80.

[58] These "agricultural representatives," as George defined them, included Diet members who held relevant offices, such as ministers and vice ministers of the Ministry of Agriculture, members of the agriculture committees in both houses, member of the party committees on agriculture, and member of the LDP agriculture *zoku*. In addition, George included Diet members who held office in agricultural organizations or registered some other connection with agriculture through education, career, or electoral ties. See George, "The Politics of Interest Representation in the Japanese Diet," 507; and George-Mulgan, "Electoral Determinants of Agrarian Power," 887–92.

[59] Hervieu, *Les Agriculteurs*, 99, 102; Boy and Dupoirier, "La Stabilité du vote de droite des agriculteurs"; Platone, *Les électorats*.

In the United States, the fragmentation of interest representation was mirrored in politics. Relations between farm groups and politicians remained ad hoc; political parties and agricultural interests never forged lasting partnerships in electoral politics. Between 1972 and 1992, the farm vote divided almost equally among the two parties, with Democrats averaging 50.2 percent over the two-decade period. In the eleven congressional elections between 1972 and 1992, a majority of farmers voted Republican in five elections, while Democrats received a majority of the farm vote in six elections.[60]

The lack of any firm ties between producers and either political party in the United States should diminish the capacity for farmers to inflict electoral retribution in matters of retrenchment. The lack of a party connection might also encourage urban and suburban politicians to view agriculture in entrepreneurial terms, since their party label does not commit them to any particular view on farm subsidies. In contrast, party links with farmers in France and Japan will diminish the likelihood of blame avoidance and entrepreneurial behavior in matters of agricultural retrenchment.

Summary: Institutions and Retrenchment

Macro political institutions in the United States divide authority over policy and diffuse responsibility throughout the political system. In France and Japan, institutions concentrate policy authority and focus responsibility in executive and party structures. Similarly, the agricultural policy process in Japan, France, and the EU concentrates policy authority within institutions that enjoy a jurisdictional monopoly over agriculture. In contrast, agricultural jurisdiction is a source of conflict in the United States. Finally, the structure of interest representation in agriculture, such as the presence of an umbrella farm union linked politically to conservative parties, magnifies the power of French and Japanese farmers in national politics and agricultural policy debates. In the United States, interest representation is fragmented along commodity lines, with neither political party holding an advantage in the farm vote.

How do these institutional differences shape retrenchment outcomes? In France and Japan, institutions will likely make blame avoidance difficult, discourage entrepreneurial activity, prevent effective venue change, and provide the opponents of retrenchment a structural advantage in the political process. In the United States, institutions should facilitate blame-

---

[60] Miller and the National Election Studies, American National Election Studies Cumulative Data File, 1952–1992.

avoidance behavior, encourage entrepreneurial activity, present opportunities for venue change, and provide proponents of retrenchment easy access to the political process. These considerations will guide the following discussion of contemporary agricultural politics.

AGRICULTURAL RETRENCHMENT IN THE UNITED STATES

As William Browne has shown, the evolution of congressional norms and procedures, an agricultural policy process characterized by overlapping and competitive policy jurisdictions, and a steady reduction in the number of congressional districts with a significant agricultural constituency have had a marked effect on congressional farm politics.[61] Agriculture, like other issue domains, has seen the number of interest groups proliferate over the past decades, many of them organized around "broad public issues" such as the environment, food safety, and other consumer concerns. As Browne remarks, "It has been the introduction of non-farm interests that has most changed agriculture. New agenda issues . . . had particularly disruptive effects within . . . Congress."[62]

Many new agenda issues were a direct response to the rising cost of agricultural commodity programs. As I examined in the previous chapter, farm politics in the early 1970s reflected a political environment dominated by consumer concerns over inflation. During discussion of the 1973 farm bill, President Nixon promised to veto any farm bill that raised food prices. Consumer organizations targeted federal commodity programs that artificially inflated food costs. The 1973 act replaced price supports that propped up commodity prices with a system of deficiency payments that supported farm incomes through direct cash grants.[63]

In the 1980s, environmentalists placed their concerns on the farm policy agenda. The 1985 farm act included measures that penalized farmers who cultivated environmentally sensitive wetlands. Farm organizations began the 1990 legislative campaign hoping to relax, if not eliminate, some of the environmental regulations on agriculture contained in the 1985 farm bill. But environmentalists enjoyed broad-based support among urban and suburban members of Congress, making it politically difficult to dilute environmental protection. In the end, the 1990 farm act strengthened environmental regulations on agriculture. As one journalist summed up, "The threat of a fight with the environmental lobby proved an effective deterrent. . . . [T]he politics of agriculture were changing. The

---

[61] Browne, *Cultivating Congress*.
[62] Ibid., 23. See also Browne, *Private Interests, Public Policy, and American Agriculture*.
[63] Hansen, *Gaining Access*, 187–201.

power of the farm coalition . . . was being challenged, even in the friendly confines of the Agriculture Committee."[64]

However, it was the budgetary impact of farm support programs that had the most disruptive effect on congressional farm politics during the 1980s and 1990s. When Congress instituted the system of direct payments in 1973, it effectively shifted the burden of federal commodity programs from consumers to taxpayers. This policy shift had important consequences during the farm crisis of the 1980s. With nearly all government supports a direct budgetary outlay, agricultural expenditures skyrocketed from $8.8 billion in 1980 to a record $31.4 billion in 1986.[65] This sudden increase in spending occurred precisely when the deficit became a politically prominent issue. As fiscal austerity took center stage in American politics, agriculture became enmeshed in political struggles over deficit reduction.

Congress proved a hospitable environment for the introduction of new issues to the agricultural policy agenda. Advocates highlighting the costs of farm subsidies for consumers, taxpayers, and the environment gained access to farm policy debates during the 1980s and 1990s. The prominence of these new issues reflected the largely urban and suburban character of the House. In addition, as Browne argues, the individualistic character of the postreform Congress also encouraged issue expansion. As individual members made their own evaluations of constituency interests and depended less on organized groups to mediate constituent demands, "congressional entrepreneurs" pushed concerns over the environment, food safety, and even fiscal austerity on to the agricultural agenda.[66]

However, even Browne acknowledges that agricultural interests still retain distinct advantages in the congressional farm policy game. With historic links to the agricultural committees in Congress, intimate knowledge of the technical complexity of farm policy, and a great deal at stake in the battles over farm subsidy provision, agricultural interests are not easily pushed aside in policy debates.[67] Despite the rising cost of agricultural supports, successful retrenchment depended on opportunities for blame avoidance, entrepreneurial issue definition, and venue change. Institutions shaped these opportunities. In particular, the congressional budget process proved to be an effective tool for agricultural retrenchment during the 1980s and early 1990s.

---

[64] "Congress Enacts Lean Farm Package," *Congressional Quarterly Almanac* 46 (1990): 334–35; Potter, *Against the Grain*, 73.

[65] Office of Management and Budget, *The Budget for Fiscal Year 2000, Historical Tables*, 52 (Budget Function 350).

[66] Browne, *Cultivating Congress*, 8–20, 133–36.

[67] Ibid., 143–45.

Fiscal Austerity and Farm Policy

Farm leaders had been aware since the 1940s that high budgetary costs could undermine political support for commodity programs. In 1949, Farm Bureau president Allan Kline opposed the Brannan Plan, in part because it placed the burden of farm program costs squarely on the shoulders of taxpayers. As Kline complained in 1949, "The income of American farmers should not be made dependent upon annual appropriations from the Federal Treasury." The *Kiplinger Washington Newsletter* suggested that Kline's sentiment was prompted by the fear that "Congress might cut it [payments] off . . . if taxpayers get tired of paying."[68] In other words, Kline realized that the shift from price supports to direct payments increased the transparency of government policy and made federal farm programs politically vulnerable.

Kline, in fact, proved highly prophetic. The shift from price supports to direct payments in the early 1970s bore strong resemblance to the Brannan Plan defeated in 1949. What Kline could not foresee was the manner in which the 1974 Congressional Budget and Impoundment Control Act centralized spending authority in Congress. Specifically, the 1974 act created new budget committees in both chambers and mandated passage of budget resolutions, which set overall targets for spending. If congressional authorizing committees did not meet these targets, the 1974 act also included a provision, known as *reconciliation*, that could effectively force congressional committees to report new legislation that would bring revenues or spending in line with the budget resolution.[69]

Although resolution and reconciliation were designed to strengthen congressional authority over the annual budget process, the Reagan administration transformed them into a useful tool to curb the spending proclivities of a Democratic Congress by forcing congressional authorizing committees to cut expenditures for most domestic programs.[70] In agriculture, the reinvigorated budget process imposed strict spending limits that significantly constrained the policy alternatives available to the House and Senate Agricultural Committees. Over the next decade, Congress rolled back federal commitments to agriculture in order to meet budget reduction targets.

In 1981, the House and Senate Agriculture Committees drafted legislation to increase farm spending by several billion dollars over the next four years. In May, however, Reagan secured his famous budget victory when

[68] "Kline Hits Brannan Plan," *Official Newsletter of the American Farm Bureau Federation*, May 2, 1949, 1; *Kiplinger Washington Letter*, April 30, 1949.

[69] Wildavsky and Caiden, *The New Politics of the Budgetary Process*, 74–79.

[70] Ibid., 98–115.

House and Senate conferees approved the president's budget resolution to slash spending for fiscal year 1982. For members of the House and Senate Agriculture Committees writing the new farm bill, the budget resolution required them to cut $3.2 billion in program costs. Rather than increase spending as initially envisioned, farm-state lawmakers were forced to rewrite the farm bill to meet the new, reduced spending targets.[71] In December 1981, Congress approved a conference committee report that ended the indexation of farm support prices to inflation, lowered price supports for milk, and relaxed production controls for peanuts and rice. All major farm organizations, except the free-market Farm Bureau, opposed the legislation.[72]

The political implications of the 1981 farm bill were more important than the substantive changes in the new legislation. Congressional budget battles weakened the positive-sum, cooperative logroll among commodity groups that had characterized farm politics since the 1960s. Subsequent debates over agricultural policy revealed the fragility of the farm coalition. With each commodity interest eager to defend its program, it became difficult to hold any coalition together. As one lobbyist remarked, "It used to be that everybody could get their piece of the pie, and if the pie was too small, then [Congress] could just make it bigger."[73] This was no longer the case after 1981 as the new deficit politics made farm policy increasingly zero-sum.

Aware that budget constraints weakened pro-spending logrolls, OMB director David Stockman encouraged the Reagan administration to favor agricultural proposals that were "unacceptable to the farm guys so that the whole thing begins to splinter."[74] Budget constraints also weakened the relationship between urban liberals and farm-state lawmakers as scarce resources made it difficult to tie an increase in farm supports with an increase in social welfare spending. Symbolically, food stamp advocates refused to support higher farm subsidies after rural members of Congress voted for a budget deal that cut aid to the poor. In the words of John Ferejohn, "By imposing relatively tight funding limits on agricultural legislation, [reconciliation] undermined the omnibus approach that characterized [farm policy]."[75]

The shadow of mandatory budget cuts loomed over every farm bill after 1981. Budget decisions now set the farm policy timetable. In 1985, as farmers suffered under the worst economic crisis since the Great

---

[71] Congressional Quarterly, *Congressional Quarterly Almanac* 37 (1981): 247–59.

[72] Ibid., 535–48; Bowers, Rasmussen, and Baker, *History of Agricultural Price Support and Adjustment Programs*, 36–40.

[73] Quoted in Wildavsky and Caiden, *The New Politics of the Budgetary Process*, 183.

[74] Greider, "The Education of David Stockman," 35.

[75] Ferejohn, "Logrolling in an Institutional Context," 248.

Depression, Congress struggled to square the circle of higher program costs in an environment of fiscal austerity. The House Agriculture Committee completed work on farm legislation by mid-July but could not report the bill until Congress voted on a budget resolution. That is, policy decisions for agriculture could take place only *after* Congress set spending targets for the coming years. Once these targets were known, the agriculture committees rewrote portions of the farm bill. The eventual Food Security Act of 1985 fell short of administration hopes, but it did freeze target prices and reduce loan rates (which set the effective price floor) to market-clearing levels.[76]

In 1990, Congress had already completed work on a new farm bill when passage of a $500 billion deficit reduction package forced the House and Senate Agriculture Committees to cut farm program costs by an additional 25 percent. Farm organizations complained that "farmers are being asked to bear so much of the burden of the federal budget deficit." The eventual Food, Agriculture, Conservation, and Trade Act of 1990 froze target prices, reduced loan rates, and lowered payment limits. As mentioned earlier, however, environmental provisions were strengthened in the 1990 act.[77]

The budget process also became an important policy mechanism in its own right *outside* the usual farm bill cycle. In 1982, Congress changed the tobacco support program so that there would be no net cost to the federal government. As part of the omnibus budget bill for 1982, Congress froze dairy support prices and authorized the secretary of agriculture to deduct up to $1.00 per hundredweight of milk from dairy farmers to help offset program costs.[78] In 1987, the Omnibus Budget Reconciliation Act reduced target prices and cut the acreage eligible for enrollment in government support programs. The 1989 Omnibus Budget Reconciliation Act reduced deficiency payments and cut funding levels for export subsidy programs (the Export Enhancement Program) at a savings of $3.5 billion in farm program costs. Finally, the 1990 Omnibus Budget Reconciliation Act, passed shortly before the 1990 farm bill, cut nearly $14 billion in agricultural spending reductions through changes in the calculation of deficiency payments and further reductions in the amount of acreage eligible for government supports.[79]

[76] Congressional Quarterly, *Congressional Quarterly Almanac* 41 (1985): 515–39.

[77] "The Budget Battle," *New York Times*, October 14, 1990, 24; "Farm Pact Cuts Outlays 25 Percent," *Washington Post*, October 17, 1990, 1; "Farm Bill Debate Is Severely Restrained in the Shadow of the Budget Ax," *Washington Post*, July 27, 1990, 6.

[78] Congress modified these changes in the 1983 Dairy and Tobacco Adjustment Act. The act froze tobacco supports, reduced dairy support prices, and added a new producer assessment to further reduce dairy program costs. Bowers, Rasmussen, and Baker, *History of Agricultural Price Support and Adjustment Programs*, 42–43.

[79] Hallberg, *Policy for American Agriculture*, 321–23.

In the 1980s and 1990s, the congressional budget process became an effective mechanism for agricultural retrenchment. First, congressional budget politics decreased the autonomy of the House Agriculture Committee over farm programs. As Weaver points out, "Budget deficits . . . have undercut the ability of clientele and policy specialists to keep decision-making within a narrow (and favorable) policy subsystem."[80] At least in agriculture, the budget process operated as an instrument of "centralizing retrenchment."[81] Second, deficit politics weakened the pro-spending logrolls and, in so doing, softened opposition to retrenchment. Stockman's strategy in 1981 was a deliberate attempt to "divide and conquer" retrenchment opponents.[82] Similarly, in 1985, urban Democrats abandoned the farm coalition completely and endorsed Reagan administration proposals for cuts in farm programs. Third, by executing agricultural retrenchment through omnibus reconciliation bills covering a wide range of programs and policies, farm-state lawmakers minimized the risk of voting for spending cuts individually. In this way, omnibus legislation provided a useful mechanism for blame avoidance.[83]

Venue Change and the 1996 Farm Bill

Budget battles over agricultural spending continued through the early 1990s; the 1993 Budget Reconciliation Act whittled away a further $3.2 billion in farm spending.[84] But with the election of a Republican majority to Congress in 1994, agricultural debates took a decidedly more partisan and ideological tone. For Republican House leaders such as Newt Gingrich and Richard Armey, the latter a vocal critic of farm subsidies, commodity programs not only were an obvious target for budget cuts but also provided an opportunity for the Republicans to illustrate their commitment to free-market principles. But other Republicans, notably Senate Majority Leader Bob Dole, remained staunch defenders of agricultural interests. Moreover, thirty-five Republicans in the House represented districts with at least 5 percent of the population employed in agriculture.[85]

---

[80] Weaver, "The Politics of Blame Avoidance," 382.

[81] Stewart, "Budget Reform as Strategic Legislative Action," 297.

[82] Pierson, *Dismantling the Welfare State?* 22–23.

[83] Weaver, "The Politics of Blame Avoidance," 384.

[84] Congressional Quarterly, *Congressional Quarterly Almanac* 49 (1993): 226.

[85] I chose 5 percent as a benchmark in this context because it is exactly one standard deviation from the district average of 2.6 percent. Winston, Hederman, and Olson, *The Congressional District Ranking Book*. By another count, thirty-three freshman Republicans out of seventy-six had "significant agricultural activity" in their districts. "The Farm Team," *National Journal*, July 1, 1995, 1708.

As Congress prepared to write new farm legislation in 1995, it became clear that agriculture would be an important test of Republican resolve.[86]

Work on agriculture began in late summer after the House and Senate Agriculture Committees received reconciliation instructions to reduce farm program costs by $13.4 billion. As in other farm bill battles since 1981, this budget number set the terms for subsequent policy debates. In the Senate, Agriculture Committee chair Richard Lugar introduced legislation that met the budget reduction target through an increase in the amount of land ineligible for subsidies from 15 to 30 percent. This mechanism was similar to the 1990 Omnibus Budget Reconciliation Act and would permit the system of government target prices and deficiency payments to remain intact. In addition, the Lugar proposal would cap the amount of subsidies available for each commodity, scale back the dairy price support program, and reduce export subsidies. Despite some initial grumbling, Lugar secured committee approval of his plan in late September.[87]

In the House, Agriculture Committee chairman Pat Roberts introduced a more radical proposal that would eliminate all acreage controls and price supports linked to production, including target prices and deficiency payments. Instead, farmers would receive "market-transition payments" that would be phased out over the next seven years. Politically, the Roberts proposed—otherwise known as the Freedom to Farm plan—gained support over other reform proposals because it cut costs, simplified regulations, and, most important, was easy to grasp by nonspecialists. In the words of a senior Republican staff member on the House Agriculture Committee, "We have come up with a farm policy people understand." These qualities made the Roberts plan an immediate favorite among the House leadership and the Republican rank and file.[88]

But within the House Agriculture Committee, the proposal touched off a rancorous debate that deeply divided members along regional and commodity lines. Representatives from corn and soybean regions of the Midwest welcomed the proposed removal of acreage controls and supported the Roberts plan. Representatives of cotton and rice farmers in the South, however, feared that the elimination of acreage controls would lead to overproduction and falling prices. When Freedom to Farm came up for a vote in committee, four Republicans joined the Democrats and

---

[86] "Farmers Brace for Stormy Debate over Subsidies," *New York Times*, February 6, 1995, 1; "Plowing a New Field," *National Journal*, January 28, 1995, 212–16.

[87] "House Torn on Agriculture; Senate Makes Progress," *Congressional Quarterly Weekly Report*, September 30, 1995, 2982–83.

[88] Press release, *House Agriculture Committee*, August 3, 1995; interview, Senate Committee on Agriculture and Nutrition, October 5, 1995; interview, House Agriculture Committee, October 6, 1995.

together defeated the Roberts bill. In the words of a senior Democratic staffer on the House Agriculture Committee reflecting upon thirteen years of experience, "We're split now like [we've] never been split before."[89]

With the Agriculture Committee unable to agree, Roberts abdicated control, and the Republican leadership shifted authority for farm legislation to the House Budget Committee, which inserted Freedom to Farm into the omnibus budget bill.[90] This move placed farm legislation in the hands of a committee with little rural representation. One lobbyist complained that "some of the people calling the shots in the entire agriculture debate had never seen a farm."[91] More important, the move tied farm legislation to the massive budget plan working its way through Congress. As one Republican staffer explained, "You can't oppose reconciliation just because of agriculture."[92] When the House approved the budget reconciliation bill in late October 1995, the measure included the agricultural provisions rejected by the House Agriculture Committee.[93]

As a conference committee worked to reconcile the House bill with the more traditional policy mechanisms contained in the Senate bill, House leaders pressed hard for inclusion of the Freedom to Farm provisions in the final version of the budget reconciliation package. House Speaker Newt Gingrich personally chaired several agriculture panels. When a dispute over dairy provisions threatened to derail negotiations, GOP leaders removed dairy from the final bill and secured a waiver from the budget committees that reduced the required cuts necessary for reconciliation. Conferees agreed on the final provisions of the agriculture title of the budget reconciliation package in November 1995. The elimination of target prices and deficiency payments for major field crops (corn, wheat, soybeans, cotton, and rice) formed the core of the agriculture provisions.[94]

When Clinton vetoed the omnibus budget bill in late 1995, a new round of farm policy negotiations began. With a majority in both chambers on record in favor of the Roberts plan, the agriculture committees turned

[89] Interview, House Agriculture Committee, October 6, 1995; "Cotton Farmers Fear Being Plowed Under by New Federal Bill," *Dallas Morning News*, October 10, 1995; "Midwest Farmers Ask for Less Government, Open Markets," *Chicago Tribune*, October 15, 1995, 11; "The Republicans' Farm Crisis," *New York Times*, October 1, 1995, 1.

[90] Interview, House Agriculture Committee, October 6, 1995; "Midwest Farmers Ask for Less Government," 11; "The Republicans' Farm Crisis," 1.

[91] *Palm Beach Post*, November 18, 1995, 1.

[92] *Roll Call*, October 2, 1995; *Washington Times*, October 19, 1995, 6; *Roll Call*, November 9, 1995, 1; interview, House Agriculture Committee, October 6, 1995.

[93] For the text of agricultural provisions in the Budget Reconciliation Act (HR 2491), see *Congressional Quarterly Weekly Report*, October 26, 1995, H11095–H11006. For the vote see H11365.

[94] "Depression-Era Programs Face Sweeping Changes," *Congressional Quarterly Weekly Report*, November 18, 1995, 3523–27.

their attention to other areas of farm policy. Dairy remained a particularly contentious issue because of regional divisions among milk producers. Under the system of regional marketing orders, support prices for milk in the Midwest are lower than in other parts of the country. Dairy Subcommittee chairman Steve Gunderson (Wisconsin) hoped to eliminate this regional differential, but he met with opposition from Northeast Republicans—particularly Rules Committee chairman Gerald Solomon. Although unsuccessful in his bid, Gunderson did secure agreement in committee to end butter and nonfat dry milk price supports and simplify the system of marketing orders.[95]

Floor debate on the omnibus farm bill began in February 1996. In the Senate, a Democratic filibuster stalled passage of the farm bill until the Senate Republican leadership agreed to expand conservation provisions and reauthorize nutrition programs.[96] Meanwhile, in the House, controversy surrounded consideration of floor amendments to the farm bill. A bipartisan coalition of urban and suburban members led by Brooklyn Democrat Charles Schumer and Florida Republican Dan Miller pressured the GOP leadership to schedule a vote on an amendment that would end the federal peanut program. Connecticut Republican Christopher Shays sponsored a similar amendment to end the sugar program. Both amendments enjoyed backing from more than one hundred cosponsors and a broad coalition of food processors, free-market conservatives, consumer groups, and environmentalists.[97]

House members from peanut and sugar districts argued that the existing bill already contained significant cuts in price supports for both commodities. More ominously, opponents warned that if the amendments passed, the entire farm bill would come undone—an unacceptable outcome for both sides. In a symbolic showdown, the House defeated the peanut amendment by three votes. The sugar amendment was defeated as well, by a nine-vote margin. On final passage of the omnibus bill containing provisions for commodity programs, conservation, nutrition, and

[95] "New Congress Sours Milk Lobby," *New York Times*, October 20, 1995, A14; "Dairy Farmers Agree on Pricing Changes," *New York Times*, January 26, 1996; "House and Senate Assemble Conflicting Farm Bills," *Congressional Quarterly Weekly Report*, February 3, 1996, 295–98.

[96] "Senators Craft Farm Bill Compromise," *Washington Post*, February 1, 1996, 8; "Farm Bill Is Stalled, but Dole Promises Action," *New York Times*, February 7, 1996, 1; "Senate Approves Bill to Phase Out Farming Subsidies," *New York Times*, February 8, 1996, 1.

[97] "Opposing Forces Fall in Line to Make or Break the Bill," *Congressional Quarterly Weekly Report*, February 17, 1996, 388–90; "The Farm Team," 1705–9; "Plowing a New Field," 212–16.

trade, the House voted in favor 270 to 155 (Republicans, 216 to 19; Democrats, 54 to 136).[98]

In March 1996, a House and Senate conference committee reconciled differences in the dairy and conservation titles of the bill, after which both chambers passed the conference report by wide margins. Although the permanent 1949 legislation authorizing commodity programs remains, the Federal Agricultural Improvement and Reform (FAIR) Act did end more than six decades of government intervention in the production and prices of wheat, cotton, corn, rice, and soybeans—commodities that account for more than half of farm output. Peanut and sugar supports survived, but changes in the FAIR Act lowered price supports and eased some aspects of the remaining controls on production. These changes effectively reduced the budgetary impact of both programs to zero. In a separate provision, Florida sugarcane producers were made to pay for environmental cleanup in the Everglades. Even dairy, which seemed intractable due to regional divisions, will see some price supports eliminated after 2000 and the system of regional pricing structures simplified.[99]

The politics surrounding the FAIR Act of 1996 illustrate how entrepreneurial politicians can facilitate retrenchment through their capacity to act as, in Young's words, "agenda setters, shaping the form in which issues are presented."[100] Newt Gingrich, Dick Armey, and other members of the House Republican leadership framed the farm bill debate in a manner that placed the defenders of farm subsidies at a rhetorical disadvantage.[101] A fortuitous boom in commodity markets in 1995 and 1996 provided a crucial advantage in this regard.[102] With prices for wheat, corn, and soybeans at record high levels, free-market liberals argued that farmers would be more productive if released from burdensome government regulations. Even President Clinton echoed this sentiment: "At long last,

[98] "House Lets Two Farm Price Supports Survive," *New York Times*, February 29, 1996, A18; "Sugar Subsidies Saved in Close Vote," *Times Picayune*, February 29, 1996, C1; "House Approves Biggest Change in Farm Policy since New Deal," *New York Times*, March 1, 1996, 1; "House OKs Measure to End Most Subsidies," *Chicago Tribune*, March 1, 1996, 1.

[99] "House, Senate Move Closer As Bills Go to Conference," *Congressional Quarterly Weekly Report*, March 2, 1996, 543–49; "House-Senate Committee Agrees on Overhaul of Farm Programs," *New York Times*, March 22, 1996, 1.

[100] Young, "Political Leadership," 294.

[101] One can argue that Pat Roberts and Richard Lugar also viewed the farm bill in entrepreneurial terms for electoral reasons: Roberts was contemplating a Senate run, and Lugar was, at the time, a presidential candidate. Charles Schumer also fits the profile of an entrepreneurial politician in his advocacy of retrenchment.

[102] Orden, Paarlberg, and Roe, "A Farm Bill for Booming Commodity Markets"; Paarlberg and Orden, "Explaining U.S. Farm Policy in 1996 and Beyond."

farmers will be free to plant for the market, not for government pro-grams."[103] High prices also made it easier to sell retrenchment to farm constituencies who, without the FAIR Act, would have seen government payments decline in 1996.[104]

More important, however, high commodity prices helped retrenchment advocates challenge the belief that government payments went to deserv-ing "family farmers." For instance, the Environmental Working Group issued a study in 1995 identifying so-called city slickers—recipients of large commodity payments residing in urban areas. According to its head, Kenneth Cook, the report was intended to dispel the myth that farm pol-icy "is about family farms, in the romantic way that Americans think about them."[105]

In other words, retrenchment advocates framed the farm policy debate in a manner that highlighted the benefits of the FAIR Act for diffuse inter-ests such as taxpayers, consumers, and environmentalists. Defending the merits of the proposed farm bill, Illinois Republican Thomas Ewing ar-gued that "rewrite of the depression-era farm programs . . . brings an end to Government control of farm markets and artificially inflated prices and limited food supplies. The environment is also helped by . . . removing current farm policy, which in some cases has been a disincentive to natural crop rotation . . . [and led to] overuse of fertilizer. Taxpayers . . . should also rejoice because there is savings in the billions in this bill for agricul-ture."[106] This emphasis on the benefits of the FAIR Act for nonfarmers broadened the coalition and increased the chances of success. In the final vote for the farm bill in both the House and the Senate, for example, Republican votes alone were not enough to secure a majority. The FAIR Act passed with the help of fifty-four Democrats in the House and twenty Democrats in the Senate.[107]

The handling of the farm bill by the House leadership also illustrates how the strategic manipulation of policy venues can enhance the chances

---

[103] The White House, Office of the Press Secretary, "Statement by the President on Farm Bill Signing," April 4, 1996.

[104] Under the old deficiency payment scheme, government payments made up the differ-ence between politically determined target prices and market prices. With market prices so high in 1996, deficiency payments would have been less than the market transition payments in the FAIR Act, which were calculated according to historic deficiency payments to farmers. *Provisions of the Federal Agriculture Improvement and Reform Act of 1996.*

[105] "Reports Describe Widespread Abuse in Farm Program," *New York Times*, October 2, 1994, 1; "Farm Aid to Chicago? Miami? Study Hit an Inviting Target," *New York Times*, March 16, 1995, 1.

[106] Statement of Congressman Thomas Ewing (R-Ill.), *Congressional Record*, 104th Cong., 2d sess., February 28, 1996, H1421.

[107] The House vote was 270 to 155: Republicans, 216 to 19; Democrats, 54 to 155. The Senate vote was 64 to 32: Republicans, 44 to 6; Democrats, 20 to 26. See note 97.

of retrenchment success. Were the House Agriculture Committee an effective veto player—"an individual or collective actor whose agreement . . . is required for a change in policy"—the Roberts proposal to eliminate target prices and deficiency payments would have failed in 1995.[108] But because of jurisdictional overlap in Congress, and specifically the rules of the congressional budget process, the House Republican leadership could shift farm policy jurisdiction to the House Budget Committee. In so doing, Gingrich and his allies circumvented recalcitrant farm-state politicians on the House Agriculture Committee. Even the unsuccessful effort to eliminate the sugar and peanut programs illustrates how House rules can be manipulated to place retrenchment proposals on the agenda. Despite the concerns of the House Agriculture Committee, the House Republican leadership scheduled floor votes on the contentious amendments.

As Baumgartner and Jones point out, "When the venue of a public policy changes, . . . those who previously dominated the policy process may find themselves in the minority, and erstwhile losers may be transformed into winners."[109] Staff members on the House Agriculture Committee interviewed during the farm bill struggle confirmed that the breakdown of committee autonomy from the House leadership resulted in a loss of control over policy outcomes. As one Democratic staff member who served as legislative director for the 1990 farm bill recalled, "In the past we did so good protecting [agricultural interests] and we were bipartisan. . . . [Former House Agriculture Committee chairman] De la Garza . . . allow[ed] no interference from the leadership," but in 1995, "the committee [suffered] under a very involved leadership." His Republican counterpart agreed that "the leadership is doing a hell of a lot of stage-managing."[110]

With the shift in policy jurisdiction upward and away from the House Agriculture Committee, farm groups lost a degree of influence. A lobbyist for the National Association of Wheat Growers, interviewed in 1995, confirmed that farm organizations "are having less influence because the leadership has control of the agenda." Even a lobbyist from the free-market Farm Bureau acknowledged, "We haven't been able to be as effective because [policy] comes straight from the [GOP] leadership."[111] According to one Agriculture Committee staff member, "Farmers don't realize the change. . . . They're not in their mothers' arms but in the hands of people who don't care [about agriculture]."[112]

---

[108] The definition of a veto player comes from Tsebelis, "Decision Making in Political Systems," 301.

[109] Baumgartner and Jones, "Agenda Dynamics and Policy Subsystems," 1047.

[110] Interview, House Agriculture Committee, October 6, 1995.

[111] Interview, National Association of Wheat Growers, October 6, 1995; interview, American Farm Bureau Federation, November 2, 1995.

[112] Ibid.

The Limits of Retrenchment

The 1996 FAIR Act was not an unqualified success for retrenchment advocates. As described earlier, the commodity regimes for dairy, sugar, and peanuts were less affected by the 1996 legislation than were field crops such as wheat, cotton, and corn. That dairy and sugar interests are major contributors to congressional campaigns provides one hypothesis for why these commodities escaped substantial reform. In fact, dairy and sugar political action committees (PACs) contribute far more than PACs representing the interests of wheat and other grains.[113] However, as Baumgartner and Leech point out in their extensive review of the literature, quantitative research that attempts to measure PAC influence on policy outcomes yields mixed results. This general finding holds true for studies that focus on agriculture. Whereas some studies do find a relationship between PAC contributions and agricultural votes in Congress, others conclude that PAC contributions have only marginal effects or make no difference at all in roll call voting on farm legislation.[114]

Although PAC contributions likely play some role, the commodity pattern of agricultural retrenchment in the United States may be due to other factors as well. As we have seen, the budget process played a central role in agricultural retrenchment during the 1980s and 1990s. Significantly, those commodities that were the least affected by retrenchment were also the least vulnerable to the budget process. Table 5.3 compares the "budget exposure" and level of producer subsidy for select U.S. commodities between 1982 and 1993.[115] Whereas only 11 percent of sugar supports and 13 percent of dairy supports were executed through budget outlays, taxpayers paid for 75 percent of wheat supports and 92 percent of corn supports. This variation is due to differences in policy mechanisms. Because dairy and sugar programs (as well as peanuts and tobacco) operate largely through price supports rather than direct payments, the cost of support falls predominantly on consumers of these commodities. Consequently, the budget exposure of these commodities is comparatively low. In contrast, the budget exposure for programs that support field crops is much higher due to the reliance on direct payments as the principal policy mechanism. We would expect commodities supported mainly by consum-

---

[113] In the 1997–1998 campaign cycle, sugar PACs contributed $1.8 million to congressional candidates, and dairy PACs contributed $1.1 million. The combined total for wheat, soybeans, corn, rice, and cotton PACs was only $724,000. For PAC contributions according the Standard Industrial Classification, see Public Disclosure Inc., *FECInfo*.

[114] For details on these studies, see Baumgartner and Leech, *Basic Interests*, 132–36.

[115] The "budget exposure" is simply the proportion of subsidies executed through direct government outlays.

TABLE 5.3
Budget Exposure and Producer Subsidy Equivalent
for Select U.S. Commodities, 1982–1993[a]

Commodity	Budget Exposure[b]	Producer Subsidy Equivalent[c]
Sugar	10.6	58.2
Dairy	12.6	48.0
Wheat	74.5	39.7
Corn	91.8	26.1
Soybeans	94.3	7.5

[a] Average.
[b] Proportion of policy transfers executed through direct budgetary outlays.
[c] Policy-related transfers as a percentage of the value of agricultural production.
Source: USDA, *Estimates of Producer and Consumer Subsidy Equivalents, 1982–1993*.

ers to be less vulnerable to budget-driven retrenchment than commodities supported by taxpayers.

This suspicion is borne out in the second column of table 5.3, which shows that there is an inverse relationship between the budget exposure of a commodity and the level of producer subsidy. Efforts to cut agricultural expenditures in the 1980s and 1990s inevitably drew congressional attention toward field crops such as corn and wheat, since changes in these commodity regimes could be executed through the budget process. In contrast, the vast majority of subsidies for dairy and sugar were "off-budget." As a result, producers of these commodities enjoyed greater immunity from the politics of fiscal austerity. Nevertheless, as I have mentioned, Congress did make changes at the margins that lowered the budgetary impact of supports for dairy, tobacco, and other heavily protected commodities.

This difference in the policy mechanisms for sugar, peanuts, and dairy made it difficult to define the subsidy issue in 1995 and 1996 in a manner that promoted retrenchment. During floor debate on the amendments, defenders of sugar and peanuts pointed to the fact that neither the sugar program nor peanut program presented a heavy burden on taxpayers. In the case of sugar, import levies actually contributed to federal revenue.[116] In addition, representatives of sugar and peanut districts possessed an effective counterattack to opponents who criticized the consumer cost of these programs. Because the principal consumers of sugar and peanuts are food processors, opponents of the amendments argued that retrenchment

[116] In the words of Patsy Mink (D-Hawaii), "No one can show me that there is one penny of taxpayers' money going into the sugar program." *Congressional Record*, 104th cong., 2d sess., February 28, 1996, H1420.

would only benefit corporate users, who were unlikely to pass on lower input costs to consumers.[117] Finally, in the case of sugar, defenders transformed the debate into a foreign policy issue rife with flag-waving and chest beating. Arguing that the sugar amendment, if passed, would mainly benefit Cuban producers, North Carolina Democrat Charlie Rose implored his colleagues, "Do not please Castro. Vote against this amendment."[118]

Agricultural debates in 1998 and 1999 also illustrate the limits of retrenchment politics. As David Orden and Robert Paarlberg emphasize, high commodity prices in 1995 and 1996 helped the Republican Congress cut farm subsidies.[119] Orden and Paarlberg predicted, with some prescience, that if commodity prices declined, so would congressional capacity for retrenchment. This proved to be the case in 1998, when the combined effects of overproduction and the Asian Crisis sent farm prices downward. In October, Congress passed a $55.9 billion agriculture appropriations bill that included $4.2 billion in additional relief payments. When Clinton vetoed the agricultural spending bill, Congress increased the emergency aid package to $5.9 billion, plus $1 billion in tax breaks over five years.[120] As low prices continued through 1999, Congress passed an agriculture appropriations bill with "emergency" farm spending in the region of $8.7 billion.[121]

Aside from low prices, another important factor that contributed to the recent increase in farm spending is that debates over agriculture in 1998 and 1999 took place under unique fiscal circumstances as Congress adjusted to the new surplus politics of the late 1990s. Since 1981, as we have seen, struggles over deficit reduction and the certainty of spending cuts severely limited the policy options available in agriculture. As a

[117] See, for example, the exchange between Christopher Shays, sponsor of the peanut amendment, and Charlie Rose, who retorted, "This amendment is for the candy manufacturer's of America." *Congressional Record*, 104th Cong., 2d sess., February 28, 1996, H1465.

[118] Ibid., H1474.

[119] Orden, Paarlberg, and Roe, "A Farm Bill for Booming Commodity Markets"; Paarlberg and Orden, "Explaining U.S. Farm Policy in 1996 and Beyond."

[120] "House Passes Agriculture Spending Bill," *Congressional Quarterly Weekly Report*, October 3, 1998, 2660–61; "Tax Breaks Are Added to Farm Aid Bill," *Congressional Quarterly Weekly Report*, October 17, 1998, 2825. Republicans defeated a Democratic plan in the Senate that would have reversed a portion of the 1996 FAIR Act and renewed supports linked to market prices. "Rift over Farm Aid Leaves Agriculture Bill Searching for Life after Veto," *Congressional Quarterly Weekly Report*, October 10, 1998, 2738.

[121] "Senate Takes Middle Ground on 'Emergency' Farm Aid As Agriculture Bill Passes," *Congressional Quarterly Weekly Report*, August 7, 1999, 1940–41; "GOP Leaders Advance Farm Aid," *New York Times*, October 1, 1999; "Senate Approves $8.7 Billion for Emergency Aid to Farmers, "New York Times, October 14, 1999; "Congress Wraps Up and Heads Home on a Trail of Broken Budget Caps," *Congressional Quarterly Weekly Report*, October 24, 1998, 2889.

USDA official remarked in 1995, "You make policy to fit the budget cap."[122] The arrival of a budget surplus in 1998 removed some of the structural impediments on agricultural spending. As an "emergency" spending item, Congress sidestepped the 1997 restrictions designed to balance the budget by 2002. Perhaps more fundamentally, the congressional budget process broke down in 1998. For the first time since passage of the 1974 Budget Act, Congress failed to pass the annual budget resolution that is supposed to serve as a spending guideline.[123]

In sum, institutions contributed to agricultural retrenchment efforts in the United States in a number of ways. The access enjoyed by a variety of nonproducer interests and the largely urban and suburban character of most congressional districts expanded the farm policy agenda and attracted the attention of political entrepreneurs, from Newt Gingrich to Charles Schumer, who seized upon agricultural retrenchment as a policy issue. The congressional budget process, meanwhile, impinged upon House and Senate agriculture committee jurisdiction over policy. This helped farm-state representatives credibly deflect blame for spending cuts as agricultural matters became enveloped in omnibus reconciliation acts. In addition, an activist leadership used the budget process to shift policy authority away from institutions, such as the House Agriculture Committee, where retrenchment opponents were strongest.

But successful retrenchment also depended on exogenous factors that influenced the magnitude of institutional effects. Framing the debate in a manner that highlighted the costs of farm subsidies for nonfarmers (and the benefits of retrenchment) depended on high farm prices, a large budget deficit, or—as in 1996—both. After 1998, when neither of these conditions held, the task of agricultural retrenchment proved much more formidable.

AGRICULTURAL RETRENCHMENT IN FRANCE

The Common Agricultural Policy cemented the union between French farmers and their conservative allies. European subsidies offered high prices, dominance in a lucrative European market, and the financial capacity to modernize underdeveloped areas of French agriculture. Without the CAP, the diverse interests within French farming could not unify under the single banner of the FNSEA. At the same time, the CAP was a cornerstone of the European project that served the foreign policy interests of

---

[122] Interview, USDA, November 1, 1995.

[123] Agriculture was not the only beneficiary of "emergency spending": the 1998 budget act included $6.8 billion for defense spending and $3.4 billion for Y2K computer problems. See "House Passes Agriculture Spending Bill."

the Gaullists and, through the transfer of policy authority to Brussels, also consolidated the expansion of executive authority under the Fifth Republic.

But unlimited European subsidies resulted in huge stocks of surplus commodities. The problem of overproduction became particularly onerous in the dairy sector. Storage costs for surplus dairy products swallowed huge portions of the European Community budget each year. Warning that continued increases in dairy supports would eventually exceed the financial resources of the EC, the Directorate-General for Agriculture (DG-VI) proposed a system of national dairy quotas in July 1983. Production in excess of the quota would receive lower support prices, thereby discouraging further increases in milk production.[124]

These problems of gross agricultural surplus and runaway CAP expenditures coincided with the socialists' climb to power in 1981. The new minister of agriculture, Edith Cresson, wanted to reorient policy toward the needs of smaller producers. In addition, Cresson heavily criticized the FNSEA as an organization of wealthy farmers and promised to incorporate the leftist farm unions such as MODEF and the CNSTP into ministerial consultations such as the *conférence annuelle*.[125]

Relations between the FNSEA and the government took a predictable turn for the worse. The FNSEA organized farm protests against Cresson's proposals during the winter of 1981–1982. A demonstration in March 1982 drew one hundred thousand farmers to Paris. In a well-publicized incident, an angry mob forced Cresson to retreat by helicopter from a speaking engagement in Calvados.[126] By 1983, Cresson's campaign to broaden agricultural representation appeared to have failed. The FNSEA continued to dominate the administrative bodies that controlled the distribution of subsidies at the national and local levels. And although the 1983 elections for the Chambers of Agriculture were conducted under a system of proportional representation to increase the electoral chances of the Left, FNSEA candidates for local chambers still received more than 70 percent of the vote.[127] By late 1983, Cresson's replacement, Michel Rocard, reinstated the representational privileges his predecessor had tried to dismantle, and the minority unions again found themselves with little or no representation on official policy bodies.[128]

---

[124] Moyer and Josling, *Agricultural Policy Reform*, 67.

[125] CNSTP stands for Confédération nationale syndicale des travailleurs-paysans. Later the CNSTP reorganized as the Confédération paysans. Keeler, *The Politics of Neocorporatism*, 234; Lagrave, "Les Gauches syndicales," 364–65; Jobert and Muller, *L'état en action*, 94.

[126] Keeler, *The Politics of Neocorporatism*, 214–28.

[127] Lagrave, "Les Gauches syndicales," 365–66; Jobert and Muller, *L'état en action*, 95.

[128] A ministerial circular announced that organizations with less than 15 percent of the vote in departmental chamber elections would be excluded from consultative bodies. Servolin, "La Gauche aux commandes," 455.

It was against this political backdrop that France struggled with the sensitive issue of dairy quotas. Although most of France's European partners appeared to support the quota proposal, the FNSEA unequivocally opposed any controls on production. Thus, French support for the quota proposal in Brussels would only exacerbate the already tense relations with the farm sector. Meanwhile, the continued downturn in the French economy had caused public approval for Mitterand and the Socialists to decline from 54 to 34 percent between June 1981 and June 1983. This decline in political support further increased the risks of a political confrontation with the FNSEA.[129]

Facing these domestic political constraints, France sought to forestall any dairy agreement. At a two-day summit of European heads of state in December 1983, President Mitterand—alone among European leaders—refused to accept the quota proposal. Mitterand's opposition caused the Athens summit to end in a deadlock, and responsibility for resolving the dairy issue now shifted to France, which was set to assume the council presidency in January 1984.[130] Observers remarked that Mitterand might have blocked progress in Athens intentionally so that CAP reform would be worked out under the auspices of French leadership. With Rocard leading the Council of Agriculture Ministers, a compromise agreement could be found beneficial to French agriculture.[131] But Rocard did not have much time to work. With European parliamentary elections slated for June 1984, Agra Europe remarked that "no French government, least of all a Socialist government with only tenuous support in the rural areas, could afford to make concessions on agriculture in the run-up to [European] elections."[132]

At first, Rocard proposed to tax dairy producers and therefore cut CAP expenses without resorting to quotas. But this alternative was rejected by the Council of Ministers as an insufficient solution to the problem of surplus production.[133] With some form of quotas now likely, Rocard looked to soften the blow for French farmers. Specifically, he demanded flexibility in the administration of quotas to account for national variation in dairy production. In practical terms, "flexibility" would safeguard the competitive advantages the efficient French milk producers enjoyed in European markets. In France, Rocard's proposal received crucial support from the National Federation of Dairy Cooperatives (FNCL) and the Chambers of Agriculture. This support, as Culpepper points out, left the FNSEA

---

[129] Parodi, "Tout s'est joué trois ans plus tôt," 26.
[130] Petit, *Agricultural Policy Formation in the European Community*, 28–34.
[131] *Agra Europe*, December 9, 1983, P/4–P/5; *Agra Europe*, January 13, 1984, E/1.
[132] *Agra Europe*, January 13, 1984, E/1.
[133] *Agra Europe*, February 10, 1984, P/2.

somewhat isolated in its opposition to quotas.[134] Following twenty-six hours of uninterrupted discussions in March 1984, the Council of Ministers reached agreement on a quota package. Although France was the largest dairy producer in Europe, the quota package required only a 2 percent reduction in French milk production, compared with 11 percent for Denmark, 9 percent for Britain, and 7 percent for Germany.[135]

The struggle over dairy quotas illustrates the political difficulties of retrenchment in France and the EC. Even the Socialists—whose electoral fortunes never depended heavily on the agricultural vote—adopted a cautious approach to CAP reform after their efforts to dismantle part of the apparatus of FNSEA dominance largely failed. Clearly, minimizing blame for the Socialist Party was a crucial component of the final agreement. By securing concessions on the calculation and distribution of the quotas, Rocard diminished the political costs of agreement. The concessions left France better off in relative terms than its European competitors. This, in turn, secured the critical support of the dairy cooperatives and the Chambers of Agriculture, leaving the FNSEA isolated in opposition. In sum, Mitterand and Rocard used the council presidency to secure side payments for domestic interests in a manner that softened the opposition to dairy quotas.

1992 CAP Reform and the Uruguay Round

When CAP expenditures increased by nearly 25 percent in 1990 and 1991, agricultural policy reform returned to the EC agenda.[136] Unlike previous reform efforts, however, agriculture was now part of the Uruguay Round on multilateral trade negotiations. The United States and other agricultural exporting nations pressed for reduced export subsidies, improved market access, and lower domestic supports—all of which implied profound changes in the CAP. As Grant observes, "The GATT Uruguay Round provided a new context for the reform debate. It brought intensified international pressure on the EC, . . . and it also brought a wider range of actors into the debate within the European Community."[137] The occurrence of multilateral trade negotiations did not make reform inevita-

---

[134] Culpepper, "Organisational Competition and the Neo-corporatist Fallacy in French Agriculture," 310.

[135] Petit, *Agricultural Policy Formation in the European Community*, 34–36, 50–52; "EEC Farm Deal: Cause for Muted Celebration," *Financial Times*, March 19, 1984, 3; "EEC Dairy Accord Boosts Summit Prospects," *Financial Times*, March 14, 1984, 2; *Agra Europe*, March 9, 1984, P/1; *Agra Europe*, March 16, 1984, P/4.

[136] Commission of the European Communities, *The Agricultural Situation in the Community*, various years.

[137] Grant, *The Common Agricultural Policy*, 151.

ble—the prospect of another budgetary crisis necessitated some change in the operation of the CAP—but trade talks did influence the content of reform proposals.

In January 1991—one month after negotiations broke down in Brussels over farm trade—DG-VI produced a set of recommendations for CAP reform that called for a 35 percent cut in cereal support prices. Farmers would receive compensation for the price cut in the form of direct payments as long as they agreed to cut crop acreage by 15 percent.[138] Although DG-VI officials denied any connection between CAP reforms and the Uruguay Round, the 1991 proposals did resemble the American system of set-asides and deficiency payments. In addition, lower support prices could reduce expenditures on export subsidies and provide a defensible position in ensuing Uruguay Round negotiations. In July, agriculture commissioner Ray MacSharry released an official reform proposal incorporating the central components of these recommendations.[139]

Throughout 1991, MacSharry stage-managed EC discussions on CAP reform while keeping an eye on renewed farm trade negotiations in Geneva. The congruence of CAP reform and the Uruguay Round presented MacSharry with both opportunities and obstacles.[140] On the downside, agriculture ministers used the Uruguay Round to justify slow progress in the CAP reform process. Lacking consensus in Geneva, some farm ministers argued that CAP reform was pointless—lest a GATT agreement require further cuts in European subsidies. Specifically, EC negotiators needed assurance from the United States and Cairns Group that the compensatory payments proposed in the MacSharry Plan would be consistent with any eventual trade agreement.[141] In addition, the Uruguay Round diminished the flexibility of the French farm ministers as well as Euro-

[138] DG-VI also recommended that compensation payments be linked to farm size. This last provision, known as *modulation*, would operate through a limit on the amount of land eligible for compensation payments—thereby reducing the size of payments for large landholders. *Agra Europe*, January 18, 1991, P/1, E/1.

[139] *Agra Europe*, June 28, 1991, P/1. The recommendations also included a controversial provision that reduce compensation for the largest farmers, thereby reorienting agricultural support in the EU toward smaller farms.

[140] Analysts are divided on whether the linkage between CAP reform and the GATT helped or hindered. Coleman and Tangermann emphasize the positive effect of CAP-GATT linkages, as does Patterson. Paarlberg, on the other hand, argues that linkages stiffened the resolve of some governments against CAP reform, lest domestic agricultural interests accuse them of "caving in" to foreign pressure. Coleman and Tangermann, "The 1992 CAP Reform, the Uruguay Round and the Commission"; Patterson, "Agricultural Policy Reform in the European Community"; Paarlberg, "Agricultural Policy Reform and the Uruguay Round."

[141] The United States agreed to this requirement at a bilateral summit in November 1991. *Agra Europe*, November 16, 1991, E/2. The Cairns Group is a group of agricultural exporters including Australia, New Zealand, and Canada that advocate farm trade liberalization.

pean Commission officials, including MacSharry and the commission's president, Jaques Delors, "who were eager to avoid the impression of reforming under American pressure."[142]

On the positive side, MacSharry used the intransigence among farm ministers and the threat of a Uruguay Round failure to bring finance and foreign ministers as well as European heads of state into discussions on agriculture. Many deemed the involvement of officials outside the Agriculture Council essential if any progress was to be made. As *Agra Europe* observed, "Without pressure from above, . . . agriculture ministers will not budge from their traditional and predictable defense of an unreformed agriculture policy." Broadening the range of participants also presented a credible threat that if farm ministers did not reach a timely compromise, they would lose influence over the contours of a final agreement.[143]

Perhaps most critically, concern that agriculture could derail the entire Uruguay Round prompted an important shift in the German position toward CAP reform and isolated France within the Council of Ministers. Historically, European agricultural policy depended on the agreement of France and Germany, and since discussion of the European Commission's proposals began in January 1991, a Franco-German alliance constituted the principal obstacle to reform.[144] But the threat of a Uruguay Round failure weakened Franco-German unity. Due to economic differences in each country's farm sector, France and Germany approached the CAP with slightly different priorities. As *Agra Europe* described succinctly, "France's overriding concerns are to maintain its position as the Community's leading farm exporter. . . . Bonn is less worried about the international competitiveness of European agriculture than about income levels for its own producers."[145] In practical terms, this meant that Germany might be prepared to accept reductions in export subsidies so long as German farmers received adequate income compensation for any price cuts. The reduction of export subsidies, of course, was anathema to French Farmers, particularly those from the Paris Basin.

In July 1991, the London meeting of the Group of Seven industrial nations resolved to successfully conclude the Uruguay Round by December, a move some interpreted as "an opaque warning to EC agriculture ministers not to put the interests of their farm constituencies before the general economic well-being of the industrialized world."[146] Facing an economic slowdown and the additional strain of unification, Chancellor

---

[142] Vahl, *Leadership in Disguise*, 157; *Agra Europe*, November 29, 1991, E/1; *Agra Europe*, September 25, 1992, P/1.

[143] *Agra Europe*, September 13, 1991, P/2; *Agra Europe*, January 31, 1992, P/2, E/2.

[144] Webber, "Franco-German Bilateralism and Agricultural Politics."

[145] *Agra Europe*, October 18, 1991, E/5.

[146] *Agra Europe*, July 18, 1991, E/8.

Helmut Kohl of Germany apparently realized that "the gains in industry from success in the GATT far outweigh the losses in the farm sector."[147] Following a cabinet meeting in October 1991, the Kohl government signaled its willingness to accept CAP reform and move ahead on the Uruguay Round so long as German farmers were compensated for any price cuts—a condition MacSharry and DG-VI promised to defend in Uruguay Round negotiations. The German shift subsequently broke the alliance opposed to reform since, as Hendriks puts it, "once German objectives were satisfied in terms of compensation, there was no longer a pressing need to support France."[148] Less than two weeks after the German cabinet meeting, France—now isolated in its opposition—announced its acceptance of CAP reform, at least in principle.[149]

Despite the breakthrough, it would take more than six months to broker a final deal on CAP reform and more than a year before resolution of the Uruguay Round impasse over agriculture. In May 1992, agriculture ministers approved a cut in cereal support prices that, although smaller than the initial MacSharry proposal, would lower European expenditures on export subsidies. In addition, the May 1992 agreement instituted an acreage set-aside and a system of compensatory payments.[150]

Although the May reforms reignited the Uruguay Round, agreement proved elusive because of French concerns that MacSharry might overstep his mandate in negotiations with the United States and agree to reduce export subsidies.[151] When Jaques Delors—a Frenchman with possible presidential aspirations—expressed similar doubts about MacSharry's handling of the negotiations, a row ensued between the commission president and the agriculture commissioner. In a deft political move, Mac-Sharry resigned as negotiator, arguing that Delors had undermined his position. The move, coupled with the announcement of U.S. sanctions against EC exports in early November, again left France isolated and "forced the German government to come out in support of MacSharry's efforts."[152] In late November 1992, MacSharry returned to the negotiat-

---

[147] *Agra Europe*, October 18, 1991, E/1.

[148] Hendriks, "German Agricultural Policy Objectives," 66–68; Vahl, *Leadership in Disguise*, 168–69.

[149] "La France ne s'oppose plus à la réforme de la politique agricole commune," *Le Monde*, October 20/21, 17.

[150] *Agra Europe*, May 22, 1992, P/2.

[151] Vahl, *Leadership in Disguise*, 191–93. Article 113 of the Treaty of Rome establishes the commission as the EU representative in trade negotiations but only under a specific mandate established by the member states: "The Commission shall conduct . . . negotiations . . . within the framework of such directives as the Council may issue to it." Nugent, *The Government and Politics of the European Community*, 84.

[152] Vahl, *Leadership in Disguise*, 194–95, 266; Grant, *The Common Agricultural Policy*, 152.

ing table with renewed authority and, joined by External Relations Commissioner Frans Andriessen, brokered an agreement with the United States that ended the deadlock over agricultural export subsidies. Under the compromise (the so-called Blair House Accord), the EC agreed to reduce the volume of export subsidies by 21 percent.[153]

The 1992 CAP reforms and the eventual breakthrough in the Uruguay Round illustrate how the occurrence of international negotiations helped retrenchment advocates frame the subsidy debate in a manner that highlighted the costs of the status quo for nonagricultural sectors. Agriculture commissioner Ray MacSharry used the Uruguay Round to his advantage in this regard while being careful not to portray the CAP reform process as simply a concession to American pressure. According to Vahl, MacSharry displayed "entrepreneurial leadership" in his handling of CAP reform, particularly in his ability to "shape the presentation of issues and the framework of deals in ways that promote agreement."[154] By highlighting the costs of an unreformed CAP and an unsuccessful Uruguay Round for European (and especially German) industry, MacSharry gained critical support from Germany and isolated France in its opposition to reform.

More important, the eventual linkage between CAP reform and the Uruguay Round momentarily altered the agricultural policy venue. Specifically, the linkage between the CAP and Uruguay Round expanded the range of participants in agricultural policy debates and temporarily shifted authority away from institutions in the EC and within the member states controlled by agricultural interests. For instance, the Agriculture Council found its authority weakened as CAP reform and Uruguay Round negotiations drew the attention of foreign ministers and European heads of state. As the stakes of agricultural agreement increased, protectionist elements within both France and Germany were momentarily weakened. In the case of Germany, MacSharry's resignation from the negotiations "strengthened the hand of . . . the Economics Minister over the Agriculture Ministry, and forced Chancellor Kohl to rethink his solidarity with France."[155] Uruguay Round disputes had a similar effect in France, where "the prime minister worked closely with powerful 'pro-GATT' ministries, and the country's stances on agriculture were largely a product of interministerial debate." This, of course, shaped the interests and con-

---

[153] The agreement included a 21 percent cut in the volume of subsidized exports. Grant, *The Common Agricultural Policy*, 76–81; Vahl, *Leadership in Disguise*, 196; Patterson, "Agricultural Policy Reform in the European Community," 135–65, 157; *CAP Weekly*, November 25, 1992, 1.

[154] Vahl, *Leadership in Disguise*, 41. In his analysis of the commission, Vahl explicitly adopts the concept of entrepreneurial leadership put forward by Young, "Political Leadership and Regime Formation."

[155] Vahl, *Leadership in Disguise*, 205.

cerns that motivated policy decisions. As Epstein concludes, "With Agriculture's voice muted by its more powerful ministerial counterparts, . . . decisions were made increasingly with the broader interests of France's economy and political security in mind."[156]

But despite the inclusion of new interests in the farm policy process, agricultural interests in France and in the EC still retained significant institutional advantages. In France, farmers' electoral influence assured that political leaders advocated retrenchment only at their peril. More political currency was to be gained by defending agriculture and denouncing U.S. pressure for farm trade liberalization. Because of the structure of European institutions, moreover, French domestic politics set limits on what was acceptable in the context of Uruguay Round negotiations. Although France could not prevent an agreement, it could extract concessions that diluted the impact of reform.

Blair House and Agenda 2000: The Limits of Retrenchment

Although the Uruguay Round presented an opportunity for retrenchment in European agriculture, the requirement that trade agreements and reform packages gain approval from the member states presented a formidable hurdle for advocates of policy change. Although many European Union matters are decided by a qualified majority, the practice of unanimous consent is a common one in agriculture and in trade matters generally. Unanimity, in the words of Garrett and Tsebelis, gives "all the decision-making power to the government with the least interest in changing the status quo."[157] Throughout much of the struggle over the Uruguay Round, this government was France.

In a September 1992 referendum, French voters narrowly approved the Maastricht Treaty.[158] Critically, 76 percent of French farmers voted against Maastricht, a verdict interpreted as a repudiation of the May 1992 CAP reform package.[159] The Blair House Accord reached in November 1992 only added to agricultural discontent as farm organizations criticized the curb on export subsidies as a substantial threat to French farm exports. And with legislative elections scheduled for the following spring, politicians of all stripes adopted a hard line against the Uruguay Round, many demanding that renegotiations take place on the export subsidy

---

[156] Epstein, "Beyond Policy Community: French Agriculture and the GATT," 364.

[157] Garrett and Tsebelis, "An Institutional Critique of Intergovernmentalism," 281.

[158] Maastricht, among other things, moved Europe toward monetary union and increased the powers of the European Parliament. See Grant, *Delors*, 181–210.

[159] "Le Referendum sur la Traite Maastricht," *Le Monde*, September 19, 1992; Platone, *Les électorats sous la Vème République*, 203.

component of the Blair House Accord. According to one estimate, 150 parliamentary seats could rest on the government's Uruguay Round position.[160] Consequently, the Bérégovoy government, "plumbing the depths of unpopularity," threatened to invoke the Luxembourg Compromise and veto the Blair House agreement.[161]

By withholding assent, the French government could postpone a Uruguay Round agreement until after the election. The Right won the election under a unified ticket of the RPR and the Union pour la démocratie française (UDF), and Edouard Balladur, leader of the new coalition government, only hardened French resolve. Again, the domestic politics of agriculture in France help explain the French position. First, as the leader of a coalition government, Balladur "was tightly constrained by the balance of opinion on agricultural trade within his Parliamentary majority . . . over which . . . he had only limited influence." Whereas a majority of Balladur's UDF party supported the Blair House Accord, the Gaullist RPR was steadfastly opposed. Balladur himself reports that he was threatened with a parliamentary revolt and a vote of no confidence if he accepted Blair House.[162] Second, Balladur had his eyes on a 1995 presidential bid and did not wish to sacrifice his long-term political aspirations by accepting a trade agreement opposed by his farmer constituents. More accurately, Balladur did not want to give his coalition partner and political rival Jacques Chirac an opportunity to advance his own presidential aspirations.[163]

In the end, French obstruction did secure concessions from France's European partners and from the United States. At a June Franco-German summit, Balladur warned Chancellor Kohl that his government would fall unless he vetoed the agreement in its current form. Apparently convinced, Kohl announced in August 1993 that "we must find a compromise acceptable to everyone," a statement widely interpreted to indicate German support for a renegotiation of Blair House. At a council meeting of foreign ministers in September 1993, Germany supported a French text that set out European Commission priorities in upcoming Uruguay Round negotiations. With their mandate defined by the September council meeting, EU negotiators secured a concession from the United States that permitted a substantial increase in the volume of subsidized exports allowed under the Uruguay Round agreement. In addition, France secured a promise from its EU partners that no additional land set-aside would be needed to comply with the Uruguay Round agreement.[164] Both conces-

---

[160] Webber, "High Midnight in Brussels," 581.

[161] Grant, *Delors*, 178.

[162] Webber, "High Midnight in Brussels," 582; Balladur, *Deux ans à Matignon*, 141.

[163] See "Gaullist Politics and the GATT," *Journal of Commerce*, September 14, 1993, 28.

[164] This was achieved by changing the base year used to calculate subsidy reductions. Webber, "High Midnight in Brussels," 589.

sions served the interests of French agricultural exporters. As Webber concluded, "The French government benefited in the Uruguay Round conflict from . . . the norm and practice of consensual decision-making."[165]

The effect of consensus decision making was also noticeable in 1999 during the struggle over the Agenda 2000 reforms. In 1998, EU agriculture commissioner Franz Fischler unveiled a CAP reform proposal to cut support prices for cereals and livestock, as well as institute reforms of the dairy quota regime. The reforms, Fischler argued, would keep the CAP within its existing WTO commitments on export subsidies, position the EU for the upcoming round of agricultural trade talks scheduled to begin in late 1999, and make possible the enlargement of the EU to include the countries of Eastern Europe.[166]

Fischler's reform plan gained an important boost in October 1998 when the Social Democratic Party won parliamentary elections in Germany. Unlike their predecessors, the Christian Democrats, the Social Democratic Party did not have historic electoral ties with farmers or with the umbrella farm organization in Germany, the Deutscher Bauernverband (DBV). This increased the range of political possibilities, and in early 1999, the new Schroeder government used its control of the rotating EU presidency to make a strong push for the reform agenda. Germany even proposed a system of "cofinancing," through which member states would pay part of the cost of farm subsidies directly from national budgets. France, as the largest beneficiary of the current CAP, steadfastly opposed any cofinancing scheme and treated the proposal as a direct affront to the Franco-German relationship that, as we have seen, is often the keystone of agreement in agriculture. In the face of French intransigence, Germany abandoned its proposal for cofinancing. With a majority of member states in favor of the Fischler package, the Council of Ministers agreed by a qualified majority to cut support prices for beef, cereals, and milk. The agreement was hailed as the most significant reform of the CAP since it was established in the 1960s.[167]

The agriculture agreement was one component of a larger reform package that required the approval of EU heads of government at the Berlin summit in late March. At the summit, French president Jacques Chirac—whose RPR party depends heavily on the farm vote—withheld agreement on the entire Agenda 2000 package unless debate was reopened on the agricultral component. With European leaders facing the twin crises of

[165] Ibid., 590.

[166] *Agra Europe*, March 20, 1998, EP1, EP3.

[167] "Bonn Keen to Reform CAP," *Financial Times*, January 2, 1999, 1; "Farm Aid: EU Talks End in Disarray," *Financial Times*, March 6, 1999, 1; "CAP: Barnyard Noises," *Financial Times*, March 3, 1999; "EU: Triumphal Mood after Farm Aid Deal," *Financial Times*, March 12, 1999.

NATO air attacks on Yugoslavia and the mass resignation of the European Commission in the wake of a corruption scandal, Chirac succeeded in his effort to water down the agriculture provisions. To the disappointment of reformers, the eventual farm reform package agreed to in Berlin included smaller cuts in support prices for beef and cereals and delayed cuts in dairy prices until 2005. Consequently, the 1999 reforms will not achieve enough budget savings to make eastward enlargement affordable or to position the EU aggressively for upcoming trade negotiations.[168]

In sum, farm subsidy retrenchment in the EU is constrained by the domestic politics of agriculture in France. Because of the political significance of the farm vote and farmers' capacity to make life difficult for governments of both the Left and the Right, reform advocates confront very real political risks in their attempt to cut subsidies or lower farm trade barriers. Consequently, French politicians look to minimize the risks from retrenchment. As experiences in the 1980s and 1990s illustrate, struggles over the CAP often revolve around the search for effective side payments necessary to placate French farm interests and, therefore, secure French assent to reform agreements. These side payments are necessary because European institutions, in particular consensus decision making, grant the least reform-minded member state an effective veto over agricultural decisions. In 1994 and 1999, France used this veto threat to extract concessions that diluted agricultural retrenchment efforts. As Germany's deputy foreign minister explained after the Berlin Summit, "The slowest ship determines the speed of the convoy." His comment neatly summarizes the effect of EU institutions on agricultural policy outcomes.[169]

AGRICULTURAL RETRENCHMENT IN JAPAN

The Japanese agricultural welfare state united an economically dominant network of cooperatives with an electorally dominant political party. This partnership yielded mutual benefits. On the strength of its rural base, the Liberal Democratic Party controlled Japanese politics for almost forty years. As a core constituency of the LDP, Nokyo solidified its central role in the agricultural economy and secured a steady flow of government funds to rural Japan.

Although the political benefits of farm subsidies were great, so too were the economic costs. Under the dual pricing structure of the food control system, the government purchased rice from farmers at one price and sold it to wholesalers at another (usually) lower price. During the period of rapid economic growth, producer prices for rice increased steadily, along

---

[168] "EU Summit: Defeat for Market Liberalisation," *Financial Times*, March 27, 1999.
[169] Günther Verheugen quoted in *Agra Europe*, 1 April 1999, EP/1.

with the rise in industrial sector wages, while wholesale prices for rice increased much more slowly. The result was a yawning deficit in the food control special account. Financial losses from rice supports contributed to rapid expenditure growth, and by the mid-1970s the agriculture budget consumed more than 15 percent of government outlays.[170] But agriculture was only one of many forms of government largesse fueled by LDP political competition. By the late 1970s, the government deficit was more than 7 percent of GDP; Finance Ministry officials warned of an impending fiscal crisis.[171]

In the 1980s, Japan embarked on a campaign of fiscal austerity. Whereas real general account expenditures increased by an annual rate of 10 percent during the 1970s, real expenditure growth slowed considerably to 3 percent per year during the 1980s.[172] Agriculture certainly felt the effect of the austerity campaign. Between 1982 and 1991, the Ministry of Agriculture budget declined by 26 percent in nominal terms, as did the budgets of other ministries that specialized in distributive pork-barrel politics. The Ministry of Construction, for example, saw its budget decline by 14 percent over the same period. In general, only defense and overseas development assistance were exempt from the austerity program of the 1980s.[173]

Upon closer examination, however, agricultural retrenchment was in fact much more limited than budget figures suggest. During the 1970s, financial losses from the purchase and sales of rice consumed around 30 percent of the Ministry of Agriculture budget.[174] As mentioned earlier, these losses were due to the great disparity between the producer price and consumer price of rice. During the late 1970s, the government began to close this price gap. Between 1975 and 1986, the nominal consumer price of rice increased by 52 percent, while the nominal producer price rose by 20 percent. After 1987, the consumer price *exceeded* the producer rice price; in 1991, the government actually made a profit of 17.2 billion yen from buying and selling rice.[175]

Accordingly, the government cost of rice supports declined considerably as the burden of policy shifted from Japanese taxpayers to Japanese consumers. Between 1982 and 1991, expenditures for food control

[170] Data on Ministry of Agriculture, Forestry, and Fisheries (MAFF) expenditures come from MAFF, *Statistical Yearbook*, various years; and IMF, *International Financial Statistics Yearbook 1990*, 445.

[171] IMF, *International Financial Statistics Yearbook 1995*, 156; Curtis, *The Japanese Way of Politics*, 71–79.

[172] IMF, *International Financial Statistics Yearbook 1993*, 441.

[173] George, "The Politics of Public Spending," 208, 213.

[174] Ogura, *Can Japanese Agriculture Survive?* 700.

[175] Curtis, *The Japanese Way of Politics*, 57–58; George, "The Politics of Public Spending," 188.

TABLE 5.4
Agricultural Expenditures in Japan, 1982–1991 (billion constant 1985 yen)

Year	General Account Expenditures on Food Control	Ministry of Agriculture General Account	Special Account Expenditures on Food Control[a]	Total Agricultural General and Special Accounts
1982	1,070	3,941	7,784	12,322
1991	343	2,565	4,348	7,811
+/–1982–1991	−726	−1,376	−3,436	−4,511
Percent of Savings from Food Control		52.8		76.2

[a] Net transfers from the General Account.
Source: George, "The Politics of Public Spending," 206, 208, 214.

(mostly rice supports) in the general account declined in real terms by 68 percent, from more than 1 trillion to 343 million yen. As indicated in table 5.4, closing the gap between producer and consumer prices alone accounts for more than half of the decline in the agriculture budget between 1982 and 1991.[176]

As students of Japanese budget politics know well, general account expenditures constitute only a part of overall government outlays. In addition, the government maintains so-called special accounts for specified projects. Special account budgets are subject to less scrutiny than general account expenditures.[177] In the case of agriculture, expenditures for rice purchases and sales are executed through the Food Control Special Account (FCSA). Between 1982 and 1991, expenditures for the FCSA decreased by 44 percent in real terms. If special accounts are included in the calculation, then reductions in the FCSA account for 76 percent of the decline in central government expenditures for agriculture between 1982 and 1991.[178]

In sum, the Japanese government achieved fiscal austerity in agriculture at the expense of prices for consumers. Although the budgetary impact of farm policy decreased during the 1980s, agricultural support levels remained relatively steady. Consequently, the cost of rice supports for consumers and industrial users of commodities (such as processors) became quite burdensome, and the net effect of budget cutbacks on agricultural income was rather minimal. Moreover, in order to sustain high domestic prices for rice and other commodities, the Japanese government strictly regulated foreign access to domestic markets.

[176] George, "The Politics of Public Spending," 206, 208.
[177] Schick, "Fiscal Externalities in U.S. and Japanese Budget Politics," 29; Campbell, Contemporary Japanese Budget Politics, 207.
[178] George, "The Politics of Public Spending," 214–15.

Political Accommodation and Party Politics

Higher wholesale prices particularly hurt the food industry, which became one of the first sectors of the business community to openly question Japan's farm policy. Import protection also cut into the profit margins of food processors, who, because of government policy, could not take advantage of a strong yen or the soft commodity markets of the early 1980s that would have lowered costs and increased profits.[179] In a 1983 policy paper entitled "The Food Industry in an Internationally Open Economic Society," the Federation of Economic Organizations (Keidanren) warned that "the Japanese food industry is losing its competitiveness with foreign products in domestic markets because of its inability to freely import raw materials. In order to cope with the situation, the government should swiftly liberalize [agriculture]."[180]

The timing of the Keidanren report coincided with renewed pressure from the United States to liberalize imports of beef and oranges. On the eve of bilateral negotiations, Nokyo organized a mass rally in Tokyo. Prominent LDP Diet members joined representatives of the nineteen regional agricultural cooperatives to protest against trade liberalization. And in a move that illustrated the sensitivity of the import issue for the LDP, officials from the Ministry of Agriculture, Forestry, and Fisheries (MAFF) pressured Keidanren in August 1983 to suppress its report on farm trade liberalization. In addition, MAFF officials persuaded the Ministry of International Trade and Industry (MITI) to remove a section on agriculture from a forthcoming white paper on trade.[181]

Political vulnerability for Prime Minister Nakasone and the LDP further heightened the sensitivity of the farm trade issue. In the December 1983 Lower House election, the LDP lost thirty-six seats, leaving the party with less than a majority.[182] And with Nakasone the leader of only the third-largest faction within the LDP, upsetting agricultural interests could shift the balance of power within the party and end Nakasone's premiership. Thus, while the prime minister managed the public side of the U.S.-Japanese negotiations, Nakasone let members of the agricultural

[179] "Free Import of Farm Produce, Keidanren Urges," *Japan Economic Newswire*, July 21, 1983.

[180] "Steps to Promote Food Industry Proposed," *Nihon Keizai Shimbun*, August 16, 1983, 1. In addition, food processors criticized the unfair tax structure that benefited Nokyo.

[181] Reich, Endo, and Timmer, "Agriculture: The Political Economy of Structural Change," 181; *Japan Economic Newswire*, January 8, 1983; "Strange Policy Debate," *Nihon Keizai Shimbun*, August 9, 1983, 6.

[182] In order to maintain control of the government, LDP party leaders offered a ministerial portfolio to the New Liberal Club—a small breakaway party of former LDP politicians. See Curtis, *The Japanese Way of Politics*, 33–35.

zoku reach their own consensus on American demands. One group of rural Diet members staunchly defended agricultural interests and took a hard line against any further liberalization. Another group stressed the need to consider agriculture within the broader contexts of foreign policy and economic growth.[183] Through the efforts of a high-ranking *zoku* member with close ties to both the bureaucracy and Nokyo, farm politicians accepted a proposed agreement to expand the import quotas for beef and citrus.[184] Successful resolution of the beef and citrus row eased bilateral relations with the United States and helped Nakasone win reelection to the party's top post.

But in the absence of foreign pressure, agricultural retrenchment and reform proved much more difficult. After three straight years of bumper rice harvests, government economists reported that a 6.6 percent cut in the producer price of rice would not adversely affect farm incomes. MAFF officials, in turn, proposed a 3.8 percent cut in the price the government paid farmers for their rice. Although smaller than the price cut initially advocated by government economists, the proposal did signal the first decline in the government rice price in thirty years. But when the government deadlocked over the proposed cut, Prime Minister Nakasone personally intervened and judged that the rice price should be left unchanged.[185]

According to journalists, factional politics within the LDP caused Nakasone to reject the price cut. With his term as LDP president again set to expire, contenders for the party leadership hoped to shift the blame of an unpopular price cut onto the prime minister. Nakasone, of course, also wanted to avoid blame and opted for a price freeze in order to protect his faction's political position. As a side payment to soften the blow of the price freeze, the government announced that Nokyo would take responsibility beginning in 1987 for the rice production control program. The move not only added to Nokyo's list of duties in the rice economy but also relieved the government of another financial burden associated with farm policy. According to Kano Yoshikazu, the transfer of policy responsibility from the government to the cooperatives "was accepted by Zenchu [Nokyo's political arm] as a quid pro quo for the price freeze."[186]

---

[183] This latter group, also known as the "comprehensive farm policy faction," first emerged in the late 1960s when the budgetary outlays for rice supports began to accelerate. Its influence in the agricultural policy process increased over the next decade, particularly with adoption of a rice acreage control program in the early 1970s. See Hemmi, "Agriculture and Politics in Japan," 240.

[184] Reich, Endo, and Timmer, "Agriculture: The Political Economy of Structural Change," 184–87; "Nakasone Praises Japan-US Accord on Beef, Orange Imports," *Jiji Press Ticker,* April 9, 1984.

[185] Kano, "Opening the Way to an Agricultural Renaissance," 10.

[186] Ibid.

The 1986 reversal stunned most observers and ignited further criticisms from the Japanese business community about the food control system and the political power of farmers. In the words of one business leader, the retracted price cut "strengthened the . . . impression that farmers are enjoying too many privileges at the expense of consumers."[187] Meanwhile, renewed bilateral tensions with the United States over agriculture added to business concerns about possible retaliation against Japanese manufacturing exports. In September, the United States Rice Millers Association filed a complaint with the U.S. government against Japan's rice import policies. The following month marked the beginning of the Uruguay Round, and in 1987 bilateral negotiations began with the United States over beef, citrus, and a host of other protected commodities.[188]

In the case of beef and citrus, the United States demanded the complete liberalization of imports and ruled out any expansion of the quota for these products as an acceptable alternative. Shortly thereafter, a GATT decision ruled that Japan's import protection regime for ten farm products contravened international trade law. Following the decision, Michio Watanabe, chairman of the LDP Policy Research Council, announced that "liberalization of some items is unavoidable."[189] However, farm protests in Hokkaido and Okinawa prompted government leaders to postpone acceptance of the GATT ruling—a decision that resulted in widespread criticism from the United States and other trading partners. According to an American observer of the U.S.-Japan farm trade dispute, international criticism "convinced the LDP political figures that a substantive solution was necessary." But resolution of the dispute could only take place once "the LDP leadership persuaded LDP agricultural Dietmen . . . that Japan could not hold out against world opinion." Members of the agriculture *zoku* eventually agreed to accept the GATT ruling so long as the two most politically sensitive products, dairy and potatoes, were not liberalized.[190]

Two months later, LDP leaders again sought party backing for a trade deal, this time to resolve the dispute over beef and oranges. Unless action was reached by May 4, the United States promised retaliation against Japanese exports. Under an accord reached in June, Japan agreed to con-

[187] "Domestic Pressure Enhances U.S. Push for Rice Imports," *Nihon Keizei Shimbun*, May 2, 1987, 1.

[188] "Debate on Agriculture Reforms Touches Sanctity of Rice Price," *Nihon Keizei Shimbun*, July 11, 1987, 8; Rapkin and George, "Rice Liberalization and Japan's Role in the Uruguay Round," 82.

[189] "Farm Product Liberalization in the Works," *Japan Economic Journal*, December 5, 1987.

[190] Porges, "Japan: Beef and Citrus," 247–48; "Farm Product Liberalization in the Works," *Nihon Keizai Shimbun*, December 5, 1987, 2; "Farmers Protest Imports, but Influence Wanes," *Nihon Keizai Shimbun*, January 23, 1988, 32.

vert beef and citrus quotas into a system of tariffs. As a palliative, LDP leaders promised a series of fiscal measures to help producers adjust to import competition. Despite the gesture, farmers complained bitterly about the trade agreement and the apparent abandonment of rural constituents by the Liberal Democrats.[191]

Agricultural politics in Japan during the 1980s illustrate the importance of blame-avoidance strategies in even moderate farm subsidy retrenchment. Although large budget deficits prompted a fiscal austerity campaign in the 1980s, the LDP found ways to diminish the budgetary impact of farm programs without a significant reduction in agricultural support. Instead, the government shifted the burden of rice price policy from taxpayers to consumers. And despite opposition to high domestic rice prices from the Japanese food industry, Japanese leaders avoided highly visible forms of agricultural retrenchment, as the 1986 price decision illustrates. However, import protection for agriculture led to trade conflicts with the United States, and pressure to open domestic markets did result in moderate liberalization in 1984 and 1988. But to ease the pain of import liberalization, Japanese leaders secured concessions for the most politically sensitive products—a side payment intended to facilitate agreement. In fact, the execution of agricultural retrenchment through international negotiations was an effective means of blame avoidance in itself, since, as Aurelia George-Mulgan points out, foreign pressure—or *gaiatsu*—enabled Japan's political leaders to "externalize the blame for market opening moves and thus reduce the political costs of the change."[192] Nevertheless, so long as the LDP continued to depend on rural votes, *gaiatsu* would have limits as a blame-avoidance strategy.

The Uruguay Round and the Limits of Retrenchment

If the LDP leadership appeared to embrace a more internationalist line toward agriculture with the 1988 beef and citrus agreement, the results of the 1989 Upper House elections revealed the political cost of import liberalization. The LDP suffered dramatic losses, losing its majority in the upper House of Councillors. In the run-up to the election, the leaders of the Japan Socialist Party (JSP) criticized the LDP for caving in to American pressure, while members of Nokyo's youth auxiliary campaigned against LDP candidates. Farmer support for the LDP dropped from 81 percent in the 1986 Upper House election to 50 percent in 1989—a margin sufficient

---

[191] Porges, "Japan: Beef and Citrus," 256–64; "High Noon Is Near for Beef, Orange Dispute," *Nihon Keizai Shimbun*, April 16, 1988, 32.

[192] George-Mulgan, "The Role of Foreign Pressure," 200.

to tip the balance in favor of JSP candidates running in the largely rural single-member districts. According to Flanagan et al., "The party's excessive seat losses were almost entirely attributable to the more rural . . . prefectural districts, where the party fell from twenty-five seats won out of the twenty-six in 1986 to only three seats in 1989."[193] In beef- and orange-producing districts, the LDP lost eighteen of twenty-two available seats.[194]

Interpreted by observers as a "protest vote" against the conservatives rather than a shift in party allegiance, the outcome of the 1989 election reminded the LDP of its continued dependence on the farm vote. And with a House of Representatives election scheduled for February 1990, party leaders made a decisive "about-face" in their position toward agricultural trade liberalization. Eager to repair its damaged rapport with farmers, the government announced it would not let "even a single grain of rice" enter the country. Once again endorsed by Nokyo, the move bolstered LDP support, and the party maintained its control of the House of Representatives. There were some notable losses for the LDP, however. In the rice-growing regions of Tohoku and Niigata, several high-ranking agriculture *zoku* members—including a former minister of agriculture—lost their seats to JSP rivals.[195]

Party leaders realized, of course, that the steady decline of agriculture in Japan would gradually sap the LDP of an important source of strength. The increasing precariousness of LDP electoral power, moreover, prompted some party members to advocate a change in strategy. By reversing the party's position on rice imports and resolving the Uruguay Round impasse, the LDP could sever ties with rural voters and engineer a realignment in Japanese politics. As one politician expressed later, "The LDP has positioned itself as an ally of farmers for too long. . . . the party should seek to regain its standing by also paying attention to the needs of city-dwelling consumers."[196]

---

[193] Half of the seats in the House of Councillors are elected every three years: fifty seats according to proportional representation, and seventy-six seats elected by a second vote cast for local candidates in forty-seven districts. Twenty-six of the forty-seven districts are single-member, winner-take-all seats in largely rural areas. Flanagan et al., *The Japanese Voter*, 432, 433 n.

[194] The Recruit scandal, in which over eighty politicians, bureaucrats, and businessmen were implicated in a vast influence-peddling scheme, and the imposition of a consumption tax were also factors in the election. George, "Prospects for Liberalizing Japan's Rice Market," 363.

[195] Rapkin and George, "Rice Liberalization and Japan's Role in the Uruguay Round," 63–64; "JSP Penetrates LDP-Dominant Rural Districts," *Japan Economic Newswire*, February 19, 1990.

[196] Ishihara quoted in "LDP Moves to Alienate Farmers from Coalition," *Nikkei Weekly*, December 13, 1993, 4; Bullock, "Explaining Rice Liberalization in Japan," 8.

In May 1991, several LDP leaders released trial balloons on the sensitive issue of rice imports. Within a three-day period, the LDP General Council chairman, the LDP chief cabinet secretary, and the LDP secretary-general suggested a limited opening of Japan's rice market to imports. Former deputy prime minister Shin Kanemaru raised the threat of trade retaliation by the United States if Japan failed to act: "What will happen to Japan's future if our dithering over rice worsens squabbles with the U.S. and leads that country to say 'no' to [Japanese] automobiles, machinery and consumer electronic products?"[197] But backbenchers remained reluctant, and Prime Minister Kaifu lacked the power to move the party forward.

Kaifu's replacement, Kiichi Miyazawa, continued the effort to shift the party's stance on rice. According to the Japanese press, Miyazawa appointed several prominent "moderates" from the agriculture *zoku* to his cabinet in late 1991, a move intended to gain support from rural backbenchers for some kind of rice import compromise.[198] However, negotiations dragged on due to U.S. insistence that Japan convert its rice import restrictions into tariffs. In early 1993, U.S. negotiators softened their stance and agreed to accept rice import quotas instead of tariffs. By this time, however, the Japanese party system had nearly unraveled completely. In June, sixty members of the LDP defected to one of three centrist parties and ran on an anti-LDP platform in the July Lower House elections. Key among the defectors was Hata Tsutomu—one of the agricultural *zoku* leaders tapped for a position in the Miyazawa cabinet before orchestrating the June revolt. Together with the JSP, the reform parties formed a Center-Left coalition government, ending thirty-eight years of uninterrupted LDP rule.[199]

Coincidentally, poor weather over the summer resulted in the worst rice harvest since the 1950s. Lacking sufficient grain stores, Japan was forced to import rice from Thailand. The food control system—the core of the Japanese agricultural welfare state—failed to meet its central purpose of self-sufficiency in rice. Newspaper surveys revealed consumer dissatisfaction with the current food control system.[200] Although the conflu-

---

[197] "International Stakes Prompt Japanese Leaders to Shift," *Nikkei Weekly*, June 8, 1991, 9.

[198] Rapkin and George, "Rice Liberalization and Japan's Role in the Uruguay Round," 73; Bullock, "Explaining Rice Liberalization in Japan," 11.

[199] Rapkin and George, "Rice Liberalization and Japan's Role in the Uruguay Round," 87–89; Bullock, "Explaining Rice Liberalization in Japan," 12.

[200] Only 13 percent of respondents to a December 1993 survey believed the system should remain unchanged. In contrast, 41 percent supported the general framework but believed some reform was necessary, while 36 percent of respondents believed the food control system should be abolished and the rice market deregulated. NHK (Japan Broadcasting Corpo-

ence of political and economic factors created a propitious time for change, most elements of the Japanese agricultural welfare state remained intact.

First, the change in government did little to disturb the agricultural decision-making process. As negotiators worked out details of a final agreement on rice, MAFF officials consulted with agriculture *zoku* leaders and Nokyo representatives, who agreed to the terms of the deal long before the agreement was made public. Leaders of the Socialist-led coalition apparently did not know the details of the rice agreement until December. Nor did the rice deal greatly alter party politics as some reformers hoped. By the time Japan ratified the Uruguay Round Agreement in October 1994, the LDP was once again in government and could claim credit for a 6 trillion yen ($60 billion) agricultural subsidy package passed as a side payment to rural interests.[201]

Second, the minimum access agreement preserved the government's role in the rice economy. U.S. demands that Japan convert rice import barriers into tariffs were anathema to Japanese negotiators in part because this would have ended the food control system—the basis of Japanese agricultural policy since 1942. As we have seen, food control was the Ministry of Agriculture's bureaucratic raison d'être and the source of Nokyo's economic rents. As Bullock points out, minimum access preserved the ministry's control over the domestic rice economy and created a new bureaucratic task—administration of rice imports. Similarly, the amendments to the Food Control Law enacted in 1994 deregulated portions of the domestic rice market (it is now possible for small shopkeepers to sell rice), but the government still operates a licensing system and exercises control over access to the wholesale rice market. Farmers may choose to sell rice outside of government-controlled channels, but the government pricing structure is still in place for the majority of farmers who continue to sell their rice to the Food Agency.[202]

Third, the influence of Nokyo, although damaged, remains formidable. As Nokyo diversified into a range of economic activities, its banking arm,

---

ration) survey of 1,183 adults conducted on December 4 and 5 1993, Roper Center, *JPOLL, Japanese Data Archive.*

[201] Under the agreement, Japan imported the equivalent of 4 percent of domestic consumption in 1995 and must increase imports to 8 percent of domestic consumption by 2000. Bullock, "Explaining Rice Liberalization in Japan," 12–13, 15–17; "LDP Moves to Alienate Farmers from Coalition," *Nikkei Weekly*, December 13, 1993, 4; "Government at Odds on Farm Budget Issue," *Daily Yomiuri*, October 15, 1994, 3.

[202] "Highlights of Package of Agricultural Measures," *Daily Yomiuri*, October 25, 1994, 8; "New Food Law Takes Effect," *Mainichi Daily News*, November 2, 1995, 7; Bullock, "Explaining Rice Liberalization in Japan," 13–14.

Norin Chukin, invested heavily in real estate ventures.[203] The end of the bubble economy in the early 1990s caused land values to drop, and many speculative real estate investments turned bad. In 1995, seven real estate–lending firms, or *jusen*, declared losses of 6.3 trillion yen in unrecoverable loans.[204] Although Norin Chukin was one of the biggest losers from the *jusen* meltdown, Nokyo used its political leverage with the LDP to soften the financial blow. Thanks to intervention by agriculture *zoku* leaders with the Ministry of Finance, Nokyo was asked to cover only 530 billion yen of these losses—even though Norin Chukin lent 5.5 trillion yen to the bankrupt *jusen*. When it became clear that taxpayers would be left to pay for these bad loans, public outcry and opposition party obstruction of the government budget forced the LDP and its coalition partners to renegotiate the *jusen* deal. In the end, the government eased the taxpayer load for the bailout, leaving the private banks to pick up the tab. But Norin Chukin maintained its special deal, and instead other financial institutions covered Nokyo's losses.[205]

The resilience of the Japanese agricultural welfare state in the 1990s illustrates the limits of retrenchment in the context of Japanese institutions. On the one hand, entrepreneurial leaders seized upon the Uruguay Round as an opportunity to redefine the agricultural issue in a manner that could hopefully reconfigure partisan politics. As George-Mulgan writes, "Emphasizing the significance of a successful outcome for the UR [Uruguay Round] . . . was common practice for . . . reformist-minded Japanese ruling party politicians." As an entrepreneurial strategy, the threat of trade retaliation "influences the domestic political equation, altering the relative balance of power between the pro– and anti–agricultural protection groups and thus changing the calculations of ruling party politicians with respect to the likely political costs and benefits of liberalization."[206]

But the extent of liberalization depended on the capacity to shift decision-making authority away from the bureaucratic, partisan, and private interests that preferred the status quo. According to Schoppa, *gaiatsu* "can expand elite-level participation as previously uninvolved bureaucratic agencies, senior party leadership, and interest groups come to have a stake in dealing with the problem."[207] Although foreign pressure may have expanded elite-level participation and influenced the decision to liberalize, actual decisions over the contours of the agreement remained in

---

[203] As of 1992, Norin Chukin was the world's seventh-largest bank in terms of assets. The Nokyo insurance company, Kyosairen, is the world's largest. Bullock, "Nokyo," 3.

[204] Ibid., 6.

[205] Rosenbluth and Thies, "The Electoral Foundations of Japan's Financial Politics," 9.

[206] George-Mulgan, "The Role of Foreign Pressure," 203–4.

[207] Schoppa, "Two-Level Games and Bargaining Outcomes," 370.

TABLE 5.5

Growth Rates of Agricultural Expenditures, 1975–1998

Year	Real Annual Growth Rates[a]		
	France[b]	Japan	United States
1975–1979/1980–1984	3.6	1.8	21.5
1980–1984/1985–1989	1.9	–4.4	1.7
1985–1989/1990–1994	2.1	0.1	–9.4
1990–1994/1995–1998	1.4	3.2	–16.3

[a]Growth rate $= \exp\left[\dfrac{\log(Y_t / Y_{t-5})}{5}\right] - 1$, where Y = five-year averages of expenditures in constant national currencies beginning at year t.

[b]Data extend only until 1996.

Sources: INSEE, *Annuaire statistique de la France*, various years; MAFF, *Statistical Yearbook of the Ministry of Agriculture, Forestry, and Fisheries*, various years; MOF, *The Japanese Budget in Brief*; OMB, *The Budget for Fiscal Year 1999, Historical Tables*.

the hands of agriculture *zoku* leaders, Nokyo representatives, and MAFF bureaucrats. Despite external pressure for open markets and domestic political uncertainty, both the Liberal Democrats and the Japanese agricultural welfare state survived.

AGRICULTURAL RETRENCHMENT: A COMPARISON

As this chapter has shown, politicians since the 1970s have been concerned largely with ways to trim the scope of the agricultural welfare state. Whether as part of a general campaign for fiscal austerity or in response to external pressure for farm trade liberalization, battles over retrenchment have taken place in all three countries. Both advocates of retrenchment and defenders of the status quo have encountered successes and failures in struggles over agriculture.

What has been the effect of retrenchment battles on the agricultural welfare state? One measure of retrenchment is simply the change in government expenditures for agriculture. Table 5.5 reports real annual growth rates, based on five-year averages, for agricultural expenditures between 1975 and 1998. For France, expenditures include national government outlays plus expenditures executed through the Common Agricultural Policy. For Japan, I use the general account budget for the MAFF. For the United States, expenditures include outlays for farm income supports and agricultural research.

Table 5.5 indicates that agricultural expenditures in the United States began to decline rapidly in the late 1980s. Although U.S. expenditures increased in the late 1990s, they remained well below the level of outlays witnessed in the previous decade. Overall, the pattern of expenditures in the United States illustrates the effect of deficit politics on agriculture. In contrast, agricultural expenditures in France have grown steadily in real terms since the 1970s. And with the exception of the period of austerity in the mid-1980s, farm expenditures have also increased in Japan. Moreover, as I described, cuts in the MAFF budget came at the cost of higher consumer prices for rice and other staples. Table 5.5 also indicates that Japanese expenditures increased in the mid-1990s. This may suggest that the LDP responded to the electoral upheaval of these years with additional subsidies for farmers, as Calder's thesis on crisis and compensation would predict.[208]

Of course, exclusive attention to government outlays will capture only part of the benefits farmers receive through agricultural policies. In particular, the effects of government programs that raise commodity prices are not reflected in table 5.5. In the EU, for example, transfers from consumers to farmers due to higher food prices constituted more than 40 percent of the total value of agricultural subsidies in 1997, which amounts to a 25 percent tax on food according to Organization for Economic Cooperation and Development (OECD) estimates. In Japan, the consumer burden of farm policy is even greater. Higher food prices account for 88 percent of all transfers to farmers, or an implicit consumer tax on food of 46 percent. By comparison, U.S. consumers paid for only 19 percent of producer subsidies, a sum equivalent to less than 8 percent of the consumer food bill.[209]

Therefore, a better measure of agricultural support would examine a variety of government policies that contribute to farm income. To date, the best measure is the Producer Subsidy Equivalent (PSE), developed by the OECD. The PSE measures the value of all transfers farmers receive through government programs. In addition to price supports and direct payments, the PSE also covers farmer tax exemptions, credit subsidies, subsidized irrigation, and other reductions in input costs. Government expenditures on research, extension, pest control, and marketing assistance are also included. In sum, the PSE is a comprehensive measure of government support to agriculture.[210] In figure 5.1, the PSE is expressed as a percentage of the value of agricultural production.

As indicated, the PSE generally increased in the early 1980s. In the United States, subsidies returned to precrisis levels in the early 1990s and

[208] Calder, *Crisis and Compensation.*

[209] OECD, *Agricultural Policies in OECD Countries 1998*, 46. Of course, the consumer/taxpayer share of farm supports varies according to commodities, as we have seen.

[210] For discussion of the PSE, see the annual OECD, *Agricultural Policies, Markets, and Trade.* For a discussion of the merits of the PSE, see Buckwell, "Some Microeconomic Analysis of CAP Market Regimes," 155–58.

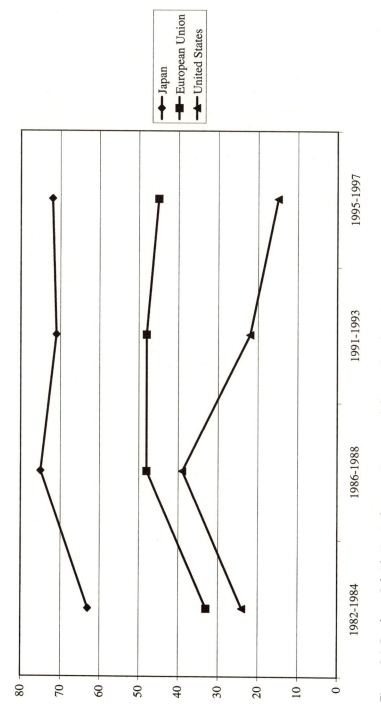

Figure 5.1 Producer Subsidy Equivalent as a Percentage of Agricultural Production, 1982–1997
Source: OECD, *Agricultural Policies, Markets, and Trade,* various years.

continued to decline.[211] In the EU and Japan, on the other hand, the PSE increased in the 1980s and remained at comparatively high levels. As of 1997, government transfers associated with agricultural programs amounted to more than 40 percent of the value of farm commodities in the EU and nearly 70 percent of the value of commodities produced in Japan. In the United States, farm policy transfers were equivalent to roughly 16 percent of agricultural production. In effect, these percentages measure the portion of agricultural income attributable to government programs.

In sum, retrenchment efforts appear to have had a greater impact in the United States than in either France or Japan. Using government expenditures on agriculture and aggregate levels of income support farmers receive as measures of retrenchment, it appears that CAP reforms in the EU or trade liberalization in Japan has had only modest effects on the agricultural welfare state. In contrast, changes to U.S. farm programs in the 1980s and 1990s appear to have had the intended effect of lowering public expenditures and increasing the exposure of agriculture to market forces.

CONCLUSION

Changes in the farm economy after 1970 contributed to rising costs associated with agricultural policies in the United States, France, and Japan. Programs designed to regulate the market and support farm incomes resulted in higher consumer prices, chronic surpluses, and rising government expenditures. Border measures such as tariffs and export subsidies intended to maintain high domestic prices produced conflicts over agricultural trade. Intensive agricultural production damaged the environment. Meanwhile, the number of farmers steadily declined. As the costs of farm policy mounted, governments faced both domestic and international pressure to dismantle portions of the agricultural welfare state.

But the capacity to reduce farm subsidies depends on a number of political factors. As Pierson reminds us, risk-averse politicians are unlikely to advocate retrenchment unless they can minimize blame for decisions that impose concentrated costs on farmers but promise only diffuse and distant benefits for taxpayers or consumers. In the United States, France, and Japan, politicians attempted to soften the blow of retrenchment through blame-avoidance strategies that obfuscated the effects of policy decisions, offered side payments to politically sensitive constituencies, and divided the opponents of retrenchment from one another.

---

[211] Again, the 1998 PSE for the United States will increase as a result of the additional supports granted that year.

But the case studies of retrenchment politics in the United States, France, and Japan also point out that blame avoidance is not the only political motivation, nor are all politicians risk-averse in matters of retrenchment. On occasion, political entrepreneurs—by definition, more risk-takers than risk-averse—will advocate retrenchment for reasons of electoral advantage or political prestige. But entrepreneurial success depends on other factors, such as the capacity to redefine the farm subsidy issue in a manner that highlights subsidy costs for nonfarm interests and manipulate policy venues so that advocates of the status quo are at a disadvantage.

Opportunities for blame avoidance and entrepreneurial success both depend on institutions. Blame avoidance is more difficult when institutions concentrate authority. Entrepreneurial behavior is more likely where parties are relatively weak and individual politicians are largely responsible for their own electoral fortunes. Entrepreneurial success, particularly with respect to venue change, is more likely in an institutional environment of jurisdictional competition than one of jurisdictional monopoly.

On balance, the policy episodes described here suggest that the conditions for successful retrenchment were more likely to be found in the United States than in France, the EU, or Japan. For instance, the 1996 farm bill illustrated how retrenchment advocates not only framed the subsidy issue in a manner that attracted broad support but also utilized the congressional budget process to shift policy authority away from the House Agriculture Committee. In France and Japan, retrenchment advocates used the occurrence of the Uruguay Round to press for policy change, but the structural advantages of agricultural interests—both in electoral contests and in the policy process—often diluted reform outcomes.

This is not to say that agricultural retrenchment in the United States was an unqualified success. The decisions to increase government aids to agriculture in 1998 and 1999 illustrate the enduring influence of appeals to an agrarian past in American politics, particularly when farm prices are low. Nor did the defenders of the status quo always win in France and Japan. Agricultural trade conflicts expanded the range of decision makers and broadened the interests involved in farm policy. In other words, exogenous factors, such as the condition of the farm economy or the occurrence of international trade negotiations, influence retrenchment outcomes as well.

When we look at measures of support, however, it is clear that agricultural retrenchment did proceed further in the United States than in Europe or Japan. At the very least, institutions shaped the extent to which exogenous factors influenced outcomes. In the United States, factors such as the Republican takeover of Congress and high commodity prices did contribute to major policy change in 1996. Because of institutions, an activist

Republican leadership intent on pleasing retrenchment-minded back-benchers could bypass a recalcitrant agriculture committee and secure far-reaching changes in the operation of farm programs. Agricultural politics in the 1990s illustrate the *vulnerability* of the U.S. agricultural welfare state to partisan and economic change.

In France, on the other hand, partisan changes such as the election of a Socialist government in 1981 did not fundamentally alter the dominance of the FNSEA. And Although the Uruguay Round negotiations on farm trade increased pressure for CAP reform, they also provided French politicians with an opportunity to dig in their heels, extract further concessions, and pander to anti-American sentiment among farmers. Similarly in Japan, there was relatively little change in agricultural politics in 1993–1994 despite the first non-LDP government in nearly forty years, the culmination of the Uruguay Round, and the failure of the food control system to guarantee rice self-sufficiency.

In conclusion, contemporary farm politics in the United States, France, and Japan illustrate the inadequacy of the mainstream view about institutions, interest group power, and policy capacity. In the United States, separated powers, congressional farm politics, and a pluralist interest group environment did not secure control of policy by rent-seeking parochial interests, nor did it prevent retrenchment decisions that inflicted concentrated costs on well-organized interests. Instead, institutions made access cheap for the critics of farm subsidies and provided advocates of retrenchment with a number of institutional avenues through which they could pursue policy goals. In France and Japan, on the other hand, institutions that concentrated authority and restricted interest group access failed to provide policy makers with autonomy from agricultural interests. Instead, institutions exposed politicians to political retribution for subsidy cuts and solidified the influence of farm organizations over the direction of policy. In some ways, contemporary agricultural politics in France and Japan displays precisely those characteristics—agency capture and policy sclerosis—supposedly found in the United States.

Conclusion

POLITICAL SCIENTISTS often argue that American institutions diminish government capacity. Central to this view is the argument that separated institutions afford interest groups with opportunities to exercise disproportionate influence over policy. American agriculture supposedly illustrated how interest groups exploit this institutional environment, and agriculture became a paradigmatic case of interest group capture. Over time, the link between institutions and interest group power first examined in the American context informed comparative studies of political institutions. Scholars argued that centralized institutions insulated policy decisions from interest group influence and augmented government capacity.

I have argued that the history of agricultural policy does not fit this standard view. In the United States, separated institutions maintained conflict and pluralism in the making of farm policy. Farmers proved unable to unify under a single organizational banner as rivalries among groups of producers preserved a high degree of conflict in agricultural policy and politics. Ultimately, interest representation in agriculture devolved to commodity-specific organizations as a way to overcome partisan and policy conflicts among farmers. But this merely institutionalized interest group pluralism in agriculture, and, beginning in the 1960s, a host of nonproducer interests gained access to the farm policy process. Coalition politics in Congress and a pluralistic interest group environment diluted the influence of farmers and their representatives over the content of agricultural policy. Capture was impossible in the context of U.S. institutions.

Second, the effects of these institutional characteristics on policy capacity were variable. At times, U.S. institutions enhanced government capacity. In the nineteenth century, party competition, bureaucratic rivalries between state and federal agencies, and a relatively unorganized interest group environment encouraged the distribution of government resources to agriculture. When policy tasks changed, institutional assets became liabilities. Unlike promotion, price supports and production controls could succeed only if farmers were somehow incorporated into the agricultural policy process. In the 1930s, party conflicts over policy alternatives, jurisdictional competition, and the lack of a corporatist client in agriculture weakened attempts to stabilize prices or reallocate market power in the farm sector. But the same institutional characteristics that inhibited market intervention and the search for a long-term farm policy after World War II facilitated retrenchment. The location of policy authority in Congress gave critics of farm subsidies access to the agricultural policy process. Budget procedures enhanced government efforts to trim farm programs.

This reassessment of institutions, interest groups, and agricultural policy is particularly instructive when we place the U.S. experience in comparative perspective. In contrast to the United States, agricultural policy in France and Japan operated through centralized institutions, a well-insulated policy process, and corporatist relations between the government and farm organizations. These institutional characteristics magnified the power of agricultural interests in France and Japan. Because of the influence wielded by farm groups, both in policy and in electoral politics, the French and Japanese agricultural welfare states more closely resemble the ideal of capture than their American counterpart.

Again, institutional characteristics afforded policy makers with both assets and liabilities. Nineteenth-century agricultural promotion in France and Japan was difficult at best, and centralized institutions impeded the distribution of resources to local areas. However, when the goal of government policy turned from promotion to regulation, close relations between centralized bureaucracies and state-sponsored farm organizations enhanced the capacity of government officials to lift farm prices and reallocate market power in agriculture. After World War II, corporatist relations established during the war evolved into political alliances between farm groups and conservative parties. This political link further secured producer dominance in the agricultural policy process. But with farm groups both a political ally and an active partner in policy making, attempts to reduce subsidies proved to be a risky political enterprise. Advocates of retrenchment often found their paths blocked by institutions that privileged farmers and their representatives in the agricultural policy process.

In sum, the history of the agricultural welfare state runs counter to standard treatments of institutions, interest group power, and government capacity. In the United States, institutions erected hurdles to farm organization mastery over the policy process. At the same time, institutions in France and Japan solidified the control of farm organizations over the contours of policy. Nor did the structure of institutions universally diminish or enhance government capacity. States are not uniformly "strong" or "weak." Institutions that facilitated regulation impeded retrenchment and vice versa.

INSTITUTIONS AND THE FUTURE OF FARM POLICY

The case of retrenchment also illustrates how institutions in France and Japan insulated the agricultural welfare state from the profound economic changes that have occurred in agriculture since the 1970s. Despite the steady decline in farming as an occupation, the transformation of agriculture into a capital-intensive sector, and the globalization of commodity markets, farmers in France and Japan retained a significant degree of political power and the capacity to fend off challenges to generous farm subsidies. An agricultural policy process dominated by farm interests and a political system that magnified the influence of rural voters beyond their numbers are important factors in explaining the resilience of the French and Japanese agricultural welfare states.

Conditions in agriculture continue to change, the number of farmers steadily declines, but attempts to map out a future direction for policy confront an institutional environment that privileges the status quo. Policy adaptation may require a change in institutions not only at the level of agricultural organizations but also perhaps even in the realm of national politics.

In France, for example, since the 1960s farm leaders and politicians have struck a balance between the interests of large- and small-scale producers, between a policy centered on price supports for the most competitive and one based on government assistance for less-developed areas. As we have seen, the CAP was critical to this balance. Should the CAP cease to remain viable due to financial implosion or external reform pressure, policy makers in France must decide whether to promote the export competitiveness of French grain producers or preserve a small-scale agriculture that is increasingly less viable. In short, should policy pursue economic or social goals?

The question divides the political parties and exposes deep divisions within French agriculture. The Socialists appear willing to embrace the social model. Speaking about CAP reform, for example, Minister of Agriculture Jean Glavany described "the expectations of society from its farmers: a vibrant rural life, preservation of the environment, management of the countryside, development of quality products." In 1999, the Socialist Jospin government passed a new agricultural law designed to keep small-scale producers on the land and encourage pro-environmental practices in agriculture.[1] Leftist farm unions, such as the Confédération paysanne, have capitalized on public concern for environmental quality in agriculture.[2] Meanwhile, politicians on the Right such as Jaques Chirac retain the productivist image of French agriculture. Along with the leaders of

[1] See, for example, the comments of agriculture minister Louis Le Pensec accompanying the *projet du loi* for the new agricultural legislation introduced on June 10, 1998, www.assemblee-national.fr/2/dossiers/agriculture/p10977.htm (1999). For the text of the *loi d'orientation*, see *Journal Officiel*, no. 158, July 10, 1999, 10231.

[2] "La Confederation paysanne cherche a marquer des points contre la FNSEA," *Le Monde*, July 24, 1997; "GM Food: Minister Hits at US Groups," *Financial Times*, August 26, 1999.

the FNSEA and the specialist producer associations, they reject the notion of farm policy cum environmental policy. FNSEA president Luc Guyau summarized this viewpoint when he told the FNSEA National Council, "Farmers want to stay producers, . . . not become gardeners or guardians of the countryside."[3]

This tension between social and economic goals is not easily reconciled. French agricultural institutions, as we have seen, are not geared toward pluralist interest representation. As the economic divisions among French producers become manifest, the FNSEA will struggle to maintain its position as a peak representative of agricultural interests. It is unclear whether the FNSEA, predicated on an earlier period of consensus, will adapt or be replaced by institutions that reflect this diversity. We can ask a similar question of French politics. It is interesting to note that an increasingly fragmented farm lobby mirrors the centrifugal tendencies in French party politics. Just as the FNSEA can no longer unite the diverse agricultural interests under the banner of modernization, neither can the Gaullists unite the French Right behind the goal of economic nationalism. The point here is that institutions constructed to be resilient to change by definition will face difficulties in adapting to new economic and political circumstances.

Parallels between agriculture and the larger political system are even more apparent in Japan, where rural economic development and political competition went hand in hand since the nineteenth century. The overlap between policy and politics reached its full expression under the leadership of the LDP after World War II. Rice subsidies and pork-barrel construction projects modernized agriculture, created a rural infrastructure, and diversified the rural economy. At the same time, of course, the steady flow of government resources also secured the political loyalty of Japanese farmers for the conservatives. Agricultural policy paid nice political dividends.

This strategy, although appropriate to the high-growth period, failed to adapt to changing economic circumstances. The problem is not simply that labor has left agriculture in droves but that those who have remained in farming do not achieve high rates of productivity. Because of generous subsidies and advances in mechanization, Japanese agriculture ossified into a sector of weekend farmers producing mainly rice on a very small scale. Even as the government spent lavishly on farmers, food imports to Japan grew steadily to meet the needs of a growing urban population. But rising food imports revealed the growing disjunction between political

---

[3] "Intervention du Président Luc Guyau devant le Ministre de l'agriculture et de la pêche Louis Le Pensec," speech delivered before the FNSEA National Council, September 9, 1998; www.FNSEA.Fr (1999).

goals and policy objectives in rural Japan. Although the government long justified expensive subsidy programs on the grounds of food security, the 1993–1994 rice shortage revealed that food control programs could not guarantee ample supplies.

One alternative to the current system would be to ease restrictions on agricultural landownership and drastically reduce rice subsidies. This would permit greater corporate investment in agriculture, make part-time farming less attractive, and encourage new, younger entrants into agriculture.[4] But a more streamlined farm sector would undermine the political basis of agricultural policy. Specifically, Nokyo's role (political and economic) in the rural economy would face a direct challenge. Part-time farmers are the core membership of local cooperatives, and rice transactions are a major source of cooperative revenues. Facilitating the exit of part-time farmers reduces membership. Easing investment, particularly for corporations, threatens Nokyo dominance in upstream and downstream sectors such as farm inputs and rice distribution.

Japan cannot restructure agriculture without touching upon long-standing political links in the countryside. Indeed, agriculture is like many other sectors of the Japanese economy that contributed to the economic malaise of the late 1990s. Economic reforms carry political costs that are unpalatable for many politicians. As a result, the status quo remains the politically expedient policy alternative. Agriculture is so exemplary of this problem because the postwar political order was founded upon links between the LDP and rural voters. Reform efforts cut directly into the government benefits that greased the LDP political machine for so long. And in the political uncertainty of the 1990s, the LDP is even more dependent on its core rural constituency and less willing to make decisions contrary to the interests of farmers or Nokyo.

Institutions in the United States are much more malleable and transmit economic and demographic changes much more faithfully into new political configurations and public policies than institutions do in France and Japan. The location of policy authority in Congress and the periodic reapportion of congressional districts steadily reduced the influence of agriculture on national politics. Attempts to institutionalize links between farmers and the government proved exceptionally difficult.

As I argued in the preceding chapter, one consequence of this institutional malleability was a reduction in the scope of the agricultural welfare state. Agricultural policy reflected demographic shifts in a fairly straightforward manner. As the number of farmers declined, so did their representation in Congress and the extent of the safety net that protected farm

---

[4] "Rural Japan Fears for Future on the Farm," *Washington Post*, November 2, 1998, A13.

incomes. The relationship is not linear, as the increases in farm spending of the late 1990s indicate. But when compared with agricultural politics in France and Japan, the political capacity of American farmers appears rather ad hoc; farmers extract benefits only when prices are extremely low and the government is running a surplus.

The ad hoc character of U.S. agricultural politics at the century's end raises interesting parallels with the 1920s, before the rise of the agricultural welfare state. As in the 1920s, American farmers in the late 1990s have endured a pronounced fall in prices while the rest of the economy boomed. A Republican Congress recognizes the need to respond to the farmers' distress but is reticent to intervene directly in agricultural markets. Without overextending the historical analogy, the agricultural crisis of the 1920s did portend a larger upheaval in the American economy. If the current downturn in agriculture spreads, the decision to end commodity programs, like the decision to scale back other forms of social insurance such as Aid to Families with Dependent Children, may prove shortsighted, and policy makers may find that the advantages of being a precocious deregulator are less than they initially thought.

AGRICULTURE AND THE AMERICAN WELFARE STATE

This begs the question of whether the recent decline in government support for agriculture can tell us anything meaningful about retrenchment politics in the United States more generally. Certainly the congressional budget process has been an effective instrument of retrenchment in policy areas other than agriculture. Paul Pierson has noted how "domestic politics in the United States had been *fiscalized*" as a consequence of political concern over the deficit.[5] Even with the arrival of a surplus, the budget process is still a central policy-making tool; fiscal concerns determine how politicians choose among policy alternatives. In agriculture, as we have seen, politicians often had to assess policy alternatives according to the projected cost of program changes. For instance, Margaret Weir describes how in the case of both welfare reform and Medicare, debates about entitlements "become intertwined with the politics of the budget."[6] Cost trumps content in a variety of policy domains, and agriculture may be one of several instances of budget-driven retrenchment.

A more interesting hypothesis is that agricultural retrenchment is part of a larger transformation that is under way in American politics. Although farmers did not rise to the same privileged political status in the United States as they did in France or Japan, they were important politi-

[5] Pierson, "The Deficit and the Politics of Domestic Reform," 127; emphasis in original.
[6] Weir, "American Politics and the Future of Social Policy," 522–23.

cally. Rural representatives in Congress influenced political outcomes through logrolls with urban members. Ad hoc coalitions between urban and rural interests produced important legislation. Farmers and workers never created a red-green coalition on a par with those in Scandinavian countries, but as partners in the New Deal coalition they did provide the political foundation for a host of social programs—from food stamps to farm subsidies—that were important components of the American welfare state.[7] If farmers were a key component of welfare state expansion in the United States, then it is possible that the decline of farming as an occupation has weakened the political foundations of the American welfare state as well.

Certainly, demographic shifts have altered the political characteristics and policy preferences in much of the United States, particularly in the South. In 1960, the vast majority of southern House members (61 percent) represented districts with at least 10 percent of their working population employed in agriculture. In 1990, not a single southern representative met this criterion, and only 12 percent of congressional districts in the South contained an agricultural labor force greater than 5 percent.[8] Southern white politicians were always conservative, but the promise of agricultural subsidies did form the basis for "progressive" logrolls as in 1965, when cotton-state Democrats supported the repeal of Section 14b of the Taft-Hartley Act to secure passage of a farm bill. The decline of agriculture eliminated the basis for the quid pro quo that constituted this urban-rural coalition. Economic development and diversity also attracted migrants from around the United States, providing fertile ground for the growth of the Republican Party that radically changed the complexion of southern political representation.[9] Prominent southern Republicans such as Newt Gingrich or Dick Armey are both "carpetbaggers" in that they were born outside the South. Forty years ago, congressmen from these areas in Georgia and Texas would have staunchly defended subsidies for peanuts and cotton. Today these "southern" Republicans are outspoken critics of government intervention in agriculture, as well as other areas of the economy.

[7] Sanders, *Roots of Reform*; Esping-Anderson agrees that, although the New Deal was premised on a similar red-green coalition, southern rural conservatism blocked the emergence of a true social democratic welfare state. However, as I have described, ad hoc logrolls between urban and rural members did fuel the expansion of the American welfare state beyond the New Deal period. See Esping-Anderson, *The Three Worlds of Welfare Capitalism*, 26–32.

[8] For 1960 data, see *Congressional Quarterly Weekly Report*, August 21, 1964, 1784–883. For 1990 data, see U.S. Bureau of the Census, *Census of Population and Housing*, Summary Tape File 3D.

[9] Johnston and Shafer, "The Transformation of Southern Politics," Polsby, "A Revolution in Congress?"

Although demographic changes have been most dramatic in the South, the effects of declining agricultural employment are national in scale. Throughout the United States, the children of farmers left rural America for nonagricultural employment in the cities. At the same time, industry and manufacturing, once concentrated in the Northeast, spread throughout the country. Former market towns in the South and West are today major metropolitan areas with diversified economies. As these fast-growing cities steadily spread outward, suburban subdivisions and housing developments replaced fields and farms. Politically, this means that formerly rural and agriculture-based congressional districts are now suburban bedroom communities often populated by white-collar professionals. One recent analysis of congressional districts found that the number of seats in the House of Representatives with at least 50 percent of its population in suburbs increased from 94 to 214 between 1963 and 1993. Over the same period, the number of rural districts declined by half, from 181 to 83.[10]

It is a question for further research whether the policy preferences of suburban voters are distinct from those of other places. If we apply the same logic used to explain agricultural retrenchment, it is plausible that suburbanization could weaken the political foundations of the welfare state as well. In the case of agriculture, institutions faithfully transmitted demographic shifts. As the number of farmers declined, so did the capacity of rural representatives to defend farm subsidies. Increasing suburban representation in Congress may have a similar consequence for social welfare programs. Most suburban voters are not welfare state "constituents"; they receive neither food stamps nor farm subsidies. We might expect that for politicians who represent these suburban constituencies, welfare state retrenchment presents fewer political costs—and potentially greater gains—than for urban or rural representatives. It is symbolic that since the Republican victory in 1994 Congress ended Great Depression era farm programs and scaled back federal welfare commitments.

Because so much policy making in the United States takes place in Congress, the apportionment of congressional seats matters for policy outcomes. If the preferences of suburban voters are distinct from voters in central cities or rural areas, then increasing suburban representation should be reflected in public policy. The changing "politics of place" may in fact be a fruitful lens with which to study post–World War II American political development.

---

[10] The number of central city districts declined from ninety-four to eighty-four over this period. See table 2 in Wolman and Marckini, "The Effect of Place on Legislative Roll Call Voting." On suburbanization, see Jackson, *Crabgrass Frontier.*

CONCLUSION

Government institutions are instruments of political control; often, they serve to consolidate power. Thus, the institutional mechanisms of agricultural policy not only secure government intervention in the farm sector but also can link producers to the larger political regime. In order for agricultural policy to serve these political functions, politicians and their allies must exercise influence over outcomes. Institutions that insulate decision making in the hands of a select few and afford stability and predictability of outcomes will further both the administrative and the political goals of market intervention.

American institutions, by design, are not well equipped to fulfill the administrative or political functions of interventionist policies. Federalism, separated powers, and other American institutions believed to fragment public authority do not merely protect private exchange from the encroachment of public power; these same institutional characteristics also protect public functions from the encroachment of private interests.[11] This is clear in the history of American agriculture. The limits of government intervention in the farm economy simultaneously set the boundaries of political power exercised by farmers and their representatives.

We find the opposite in France and Japan, where institutions, again by design, are well equipped to fulfill the administrative and political functions of interventionist policies. The centralization of authority within national governments and individual line agencies facilitated intervention in the farm economy. After World War II and the incorporation of farm organizations into conservative politics, agricultural policies were subordinated to the political concerns of politicians and producers. Effective intervention, therefore, increases the likelihood of eventual capture.

I have argued that the effects of these institutional differences on policy capacity are quite variable. Divorced from the specific context of government tasks and the changing circumstances of public policy, pronouncements about the effects of institutions or the strengths and weaknesses of state structures become meaningless. As we have seen, institutional configurations that facilitate promotion can impede regulation. Poor regulators may become precocious deregulators. Unless we evaluate institutions in a variety of policy contexts, our conclusions will suffer from a problem of selection bias.

Appreciation for the variability of effects also points our attention to the political consequences of institutional differences. In the United States,

---

[11] The Framers had to balance the fears of an interventionist state against the danger that a weak government would easily succumb to the will of a particular faction. James Madison, "Federalist #51."

politicians, bureaucrats, and producers failed to create an environment that restricted access to agricultural policy decisions. This illustrates a fundamental characteristic of American politics. Because of institutions, momentary winners in the political process face difficulties consolidating control over the instruments of government. Access remains cheap; winners are unlikely to ever completely exclude opponents from policy decisions. With politicians unable to effectively manipulate policy for purely partisan gain, American politics remains fluid; partnerships between political parties and producers are often ad hoc and unstable. This contrasts quite clearly with French and Japanese institutions, in which access to policy decisions is often restricted to the political insiders who have consolidated control over the instruments of government. Stable partnerships between political parties and privileged constituencies, such as farmers, enables politicians to manipulate policies for partisan gain. Although this solidified the dominant electoral alignment of each country, public policy today is inseparable from the postwar political orders in these nations.

If the structure of American institutions preserves access for political outsiders and militates against the manipulation of public policies for partisan gain, why the concern of Lowi, McConnell, and others with the phenomenon of capture? The conclusions of these scholars may have been different if they had placed their observations in comparative perspective or appreciated how different policy functions suggest different relations between government and society. There is another reason: the transparency of political deliberation in the United States can create the false impression of interest group dominance. Even the mere appearance of close relations between politicians and producers, between the regulators and the regulated, disturbs Americans who are ever vigilant for signs of corruption in the exercise of public functions. Such vigilance, however, results in the mistaken presumption that access secures influence. In this study, I have suggested that it is in those countries where political deliberation is much less transparent and access is much more restricted that private interests exercise greater control over policy outcomes. Here in the United States, political access may be cheap, but you get what you pay for.

Bibliography

The sources used in this study have been divided into four categories: general background, the United States, France, and Japan. In addition, sources for specific country cases have been divided into three categories: politics and institutions, agriculture, and primary sources such as government documents, data sources, and periodicals.

General Background

Anderson, Kym, Yujiro Hayami, and Masayoshi Honma. "The Growth of Agricultural Protection." In *The Political Economy of Agricultural Protection: East Asia in International Perspective*, edited by Kym Anderson and Yujiro Hayami. Sydney: Allen and Unwin, 1986.

Atkinson, Michael M., and William D. Coleman. "Strong States and Weak States: Sectoral Policy Networks in Advanced Capitalist Economies." *British Journal of Political Science* 19 (1989): 48–67.

Baumgartner, Frank R., and Beth L. Leech. *Basic Interests: The Importance of Groups in Politics and in Political Science*. Princeton, N.J.: Princeton University Press, 1998.

Becker, Gary. "A Theory of Competition among Pressure Groups for Political Influence." *Quarterly Journal of Economics* 98 (1983): 371–400.

Beer, Samuel H. *Britain against Itself*. London: Faber and Faber, 1982.

Berlon, Jean-Pierre. "The Historical Roots of the Present Agricultural Crisis." *In Towards a New Political Economy of Agriculture*, edited by William H. Friedland, Lawrence Busch, Frederick H. Buttel, and Alan P. Rudy. Boulder, Colo.: Westview Press, 1991.

Cawson, Alan. "Introduction: Varieties of Corporatism: The Importance of the Meso-Level in Interest Intermediation." In *Organized Interests and the State: Studies in Meso-Corporatism*, edited by Alan Cawson. London: Sage, 1985.

Coleman, William D. "Assessing the Changing Political Influence of Farmers: A Comparative Study." Paper prepared for the conference on *Liberalizing Agricultural Trade?* European Union Center, University of Washington, Seattle, May 14, 1999.

Derthick, Martha, and Paul J. Quirk. *The Politics of Deregulation*. Washington, D.C.: Brookings Institution, 1985.

Dunlavy, Colleen A. "Political Structure, State Policy, and Industrial Change: Early Railroad Policy in the United States and Prussia." In *Structuring Politics: Historical Institutionalism in Comparative Analysis*, edited by Sven Steinmo, Kathleen Thelen, and Frank Longstreth. Cambridge: Cambridge University Press, 1992.

Esping-Anderson, Gosta. *The Three Worlds of Welfare Capitalism*. Cambridge: Polity Press, 1990.

Friedland, William H., Lawrence Busch, Fredrick H. Buttel, and Alan P. Rudy, eds. *Towards a New Political Economy of Agriculture*. Boulder, Colo.: Westview Press, 1991.

Friedmann, Harriet, and Philip McMichael. "Agriculture and the State System: The Rise and Decline of National Agricultures, 1870 to the Present." *Sociologia Ruralis* 29 (1989): 93–117.

Hall, Peter. "Policy Paradigms, Social Learning, and the State." *Comparative Politics* 25 (1993): 275–96.

Hansen, John Mark. "The Political Economy of Group Membership." *American Political Science Review* 79 (1985): 79–96

Hayami, Yujiro, and Vernon W. Ruttan. *Agricultural Development: An International Perspective*. 2d ed. Baltimore: Johns Hopkins University Press, 1985.

Hayes, Michael T. "The Semi-sovereign Pressure Groups: A Critique of Current Theory and an Alternative Typology." *Journal of Politics* 40 (1978): 134–61.

Hollingsworth, J. Rogers, and Wolfgang Streeck. "Countries and Sectors: Concluding Remarks on Performance, Convergence, and Competitiveness." In *Governing Capitalist Economies: Performance and Control of Economic Sectors*, edited by J. Rogers Hollingsworth, Philippe C. Schmitter and Wolfgang Streeck. Oxford: Oxford University Press, 1994.

Honma, Masayoshi, and Hayami Yujiro. "The Determinants of Agricultural Protection Levels: An Econometric Analysis." In *The Political Economy of Agricultural Protection: East Asia in International Perspective*, edited by Kym Anderson and Yujiro Hayami. Sydney: Allen and Unwin, 1986.

Janoski, Thomas, and Larry W. Isaac. "Introduction to Time-Series Analysis." In *The Comparative Political Economy of the Welfare State*, edited by Thomas Janoski and Alexander M. Hicks. Cambridge: Cambridge University Press, 1994.

Johnson, D. Gale. *World Agriculture in Disarray*, 2d ed. London: Macmillan, 1991.

Katzenstein, Peter J. "Conclusion: Domestic Structures and Strategies of Foreign Economic Policy." In *Between Power and Plenty: Foreign Economic Policies of Advanced Industrial States*, edited by Peter J. Katzenstein. Madison: University of Wisconsin Press, 1978.

Kim, Chul-Kyoo, and James Curry. "Fordism, Flexible Specialization and Agri-Industrial Restructuring." *Sociologia Ruralis* 33 (1993): 61–80.

Kingdon, John W. *Agendas, Alternatives, and Public Policies*. 2d ed. New York: HarperCollins, 1995.

Kitschelt, Herbert. "Industrial Governance Structures, Innovation Strategies, and the Case of Japan: Sectoral or Cross-National Comparative Analysis." *International Organization* 45 (1991): 453–93.

Kloppenburg, Jack. *First the Seed: The Political Economy of Plant Biotechnology, 1492–2000*. Cambridge: Cambridge University Press, 1988.

Krasner, Stephen D. "United States Commercial and Monetary Policy: Unraveling the Paradox of External Strength and Internal Weakness." In *Between Power and Plenty: Foreign Economic Policies of Advanced Industrial States*, edited by Peter J. Katzenstein. Madison: University of Wisconsin Press, 1978.

Lindert, Peter H. "Historical Patterns of Agricultural Policy." In *Agriculture and the State: Growth, Employment, and Poverty in Developing Countries*, edited by C. Peter Timmer. Ithaca, N.Y.: Cornell University Press, 1991.

Lowi, Theodore J. "American Business, Public Policy, Case-Studies, and Political Theory." *World Politics* 16 (1964): 676–715.

———. "Four Systems of Policy, Politics, and Choice." *Public Administration Review* 32 (1972): 298–310.

———. *The End of Liberalism: The Second Republic of the United States*. 2d ed. New York: Norton, 1979.

Lustick, Ian S. "History, Historiography, and Political Science: Multiple Historical Records and the Problem of Selection Bias." *American Political Science Review* 90 (1996) 605–18.

Malenbaum, Wilfred. *The World Wheat Economy, 1885–1939*. Cambridge, Mass.: Harvard University Press, 1953.

Mayhew, David R. *Congress: The Electoral Connection*. New Haven, Conn.: Yale University Press, 1974.

McConnell, Grant. *Private Power and American Democracy*. New York: Knopf, 1966.

McCubbins, Mathew D., and Talbot Page. "A Theory of Congressional Delegation." In *Congress: Structure and Policy*, edited by Mathew McCubbins and Terry Sullivan. Cambridge: Cambridge University Press, 1987.

Milner, Helen. "Maintaining International Commitments in Trade Policy." *Government Capabilities in the United States and Abroad*, edited by R. Kent Weaver and Bert A. Rockman. Washington, D.C.: The Brookings Institution, 1993.

Mitchell, Timothy. "The Limits of the State: Beyond Statist Approaches and Their Critics." *American Political Science Review* 85 (1991): 77–96.

Noël, Alain. "Accumulation, Regulation, and Social Change: An Essay on French Political Economy." *International Organization* 41 (1987): 303–33.

Offer, Avner. "Between the Gift and the Market: The Economy of Regard." *Economic History Review* 50 (1997): 450–478.

Olson, Mancur. *The Logic of Collective Action: Public Goods and the Theory of Groups*. Cambridge, Mass.: Harvard University Press, 1971.

———. *The Rise and Decline of Nations*. New Haven, Conn.: Yale University Press, 1982.

Peltzman, Sam. "Toward a More General Theory of Regulation." *Journal of Law and Economics* 19 (1976): 211–40.

———. "Constituent Interest and Congressional Voting." *Journal of Law and Economics* 27 (1984): 181–210.

———. "The Economic Theory of Regulation after a Decade of Deregulation." *Brookings Papers on Economic Activity*, special issue supplement (1989): 1–59.

Pierson, Paul. "When Effect Becomes Cause: Policy Feedback and Political Change." *World Politics* 45 (1993): 595–628.

———. *Dismantling the Welfare State? Reagan, Thatcher and the Politics of Retrenchment*. Cambridge: Cambridge University Press, 1994.

Pincus, Jonathan. "Pressure Groups and the Pattern of Tariffs." *Journal of Political Economy* 4 (1975): 757–78.

Pugliese, Enrico. "Agriculture and the New Division of Labor." In *Towards a New Political Economy of Agriculture*, edited by William H. Friedland, Lawrence Busch, Frederick H. Buttel, and Alan P. Rudy. Boulder, Colo.: Westview Press, 1991.

Salisbury, Robert. "The Analysis of Public Policy: A Search for Theories and Rules." In *Political Science and Public Policy*, edited by Austin Ranney. Chicago: Markham, 1968.

———. "Why No Corporatism in America?" In *Trends Toward Corporatist Intermediation*, edited by Philippe C. Schmitter and Gerhard Lehmbruch. Beverly Hills, Calif.: Sage, 1979.

Salisbury, Robert, and John Heinz. "A Theory of Policy Analysis and Some Preliminary Applications." In *Policy Analysis in Political Science*, edited by Ira Sharkansky. Chicago: Markham, 1970.

Schattschneider, E. E. *Politics, Pressures, and the Tariff*. New York: Prentice-Hall, 1935.

———. *The Semisovereign People*. New York: Holt, Rinehart, and Winston, 1960.

Schick, Allen. "Governments versus Budget Deficits." In *Do Institutions Matter? Government Capabilities in the United States and Abroad*, edited by R. Kent Weaver and Bert A. Rockman. Washington, D.C.: The Brookings Institution, 1993.

Schmitter, Philippe. "Still the Century of Corporatism?" In *Trends Toward Corporatist Intermediation*, edited by Philippe C. Schmitter and Gerhard Lehmbruch. Beverly Hills, Cali.: Sage, 1979.

Schonhardt-Bailey, Cheryl. "Lessons in Lobbying for Free Trade in Nineteenth-Century Britain: To Concentrate or Not." *American Political Science Review* 85 (1991): 37–58.

Schultz, Theodore W. *The Economic Organization of Agriculture*. New York: McGraw-Hill, 1953.

Scott, James C. "Patron-Client Politics and Political Change in Southeast Asia." *American Political Science Review* 66 (1972): 91–113.

Shafer, D. Michael. *Winners and Losers: How Sectors Shape the Developmental Prospects of States*. Ithaca, N.Y.: Cornell University Press, 1994.

Shonfield, Andrew. *Modern Capitalism: The Changing Balance of Public and Private Power*. 3d ed. Oxford: Oxford University Press, 1976.

Stigler, George J. "The Theory of Economic Regulation." *Bell Journal of Economics and Management Science* 2 (spring 1971): 3–21.

Streeck, Wolfgang, and Philippe C. Schmitter, eds. *Private Interest Government: Beyond Market and State*. London: Sage, 1985.

Tolley, George, Vinod Thomas, John Nash, and James Snyder. "What We Know about Agricultural Prices: Policies, Politics, and Supply." In *The Economics of Agriculture: Papers in Honor of D. Gale Johnson*. Vol. 2, edited by John M. Antle and Daniel A. Sumner. Chicago: University of Chicago Press, 1996.

Truman, David B. *The Governmental Process: Political Interests and Public Opinion*. 1951; Westport, Conn.: Greenwood Press, 1981.

Tsebelis, George. "Decision Making in Political Systems: Veto Players in Presidentialism, Parliamentarism, Multicameralism and Multipartyism." *British Journal of Political Science* 25 (1995): 289–325.

Van Waarden, Frans. "Dimensions and Types of Policy Networks." *European Journal of Political Research* 21 (1992): 29–52.

Walker, Jack L. "The Origins and Maintenance of Interest Groups in America." *American Political Science Review* 77 (1983): 390–406.

Weaver, R. Kent. "The Politics of Blame Avoidance." *Journal of Public Policy* 6 (1984): 371–98.

Weaver, R. Kent, and Bert A. Rockman. "Assessing the Effects of Institutions." In *Do Institutions Matter? Government Capabilities in the United States and Abroad*, edited by R. Kent Weaver and Bert A. Rockman. Washington, D.C.: The Brookings Institution, 1993.

———. "When and How Do Institutions Matter?" In *Do Institutions Matter? Government Capabilities in the United States and Abroad*, edited by R. Kent Weaver and Bert A. Rockman. Washington, D.C.: The Brookings Institution, 1993.

Wilson, Graham K. *Interest Groups*. Oxford: Basil Blackwell, 1990.

Wilson, James Q. *Political Organizations*. New York: Basic Books, 1973.

———. "The Politics of Regulation." In *The Politics of Regulation*, edited by James Q. Wilson. New York: Basic Books, 1980.

Young, Oran R. "Political Leadership and Regime Formation: On the Development of Institutions in International Society." *International Organization* 45 (1991): 281–308.

Yee, Albert S. "The Causal Effects of Ideas on Policies." *International Organization* 50 (1996): 69–111.

United States

Politics and Institutions

Baumgartner, Frank R., and Bryan D. Jones. "Agenda Dynamics and Policy Subsystems." *Journal of Politics* 53 (1991): 1044–74.

———. *Agendas and Instability in American Politics*. Chicago: University of Chicago Press, 1993.

Baumgartner, Frank R., Bryan D. Jones, and Michael C. MacLeod. "Policymaking, Jurisdictional Ambiguity, and the Legislative Process." Policy Agendas Project, discussion paper no. 4, October 1998.

Bensel, Richard F. *Yankee Leviathan: The Origins of Central State Authority in America, 1859–1877*. Cambridge: Cambridge University Press, 1990.

Brady, David W. *Critical Elections and Congressional Policy Making*. Stanford, Calif.: Stanford University Press, 1988.

Campbell, Angus, Philip E. Converse, Warren E. Miller, and Donald E. Stokes. *The American Voter*. New York: Wiley, 1960.

Curry, Leonard. *Blueprint for Modern America: Nonmilitary Legislation of the First Civil War Congress*. Nashville, Tenn.: Vanderbilt University Press, 1968.

The Federalist Papers. Ed. Clinton Rossiter. New York: Penguin, 1961.

Foner, Eric. *Reconstruction: America's Unfinished Revolution, 1863–1877*. New York: Harper and Row, 1988.

Greider, William. "The Education of David Stockman." *Atlantic*, December 1981.

Hawley, Ellis. "Herbert Hoover, the Commerce Secretariat and the Vision of an 'Associative State,' 1921–1928." *Journal of American History* 61 (1974): 117–37.

Heclo, Hugh. "Issue Networks in the Executive Establishment." In *The New American Political System*, edited by Anthony King. Washington, D.C.: American Enterprise Institute, 1978.

Hofstadter, Richard. *The Age of Reform: From Bryan to FDR*. New York: Knopf, 1955.

——. *The Idea of a Party System*. Berkeley: University of California Press, 1969.

Jackson, Kenneth T. *Crabgrass Frontier: The Suburbanization of the United States*. New York: Oxford University Press, 1985.

Johnston, Richard G.L., and Byron E. Shafer. "The Transformation of Southern Politics, Revisited: The House of Representatives as a Window." Unpublished manuscript, Nuffield College, Oxford, 1999.

Jones, Charles O. "American Politics and the Organization of Energy Decision Making." *Annual Review of Energy* 4 (1979): 99–121.

Josephson, Matthew. *The Politicos, 1865–1896*. New York: Harcourt, Brace, 1938.

Keller, Morton. *Affairs of State: Public Life in Late Nineteenth-Century America*. Cambridge, Mass.: Harvard University Press, 1977.

Kleppner, Paul. *The Third Electoral System, 1853–1892: Parties, Voters, and Political Cultures*. Chapel Hill: University of North Carolina Press, 1979.

Loomis, Burdett A. "The Congressional Office as a Small Business: New Members Set Up Shop." *Publius* 9 (summer 1979): 35–55.

Lowi, Theodore J. "Party, Policy and Constitution in America." In *The American Party Systems: Stages of Political Development*, edited by William Nisbet Chambers and Walter Dean Burnham. New York: Oxford University Press, 1967.

Marcus, Robert. *Grand Old Party: Political Structure in the Gilded Age, 1880–1896*. Oxford: Oxford University Press, 1971.

Mayhew, David R. *Party Loyalty among Congressmen: The Difference between Democrats and Republicans, 1947–1962*. Cambridge, Mass.: Harvard University Press, 1966.

McCormick, Richard L. *The Party Period and Public Policy: American Politics from the Age of Jackson to the Progressive Era*. Oxford: Oxford University Press, 1986.

McCubbins, Mathew D., and Thomas Schwartz. "Congress, the Courts, and Public Policy: Consequences of the One Man, One Vote Rule." *American Journal of Political Science* 32 (1988): 388–415.

Pierson, Paul. "The Deficit and the Politics of Domestic Reform." In *The Social Divide: Political Parties and the Future of Activist Government*, edited by Margaret Weir. Washington, D.C.: Brookings Institution Press, 1998.

Polsby, Nelson W. "A Revolution in Congress?" Inaugural lecture, Oxford University, December 1, 1997.

Rohde, David W. *Parties and Leaders in the Postreform House*. Chicago: University of Chicago Press, 1991.

Salisbury, Robert H. "The Paradox of Interests in Washington, D.C.: More Groups and Less Clout." In *The New American Political System*, ed., edited by Anthony S. King. Washington, D.C.: American Enterprise Institute, 1990.

Salisbury, Robert H., and Kenneth A. Shepsle. "U.S. Congressmen as Enterprise." *Legislative Studies Quarterly* 6 (1981): 559–76.

Schick, Allan. "Fiscal Externalities in U.S. and Japanese Budget Politics." Maryland/Tsukuba Papers on US-Japanese Relations, University of Maryland, March 1996.

Shefter, Martin. "Party, Bureaucracy and Political Change in the United States." In *Political Parties: Development and Decay*, edited by Louis Maisel and Joseph Cooper. Beverly Hills, Calif.: Sage, 1978.

Shepsle, Kenneth A. "Institutional Arrangements and Equilibrium in Multidimensional Voting Models." *American Journal of Political Science* 23 (1979): 27–59.

Skocpol, Theda. *Protecting Soldiers and Mothers: The Political Origins of Social Policy in the United States*. Cambridge, Mass.: Harvard University Press, 1992.

Skowronek, Stephen. *Building a New American State: The Expansion of National Administrative Capacities, 1877–1920*. Cambridge: Cambridge University Press, 1982.

Sniderman, Paul J., Henry E. Brady, and Philip E. Tetlock. *1994 Multi-investigator Survey*. Survey Research Center, University of California-Berkeley, 1994.

Stewart, Charles H. III. "Does Structure Matter? The Effects of Structural Change on Spending Decisions in the House, 1871–1922." *American Journal of Political Science* 31 (1987): 585–605.

———. "Budget Reform as Strategic Legislative Action: An Exploration." *Journal of Politics* 50 (1988): 292–321.

———. "Lessons from the Post–Civil War Era." In *The Politics of Divided Government*, edited by Gary W. Cox and Samuell Kernell. Boulder, Colo.: Westview Press. 1991.

Weir, Margaret. "American Politics and the Future of Social Policy." In *The Social Divide: Political Parties and the Future of Activist Government*, edited by Margaret Weir. Washington, D.C.: Brookings Institution Press, 1998.

White, Leonard. *The Republican Era, 1869–1901: A Study in Administrative History*. New York: Macmillan, 1958.

Wildavsky, Aaron, and Naomi Caiden. *The New Politics of the Budgetary Process*. 3d ed. New York: Longman, 1997.

Wilson, Graham K. "Why Is There No Corporatism in the United States?" In *Patterns of Corporatist Policy-Making*, edited by Gerhard Lehmbruch and Philippe Schmitter. London: Sage, 1982.

Wolman, Harold, and Lisa Marckini. "The Effect of Place on Legislative Roll Call Voting: The Case of Central City Representatives in the U.S. House." Paper presented at the annual meeting of the American Political Science Association. Boston, Massachusetts, 1998.

Agriculture

Baker, Gladys L., Wayne D. Rasmussen, Vivien Wiser, and Jane M. Porter. *Century of Service: The First 100 Years of the United States Department of Agriculture.* Washington, D.C.: United States Department of Agriculture, 1963.

Barton, Weldon W. "Coalition-Building in the United States House of Representatives: Agricultural Legislation in 1973." In *Cases in Public Policy-Making*, edited by James E. Anderson. New York: Praeger, 1976.

Batie, Sandra. "Hogs, Chickens and Agrarian Values: Implications of an Industrialized Agriculture." Paper prepared for the Program in Agrarian Studies, Yale University, October 13, 1995.

Benedict, Murray R. *Farm Policies of the United States, 1750–1950.* New York: Twentieth Century Fund, 1953.

Benedict, Murray R. and Oscar C. Stine. *The Agricultural Commodity Programs: Two Decades of Experience.* New York: Twentieth Century Fund, 1956.

Black, John D. "The McNary-Haugen Movement." *American Economic Review* 18 (September 1928): 405–27.

Block, William J. *The Separation of the Farm Bureau and the Extension Service: Political Issue in a Federal System.* Illinois Studies in the Social Sciences, vol. 47. Urbana: University of Illinois Press, 1960.

Bonnen, James T., and William P. Browne. "Why Is Agricultural Policy So Difficult to Reform?" In *The Political Economy of U.S. Agriculture: Challenges for the 1990s*, edited by Carol S. Kramer. Washington, D.C.: Resources for the Future, 1989.

Browne, William. *Private Interests, Public Policy, and American Agriculture.* Lawrence: University Press of Kansas, 1988.

————. *Cultivating Congress: Constituents, Issues, and Agricultural Policymaking.* Lawrence: University Press of Kansas, 1995.

Buck, Solon. *The Agrarian Crusade: A Chronicle of the Farmer in Politics.* New Haven, Conn.: Yale University Press, 1920.

————. *The Granger Movement: A Study of Agricultural Organization and Its Political, Economic and Social Manifestations, 1870–1880.* 1912; Lincoln: University of Nebraska Press, 1969.

Buttel, Frederick H., and Pierre LaRamee. "The 'Disappearing Middle': A Sociological Perspective." In *Towards a New Political Economy of Agriculture*, edited by William H. Friedland et al. Boulder, Colo.: Westview Press, 1991.

Campbell, Christiana M. *The Farm Bureau and the New Deal.* Urbana: University of Illinois Press, 1962.

Christenson, Reo. *The Brannan Plan: Farm Politics and Policy.* Ann Arbor: University of Michigan Press, 1959.

Clarke, Sally H. *Regulation and Revolution in United States Farm Productivity.* Cambridge: Cambridge University Press, 1994.

Clemens, Elisabeth S. *The People's Lobby: Organizational Innovation and the Rise of Interest Group Politics in the United States, 1890–1925.* Chicago: University of Chicago Press, 1997.

Cochrane, Willard. *The Development of American Agriculture: A Historical Analysis.* Minneapolis: University of Minnesota Press, 1979.

Cochrane, Willard, and Mary Ryan. *American Farm Policy, 1948–1973*. Minneapolis: University of Minnesota Press, 1976.

Cohn, Theodore H. "The Changing Role of the United States in the Global Agricultural Trade Regime." In *World Agriculture and the GATT*, edited by William P. Avery. London: Lynne Rienner, 1993.

Coleman, William D., Grace D. Skogstad, and Michael M. Atkinson. "Paradigm Shifts and Policy Networks: Cumulative Change in Agriculture," *Journal of Public Policy* 16 (1996): 273–301.

Crampton, John A. *The National Farmers Union: Ideology of a Pressure Group*. Lincoln: University of Nebraska Press, 1965.

Cronon, William. *Nature's Metropolis: Chicago and the Great West*. New York: Norton, 1991.

Danbom, David. "Romantic Agrarianism in Twentieth-Century America." *Agricultural History* 65 (1991): 1–12.

Davenport, Eugene. "The Relations between the Federal Department of Agriculture and the Agricultural Colleges and Experiment Stations." In *Proceedings of the American Association of Agricultural Colleges and Experiment Stations*, twenty-seventh annual convention (1913).

Ferejohn, John A. "Logrolling in an Institutional Context: A Case Study of Food Stamp Legislation." In *Congress and Policy Change*, edited by Gerald C. Wright Jr., Leroy N. Rieselbach, and Lawrence C. Dodd. New York: Agathon Press, 1986.

Finegold, Kenneth, and Theda Skocpol. *State and Party in America's New Deal*. Madison: University of Wisconsin Press, 1995.

Fite, Gilbert C. *George N. Peek and the Fight for Farm Parity*. Norman: University of Oklahoma Press, 1954.

Gardner, Bruce L. "Causes of U.S. Farm Commodity Programs." *Journal of Political Economy* 95 (1987): 290–310.

Gates, Paul W. *Agriculture and the Civil War*. New York: Knopf, 1965.

Gaus, John M., and Leon O. Wolcott. *Public Administration and the United States Department of Agriculture*. Chicago: Social Science Research Council, 1940.

Gilbert, Jess, and C. Howe. "Beyond 'State vs. Society': Theories of the State and New Deal Agricultural Policies." *American Sociological Review* 56 (1991): 204–20.

Gilpatrick, Thomas V. "Price Support Policy and the Midwest Farm Vote." *Midwest Journal of Political Science* 3 (1959): 319–35.

Goodwyn, Lawrence. *Democratic Promise: The Populist Moment in America*. New York: Oxford University Press, 1976.

Hadwiger, Don F., and Ross B. Talbot. *Pressures and Protests: The Kennedy Farm Program and the Wheat Referendum of 1963*. Ames: Iowa State University Press, 1965.

Hallberg, M. C. *Policy for American Agriculture: Choices and Consequences*. Ames: Iowa State University Press, 1992.

Hamilton, David E. "Building the Associative State: The Department of Agriculture and American State-Building." *Agricultural History* 64 (1990): 207–18.

———. *From New Day to New Deal: American Farm Policy from Hoover to Roosevelt, 1928–1933*. Chapel Hill: University of North Carolina Press, 1991.

Hansen, John Mark. *Gaining Access: Congress and the Farm Lobby, 1919–1981.* Chicago: University of Chicago Press, 1991.

Hardin, Charles M. *The Politics of Agriculture.* Glencoe: Free Press, 1953.

———. "The Republican Department of Agriculture: A Political Interpretation." *Journal of Farm Economics* 36 (1954): 210–27.

Heinz, John. "The Political Impasse in Farm Support Legislation." *Yale Law Journal* 71 (1961): 952–78.

Hicks, John D. *The Populist Revolt: A History of the Farmers' Alliance and the People's Party.* Minneapolis: University of Minnesota Press, 1931.

Hoffman, Elizabeth, and Gary D. Libecap. "Institutional Choice and the Development of U.S. Agricultural Policies in the 1920s." *Journal of Economic History* 51 (1991): 397–411.

Hooks, Gregory. "From an Autonomous to a Captured State Agency: The Decline of the New Deal in Agriculture." *American Sociological Review* 55 (1990): 29–43.

Hoover, Herbert. "Message to the Special Session of the Congress on Farm Relief, Tariff and Certain Emergency Measures." April 16, 1929. *Public Papers of the Presidents of the United States.* Washington, D.C.: Government Printing Office, 1974.

Huffman, Wallace E., and Robert E. Evenson. *Science for Agriculture: A Long-Term Perspective.* Ames: Iowa State University Press, 1993.

Jones, Charles O. "Representation in Congress: The Case of the House Agriculture Committee." *American Political Science Review* 55 (1961): 358–67.

Kelley, Oliver H. *Origin and Progress of the Patrons of Husbandry in the United States: A History of 1866–1873.* Philadelphia: J. A. Wagenseller, 1875.

Kile, Orville Merton. *The Farm Bureau through Three Decades.* Baltimore: Waverly Press, 1948.

Kirkendall, Richard. *Social Scientists and Farm Politics in the Age of Roosevelt.* Columbia: University of Missouri Press, 1966.

Kursman, Nancy. "Structure and Policy Shifts: The U.S. House Committee on Agriculture, 1862–1942." Ph.D. dissertation, Rice University, 1986.

Lyons, Michael S., and Marcia W. Taylor. "Farm Politics in Transition: The House Agriculture Committee." *Agricultural History* 55 (1981): 128–46.

Marcus, Alan. *Agricultural Science and the Quest for Legitimacy: Farmers, Agricultural Colleges, and Experiment Stations, 1870–1890.* Ames: Iowa State University Press, 1985.

Matusow, Allen J. *Farm Policies and Politics in the Truman Years.* Cambridge, Mass.: Harvard University Press, 1967.

McConnell, Grant. *The Decline of Agrarian Democracy.* 1953; New York: Atheneum, 1969.

Nourse, Edwin G. *Marketing Agreements under the AAA.* Washington, D.C.: The Brookings Institution, 1935.

Nourse, Edwin G., Joseph S. Davis, and John D. Black. *Three years of the Agricultural Adjustment Administration.* Washington, D.C.: The Brookings Institution, 1937.

Orden, David, Robert Paarlberg, and T. Roe. "A Farm Bill for Booming Commodity Markets." *Choices*, second quarter, 1996, 39–40.

Paarlberg, Robert, and David Orden. "Explaining U.S. Farm Policy in 1996 and Beyond: Changes of Party Control and Changing Market Conditions." Paper presented to the Conference on Globalization, Agricultural Policy, and Agrarian Change, Yale University, April, 1997.

Palmer, Bruce. *Man over Money.* Chapel Hill: University of North Carolina Press, 1980.

Rosenberg, Charles E. "The Adams Act: Politics and the Cause of Scientific Research." *Agricultural History* 38 (1964): 3–12.

Ross, Earle D. "The United States Department of Agriculture during the Commissionership: A Study in Politics, Administration, and Technology." *Agricultural History* 20 (1946): 129–43.

Rowley, William D. *M. L. Wilson and the Campaign for Domestic Allotment.* Lincoln: University of Nebraska Press, 1970.

Saloutos, Theodore. *The American Farmer and the New Deal.* Ames: Iowa State University Press. 1982.

Saloutos, Theodore, and John D. Hicks. *Agricultural Discontent in the Middle West, 1900–1939.* Lincoln: University of Nebraska Press, 1951.

Sanders, Elizabeth. *Roots of Reform: Farmers, Workers, and the State, 1877–1917.* Chicago: University of Chicago Press, 1999.

Schapsmeier, Edward L., and Frederick H. Schapsmeier. *Ezra Taft Benson and the Politics of Agriculture: The Eisenhower Years, 1953–1961.* Danville, Ill.: Interstate Printers and Publishers, 1975.

Schwartz, Michael. *Radical Protest and Social Structure.* Chicago: University of Chicago Press, 1988.

Simon, John Y. "The Politics of the Morrill Act." *Agricultural History* 37 (1963): 103–11.

Skocpol, Theda, and Kenneth Finegold. "State Capacity and Economic Intervention in the Early New Deal." *Political Science Quarterly* 97 (1982): 255–78.

Skogstad, Grace. "Ideas, Paradigms and Institutions: Agricultural Exceptionalism in the European Union and the United States." *Governance* 11 (1998): 463–90.

Summers, Mary. "Putting Populism Back In: Rethinking Agricultural Politics and Policy." *Agricultural History* 70 (1996): 395–414.

Tontz, Robert L. "Memberships of General Farmers' Organizations, United States, 1874–1960." *Agricultural History* 38 (1964): 136–43.

True, Alfred C. "History of the Hatch Experiment Station Act of 1887." In *Proceedings of the Association of Land-Grant Colleges and Universities*, fortieth annual convention (1926).

———. *A History of Agricultural Extension Work in the United States, 1785–1923.* Washington, D.C.: USDA Miscellaneous Publication no. 15, 1928.

———. *A History of Agricultural Experimentation and Research in the United States, 1607–1925.* USDA Miscellaneous Publication no. 251, 1937.

Wanlass, William. *The United States Department of Agriculture: A Study in Administration.* Baltimore: Johns Hopkins University Press, 1920.

Wilcox, Walter W. *The Farmer in the Second World War.* Ames: Iowa State University Press, 1947.

Wilson, Graham K. *Special Interests and Policymaking: Agricultural Policies and Politics in Britain and the United States of America, 1956–1970.* London: Wiley, 1977.

Young, Brigitte. "The Dairy Industry: From Yeomanry to the Institutionalization of Multilateral Governance." In *Governance of the American Economy,* edited by John L. Campbell, J. Rogers Hollingsworth, and Leon N. Lindberg. Cambridge: Cambridge University Press, 1991.

Young, James T. "The Origins of New Deal Agricultural Policy: Interest Groups' Role in Policy Formation." *Policy Studies Journal* 21 (1993): 190–209.

Primary Sources

Agricultural Adjustment Administration. *Agricultural Adjustment, 1937–1938.* Washington, D.C.: Government Printing Office, 1938.

Baumgartner, Frank R., and Bryan D. Jones. *Congressional Hearings Dataset.* Policy Agendas Project, University of Washington. http://weber.u.washington. edu/~ampol/ (1999).

Bowers, Douglas E., Wayne D. Rasmussen, and Gladys L. Baker. *History of Agricultural Price Support and Adjustment Programs, 1933–84.* Agriculture Information Bulletin No. 485. Economic Research Service, U.S. Department of Agriculture, 1984.

Bureau Farmer.

Chicago Tribune.

Columbia Oral History Project. *Reminiscences of Chester C. Davis.*

———. *Reminiscences of Mordecai Ezekial.*

Committee on Agriculture. House of Representatives. *Hearing before the Committee on Agriculture, House of Representatives.* "Agricultural Relief." 71st Cong., 1st sess. Serial A-Part 7, 1929.

———. *Hearing before the Committee on Agriculture, House of Representatives.* "Agricultural Adjustment Program." 72d Cong., 2d sess. Serial M, 1932.

———. *Hearings before the House Agriculture Committee, House of Representatives.* "Agricultural Act of 1961." 87th Cong., 1st sess. Serial E, 1961.

———. *Hearings before the House Agriculture Committee. Subcommittee on Livestock and Feed Grains and Subcommittee on Wheat.* "Wheat and Feed Grains." 89th Cong., 1st sess. Serial J, 1965.

———. "Press release." August 3, 1995.

Congressional Quarterly, *Congressional Quarterly Almanac.* Washington, D.C.: CQ Press, various years.

Congressional Quarterly Weekly Report.

Dallas Morning News.

Federal Farm Board. *Second Annual Report of the Federal Farm Board.* Washington, D.C.: Government Printing Office, 1931.

———. *Third Annual Report of the Federal Farm Board.* Washington, D.C.: Government Printing Office, 1932.

Interview. American Farm Bureau Federation. November 2, 1995.

Interview. House Agriculture Committee. October 6, 1995.

Interview. National Association of Wheat Growers. October 6, 1995.

Johnson, Donald B., and Kirk H. Porter, eds. *National Party Platforms, 1840–1972.* Urbana: University of Illinois Press, 1973.

Journal of the United States Agricultural Society 1, no. 1 (1852).

Kiplinger's Washington Newsletter.

Miller, Warren E., and the National Election Studies. American National Election Studies Cumulative Data File, 1952–1992 [computer file]. 6th release. Ann Arbor: University of Michigan, Center for Political Studies, 1994.

Mitchell, B. R. *International Historical Statistics: The Americas.* New York: Stockton Press, 1993.

National Grange Executive Committee. *Proceedings of the Sixth Session of the National Grange.* 1874.

National Journal.

Nation's Agriculture.

New York Times.

Office of Management and Budget. *The Budget for Fiscal Year 2000, Historical Tables.* Washington, D.C.: Government Printing Office, 1999.

Official Newsletter of the American Farm Bureau Federation.

Public Disclosure, Inc. *FECInfo.* http://www.tray.com/fecinfo/_pac.htm (1999).

Roll Call.

Times Picayune.

"The Truth about the Wheat Situation." *Federal Farm Board Press Release.* July 21, 1931.

United States Bureau of the Census. *Historical Statistics of the United States, Colonial Times to 1970.* Washington, D.C.: Government Printing Office, 1976.

———. *Congressional Districts of the U.S., 104th Congress.* Washington, D.C.: Bureau of the Census, 1995.

———. *Statistical Abstract of the United States.* Washington, D.C.: Government Printing Office, 1992.

United States Congress. *Congressional Globe.*

USDA. *Annual Reports of the Department of Agriculture, 1914.* Washington, D.C.: Government Printing Office, 1914.

———. *Yearbook of Agriculture, 1926.* Washington, D.C.: Government Printing Office, 1926.

———. *Yearbook of Agriculture, 1935.* Washington, D.C.: Government Printing Office, 1935.

———. *Agricultural Statistics, 1942.* Washington, D.C.: Government Printing Office, 1942.

———. *1992 Census of Agriculture.* Washington. D.C.: Government Printing Office, 1992.

———. *Estimates of Producer and Consumer Subsidy Equivalents, 1982–1993.* Washington, D.C.: Government Printing Office, 1994.

———. *Provisions of the Federal Agriculture Improvement and Reform Act of 1996.* Edited by Frederick J. Nelson and Lyle P. Schertz. Economic Research Service, U.S. Department of Agriculture. Agriculture Information Bulletin No. 729.

USDA. Historical Budget Outlays, 1962–1996. Economic Research Service.usda. mannlib.cornell.edu/data-sets/general/95004.

———. *1997 Census of Agriculture.* Washington, D.C.: Government Printing Office, 1997.

————. *Track Records: United States Crop Production*. National Agricultural Statistics Service. usda.mannlib.cornell.edu/data-sets/crops/96120/ (1999).

Wall Street Journal.

Wallace's Farmer.

Washington Post.

Washington Times.

Winston, David, Rea Hederman, and Christine Olson. *The Congressional District Ranking Book*. The Heritage Foundation. http://www.heritage.org/cd_ranking/i-cdrank.html (1997).

France

Politics and Institutions

Agulhon, Maurice. *The French Republic, 1879–1992*. Translated by Antonia Nevill. Oxford: Blackwell, 1993.

Balladur, Edouard. *Deux ans à Matignon*. Paris: Plon, 1995.

Chapman, Brian. *The Prefects and Provincial France*. London: George Allen and Unwin, 1955.

Chapman, Guy. *The Third Republic of France: The First Phase, 1871–1894*. London: Macmillan, 1962.

Cole, Alistair. "The Evolution of the Party System, 1974–1990." In *French Political Parties in Transition*, edited by Alistair Cole. Brookfield, Vt.: Dartmouth, 1990.

Debré, Michel. "The Constitution of 1958: Its Raison d'Etre and How It Evolved." In *The Fifth Republic at Twenty*, edited by William Andrews and Stanley Hoffman. Albany: State University of New York Press, 1981.

Duverger, Maurice. *Political Parties: Their Organization and Activity in the Modern State*. Translated by Barbara North and Robert North. London: Methuen, 1954.

Elbow, Mathew. *French Corporative Theory, 1789–1948*. New York: Columbia University Press, 1953.

Elwitt, Sanford. *The Making of the Third Republic: Class and Politics in France, 1868–1884*. Baton Rouge: Louisiana State University Press, 1975.

Feigenbaum, Harvey B. "Recent Evolution of the French Executive." *Governance* 3 (1990): 264–78.

Frears, John. "The French Parliament: Loyal Workhorse, Poor Watchdog." *West European Politics* 13 (1990): 32–51.

Gaffney, John. "The Emergence of a Presidential Party: The Socialist Party." In *French Political Parties in Transition*, edited by Alistair Cole. Brookfield, Vt.: Dartmouth, 1990.

Garrett, Geoffrey, and George Tsebelis. "An Institutional Critique of Intergovernmentalism." *International Organization* 50 (1996): 269–99.

Goguel, François. *La Politique des partis sous la Troisième République*. Paris: éditions du Seuil, 1946.

————. *Géographie des élections françaises de 1870 à 1951*. Paris: Armand Colin, 1951.

Hazareesingh, Sudhir. *Political Traditions in Modern France*. Oxford: Oxford University Press, 1994.

Keeler, John T. S. "Executive Power and Policy-Making Patterns in France: Gauging the Impact of Fifth Republic Institutions." *West European Politics* 16 (1993): 518–44.

Knapp, Andrew. "*Un Parti comme les autres*: Jacques Chirac and the Rally for the Republic." In *French Political Parties in Transition*, edited by Alistair Cole. Brookfield, Vt.: Dartmouth, 1990.

Lebovics, Herman. *The Alliance of Iron and Wheat in the Third French Republic, 1860–1914: Origins of the New Conservatism*. Baton Rouge: Louisiana State University Press, 1988.

Lequesne, Christian. *Paris-Bruxelles: Comment se fait la politique européenne de la France*. Paris: Presses de la Fondation Nationale des Science Politiques, 1993.

Menon, Anand. "French-EU Policy Making." Mimeo, Oxford University, 1998.

Nugent, Neill. *The Government and Politics of the European Community*. Durham, N.C.: Duke University Press, 1989.

Petot, J. "L'Europe, la France, et son président." *Revue du Droit Publique et de la Science Politique en France et à l'Etranger* 109 (1993): 325–95.

Pierce, Roy. *French Politics and Political Institutions*. 2d ed. New York: Harper and Row, 1973.

Platone, François. *Les électorats sous la Vème République: Données D'enquête 1958–1995*. Paris: CEVIPOF, 1995.

Schmidt, Vivien A. *Democratizing France: The Political and Administrative History of Decentralization*. Cambridge: Cambridge University Press, 1990.

Siegfried, André. *Tableau politique de la France de l'Ouest sous la Troisième République*. Paris: Armand Colin, 1913.

Smith, Michael S. *Tariff Reform in France, 1860–1900: The Politics of Economic Interest*. Ithaca, N.Y.: Cornell University Press, 1980.

Suleiman, Ezra. *Politics, Power and Bureaucracy in France*. Princeton, N.J.: Princeton University Press, 1974.

Williams, Philip M. *Crisis and Compromise: Politics in the Fourth Republic*. Garden City, N.Y.: Doubleday, 1966.

Wilsford, Douglas. "Tactical Advantages versus Administrative Heterogeneity: The Strengths and Limits of the French State." *Comparative Political Studies* 21 (1988): 126–68.

Wright, Vincent. *Government and Politics of France*. 2d ed. New York: Holmes and Meier, 1983.

Agriculture

Agulhon, Maurice. "Attitudes politiques." In *Histoire de la France rurale*, edited by Georges Duby and Armand Wallon. Vol. 3. Paris: éditions du Seuil, 1976.

———. "LesPaysans dans la vie politique." In *Histoire de la France rurale*, edited by Georges Duby and Armand Wallon. Vol. 3. Paris: éditions du Seuil, 1976.

Alphandéry, Pierre, Pierre Bitoun, and Yves Dupont. *Les Champs du départ: Une France rurale sans paysans?* Paris: Editions La Découverte, 1988.

Augé-Laribé, Michel. *Syndicats et coopératives agricoles*. Paris: Libraire Armand Colin, 1920.

Augé-Laribé, Michel. *La Politique agricole de la France de 1880 à 1940*. Paris: Presses Universitaire de France, 1950.

Barral, Pierre. *Les Agrariens français de Méline à Pisani*. Paris: Libraire Armand Colin, 1968.

———. "Agrarisme de gauche et agrarisme de droite sous la Troisième République." In *L'Univers politique des paysans dans la France contemporaine*, edited by Yves Tavernier, Michel Gervais, and Claude Servolin. Paris: Armand Colin, 1972.

Berger, Suzanne. *Peasants against Politics: Rural Organization in Brittany, 1911–1967*. Cambridge, Mass.: Harvard University Press, 1972.

Blanc, Michel, André Brun, Bernard Delors, and Philippe Lacombe. "L'Agriculture française est-elle encore familiale?" In *Les Agriculteurs et la politique*, edited by Pierre Coulomb et al. Paris: Presses de la Fondation Nationale des Science Politique, 1990.

Blanc-Gonnet, Pierre. *La Réforme des services extérieurs du ministère de l'agriculture*. Grenoble: Editions Cujas, 1967.

Bourdon, Michel. "L'Agriculture française dans la récession économique." In *Les Agriculteurs et la politique*, edited by Pierre Coulomb et al. Paris: Presses de la Fondation Nationale des Science Politique, 1990.

Boussard, Isabel. *Vichy et la Corporation paysanne*. Paris: Presses de la Fondation Nationale des Science Politique, 1980.

———. *Les Agriculteurs et la république*. Paris: Economica, 1990.

Boy, Daniel, and élisabeth Dupoirier. "La Stabilité du vote de droite des agriculteurs." In *Les Agriculteurs et la politique*, edited by Pierre Coulomb et al. Paris: Presses de la Fondation Nationale des Science Politique, 1990.

Bruneteau, Bernard. *Les Paysans dans l'état: Le gaullisme et le syndicalisme agricole sous la Ve République*. Paris: Harmattan, 1994.

Buckwell, Allan. "Some Microeconomic Analysis of CAP Market Regimes." In *The Common Agricultural Policy*, edited by Christopher Ritson and David Harvey. 2d ed. Wallingford, U.K.: CAB International, 1997.

Cépède, Michel, and Gérard Weill. *L'Agriculture*. Paris: Presses Universitaires de France, 1965.

Cleary, M. C. *Peasants, Politicians, and Producers: The Organisation of Agriculture in France since 1918*. Cambridge: Cambridge University Press, 1989.

Clerc, François. "FNSEA-CNJA: Les conflicts de l'unité." In *Les Agriculteurs et la politique*, edited by Pierre Coulomb et al. Paris: Presses de la Fondation Nationale des Science Politique, 1990.

Clout, Hugh D. *The Land of France, 1815–1914*. London: George Allen and Unwin, 1983.

Coleman, William D., Michael M. Atkinson, and Eric Montpetit. "Against the Odds: Retrenchment in Agriculture in France and the United States." *World Politics* 49 (1997): 453–81.

Coleman, William D., and Stefan Tangermann. "The 1992 CAP Reform, the Uruguay Round and the Commission: Conceptualizing Linked Policy Games." *Journal of Common Market Studies* 73 (1999): 385–405.

Coulomb, Pierre. "La Cogestion: Une nouvelle corporatiste?" In *Les Agriculteurs et la politique*, edited by Pierre Coulomb et al. Paris: Presses de la Fondation Nationale des Science Politique, 1990.

———. "Les Conférences annuelles: Entre corporatisme et populisme." In *Les Agriculteurs et la politique*, edited by Pierre Coulomb et al. Paris: Presses de la Fondation Nationale des Science Politique, 1990.

Coulomb, Pierre, and Henri Nallet. "Les Organisations syndicales agricoles à l'éprouve de l'unité." In *L'Univers politique des paysans dans la France contemporaine*, edited by Yves Tavernier, Michel Gervais, and Claude Servolin. Paris: Armand Colin, 1972.

Culpepper, Pepper D. "Organisational Competition and the Neo-corporatist Fallacy in French Agriculture." *West European Politics* 16 (1993): 295–315.

Cusson, Georges. *Origines et évolution du Ministère de l'agriculture*. Paris: Les Presses Modernes, 1929.

Daugbjerg, Carsten. "Policy Networks and Agricultural Policy Reforms: Explaining Deregulation in Sweden and Re-regulation in the European Community." *Governance* 10 (1997): 123–42.

Debatisse, Michel. *Agriculture: Les temps difficiles. . . .* Paris: Economica, 1986.

De Bresson, Jacques. *L'Office du blé*. Paris: Libraire technique et économique, 1937.

Delorme, Hélène. "L'Emergence d'un coporatisme agro-alimentaire dans l'Union europeene." Paper presented to the conference "Organized Interests in the European Union." Nuffield College, Oxford, October 2, 1999.

Dogan, Mattei. "La Représentation parlementaire du monde rural." In *Les Paysans et la politique dans la France contemporaine*, edited by Jacques Fauvet and Henri Mendras. Paris: Armand Colin, 1958.

Duby, Georges, and Armand Wallon, eds. *Histoire de la France rurale*. Vol. 3. Paris: éditions du Seuil, 1976.

Eizner, Nicole. *Les Paradoxes de l'agriculture Française*. Paris: Editions l'Harmattan, 1985.

Emeri, Claude. "La CGA." In *Les Paysans et la politique dans la France Contemporaine*, edited by Jacques Fauvet and Henri Mendras. Vol. 94 of *Cahiers de la Fondation Nationale de Sciences Politique*. Paris: Armand Colin, 1958.

Epstein, Paul J. "Beyond Policy Community: French Agriculture and the GATT." *Journal of European Public Policy* 43 (1997): 355–72.

Golob, Eugene. *The Méline Tariff: French Agriculture and Nationalist Economic Policy*. New York: Columbia University Press, 1944.

Grant, Charles. *Delors: Inside the House That Jacques Built*. London: Nicholas Brealey, 1994.

Grant, Wyn. "Pressure Groups and the European Community: An Overview." In *Lobbying in the European Community*, edited by Sonia Mazey and Jeremy Richardson. Oxford: Oxford University Press, 1993.

———. *The Common Agricultural Policy*. London: Macmillan, 1997.

———. "Biotechnology: A Source of Tension in US-EU Trade Relations." Paper prepared for the conference Liberalizing Agricultural Trade? University of Washington, May 1999.

Halévy, Daniel. *Le Fin des notables*. Paris: Grasset, 1930.

Harris, Simon. "The Food Industry Perspective." In *Agriculture in the Uruguay Round*, edited by Kenneth A. Ingersent, A. J. Rayner, and R. C. Hine. Basingstoke: Macmillan, 1994.

Hendriks, Gisela. "German Agricultural Policy Objectives." In *Renationalisation of the Common Agricultural Policy?* edited by Rasmus Kjeldahl and Michael Tracy. Copenhagen: Institute of Agricultural Economics, 1994.

Hervieu, Bertrand. "Pluralité reconnue, pluralisme contesté." In *Les Agriculteurs et la Politique*, edited by Pierre Coulomb et al. Paris: Presses de la Fondation Nationale des Science Politique, 1990.

———. *Les Agriculteurs*. Paris: Presses Universitaires de France, 1996.

Jobert, Bruno, and Pierre Muller. *L'état en action: Politique publiques et corporatismes*. Paris: Presses Universitaires de France, 1987.

Keeler, John T. S. *The Politics of Neocorporatism in France: Farmers, the State, and Agricultural Policy Making in the Fifth Republic*. New York: Oxford University Press, 1987.

———. "Agricultural Power in the European Community: Explaining the Fate of CAP and GATT Negotiations." *Comparative Politics* 28 (1996): 127–49.

Klatzmann, Joseph. "Géographie electorale de l'agriculture française." In *Les Paysans et la politique dans la France contemporaine*, edited by Jacques Fauvet and Henri Mendras. Paris: Armand Colin, 1958.

Lagrave, Rose-Marie. "Les Gauches syndicales (MODEF, CNSTP, FNSP). "In *Les Agriculteurs et la politique*, edited by Pierre Coulomb et al. Paris: Presses de la Fondation Nationale des Science Politique, 1990.

Laligant, Marcel. *L'Intervention de l'etat dans le secteur agricole*. Paris: Libraire Generale de Droit et de Jurisprudence, 1970.

Leveau, Rémy. "L'Enseignement et la vulgarisation agricoles." In *Les Paysans et la politique dans la France contemporaine*, edited by Jacques Fauvet and Henri Mendras. Paris: Armand Colin, 1958.

Mendras, Henri, and Yves Tavernier. "Les Manifestations de Juin 1961." *Revue Française de Science Politique* 12 (September 1962): 647–71.

Miette, Roland. *L'Evolution de l'agriculture algerienne*. Paris: Centre de hautes etudes sur l'Afrique et l'Asie Moderne, 1980.

Ministère de L'Agriculture. *Cent ans de ministère de l'agriculture*. Paris: Ministère de L'Agriculture, 1982.

Morel, Léopold. "L'économie dirigée en viticulture." Ph.D. dissertation, University of Paris, 1939.

Moulin, Annie. *Peasantry and Society in France since 1789*, translated by M. C. Cleary and M. F. Cleary. Cambridge: Cambridge University Press, 1991.

Moyer, H. Wayne, and Timothy E. Josling. *Agricultural Policy Reform: Politics and Process in the EC and USA*. New York: Harvester Wheatsheaf, 1990.

Muth, Hanns Peter. *French Agriculture and the Political Integration of Western Europe*. Leyden: A. W. Sijthoff, 1970.

Naylor, Eric L. *Socio-Structural Policy in French Agriculture*. O'Dell Memorial Monograph no. 18. Department of Geography, University of Aberdeen, 1985.

Neville-Rolfe, Edmund. *The Politics of Agriculture in the European Community*. London: Policy Studies Institute, 1984.

Noly, Pierre-J. "Le Role des coopératives agricoles des producteurs de blé." Ph.D. dissertation, Paris, 1938.

Paarlberg, Robert. "Agricultural Policy Reform and the Uruguay Round: Synergistic Linkage in a Two-Level Game?" *International Organization* 51 (1997): 413–44.

Parodi, Jean-Luc. "Tout s'est joué trois ans plus tôt." In *Mars 1986: La drôle de défaite de la gauche*, edited by élisabeth Dupoirier and Gérard Grunberg. Paris: Presses Universitaires de France, 1986.

Patterson, Lee Ann. "Agricultural Policy Reform in the European Community: A Three-Level Game Analysis." *International Organization* 51 (1997): 135–65.

Petit, Michel. *Agricultural Policy Formation in the European Community: The Birth of Milk Quotas and CAP Reform.* Amsterdam: Elsevier, 1987.

Potter, Clive. *Against the Grain: Agri-Environmental Reform in the United States and the European Union.* Wallingford, U.K.: CAB International, 1998.

Price, Roger. *The Modernization of Rural France: Communications Networks and Agricultural Market Structures in Nineteenth-Century France.* London: Hutchinson, 1983.

Prugnaud, Louis. *Les Etapes du syndicalisme agricole en France.* Paris: Editions de l'épi, 1963.

Rémy, Pierre. "Le Gaullisme et les paysans." In *L'univers politique des paysans dans la France contemporaine*, edited by Yves Tavernier, Michel Gervais, and Claude Servolin. Paris: Armand Colin, 1972.

Ritson, Christopher. "The CAP and the Consumer." In *The Common Agricultural Policy*, edited by Christopher Ritson and David Harvey. 2d ed. Wallingford, U.K.: CAB International, 1997.

Rogers, Susan Carol. "Farming Visions: Culture and Agriculture in France." Paper presented to the Program in Agrarian Studies, Yale University, 1994.

Roudié, Philippe. *La France: agriculture, forêt, pêche depuis 1945.* Paris: Sirey, 1985.

Roussillon, Henry. *L'Association générale des producteurs du blé.* Paris: Armand Colin, 1970.

Rouveroux, Pierre. "La Représentation professionnelle de l'agriculture." Ph.D. dissertation, University of Paris, 1938.

Servolin, Claude. "*La Gauche aux commandes.*" In *Les Agriculteurs et la Politique*, edited by Pierre Coulomb et al. Paris: Presses de la Fondation Nationale des Science Politique, 1990.

Tavernier, Yves. "Le Syndicalisme paysan et la politique agricole du gouvernement." *Revue Française de Science Politique* 12 (1962): 599–646.

———. "Le Syndicalisme paysan et la cinquième république." *Revue Française de Science Politique* 16 (1965): 869–912.

———. *Le Syndicalisme paysanne.* Paris: Armand Colin, 1969.

Tracy, Michael. *Government and Agriculture in Western Europe, 1880–1988.* 3d ed. New York: Harvester Wheatsheaf, 1989.

Vahl, Remco. *Leadership in Disguise: The Role of the European Commission in Decision-Making on Agriculture in the Uruguay Round.* Aldershot: Ashgate, 1997.

Vaugelas, Charles. "Le Ministère de l'agriculture." In *Les Paysans et la politique dans la France contemporaine*, edited by Jacques Fauvet and Henri Mendras. Paris: Armand Colin, 1958.

Warner, Charles K. *The Winegrowers of France and the Government since 1875.* New York: Columbia University Press, 1960.

Webber, Douglas. "High Midnight in Brussels: An Analysis of the September 1993 Council Meeting on the GATT Uruguay Round." *Journal of European Public Policy* 5 (1998): 578–94.

———. "Franco-German Bilateralism and Agricultural Politics in the European Union." *West European Politics* 22 (1999): 45–67.

Wright, Gordon. *Rural Revolution in France: The Peasantry in the Twentieth Century.* Stanford, Calif.: Stanford University Press, 1964.

Primary Sources

Agra Europe.

Archives Nationale. F10 2170. "Office Nationale Interprofessionel du Blé."

Assemblée Nationale. *Journal Officiel.*

Commission of the European Communities. *Bulletin of the European Communities.* Brussels: Commission of the European Communities, December 1983.

———. *The Agricultural Situation in the Community.* Brussels: Commission of the European Communities, various years.

De Gaulle, Charles. *Lettres, notes, et carnets, Juin 1958–Décembre 1960.* Paris: Plon, 1984.

European Economic Community. *Second General Report.* Brussels: European Economic Community, 1969.

Financial Times.

Food and Agriculture Organization of the United Nations. *Trade Indices: Crops and Livestock, Primary and Processed.* FAOSTAT Database collection. http:// apps.fao.org (1999).

INSEE. *Annuaire Statistique de la France.* Paris: INSEE, various years.

Interview. Bureau du Budget, Ministère de l'agriculture, pêche, et l'alimentation. October 11, 1996.

Ministère de l'Agriculture. "Les concours publics â l'agriculture, 1990–1994." *Projet de loi de finances pour 1996.* Paris: Ministère de l'agriculture de la pêche et de l'alimentation, 1996.

Le Monde.

Organization for Economic Cooperation and Development. *Agricultural Policies in OECD Countries.* Paris: OECD, various years.

———. *Agricultural Policies, Markets, and Trade.* Paris: OECD, various years.

Japan

Politics and Institutions

Akita, George. *Foundations of Constitutional Government in Modern Japan, 1868–1900.* Cambridge: Cambridge University Press, 1967.

Baerwald, Hans H. *The Purge of Japanese Leaders under the Occupation.* Berkeley: University of California Press, 1959.

Beasley, W. G. "Meiji Political Institutions." In *The Nineteenth Century*. Vol. 5 of *The Cambridge History of Japan*, edited by Marius B. Jansen. Cambridge: Cambridge University Press, 1989.

Calder, Kent. *Crisis and Compensation: Public Policy and Political Instability in Japan, 1949–1986*. Princeton, N.J.: Princeton University Press, 1988.

Campbell, John C. *Contemporary Japanese Budget Politics*. Berkeley: University of California Press, 1977.

Cole, Allan, George Totten, and Cecil Uyehara. *Socialist Parties in Postwar Japan*. New Haven, Conn.: Yale University Press, 1966.

Curtis, Gerald L. *The Japanese Way of Politics*. New York: Columbia University Press, 1988.

Dower, John W. "The Useful War." In *Showa: The Japan of Hirohito*, edited by Carol Gluck and Stephen R. Graubard. New York: Norton, 1992.

Eisuke Sakakibara, "The Japanese Politico-Economic System and the Public Sector." In *Parallel Politics: Economic Policymaking in Japan and the United States*, edited by Samuel Kernell. Washington, D.C.: The Brookings Institution, 1991.

Flanagan, Scott C., Shinsaku Kohei, Ichiro Miyake, Bradley M. Richardson, and Joji Watanuki. *The Japanese Voter*. New Haven, Conn.: Yale University Press, 1991.

Fraser, Andrew, R. H. Mason, and Philip Mitchell. *Japan's Early Parliaments, 1890–1905: Structure, Issues, and Trends*. London: Routledge, 1995.

Iwasaki, Uichi. *The Working Forces in Japanese Politics: A Brief Account of Political Conflicts, 1867–1920*. Vol. 97 of *Studies in History, Economics, and Public Law*. New York: Columbia University Press, 1921.

Johnson, Chalmers. *MITI and the Japanese Miracle: The Growth of Industrial Policy in Japan, 1925–1975*. Stanford, Calif.: Stanford University Press, 1982.

Junnosuke, Masumi. *Postwar Politics in Japan, 1945–1955*. Translated by Lonny E. Carlile. Berkeley: Institute of East Asian Studies, 1985.

———. "The 1955 System: Origin and Transformation." In *Creating Single-Party Democracy: Japan's Postwar Political System*, edited by Tetsuya Kataoka. Stanford, Calif.: Hoover Institution Press, 1992.

Kohno, Masaru. "Rational Foundations for the Organization of the Liberal Democratic Party in Japan." *World Politics* 44 (1992): 369–97.

Lewis, Michael. *Rioters and Citizens: Mass Protest in Imperial Japan*. Berkeley: University of California Press, 1990.

McCubbins, Mathew, and Gregory W. Noble. "Perceptions and Realities of Japanese Budgeting." In *Structure and Policy in Japan and the United States*, edited by Peter F. Cowhey and Mathew D. McCubbins. Cambridge: Cambridge University Press, 1995.

Muramatsu, Michio. "Bringing Politics Back into Japan." In *Showa: The Japan of Hirohito*, edited by Carol Gluck and Stephen R. Graubard. New York: Norton, 1992.

———. "Patterned Pluralism under Challenge: The Policies of the 1980s." In *Political Dynamics in Contemporary Japan*, edited by Gary D. Allinson and Yasunori Sone. Ithaca, N.Y.: Cornell University Press, 1993.

Muramatsu, Michio, and Ellis Krauss. "The Conservative Policy Line and the Development of Patterned Pluralism." In *The Political Economy of Japan*. Vol. 1, *The Domestic Transformation*, edited by Kozo Yamamura and Yasukichi Yasuba. Stanford, Calif.: Stanford University Press, 1987.

Najita, Tetsuo. *Hara Kei in the Politics of Compromise, 1905–1915*. Cambridge, Mass.: Harvard University Press, 1967.

Park, Yung H. *Bureaucrats and Ministers in Contemporary Japanese Government*. Berkeley: University of California Press, 1986.

Ramseyer, Mark, and Frances Rosenbluth. *Japan's Political Marketplace*. Cambridge, Mass.: Harvard University Press, 1993.

———. *The Politics of Oligarchy: Institutional Choice in Imperial Japan*. Cambridge: Cambridge University Press, 1995.

Rosenbluth, Frances, and Michael F. Thies. "The Electoral Foundations of Japan's Financial Politics: The Case of Jusen." Paper presented at the annual meeting of the American Political Science Association, Boston, 1998.

Scalapino, Robert A. *Democracy and the Party Movement in Prewar Japan: The Failure of the First Attempt*. 1953; Berkeley: University of California Press, 1967.

Schoppa, Leonard J. "Zoku Power and LDP Power: A Case Study of the Zoku Role in Education Policy." *Journal of Japanese Studies* 17 (1991): 79–106.

———. "Two-Level Games and Bargaining Outcomes: Why *Gaiatsu* Succeeds in Japan in Some Cases but Not Others." *International Organization* 47 (1993): 353–86.

Silberman, Bernard S. "Bureaucratic Development and the Structure of Decision-Making in Japan, 1868–1925." *Journal of Asian Studies* 29 (1970): 347–62.

———. "The Bureaucratic State in Japan: The Problem of Authority and Legitimacy." In *Conflict in Modern Japanese History: The Neglected Tradition*, edited by Najita Tetsuo and J. Victor Koschmann. Princeton, N.J.: Princeton University Press, 1982.

Tani, Satomi. "The Japan Socialist Party before the Mid-1960s: An Analysis of Its Stagnation." In *Creating Single-Party Democracy: Japan's Postwar Political System*, edited by Tetsuya Kataoka. Stanford, Calif.: Hoover Institution Press, 1992.

Ward, Robert. "Conclusion." In *Democratizing Japan: The Allied Occupation*, edited by Robert Ward and Sakamoto Yoshikazu. Honolulu: University of Hawaii Press, 1987.

Agriculture

Bullock, Robert. "Explaining Rice Liberalization in Japan." USJP Occasional Paper. Cambridge: Program on U.S.-Japan Relations, 1995.

———. "Nokyo: A Short Cultural History." Japan Policy Research Institute working paper no. 41. Cardiff, Calif.: Japan Policy Research Institute, 1997.

Donnelly, Michael W. "Setting the Price of Rice: A Study in Political Decision Making." In *Policy-making in Contemporary Japan*, edited by T. J. Pempel. Ithaca, N.Y.: Cornell University Press, 1977.

———. "Political Management of Japan's Rice Economy." Ph.D. dissertation, Columbia University, 1978.

———. "Conflict over Government Authority and Markets: Japan's Rice Economy." In *Conflict in Japan*, edited by Ellis S. Krauss, Thomas P. Rohlen, and Patricia G. Steinhoff. Honolulu: University of Hawaii Press, 1984.

Dore, Ronald. *Land Reform in Japan*. 1984; London: Athlone Press, 1984.

Francks, Penelope. *Technology and Agricultural Development in Pre-war Japan*. New Haven, Conn.: Yale University Press, 1984.

Fukutake, Tadashi. *Japanese Rural Society*. Translated by Ronald Dore. Ithaca, N.Y.: Cornell University Press, 1967.

George, Aurelia. "Rice Politics in Japan." Pacific Economic Papers, no. 159. Canberra: Australia-Japan Research Centre, 1988.

———. "Prospects for Liberalizing Japan's Rice Market." *Pacific Review* 4 (1990): 363–67.

———. "The Politics of Interest Representation in the Japanese Diet: The Case of Agriculture." *Pacific Affairs* 4 (1991): 506–28.

———. "The Politics of Public Spending in the Agriculture, Forestry and Fisheries Sector." In *Japanese Agricultural Policy Reconsidered*, edited by Ogura Takekazu. Tokyo: Food and Agricultural Policy Research Center, 1993.

George-Mulgan, Aurelia. "The Role of Foreign Pressure (*Gaiatsu*) in Japan's Agricultural Trade Liberalization." *Pacific Review* 10 (1997): 165–209.

———. "Electoral Determinants of Agrarian Power: Measuring Rural Decline in Japan." *Political Studies* 45 (1997): 875–99.

———. *The Politics of Agriculture in Japan*. London: Routledge, 2000.

Havens, Thomas R. H. *Farm and Nation in Modern Japan: Agrarian Nationalism, 1870–1940*. Princeton, N.J.: Princeton University Press, 1974.

Hayami, Yujiro. *A Century of Agricultural Growth in Japan: Its Relevance to Asian Development*. Minneapolis: University of Minnesota Press, 1975.

Hayami, Yujiro, and Yamada Saburo. "Agricultural Research Organization in Economic Development: A Review of the Japanese Experience." In *Economic Growth: The Japanese Experience since the Meiji Era*, edited by Lawrence Klein and Ohkawa Kazushi. Homewood, Ill.: Irwin, 1968.

Hemmi, Kenzo. "Agriculture and Politics in Japan." In *U.S.-Japanese Agricultural Trade Relations*, edited by Emery Castle and Kenzo Hemmi. Washington, D.C.: Resources for the Future, 1982.

Johnston, Bruce F. *Japanese Food Management in World War II*. Stanford, Calif.: Stanford University Press, 1953.

Kano, Yoshikazu. "Opening the Way to an Agricultural Renaissance." *Japan Echo* 14, no. 1 (1987): 9–13.

Kuroda, Yoshima. "The Present State of Agriculture in Japan." In *U.S.-Japanese Agricultural Trade Relations*, edited by Emery Castle and Kenzo Hemmi. Washington, D.C.: Resources for the Future, 1982.

Moore, Richard. *Japanese Agriculture: Patterns of Rural Development*. Boulder, Colo.: Westview Press, 1990.

Ogura, Takekazu. *Agricultural Development in Modern Japan*. 1963; Tokyo: Fuji, 1967.

———. *Can Japanese Agriculture Survive? A Historical and Comparative Approach*. Tokyo: Agricultural Policy Research Center, 1982.

Porges, Amelia. "Japan: Beef and Citrus." In *Reciprocity and Retaliation in U.S. Trade Policy*, edited by Thomas Bayard and Kimberly Ann Elliott. Washington, D.C.: Institute for International Economics, 1994.

Rapkin, David P., and Aurelia George. "Rice Liberalization and Japan's Role in the Uruguay Round: Evolving Strategies in a Two-Level Game." In *World Agriculture and the GATT*, edited by William P. Avery. London: Lynne Rienner, 1993.

Reich, Michael R., Yasuo Endo, and C. Peter Timmer. "Agriculture: The Political Economy of Structural Change." In *America Versus Japan*, edited by Thomas McCraw. Boston: Harvard Business School Press, 1986.

Smith, Patrick. "Letter from Tokyo." *New Yorker*, October 14, 1991, 105–18.

Tobata, Seiichi. *Control of the Price of Rice*. Tokyo: Institute of Pacific Relations, 1933.

Waswo, Ann. *Japanese Landlords: The Decline of a Rural Elite*. Berkeley: University of California Press, 1977.

Yamada, Saburo. "Changes in Output and in Conventional and Nonconventional Inputs in Japanese Agriculture since 1880." *Food Research Institute Studies* 7 (1967): 371–413.

Primary Sources

Bank of Japan. *Economic Statistics of Japan*, various years.

———. *Historical Statistics of the Japanese Economy*. Tokyo: Bank of Japan, 1965.

Daily Yomiuri.

Far Eastern Survey.

Food and Agriculture Organization of the United Nations. *Population: Long-Term Series (Decennial)*. FAOSTAT Database collection. http://apps.fao.org (1999).

Harada Kumao. *The Saionji-Harada Memoirs, 1931–1940*. Washington, D.C.: University Publications of America, 1978.

International Monetary Fund. *International Financial Statistics Yearbook*. Washington, D.C.: International Monetary Fund, various years.

Japan Economic Newswire.

Japan Times and Mail.

Okawa, Kazushi, Shinohara Miyohei, and Umemura Mataji. *Estimates of Long-Term Economic Statistics of Japan since 1868*. Vol. 7. Tokyo: Tokyo Keizai Shimposha, 1965.

Mainichi Daily News

Ministry of Agriculture, Forestry, and Fisheries. *Statistical Yearbook of the Ministry of Agriculture, Forestry, and Fisheries*. Tokyo: Norin Tokei Kyokai, various years.

———. "Summary of the Survey on Agricultural Structure and Movement (Basic Structure), as of January 1, 1998." http://www.maff.go.jp/esokuhou/index.htm (1999).

Ministry of Finance. *The Japanese Budget in Brief, 1999*. Tokyo: Budget Bureau, 1999.

Mitsubishi Economic Research Bureau, *Monthly Circular*, various years.

Nihon Keizei Shimbun.
Nikkei Weekly.
Oriental Economist.
Reuters.
Roper Center. *JPOLL, Japanese Data Archive.* www.ropercenter.uconn.edu, March 1999.
Supreme Commander for Allied Powers, Natural Resources Section. *Agricultural Programs in Japan, 1945–51.* Washington, D.C.: Government Printing Office, 1952.
Trans Pacific.
Yomiuri Shimbun.